INTEGRATED MARITIME SECURITY
Governing the Ghost Protocol

Prabhakaran Paleri

(Established 1870)
United Service Institution of India
New Delhi

Vij Books India Pvt Ltd
New Delhi (India)

Published by

Vij Books India Pvt Ltd
(Publishers, Distributors & Importers)
2/19, Ansari Road
Delhi – 110 002
Phones: 91-11-43596460, 91-11-47340674
Fax: 91-11-47340674
e-mail: vijbooks@rediffmail.com

ISBN: 978-93-82652-67-0

Price in India: Rs 1495/-

Dedicated to the memory of

Vice Admiral Mihir Kumar (Mikki) Roy, PVSM, AVSM (Retd.)

Miss you, sir; you encouraged me to think differently.

Contents

Preface

The title of this book is a macro level statement. This is a composite and continuing work examining the land centred national security governance and its relation with the ocean. People have taken the ocean as a realm of mystery and perils since the very beginning. There were many catchphrases and statements of the "he-who-rules-the-ocean-will-rule-the-world" kind about the ocean and ocean governance. They were seemingly true according to the respective periods. That is, provided anybody could rule the ocean. It was the ocean that always ruled the world. It is next to impossible for any geopolitical entity to rule the ocean especially in modern times. Every geopolitical entity can exercise its right over it. Hegemonic ambitions and colonialism over the sea have become things of the past. An entity will have to tame the ocean appropriate to its rights. Taming the ocean for relative benefits is what the governments can attempt. The theme of this book revolves around it—taming the ocean. It is (more than) the chronicle of *sagar manthan*[1] and the symbolism concealed in it, yet in another form. It is new; it is different as a concept. It is also difficult to implement right away unless the government is daring to break the method inertia of governance associated with it. For these reasons the idea may not find immediate acceptance. But the findings, it is expected, may carve a niche in strategic appreciation not only in national governance but also in governing any human system where wellbeing, not the doled out welfare or selective political anointment, is the end objective. It is expected to pick up in the natural way as the art and science of national governance evolves.

The examination of the concept of national security clearly indicates that the idea is practised in a fragmented manner all over the world taking the physical security of a nation as the prime requirement

1 See annexure.

for any government to meet in national governance. It becomes the leading objective and reinforces the view that national security means the physical security of a nation against external and internal threats. This is far from truth. Since the late 18th century scholars have identified national security as a much broader concept, but in a world troubled by war, violence and crime, the governance got focused on survival against physical threats. The concept of national security lap dissolved in military affairs and internal problems of security in the name of national security. The practice is continuing.

This book examines the evolution of the wholesome concept of national security and its definition, and showcases governance aimed at maximising national security through the identified interactive elements of it. Governance of human system is naturally land centred and thereby the terrain specific national security external to land gets isolated, though may receive selective attention of governments. This is largely visible in governing the ocean. The governments can overcome this situation and the ocean can be governed more effectively by integrating maritime security with national security. The study confirms it.

Like any other task, national governance too gravitates through familiar and beaten tracks in any political system. Altering the course of governance has to be done carefully and slowly. It is like wheeling over a fully laden ultra large crude carrying tanker in restricted water, though there is room to manoeuvre. There is massive inertia, hence no quick remedy in governance. Altering course of governance takes time.

The idea of integrated maritime security originated from my professional experience, previous research studies, and discussions and interactions with various veterans and scholars on the subject. Standing atop the bridge of a ship in absolute command watching the restlessly manic and endless sea, one gets into an orgasmic spin of superhuman spirit with the awareness of unlimited accountability towards the safety of the ship and the lives on board. It would have happened to many commanders and masters who were fortunate to encounter the perils of the sea very early in life. Yes, fortunate. It is an experience that defies explanation. The spin continues for the rest of one's life even after "finishing with main engines."

Whether the situation is close quarter or open quarter, one has to love the sea to "feel" the dread of it before taming it.

Every researcher and practitioner will have his or her own perspectives. This study carries my perspective of the ocean and the concept of national security, not maritime security, as an exclusive idea in isolation. For this, I respect the research findings of many scholars on the subject. Their findings not only enlightened me but also encouraged me to delve deeper. I practiced it at every turn of my career. The idea of this book is to present the findings and suggestions to the executors and researchers for application and further research. Being a new concept, the ideas may find reiterated in various chapters in different forms for familiarity and reinforcement while reading through.

The study is not specific to any country. But there are references to many countries for driving the point home. The study takes into consideration every geopolitical entity, each one different from the other and governed differently. The idea suggested here is national governance with the sole objective of maximisation of national security, as the way it is defined here, by integrating the terrain specific maritime security for better yield from the ocean. To that extent integrated maritime security is the absolute assimilation of the terrain specific aspects of the ocean related to a geopolitical entity with its national security elements for maximising the benefits to the people by governance.

The book is global in scope. It is about bringing the ocean over land for governing it. The findings are applicable to any entity, including the landlocked and geographically disadvantaged, provided it can understand and appreciate its part of the ocean. It will be useful even to prevent the damages when the ocean comes over to lunch uninvited if and when the sea level rises. When it happens, the low lying nations do not actually sink or drown; they get choked by the ocean riding them commandingly. This is what a tsunami does, though temporarily. Sea level rise is much worse.

This book goes along with the design of my previous research on national security, a concept I believed was much larger than the idea of national security that has been practiced all around the world. It was a revelation. Building further on the research, one reaches a state of sanguine confidence that the world doesn't have to struggle so much to achieve wellbeing or do all that to safeguard whatever it wants to safeguard. An alteration of course, perhaps, is all what is necessary which anyway will happen when the decks are open. This book may throw some wild cards when it happens.

I have been encouraged by the United Service Institution of India (USI) and its Centre for Strategic Studies and Simulation (CS3) for examining the topic. It is an honour. The Institution with an outstanding reputation of more than 140 years became one of my mentors in strategic research when it awarded me a project a decade ago. The research had found great application subsequently. This time the subject is new and very futuristic. I am grateful to its visionary director Lt Gen P. K. Singh, PVSM, AVSM (Retd.), the sensuously acute and dedicated research head at the CS3 Maj Gen Y. K. Gera (Retd.) and all the veterans of the Institute for the faith they bestowed in me.

I am sure the findings of this research will be useful to those in governance who dare to experiment with the new. If they do, they could gain headway in governance relative to others engaged in similar tasks around the world.

Being a sailor most of my life, I feel comfortable with nautical terms of expression even in normal dialogues. I have taken extreme care in avoiding such terms in this study. Still I have dabbled in some. I couldn't help it. Please disregard, if you find them uncanny. The same goes for mathematical expressions. I have been careful to steer clear of them. The reader may skip through the limited parts where I was compelled to highlight some.

Chapter 1

INTRODUCTION—THE CURIOUS CASE OF MARITIME SECURITY

It is impossible for humans[1] to appreciate existential security beyond the territorial realm of land; it is not because they are ignorant about the importance of the ocean…

The much talked about "maritime security" is a curious case, a kind of ghost protocol; GP for short. Giving shape to a ghost protocol is a difficult task. But, it is part of governance. Individuals and governments who attempt to manage maritime security often perform it irresolutely. The outcomes fall short of expectations in the miasma of lapses and consequences while chasing the objectives.

They are often unaware that ghost protocols are to be shaped and prepared before handling.

There are many ghost protocols in a social system under governance. Maritime security is a high-flier among them. This study examines the idea of maritime security and its governance for maximising national security. In the process, both the concepts and their associated aspects need to be understood by reductionist analysis for clarity of differentiation which is the prime requirement for integration of the whole system for better results. Reductionism reflects the perspectives of causality. It is a complex process, especially when it is about social systems that have been practiced for a very long time. The problem will be about acceptance.

When "Terra" is "Firma"

For humans, the world is over land, the terra firma. They live and multiply on it. They have been more interested with the vital aspects of the solid terrain and the associated geoproperty rights[2] over it than the surrounding ocean water. They feel secure over land. As on date, if anyone wants to own a piece of land, he or she will have to acquire it from someone or a government. People fought and brawled over land individually and in groups in every which way they could. Authors wrote stories of human saga and conflicts with the land all over the world. Today, there is no land on the planet that doesn't belong to someone or some group including governments as private or public property. No one can walk into a piece of land and occupy it legally today. There is also land that is claimed by more than one country. They remain under dispute or informally declared as "no-man's land."[3] A small piece of land at the South Pole still remains "unsold" or not permanently occupied. It is the only piece of land available for all.[4] It is precariously placed in the list of the global commons surrounded by frozen ocean waters. It is the remaining piece of the original and the last known supercontinent, the mother of all the occupied land territories today—Pangaea. The rest of the world broke away in pieces from Pangaea to settle elsewhere in the ocean as decided by the spin of the Earth and the momentum of the drifting pieces. They were all bought or occupied. They still carry the pangs to rejoin.

To that extent the populated world of today is still wandering like dump barges broken loose in the ocean.

Humans remain precariously perched over the various pieces of floating landmass. They cannot live elsewhere. They are aware of it. They can slip into the water if they walk out of the gunwale of their land-barge, and die. So, they feel. They know gravity is stronger than buoyancy. Their minds play with them, scaring them subconsciously. They consider, the ocean is separate from their land. The do not know that the water too is drifting along with the land as part of Earth's crest, part of their land. What they know is that water can kill them; only land can protect them.

Humans feel secure when *terra* is *firma*—the land over which they stand is solid. This feeling is clear and present in everything they do, including governance.

Human affinity with the land from the very beginning is understandable. There are quick takes on why people cling on to land so vehemently. First, being humans, they feel physically secure with life only over land where they can breathe effortlessly. Humans cannot breathe underwater. Though not a new or clever discovery of this study, it is as simple as that. Second, humans are psychologically insecure to the hilt when their complex neural systems get unleashed on the security aspects of the future. Security is identified, among others, with the life supporting land. Everyone pines for a piece of land with a house on it. In a high-rise apartment, the land becomes the floor space in virtual reality. People even plant trees and grass on their skyscraping terraces and interiors; they miss the piece of real land which is their security blanket. With all these fixations over land, it is natural for humans to clasp it virtually or otherwise, and forget everything else including the ocean. Humans are preoccupied with land and the associated *terra tactus*. Their thinking is land based. They need to touch land to feel comfortable.

They clasp the land for survival. They cling on to it for dear life. It is a primordial instinct by default for continued existence of life created to survive over land alone. Humans are endowed with advanced brains relative to other life forms. Their survival tool is supposed to be the brain, not jaws, claws and size. The craze for land drives people fanatically. They can't think of anything else without land under their feet and dissolved in their mind. Every religious and political system has its vehement dogma on land, and the possession and use of it. Not so passionately about the ocean. In contrast, the ocean remained free and unoccupied. One can sail into even the territorial sea of a country easily and get away with it, but not across the land border. Why is it so?

The Landclasp Syndrome

The landclasp syndrome reflects in every human activity on the planet but is much more amplified in national governance. The syndrome is robust and pervasive. In contrast, ocean remains secondary. It is evident in the maritime disputes that prevail all over. The disputes, on the first hand, were caused by the landclasp syndrome. The parties involved did not realise the disputes at sea were that serious until the law of the sea demarcated the points for assessing ocean rights that also covers ocean bed and beneath—the land underwater legally called the subsoil. This makes the ocean a part of the land for argument. The disputes at sea between nations remained unresolved or did not project the necessary urgency as in the case of issues over land. The landclasp syndrome was inimical to appreciating the ocean and everything associated with it. The people and the governments were hooked on to land. A breach over land is much more serious even today than a breach on the ocean water from the public point of view.

There is no need for humans to unclasp the land and dive into the ocean. Hugging the land is a natural choice. It is more comfortable and natural. The hold over land is essential. It is impossible to get rid of this feeling anyway unless humans develop gills and learn to breathe underwater as comfortably as over land. Hence the idea of maritime security has to be within this clasp over land. Every issue of maritime security, therefore, has to be resolved over land. Nations have admitted it openly. Though, ultimately, it is the ocean that will decide the destiny of land and people over it—an irony of sorts.

To understand the landclasp syndrome of humans, it is necessary to examine human bondage to land in matters related to security for which the stage was set much before human life originated over land. It is also essential to understand why ocean, in spite of being a very dominating terrain of the planet, is secondary to humans in their immediate existence.

All these... from a strategic perception of security.

World in Distant Past

There are clear evidences of the past, one of them in the distribution of fossils, at least as far as the time when the land masses were cloistered in a more or less human embryonic shape at one point as a supercontinent with the expansive ocean around it. The single supercontinent lay cosseted there in time between the late Paleozoic era (541-252.2 Ma) and the beginning of the Mesozoic era (252.2-66 Ma). The supercontinent was called Pangaea. Between the periods, the Pangaean existence was dated around 300 million years ago. Scholars believe there would have been various other supercontinents even before that. That is not a concern for this study.

The study is concerned about governing the human system. Human life originated many millennia after the Pangaean breakup about 200 million years ago. Pangaean break up is important to understand the ocean distribution. The ocean that surrounded the supercontinent of Pangaea is called Panthalassa or Panthalassic Ocean. An interesting fact is that the ocean has no name today. Whereas, the world has named the ocean that existed many millennia into the past. The ocean has changed in shape, size, volume, temperature and salinity. But it is still single and surrounds all the continents as a continuum. In some cases it is called the World Ocean with various geographical divisions under different names.

The period of existence of a supercontinent was comparatively short in relation to the life of the planet, which is estimated to be around four billion years. All these studies will be quite trivial when the planet finally succumbs one day to become a cosmic speck, or whatever it is going to be, at the end of its life. A researcher interested in ocean strategy is not concerned about such a long period of study. More than that, it is the human beings survival instinct that is important for such research. The centre of gravity of the survival instinct was laid over land in the past. There are reasons to believe that it is not likely to change considering humans are designed for land. That is the fact that has to be established. Whatever may be the influence the ocean has on sustaining life on land in addition to the waterworld of the ocean itself, the humans will always be concerned about their existence primarily over land. They will view the ocean from the land and not on the reverse. If that is so, human wellbeing will ever remain a land based concept. Any other terrain based security, therefore, has to be part of it and not external or exclusive to it.

The name Pangaea was coined in 1927 in a symposium discussing continental drift. The findings about the supercontinent were postulated by Alfred Wegener (1880-1930) in his book *Die Endstehung der Continent und Ozeane*.[5] The perception that the ocean was different from the land originated from this finding among other thought processes. The human tendency to look at land as a separate entity different from ocean can be seen in visualising the supercontinent exclusive of the ocean. In reality, the ocean was part of the single supercontinent on the Earth's crest. It is the geological plates that moved floating on Earth's molten interior, not the ocean. They moved carrying the "single" ocean. The ocean thereby becomes part of the land that drifts but, being fluid, takes different spatial shapes. This process is still continuing.

Land is a solid, fluid, gaseous and plasmic combination. It also means ocean is part of land and not different from it.

World Today

The world we know today lies in the centre of the study of any scholar. Everything about the world related to the past and present emanates outwardly from the world today as appreciated by the individual scholar. The world today is important for the study of national security governance from this sense. The supercontinent of yesterday lie staggered with the ocean still surrounding the widely separated land masses that thrust above it like gargoyles. The land masses comprise various geopolitical entities with people of varying ethnicity, belief systems and concerns. The common concern for all is security that they are yet to define seriously.

The world today is heavily populated with human beings who live in large complex groups and use communication thankfully better than any other live forms for individual and group expression. The population is estimated to be 7.1 billion with a density of 43.6 people per square kilometer over land (2013). This is not a precise measurement but a statistical approximation that keep changing (normally increasing in spite of every calamity) in time. Humans belong to the prime life system that is not yet endangered probably being at the top of the life system pyramid. They generally follow the family group system which in course of time has thinned down to molecular family system at the lower level. Family group system collectively cares for security at the bottom level of the human society. Starting with the family, the group living extends to nations and in special cases collectively to global society. The global society concept in human system is not a reality but an elusive desire in some quarters if not an illusory concept. [6] The concept lacks universal acceptance for obvious reasons. The idea is a hard sell.

All these are governed by belief systems stored in human brain mostly interactive with primordial instincts of survival. The resulting behaviour at times becomes extremely intricate. It is from this point one has to understand the complexity of governance of a human system. The entire system of governance today is naturally land-centric. The pace at which human belief system changes is very much slower than the changes in human ingenuity. This causes a lag in human adaption to ingenuity. The change in belief system is not visible on the go but the change brought out by ingenuity is instant. For this reason "change" for humans is innovation using the skills which is only temporary transformation, not a change in human perception of security for this study. Hence the study of human security remains affirmed in the law of invariance—nothing changes since the change is not noticeable at the moment of change.[7]

Under the law of invariance, however vital the ocean may be for human security, the governing mindset will still remain primordial and land based.

World in Distant Future

Examining how the world is going to be millions of years from now may not be a subject of interest in the study of maritime security, right? Wrong. The most vital aspect in the study of maritime security is the changes taking place in the ocean and about the ocean within the application of the law of invariance. The changes in the ocean also cause changes in the outlook of land and the humans who inhabit it. To understand the changes, one has to appreciate that it exists, though not visible immediately. One of the testimonies that the world will change in distant future lies in the geological confirmation that the formation of supercontinents is a cyclical process. Earth's crest gets reconfigured constantly. Scholars believe from the available evidences that there were other supercontinents much before Pangaea. It also means that the land masses of the present will come closer to become another supercontinent one day in the process of cyclical contraction and separation. If that is so, the cyclical process that is on at this moment will keep changing the profile of the world continuously. Anything that has to happen to the planet such as climate change or even an ice age will overlap within the process of this cyclical contraction and expansion. The changes are not commonly observable since the world is creeping slower than the growth of a finger nail.[8] They can be made visible for human perception only by visualising the future, millions of years from now. It will be amazing, even as a fun study, as the forecasters put it, to observe the world entirely different from now in its new shape similar, though not exactly, to the old Pangaea.

The continents and the ocean will look different in around 250 million years or earlier, which is only a brief moment in the life of the planet.

All these show that the floating land mass on the Earth behaves more strangely than the ocean. Humans live on the landmass clasping to it, oblivious to the dynamics going through in an endless manner. There is no reason why the world is not with humans even after 250 million years from now. But if they are there, they will still hold on to the available land under the landclasp syndrome.

Humans and Human Saga

Complexity is in the mind of the non-committal. Understanding about the humans and how and why they are on the planet are simple. Anyone can appreciate it with a little bit of commitment towards groping it through clarifying questions. When a research activity examines security, it is also necessary to understand the central target. The security envisaged here is for the humans, not for any other life form. The security is not just physical. Humans have brains in which emotions are cooked and digested. Human mind is a cauldron and a digester of intellect. This is not a philosophical sentiment, but sheer direct and simple biological statement. The neural networks in the human brain give the life form a status that is beyond mere physique—beyond claws, jaws and size. This is where the scenario changes. Security for humans, to that extent, any feeling or emotions, is a body-mind relationship where one cannot be separated from the other. It will be understood better when the human saga is examined.

According to anthropologists, present day humans are primates who belong to the species *Homo sapiens* (*H. sapiens*). Humans are the only extant species since originated along the *Homo* lineage. Humans were never extinct or under threat of extinction. The peculiarity of humans is their large and relatively well developed brains that increase mental capabilities. They are intelligent species who can use their brains to survive. Humans are the first of such species and therefore remain at the apex of present day evolution.

It is believed through scientific investigation that humans originated in Africa about 200,000 years ago. They began to show behavioural modernity only around 50,000 years back. The life-span of the species so far is relatively short and even negligible mathematically with respect to another short and recent event in the course of the planet—

the Pangaean breakup— that seemingly happened "yesterday." Well, not exactly; may be a couple of days ago relative to the life of the planet. This comparison of human-earth relativity is relevant for this study.

The anthropologists have an interesting find though not spoken loudly. Humans cannot call or designate apes as their ancestors because they just parted ways from them very seriously, that too from a sole species, the chimpanzees, some five million years ago, evolving into *Australopithecines*. Humans can categorically say that they have nothing (serious) to do with apes. *Australopithecines* were not apes in that sense. They were much ahead of apes. Apes still exist today in the more or less similar state. *Australopithecines* ultimately evolved into the genus *Homo*. Today the researchers believe that humans may have evolved from *Australopithecine* ancestors. So, discount the fad on apes forever.[9] No, the great grandfathers of human species did not live on trees. Probably, they climbed them.

The first *Homo* species was considered to be the *Homo erectus* from Africa who along with *Homo hiedlebergensis* (Africa and Eurasia) and the later find of Neanderthals, is taken as the immediate ancestor of the modern human. *Homo erectus* lived around 180,000,000 years ago whereas *Homo hiedlebergensis* is considered to be 1,300,000 to 600,000 years old. But there are doubts around here as the time gap between *Homo erectus* and *Homo hiedlebergensis* shows. The evolution into the modern human began with *Homo erectus*, the African upright humanoid through other humanoids such as the *Homo hiedlebergensis*, Neanderthals (believed to have existed in Europe 600,000 to 300,000 years ago), *Homo sapiens* to the present day *Homo sapiens*. The date of the process could be two million years to the date the ocean levels rose to the brim of the present day. The latter date is more important. These dates give some mathematical accuracy for human origin. Mathematics too cannot be taken for granted. But the fact remains that humans are evolutionary entities in life form meaning assured death and biodegradation, if born. Humans are presently at the apex and there are all chances of modern humans evolving into the "next' species. That will take too long a time, but cannot be neglected as the present has been too long from Pangaean break up. And the day has arrived to discuss about it. A million years can pass in a jiffy. The human saga does not end here. It will only end when the human species is extinct as the last species or the first of a new kind of species to evolve, like the *Homo erectus* or if one would like to choose closer, the Neanderthals, for the humans.

Human Migration and Occupation of Land

Human beings migrated taking the first step on foot and extended all over the world they could reach out from the period of *Homo erectus*. This is important to appreciate. Dating human migration has to be relative to the type of people who moved out first. *Homo erectus* moved out to Eurasia more than a million years ago.[10] This was followed by *Homo sapiens* from Africa more than 70,000 years ago. Migration modified them genetically by evolution based on the necessities and situations of life. The migratory instinct of humans driven by the primordial instinct of survival still continues. Only the forms and methods have altered. Human migration from one place to another mostly in groups is a fact of life. The process is different today but the practice continues. A human is a primordial migrant.

Migration causes conflict with the population existing in the new place. The immigrants will have to bear with it or they may have to clash with those already there. It is visible even today. There will be cultural displacement or assimilation. It is also applicable to the natives whose lives change forever when migrants arrive to settle down in their domain even if they are temporary settlers. The land gets affected first that changes the environment and resource exploitation and sustainability. Migration was predominantly voluntary in the early times but there were induced migrations in the forms of slave trade, human smuggling, human trafficking, ethnic cleansing, etc. There is no end in terms of time and distance for migration. Migration will continue indefinitely as long as the survival instinct is dominant in humans. People will roam around the world in the lookout for better lives rationalising their behaviour. Though scholars may disagree with this view points and insist on only nomadic humans are migrating across land today, long queues in embassies or in the traffickers' alleys across the world are indicators of the continuing tendency of people to look for perceived greener and safer pastures towards alien landscapes. Migration under international law matters with those who are willingly choosing to emigrate to another geographical entity from one's own. The decision to migrate has to be taken under freewill and not under duress. It was so when humanities moved across in ancient times and before the laws related to migration arrived. But the fact is, migration, whether under freewill or deceptive or coercive circumstances, is always from land to a better land as perceived. The hold over land is ever present. No one has moved out or escaped to ocean yet. Though may sound strange, this is a key point about human affinity towards land.

Migrations were in quest of improving quality of life. Modern migration too is no different. Industrialisation was a powerful driving force of migration to where it appeared. This is also the most resilient factor that finds a place in the modern or neoclassical macroeconomic theory where in migration of skilled and unskilled workers is motivated by wage differences for the same work at different geographical points. People tend to move from low state to higher state of economics and wellbeing in search of perceived security.

In 2010, the number of international migrants was estimated at 214 million. It is expected to reach 405 million in 2050.[11] The causes for migration are war, ethnic disturbances, opportunities, income disparity for similar work, disasters, etc. There are many illegal migrants in various parts of the world. People also migrate within a country. It is called internal migration. Of course, internal migration is limited to large countries. Industrial economics, based on migration, created the labour force as a factor of production very early. The labour force becomes dynamic under migratory tendencies.

Theories on migration do not end here. Migration for this study is about the perceived security factor in the minds of a human being or a group in which he or she belongs. It is movement over land in search of new opportunities for assured security in life. The land is the key. Nowhere the human being had thought about settling in the ocean with vast opportunities and resources. The reasons can be far too many. But the real reason is that their attachment with the land is stronger than with the ocean from the primordial instinct itself. Hence, it is even possible that human beings may think and talk of migrating to other planets in future where the "*terra* is *firma*" in spite of them being more hostile than the ocean of their mother planet called Earth.

Human Domination of Land

Humans, the last to arrive on the scene of evolution, dominated the land in spite of other life forms before them. This, the humans did in many ways. One of the methods was snatching the land from those who owned them by various means including war and plunder. People invaded and stole land from indigenous humans.

Human domination of land is not a study that can be analysed precisely. It has to be done in staccato fashion with interruptions on the way. But in a study to understand the human affinity to land these interludes do not matter. First, it is clear that humans took over land by various means from others after the initial entry and ownership. The formation of human settlements under various forms of governance till the nation-state arrived after the Westphalian Treaties in 1648 with sovereign rights was in great randomness and, thereby, chaotic. But chaos is an essential part of any system and sometimes very essential for the system to break the routine for survival. It can be seen that chaos did not settle down even after the formation of the sovereign states post Westphalia. Chaos reigns in human systems by default.

The second interesting aspect of land is that still there are human systems, some of them extremely thin compared to the world population that holds on to the land without allowing anyone else to enter their "property." It is one of the most amazing find of this study where the real reason perhaps is evasive to the extent that when time changes and even the presumed reason is gone, still the society survives with their land as their exclusive world. How could this situation be analysed?

Enter India; it is the world by itself. Everything about the human system in the world is visible in India. It is a bio-model for the world suitable for reductionist study. It is a unique country for analysing the human saga in conformity of the landclasp syndrome as the most dominant force that drives security thinking among humans. There are other samples too.

Hostility and determined projection and application of it by the inhabitants to anyone who enters a territory of land hold the key to assert the landclasp syndrome. This is visible everywhere in India and Indian governance. Hostility over land is one of the driving forces in politics and religious belief systems. To that extent politics in modern day is another form of religion. Politics too thrives on intense beliefs and archaic regimentation. But instead of a detailed examination, a simple look at the behaviour pattern of a bunch of islanders in India's

Andaman and Nicobar islands will confirm the conditioned landclasp syndrome of human beings.

North Sentinel Island is one of the 572 islands in the Andaman and Nicobar group. The island with an area of about 71 square kilometers is thickly vegetated and surrounded by coral reefs. Even though lying on the west of the main islands on the lee side of the normal tsunami propagation from the Java trench of the Indonesian tectonic belt, it is also opened to the fury of nature and has been shaped virtually by earthquakes and tsunamis. The Asian tsunami of 2004 had uplifted the island along with others in the Andaman and Nicobar group like a seesaw. The island is home for one of the few remaining primitive hunter-gatherer tribes that has no contact with the world outside "their" land. The islanders, called the North Sentineleses, who are hunter gatherers and believed to speak the Sentinelese language[12] violently disdain any external attempt at contact. The government of India has prohibited visitors into the island. But the islanders have been, from the very old times keeping their land from alien entry and domination much before such declaration. It has been a unique landclasp syndrome. They do not show such possessiveness about the ocean around them though they may venture out to visit an abandoned shipwreck, if accessible, bodily. They may fish with their hand crafted harpoons from the security of the land. They do not otherwise venture out into the sea to other islands. It is a bio-model[13] for this study.

The Sentinelese mindset about land and solid space can be seen in every human in whatever he or she does as what the sociologists say the territorial instinct. Yes, there is a difference; the Sentinelese behaviour is more a group show than individual act. That is the way nations behave. The China-India logjam in the Himalayas in April 2013 is simply North Sentinelese behaviour—"you have crossed the border, please go back."[14] Of course, there are rational arguments to suite the modern times. The deep rooted reason is the landclasp syndrome.

North Sentineleses are not at all possessive about the ocean around them. Anybody can take it as long as they keep away from their land. People who attempt to land on the beach will be resisted with long spears and arrows, the only weapons they use, by the natives who count between 50 and 400 according to reports (2012). Miles away from them on the other side there is a country that is said to be the epitome of modern in everything which many in the world consider the final destination for secured life. That is the perception. But they too behave the same way when illegal immigrants from elsewhere attempt to land on the beach over the long stretch of the coast at the south end. The only difference is that it will be blocked or landing will be resisted by the coast guard, a force of the government and not by the people residing there. In the North Sentinelese Island it is the people who will do it, not the representatives of an armed force of a government. That is the difference and to think of it that is the only stretch of modernisation from people doing it themselves directly or doing it through their representatives. In the modern state, the rules change as soon as the illegal immigrants touch the land or step on the beach. They can meet a lawyer thereafter. In water the rules are different. They are chased away. It is a kind of Indian *kabaddi* a game where touching the line over land is the time when the rules of the game change. Land is the ultimate in security perception.

On 26 January 2006 two fishers from a nearby island drifted into the North Sentinelese Island. They were killed and buried under sand by the locals according to a report from Indian Coast Guard.[15] Investigation related to the incident also proved that the North Sentineleses were not cannibals as presumed earlier, according to the coast guard regional commander S.P.S. Basra, an authority on the security of Andaman and Nicobar islands.

Sentineleses belong to the lost people according to the modern sociologists. They are not lost. They are actually not contactable. The world knows them. They remain isolated by their own choice. There are many such people at the tail end of the "worm train"[16] civilisation process in terms of modernisation and survivability. It calls for a different study. Here it is only asserted to establish how human beings feel for their land territory. The non-contactable or isolated people exist in various parts of the world. Some call them lost tribes. But they are basically indigenous peoples who clasp their land dearly and vehemently. They are not just hunter gatherers alone; many engage in farming too.

The world is made of land and ocean with a supporting air column. Human domination is only over land which is about 29 per cent and reducing gradually. The human inhabited land is a combination of agricultural and urban areas. It is about 43 per cent of the land (2005). That is to put it roughly without consideration for overlapping areas.[17] According to World Bank's World Development Report, 95 per cent of world population is concentrated on 10 per cent of world surfaces while only 10 per cent of world's land is classified as remote (2009).[18] Human domination of land is not uniform. It is not because of remoteness or terrain unsuitability in strict sense. But migratory tendencies make people keep moving and concentrating like flies around the honey pot. The general conclusion is that almost the entire land is possessed by people or governments. The density of occupancy varies and is limited to opportunities. The area occupied by Antarctica, generally appreciated as global commons, is nine per cent of the total land area.[19]

But more than the human domination of the land as compulsive possession, it is the establishment of right over it by those who dominated the acquisition that calls for attention. Humans have altered the land considerably after domination. There are no other species on Earth that had altered the face of the planet the way humans have done. Intentional alteration shows how vehement is the possessiveness that humans express towards land. Of course, there are other life forms that alter the land they occupy to suit their purposes. But such changes do not harm the land or change its nature. Compared to the land, the ocean remains unaltered in its natural profile. The changes in the ocean profile are over the land near to it. The life forms that live in the ocean never change it. Any major alteration to the ocean profile is by human intervention. The contrast in the alteration of land and the ocean also shows the seriousness of the landclasp syndrome.

The alteration of the ocean, where it exists, is collateral to land alteration. Terrestrial alteration dates back to the beginning of farming and agriculture about 10,000 years ago. The pace of alteration has accelerated today. But the alteration of the ocean is absolutely negligible compared to the land. The repercussions of the unregulated alterations of land could be extremely serious unless compensated with nature. Cities arose 9,000 years ago from the Mesopotamian planes. Today the cities attract heavy human flow from rural areas. There is also reverse migration when the economy is on the brink. People who return to their rural base often find their land is either gone or turned unsuitable for tilling.[20]

Human Systems and Land-centric Civilisation

The human systems existed in groups, relatively civilised within the absolute system.[21] Many human settlements advanced naturally within the constraints of the period they existed, vanished without trace under unforeseen circumstances. The circumstances, obviously, were beyond their control. These settlements were in the form of societies, not nations.[22] Historians used societies as the intelligible units of human settlements for their studies.[23] The ancestors of the people of today's nations belonged to these societies.

Civilisation, for some scholars, means an advanced human society.[24] Another way to look at the term is as the total product of human creativity and intellect at a given time. The civilisation took the land route. People migrated passing over land. It was land-centric. The migration over land was relatively easy as the sea level was far below and one could walk from land to land across the world. Historians mention about various civilisations. They were right, because for them civilisation meant an advanced form of society. Others were called primitives. Advancement is a relative expression. But this study looks civilisation from a unitary perspective of human development. The "worm train" mentioned earlier may be recalled here, for a moment, for a better appreciation.

The accentuation on the unitary civilisation in the author's study[25] is based on the fact that the entire human system evolves and develops as one unitary chain of incidents of all kinds including those created by chance variables. The human systems evolved and continue evolving from one stage or another. In all circumstances the process is likely to go on in future in a similar manner without any difference. In the unitary civilisation concept, neither the rate of development nor the relative advancement of the human system is the focus. The civilisation model is that of a long "worm train" that envelop the entire human system with graduating sections of development the world witnesses at any one time—a "train" with differently graded compartments of human systems. Under such perception, it can be visualised that in any age of historically recognised divisions of civilisations, the world also had comparatively less advanced societies within them. It may not be considered an imbalance, but actually it is the way the human society creeps towards evolution between two different ends—the head and the tail on either end of a long middle section with interconnecting vestibules. The vestibules are the migratory passages from one compartment to another. Each compartment or wagon is at different level of advancement. Under the unitary concept of civilisation every human being is recognised as part of the civilisation. There is nobody who is uncivilised. Civilisation is not restricted only to the selective groups under the falsie of advancement. The worm train should be visualised external to the nation state concept and seen as different levels of human system in their livelihood and knowledge acquisition.

The question is "What if an element or a section of the worm train remains static or destroyed?" Static or arrested societies can be seen at different sections especially at the tail end of the train, but they also have motion forward, though relatively at a lesser momentum than certain other sections that may go past of the one ahead. Even at the end, there is motion forward if there is no destruction by extinction. Yet, if the sections remain static, the worm train of civilisation has the capacity to stretch. It continues to crawl forward in history by regeneration if destroyed at sections or compartments. The train of civilisation grows like the amputated tail of a lizard. Human beings have repeatedly shown that they are determined to stay against all odds. The worm design is perhaps the secret by which they achieve this feat. If the human systems developed uniformly and concurrently, the shape of the worm would have changed into that of a globule. In such a state, the humans as a whole would be most vulnerable. If perished, there might not be another opportunity.

Historically, the idea of civilisations was different. To shift into a more systematic and reader friendly presentation of the case of the unitary civilisation, it can be said that in any age of historically recognised civilisations, there were less civilised societies within them. They were called primitive societies in some cases though it is not an acceptable terminology in this study except for offering an explanation. "How primitive is primitive?" is a serious question. It cannot be defined to a consensus. Relatively civilised societies existed within a human civilisation all the time. The only difference today is that they exist within the boundaries of a nation state and not in a society of disjointed settlements. Study of societies at various stages of development also shows that they were different from each other and from the lesser-civilised societies that existed during the period. There were other differences too. The asymmetries of lifestyles continue today.[26]

Studies on humans have to see people as whole, not as different groups but a single civilisation with people at different stages of development. This study does not intend to challenge the theories of experts on the subject. But it perceives civilisation as a whole unit with respect to time. It makes the passage to identify the concept of this book easy and practical. It is important for this study. From the viewpoint of historical studies, some civilisations were seen as arrested by their nature under the, multi-civilisation studies. Examples quoted by noted historian Arnold J. Toynbee are the Eskimos, Polynesians, Nomads, etc. While the Eskimos confined to the Arctic ice, the Polynesians faced the challenges of the sea around them. They remained static by the limitations caused by the sea. Those who developed had the land to support them. The Nomads were the wanderers of the desert steppes. Their land was not tillable for farming crops. It was as good as ocean. Toynbee compared the oasis in the deserts to islands in the ocean.[27] Such terrains impose restrictions that pulled the people back at a particular stage of their development to a restricted life style that limited their further growth, but balanced them with the terrain.

A historian of the caliber of Toynbee when compares an oasis with an island, there is also an implicit understanding of the landclasp dilemma where the desert around the oasis was compared with the ocean symbolically as uncommon for human habitation. That was the implied suggestion of original thinking.

Though not critically relevant to this study, the much talked about "clashes between civilisations" under the multi-civilisation argument becomes "clashes within civilisation" according to the argument based on unitary civilisation. The concept of unitary civilisation put forward is based on a previous finding of the author. The human clashes within the unitary civilisation can be compared to the turbulence within the high column of a cumulonimbus cloud in its prime. That is how the unitary system of the world civilisation behaves in its interactive matrix between various human systems in different compartments on the worm train. There will be clashes. The clashes will be within the unitary civilisation, not between civilisations. The world is one single civilisation. That is more than just an affirmation of this study.

The discussion is on the landclasp syndrome the humans exhibit in relation to the ocean. The study necessitates major shift in governance of a country in terms of maritime security. The examination is how civilisation impacted on the behaviour of humans with respect to land and to some extent the ocean. For this purpose the idea of unitary civilisation, the way humans advanced within a unitary system in the world, is important.

The human civilisation today is holding over land more than any other valued assets. Land holdings are a much bigger issue from the human concentration perspective. This is especially so with respect to rural households all over the world. Rural households look more at physical assets than financial assets that will give them security according to their perception in the old age. Land also gives inflation protection. Land as an asset is multidimensional. One's land is one's final place to live, till and die. Land is costlier in urban settlements. The urbanites accept it and look for other assets for security. But the land-centricity still remains with them.

The land-centric approach of the people has made land unsuitable for agriculture especially in urban areas. Soil is degraded and disbursed by wind and water, water tables are receding and agricultural productivity can decline and give way to other forms of production that may not sustain fertility of land. According to sociologist William Catton, prognosis for the future is an overshoot that occurs when populations exceed the local carrying capacity.[28] Only a population that is equal or less than the carrying capacity is sustainable. That will also be the optimum population for a country today.[29] Ideally, sustainable population of a particular species should be consuming renewable resources at a rate less than they are renewed, non-renewable resources at a rate less than the rate at which substitutes can be found and emitting pollution at a rate less than the capacity of the environment to absorb that pollution. If not, their survival in harmony with their land will be at risk.

It is straight line thinking all over. Actually nature and human intellect will not behave, as we see in our daily affairs, in that way. It may be so for other life forms. Most of the life forms as we know today can be extinct or endangered. But so far there is no indication for human extinction. Hence the theories applicable for sustainability of other species may not be applicable for human life forms with intellect. National and international governance should be ideally aimed at maximising human wellbeing. Governance for maximising national security is applicable at this juncture. The question is which is the focal terrain for governing national security? It has to be land as humans are land based species. Their affinity towards land is not an obsession; it is a natural instinct that cannot be changed. At least for now. Hence every aspect of security has to be integrated with national security governance which is a land based concept.

In this quest there can be many questions related to land, population, environment and resources. It is the role of the government to handle them to maximise the wellbeing of the people with the participation of the people. In all these aspects, the relationship between land and population is vital, not the ocean and population in spite of the fact both have resources and environmental affinity. Land is more important than ocean in national security governance. But still it is the ocean that will show the way for humans to survive over land. The maritime security is about the ways of using the ocean to survive over land, not in the ocean. That is what makes the maritime security a curious case.

Land and Maritime Issues—Comparison

The long border between China and India is disputed. There is no firmly respected demarcation along the border. The area is not an economically viable terrain, but of great strategic significance with vantage points especially when the two countries are connected to the security ventilator of confidence building measures (CBM) since very long. The border gets breached repeatedly and the countries blame each other in different ways. In one such incident there were reports in April 2013 that the Chinese troops intruded into India at Ladakh's Daulat Beg Oldi (DBO) sector. It raised acrimonious animosity against China in India—parliament, media and the public. The Chinese scholars and the military too had their shares of volleys against India. The governments and their diplomatic officialdom were careful and took cautious stand. The standoff continued for about three-weeks.

According to reports in India, a battalion of Chinese troops accompanied by vehicles and dogs came 19 km into India on 15 April 2013 and erected five tents. Indian troops responded facing the Chinese at about 300 meters by putting up tented posts. India's demand was that the Chinese should withdraw all the way back across the line of actual control (LAC). Indian troops, as reported, agreed to move back to Burste where they were stationed before.

The Chinese premier Li Keqiang was to visit India from 20 May 2013. India's foreign minister was to visit China on 9 May 2013 as a prelude to the premier's visit. The troop excess ended just four days before that. According to India's foreign minister, India would have expected a much better response from China. He harped on it continuously. There were growing calls in India that both the visits should be cancelled. China refused to budge and insisted that Indian troops should pull back. There were four flag meetings during the course between the senior military officials of the two countries. During discussions, China reiterated their demand that India should pull out of the bunkers they constructed in Phuktsay and Chumar areas to which India contended that similar activities were carried out by the Chinese on their side. The Chinese maintained that the activities on their side were merely developmental work and India should stop pushing its grazers in Chumar division southeast of Ladakh.

Initial Chinese intrusion was about 27 km. But an early detection and aggressive patrolling by Indian troops posted in the sector managed to make them pull back to the old patrol base at the DBO sector which was still 19 km from the LAC, as reported. Subsequently China and India followed diplomatic efforts to handle the issue. A veteran Indian analyst stated in the visual media that first of all it was not an intrusion but a transgression. Intrusion was a more serious word to use in the context. Some Indian media went to the extent of stating the government surrendered national interests to China out of fear. This was denied by the analyst who repeated it was only a transgression and not encroachment or intrusion. The analyst did not feel India received a slap from the Chinese as the media wanted to probe. The media also highlighted that China kept intruding into Indian territories to show its might before pulling back especially when its leaders were about to visit India. The media also added the visit of the new Chinese premier was not exclusive to India as a special case but a passing show after a visit to its most favoured ally and a mentee of sorts, Pakistan, whose rivalry with India was known, to congratulate the new government immediately after elections in May 2013.

But there was nothing new about the incident. According to Indian military sources such "transgressions" were common along LAC. They were probably right because it was quite usual under the landclasp syndrome of humans. But it is not so forceful at the maritime borders anywhere in the world, especially where land is not explicitly involved.

The observant New York Times reported the news as the Chinese sending an unusual number of military patrols into the remote high altitude mountainous desert of Ladakh.[30] According to the spokesperson of the ministry of external affairs of India, undoubtedly, it was a serious concern for the entire country. The politicians in India excluding the prime minister who kept his cool continued to be jingoistic and high pitched. The sensitivity of land intrusion was extremely high and intolerable to people. In China, there were mixed reactions and majority wanted to deal diplomatically without giving in to India's bad habits and media lies.[31] According to New York times, what puzzled Indian analysts, was why China squabbled on a barren moonscape frequented only by nomadic cattle grazers more than its maritime disputes in South China Sea with Japan, the Philippines and Vietnam among others. The answer lies on the aspect of the landclasp syndrome of humans and human societies. The sensitivity issues here are associated with the seriousness of land occupation which the other party considers totally unacceptable, whereas a maritime discord can wait.

Later on 23 October 2013 the prime ministers of China and India met in Beijing and signed a key agreement in the hope of resolving border and river water issues. The agreement known as Border Defence Cooperation Agreement (BDCA) is expected to strengthen the relations between the two countries in political relations and mutual cooperation.[32]

India and Bangladesh are in the process of settling down its disputes over sections of land border though the entire maritime boundary is under dispute. Maritime disputes do not show the urgency like the disputes along the land border. The minister for external affairs was to submit a bill in the Rajya Sabha (Upper House) of Indian Parliament on 7 May 2013, when Assam Gana Parishad (AGP), a local political party of the state of Assam in India bordering Bangladesh vehemently opposed it. The Bill was snatched from the minister violently in a discourteous manner. It happened when the minister got up to present the bill seeking constitutional amendments (No. 119). It was based on the agreement between India and Bangladesh signed a year back. The proceedings were stalled. The provocateurs were adamant and reiterated it is a national security issue and not that of the state of Assam alone.[33] A slight modification of the maritime boundary would not have invited such a wrath from the opposition unless it is exclusively guided by opportune politics. It was evident when India demarcated the maritime boundary with Sri Lanka in Palk Bay and Gulf of Mannar. There was no voice against it in India. But lately, the government of the state of Tamil Nadu, India woke up to the "handing over" of a small uninhabited island of 1.15 sq km, Kachchatheevu, under the bilateral delimitation agreements. The state politicians very well know that international agreements cannot be revoked by a single party to the agreement. The issue would not have been there if the tiny island had not come into focus, one may say.

India shares its boundaries with 10 countries—Bangladesh, Bhutan, China, Indonesia, Maldives, Myanmar, Nepal, Pakistan, Sri Lanka and Thailand. India shares maritime boundaries with seven out of them; among them three shares land boundaries also—Bangladesh, Myanmar and Pakistan—with India. India's maritime disputes are only with Bangladesh and Pakistan. It has also land disputes with both these countries. Maritime disputes remain unresolved, according to political analysts, because of the land disputes. It need not be exact when viewed under the landclasp syndrome. In fact, the maritime disputes have much more economic values than the land disputes and more or less equal strategic values. But still the land disputes gain more attention and volatility than the maritime disputes. The marine borders are relatively unguarded with respect to land borders. India will also have another neighbour across the legal continental shelf once the area is approved legally—Sultanate of Oman. Considering it is a continental shelf domain within the maritime security perspective, demarcating it is not likely to cause any serious issues between the two countries. It would, if it was over dry land.

While China-India relations were getting glaringly rubbed on the Himalayan icy desert, the South China Sea was getting clobbered over the disputed Senkaku (Diaoyu) Island claimed by Japan, China (PRC) and Taiwan (ROC). It did not reach the proportion of the land fury between China and India, especially among the public of both the countries, though the area and the repercussions were very much larger in the China-Japan and Japan-Taiwan maritime issues. Here one country faces two claimants. Still the issue does not surpass the seriousness of a land breach. There are many such situations that make maritime security a curious case.

There are large number of land and maritime disputes in the world today. Disputes along airspace tags or dissolves in land and maritime disputes. Almost all the land and maritime disputes are carried forward from history, long and short of it. The disputes are international as well as within the nations. The latter disputes are mainly over land territory. The disputed territories in some cases are under the total control of one of the claimants, or partial control of more than one claimant. Some are no man's land. Some of the internal disputes are between the state and the sub-national entities and in some cases between the sub-national entities. There are also disputes in the Antarctic territory. Though the Antarctic Treaty freezes all the territorial claims, Antarctic is considered to be global commons. The Antarctic disputes are globally unresolved because the treaty is not strictly competent to handle them. Any state can still lay claim to Antarctica as *terra nullius* on the grounds of the land not being part of any existing state's legal and effective territory.

War, Society, Land and Greed

Warfare has been an integral aspect of human systems. War was fought for resources, primarily land, for the foothold of the society. The first war ever fought, probably, was for fire.[34] If that is so, that was the only war where land was not the cause. But the wars for "fire" were still fought over land. The assumption about the war for fire, not a critical finding, emphasises the human need for resources for perceived security. Resources are primarily associated with land. This is reflected even when environment, resources and explorations are concerned, wherein the nodal agencies or the resource agents are land based.

War and resources are linked intimately. War is primarily meant for gathering and controlling resources. Behind every war there is a resource motive. The Trojan War, some believe, was a reality. The Greek epic *Iliad,* written by Homer (850 B.C.), according to them, would have been based on an actual war fought for tin, a precious strategic resource in those days, not exactly to rescue Helen, the runaway wife of Agamemnon, the king of Mycenae and the leader of the Greek in the coalition war. The war lasted ten years and the Greek established control of Troy and its resources over land. Helen could have been an excuse. Ten year span could be too long a wait. Excuses follow wars. In modern times tin may be replaced with oil under veritable excuses to ignite a war. The maritime forces will be involved in sealift and naval landings as in the Trojan War. But the wars were generally fought to gain ground and dominate over land, not the ocean, even if that land is a tiny speck of ground. The resources are associated with land though ocean is a great reservoir of them. The not so thought about fact is that the ocean that holds vital resources is land just happened to be under water.

War is violent conflict between human systems. War is lethal even for close noncombatants who get involved in the ensuing violence after it breaks out. The victory in war is decided by the quantum of ground occupied. The ground that is occupied by the victor once belonged to the opponent. That was before the commencement of war. The dominance in ocean may help in war by movements and manoeuvres. But the ultimate factor in deciding victory over the opponent is based on the ground (land) held. War is also different from conflicts, brawls, riots, revolts, etc., which are not necessarily meant for occupancy of land. A revolution may or may not involve warfare. The objective is to occupy land that has been denied to the revolutionaries who were subjugated in their own land. The objective of a revolution is to take over power of governance. But war is fought for land primarily under issues of sovereignty and assorted benefits that include resource conformity for own society and denial to others. In the last century, it is estimated that between 167 and 188 million people perished as result of war for land and associated benefits.[35] War gets support from other terrains under the terrain specificity principle of national security.[36] Ocean is just one among the terrains. Land dominates all terrains. Everyone wants it. No one is satisfied with what is held as far as the land holdings are concerned.

The theories of war from the times of Sun Tzu and even before were based on land and occupying the territory. The theorists concluded that war was one of the means of political intercourse and, thereby, an instrument of geostrategic policy. It is seemingly true in a world that approves war as a means of sorting out difficulties in a difficult way. That makes war another form of international relations in which violence is used to influence the other country. Even if this theory of negative diplomacy has the approval of the society, it is applicable only when the parties involved in war are recognised countries. Interestingly even modern society approves it as a means of resolving disputes between countries. War mongering by people and governments are still in fashion. The media too support it in certain cases. But there could be conflicts similar to war with extreme violence where one party is attempting to subjugate another to its will. But in reality, it is impossible for parties to be independent of any country. They may be called non-state actors but certainly it could be seen historically that every "non-state actor" had one or more state actors as support. Under such circumstances the theories of war, especially those postulated by Carl Von Clausewitz is applicable in every conflict regardless of state and non-state participants, if the emphasis is on violence and interaction is based on assault with overwhelming force or impact. Such wars are fought presently in various parts of the world where terrorism, rogue states, ethnic cleansing, insurgency, etc., turns out to be abstractionist expressions of the political kind. In reality, war is fought with state machinery even if it is by proxy or through non-state actors. Modern conflicts are all indirect wars under various names and approbations. All these conflicts are land-centric. The maritime elements of such conflicts are very feeble and, if at all there, are limited to sealift and reach. It is long since a ship sank another in direct conflict at sea. Of course, this doesn't limit maritime operations within the domain of logistics or reach. In a scenario of mutually assured destruction (MAD), humans will need ocean to hide and strike. The terrain could be exclusively the expansive ocean. The big picture of the maritime domain of the ocean terrain cannot be pulled down from the operations rooms and control centres till then. When it happens, the ocean could be the prime terrain where the final destiny will be laid out unless outer space had already gained prominence or a major terrain shift had taken place as a more hideous game zone than the ocean or outer space.

On an afterthought, it is doubtful for the outer space to replace the ocean ever in the gravity of human survival.

No major theories of war postulated by military or political strategists mention about maritime warfare or maritime strategy. It is limited to a handful of professionals and scholars within their limited space. But the two world wars were fought seriously at sea. The third one, the Cold War, was seriously ocean centric. Ships of bipolar powers playing chicken at sea, nuclear arms race at sea, underwater nuclear explosions, Cuban missile crisis, Bay of Pigs, Arctic hideouts, etc., were all based on the ocean. The primarily ocean bred marines of modern warfare in the US military are those who fight the war over land and basically meant for preemptive surgical strikes or advanced clean up and hold before the war erupts seriously. An amphibious landing is a vital component of land war. It is not a war at sea.

War is an extreme human activity that has the approval of the social systems of yore. Things may be slowly changing today with the people able to understand the overall impact of war in every field. But it is not going to end war but may transform it into more vicious conflicts within the domain of the powerful. The powerful needs wars to retain power. War was the actual projection of power. The world is still witnessing such power projections for domination over land and resources. The psychology of human greed fuels this behaviour.

The famous Russian philosopher and writer Leo Tolstoy (1828-1910) wrote a short story in 1886—*"How Much Land does a Man Need?"* The story was acclaimed the greatest piece of literature by none other than James Joyce (1882-1941), one of the influential writers in the modernist avant-garde of early 20th century. It was admired by various other writers and entertainment media producers. In the story, the protagonist Pahóm, a peasant, decided to acquire as much land as possible as his wife always complained that they did not have enough land to satisfy them. He felt he did not even have to fear the devil if he had enough land. Satan overheard it and decided to accept the challenge. The rest of the story was how Pahóm went around acquiring land in his manic obsession and finally got his hands on a huge acreage, the bargain of a lifetime, only to die of exhaustion the day he contracted it. His servant buried him on the land in a grave that measured six feet. It was a great story of the period with a solemn message that, however, cannot be followed as human greed surpasses wisdom and right discrimination when driven by the primeval instinct for perceived security. Nations are made that way. "We, the People" think based on land, the mirror of perceived security. Nations are governed through land based thinking. The problem is when a terrain different from land, for example the ocean, matters for national security. How do we think; how do we govern?

Is landclasp syndrome an obsession? It doesn't seem so. But people value land as the one that provide them security. People try to grab everything that provides a feeling of security. In the quest for security, even a small security blanket will satisfy a child. Land is the high point in the quest for security. Acquiring land is a survival instinct by default in humans. It is not a pervasive obsession. Land is everything. The landclasp syndrome figures in everything that humans do, even in national or international governance. Natural, it is. It is within this paradigm, maritime security becomes a curious case.

Examining Maritime Security

According to *Rig Veda,* the ancient Indian verse, ocean is the reservoir of rivers.[37] Ocean in that sense leads to the lowest point on the earth as part of the land unless it covers it totally. How was it formed; what does it contain? Who knows?

According to scholars and historians, World Ocean was at a very low level around 20,000 B.C. Today's continents were connected over land.[38] People walked across them. Today's busy ports were located far deep into the land as stoned interiors. Most of the people never saw the sea. The movement of people was much inside relative to the ocean then existed. The world became warmer around 15,000 B.C. Icy glaciers melted. The people were a bit puzzled, but they didn't reason or debate over climate change. They watched the sea level rising persistently without knowing the reason or trying to figure it out. They retreated as the water came up. The sea level gradually rose for about 4,000 years until it stopped around by 8,000 B.C. By then, the sea level had risen by about 140 metres. Historian Geoffrey Bellaney recapitulates it as the most extraordinary event in human history during the last 100,000 years and far more influential than all the combined events of the 20th century.[39]

The rising seas transformed human life and altered their behaviour in relation to the ocean and the land forever. The land sank under the rising sea level. People became aware of the ocean that surrounded them, though they didn't understand it. The mystery began.

Bellaney wrote that the seas caused a peculiar phenomenon of proximity and isolation that according to him were the two powerful determinants of history.[40] Today the oceans cover around 360 million square kilometers, about 71 per cent of the earth's surface. The land adjoining the oceans has a total coastline of 504,000 kilometres according to certain estimates.[41] Though it appears to divide the nations, the ocean, in fact unites them geographically. It binds the continents. It is a medium that humans have ventured out for centuries to discover, conquer, trade and harvest. The average depth of the ocean is four kilometers. Ocean is a common challenge for humans. Those who traversed it depended on each other, helped and developed special bonds.

All these, and the topping proclamation that the ocean sustains life on the earth, could be ideological statements. What exactly is the value of the ocean to humans who cling on to land? How to understand it with precision accuracy? To that extent the ocean as understood today is much more than the quoted text from *Rig Veda*. It is not just a reservoir of rivers that flow down over land; it is a treasure house of everything that humans can use and are using in a limited way to transform their lives for the better. The contents of the ocean and the benefits the humans can accrue from it are yet to be identified and calculated precisely. It is a geophysical terrain similar to land where the game can be played to maximise national security.

Ocean Property

The best way to govern the ocean from the land-centric posture is by converting it into a unitary parameter by integrating everything associated with it in relation to the purpose. The purpose is national governance. The unitary term used in this study to explain the combinations of the ocean factors in human life and related national security aspect is ocean property.[42] Ocean property is a singular term identified to assess the value of the ocean as in the case of geoproperty rights. Ocean property is the result when the parameters of ocean are consolidated under a unitary concept for ease of governance. Ocean property should allow for identifying and measuring the complementary components towards national security and establishing the rights over them.

The ocean property comprises four components according to a study[43] ac. They are,

- ocean advantage,
- ocean resources,
- ocean environment and
- oceanic islands.

Threats to these components can interplay with the national security regime. Maximising national security, therefore, includes maximising the returns from the ocean property components by minimising the threats closing on them under the force of threat attraction.[44] It is possible only by establishing an appropriate ocean property regime for a nation. Any geopolitical entity, including landlocked or geographically disadvantaged can make an estimate of its ocean property rights. The estimates will be different for different entities. To that extent it is also important to understand that ocean property is not exclusive to littorals and islands, but to landlocked and geographically disadvantaged entities too. This is an important aspect reiterated further in this study.

The ocean property components together contribute to the ocean property regime for maximising returns for the select geopolitical entity. The maritime security component is hidden in the ocean property regime at the macro level. To understand ocean property it is necessary to examine and appreciate its constituents.

Ocean Advantage

Ocean advantage is hidden in the multidimensionality of the ocean as a terrain, among other aspects. It is similar to terrain advantage over land to some extent. The terrain advantage is emphasised by the adopted manoeuvres according to the appreciated context. The operations or activities that demand manoeuvres in the ocean can be,

- geostrategic during other-than-war situations,
- wartime as in strategic and tactical military operations,
- socio-econo-political as in commercial shipping,
- ocean research,
- law enforcement and

- even unlawful as in maritime crimes, etc.

In all the manoeuvres related to an operation or an activity at sea, ocean advantage is the key element that is put to use. Every operation or activity at sea or related to the sea has to take into consideration the associated ocean advantage to maximise its effectiveness, whether lawful or unlawful. Ocean advantage is the way ocean can be put to use to the maximum benefit with respect to an ocean related activity the country or any other entity is engaged in.

The uniqueness of the ocean is its multidimensionality. It is one of the contributing factors of ocean advantage. It has the surface, the layer, interfacial zones with air and land, and finally the depth, the large abyss of hidden treasure. All these dimensions together contribute to the ocean advantage. Ocean provides movement and transportation through common areas with freedom of navigation. Stealth is a key factor in ocean movement that has been very well emphasised in submarine or underwater manoeuvres. Stealth is greatly advantageous for military security from the time submarines entered the war zone. The submarine is a weapon by itself to counter asymmetric threats. It proved its worth as for the classical *guerre de course.*[45] Submarines can penetrate deep littoral waters immune to nuclear, biological, and chemical attacks, if well equipped with countermeasures to face the threats of attack submarines and mines. They can provide an efficient platform for nuclear attack on the second strike mode for balance of power in a nuclear scenario, and force the world to resort to conventional warfare. Submarines are unique combination of mobility, stealth, endurance and versatility for offensive operations. Surface and air forces are more vulnerable than submarines. Ocean is the only geographical terrain that provides this advantage under heightened emphasis. It is a critical aspect of ocean advantage that is expected to be exploited further with the advent of ocean robotics especially of the underwater variety. A simple wave rider robotic design that can go across the ocean submerging when necessary to avoid detection can prove more fatal than an unmanned aerial vehicle or even a submarine tomorrow. Underwater robots distributed worldwide can be strategic sensing platforms and could also aid the second strike doctrine under absolute stealth.

Ocean advantage is not just about stealth, submarines or underwater robotics. They are applications of ocean advantage. The ocean advantage could be any kind of ocean support with which a nation or a geopolitical entity is at an advantage in relation to another. Maritime transportation is an ocean advantage. It is left to the entity to identify and decide on it. Ocean provides the facility. Any country can progress in sea transportation for carriage of goods. Landlocked and geographically disadvantaged countries and other geopolitical entities could engage in commercial shipping. It doesn't have to be the monopoly of coastlands[46] or island nations. But surprisingly no such nation has ever thought of venturing into shipping seriously. Any geopolitical entity can engage in it. Somalia with its mega piracy adventures has taken absolute benefit of ocean advantage to partially avoid poverty in the absence of a government for 21 years even remaining as a member of the United Nations.[47] The world could not contain their piratical activities in spite of spending billions from national economies. Somali pirates were at a higher advantage—the ocean advantage—in relation to their adversaries. Somali piracy will come to an end only when Somalis decide it unless their adversaries turn the ocean advantage against them. The power of ocean advantage should not be underestimated. The terrorists who attacked India at Mumbai on 26 November 2008, very effectively manoeuvred under the ocean advantage for reach. Regrettably history reveals that an entity had effectively used ocean advantage to its benefit only in war or for committing unlawful activities. That is one of the reasons why the unlawful activities based in the ocean terrain cannot be contained easily. The landclasp syndrome prevents a nation in absorbing ocean advantage positively to enhance maritime security.

But there is more to mention about ocean advantage than war, unlawful and clandestine activities.

Ocean advantage, in this study, is similar to terrain advantage with a slight difference. Terrain advantage is the advantage an entity gains over the adversary, real or virtual, by manipulating or utilising it. For that the terrain should have certain peculiarities that suit the purpose and allows the entity to take advantage in a situation. For example a high ground can provide certain advantage in a land operation; a naturally fertile plain can be useful for high yield farming. However, it depends on the way the entity utilises the terrain. What the entity can utilise for an identified purpose is the terrain advantage. A terrain is where the game is played and the outcome is decided. It is quite important in national security governance. The ocean as a terrain provides immense advantage to every nation in maximising their national security or for any entity to maximise the return in their ocean based activity. This aspect is termed as ocean advantage and is included in the overall concept of ocean property as one of its elements. Ocean property like geoproperty has legal connotation since every geopolitical entity has rights over the ocean including the rights over the global commons. The property rights in the ocean encompass the concept of ocean property. A nation that can maximise its ocean advantage can gain seriously from its maritime security.

The ocean attains the ocean advantage by its,

- expansiveness,
- stealth nature,
- global commons,
- dynamic energy that can be converted into useful energy and
- multidimensional profile.

It is the ocean advantage that promotes transportation by sea and associated industries. Military operations at sea heavily depend on ocean advantage. The possibility of using the sea for a response to first strike in nuclear attack keeps the balance to some extent between the potential nuclear adversaries of the tremulous world. This operational attitude derives from the ocean advantage. Perpetrators of unlawful activities at sea and from the sea use ocean advantage to their benefit. Ocean advantage is different from ground or field advantage over land though has theoretical similarities. It is a distinct advantage as part of ocean property, a concept that is very much terrain specific.

Ocean advantage is inherent to ocean as part of ocean property. Strategically or tactically an entity may not be able to deny ocean advantage to another. But it can gather it more than the adversary if both are placed similar in ocean advantage.

Ocean Resources

There are various opinions while defining ocean resources. Resource is a source of support or help for definite purposes. Ocean as a supporting entity for life is a resource by itself. But a macro level appreciation is not a practical idea for national governance. Resource identification should be arrived by analytical reductionism reaching at the smallest unit of the resource. The resource thereby is the smallest standalone unit that supports a purpose. It has been mentioned earlier that the first war was fought by humans probably for fire. The Trojan War was probably fought for tin, an important metallic element of that period—the Bronze Age—for making the alloys of bronze by melting with copper. Both the fire and tin were valuable resources of the respective periods and sufficient excuses for indulging in war. The resource cannot be anything, but the one that has value to the envisaged purpose. The higher the value, the more important the resource will be. The value will also depend upon the period when it is considered. The ocean contains many such resources that a user may perceive as a support requirement. The resources can be classified in various ways. A common appreciation is as living and non-living resources.

The living resources of the ocean comprise the food resources—fish and sea weeds. The non-living resources are water, oil, gas, lime, mud deposit and a variety of minerals. The identified minerals in the ocean are magnesium, bromine, sand, gravel aggregates, placer deposits, phosphate, calcareous deposits, manganese, copper, cobalt and nickel. There are also hydrothermal mineral deposits containing zinc, copper, iron, silver, cobalt and gold. But the issue here is identifying the ocean resources. From the land based perspective, all the identified resources on the seabed or beneath including the continental shelf unless they are exclusively ocean generated like shell fish or sea weeds, could be viewed as land resources and not as ocean resources. The ocean resources could be segregated as those in other dimensions of the ocean other than seabed or beneath and exclusive to ocean for their sustenance. In that case oil, gas, mineral nodules, etc. becomes land resources under the hardcore landclasp syndrome.

Ocean Environment

Environment has many definitions. One of the definitions mentions environment as the aggregate of all external conditions and influences affecting life and development of organisms.[48] There is life in the ocean supported by the marine environment. Ocean supports life on the earth through the conducive natural environment sustained by it. The ocean environment as a part of ocean property comprises:

- coastal zones,
- marine environment and
- climate dynamics.

They are influential in designing an ocean property regime. Governing the ocean environment means managing all the three constituents. People's participation is essential for it. It is more than a national task. It has to have a global approach as environment is not bounded by national boundaries.

Coastal Zones

Coastal zone is the meeting and interacting point of the atmosphere, the sea and the land. It is a land-sea-air concept. Human activity under the landclasp syndrome in the name of development is predominant in coastal zone. But coastal zone as part of ocean environment has an environmental signature. Because, it is an area that has abundant biodiversity in terms of flora and fauna. The environment that sustains this biodiversity is a combination of marine, land and air based environment. It will be difficult to separate them precisely. Any change in the environmental stasis can alter the biodiversity. The thrust areas of coastal zone biodiversity are wet lands, mangrove areas, coral reefs, etc. that lie partially over land and partially in water.

The coastal zone is the area as decided and approved by the competent authority on either side of the coastline. The profile of the coastline shows at least three paradoxical behaviours. In one, the coastline changes its profile every moment by wave action and other geological changes. Secondly, it exhibits a mathematical ambiguity in measurement. The coastline is a fractal. It means, in short measures, the coastline will appear longer than in long measures. Third, the coastline is not at the same level around the world as the sea level varies at different places though the entire ocean is a continuum without a break. The sea level normally taken as the mean sea level for altitude calculation is for this reason. The sea level alters at different part of the world because of Earth's spin, gravitational pull of the moon, underwater disturbances, the difference in the quantity of the water that leaves and returns to a particular sea, etc.

The length of the world coastline is an approximation at a particular time by a particular measurement. Under the international law, instead of the coastline, it is the surveyed baseline that is accepted by governments as a reference line to decide the dividing line of land and water with respect to the ocean. The baseline also loses its sanctity unless legally recognised. Countries can oppose the baseline of another especially at disputed boundaries. Internally, a government can face issues in determining the baseline based on developmental activities.

Marine Environment

Marine environment, sustains life in the ocean. Marine environment is that part of ocean environment that directly impacts life systems on the Earth. Ocean environment is the absolute environment of the ocean comprising the three constituents—coastal zone, marine environment and climate dynamics.

Any damage to marine environment will not only impact on life in the ocean but also the ocean environment as a whole with a larger impact over the land. The marine environment should be free from pollution and other damages. Other damages can be caused when ocean loses its balance by changes caused by global warming or other unforeseen situations. Failing to tackle global warming may weigh heavily on the governments in future. Ocean is a sink for carbon. Unchecked carbon emission can cause imbalance in the carrying capacity of the ocean. According to researchers it can cost the world around £1.3 trillion a year by 2100, which is a very conservative assessment.[49] The state of the marine environment is bad. It is facing serious problems due to pollution, overfishing, oxygen depletion, acidness and rising sea levels.

The marine environment holds and sustains the marine ecosystems which belong to the largest aquatic system in the world. It is extremely difficult to study and understand the marine ecosystem due to the multidimensional nature and expansiveness of the ocean. The study is best undertaken by dividing the open ocean into vertical and horizontal divisions.[50] The entire area of the open ocean is the pelagic realm whereas the benthic realm is the sea bottom, the "land" part of it for this study.

The circulation of rainwater and the huge preservation capability of the ocean have contributed immensely to purifying the environment.

And also, it would be difficult for the proper air temperature to be maintained without great sea currents. All these and more including the yet to be identified factors govern the ocean environment.

Climate Dynamics

Earth is a beautiful blue marble. The soothing colour it acquired is from the ocean and atmosphere. The vivacity of the planet reflects in its manifestation as the blue marble. It is made possible by the climate mostly and regularly designed by the ocean. A healthy ocean environment will give the planet the blue marble look. Ocean is primarily responsible for the climate around the planet which changes seasonally. Ocean has shaped the earth and its climate in profound ways. Sometimes it unleashes fiendish forces that also contribute in shaping the earth. The ocean is a storehouse for mega energy and the heat exchange between ocean and the atmosphere drives the winds across the world. Winds create atmospheric circulation and ocean surface currents. The heat exchange also drives the currents inside the ocean from one end to another. The ocean is the moderator of climate. It does it by absorbing excess heat and carbon dioxide thereby slowing the warming of the atmosphere due to rising levels of greenhouse gases. Without ocean, Earth would not have been a blue marble. Its colour would have been amber, like Mars or Venus.

The ocean environment is the driver of climate on the planet. Ocean absorbs heat when the air is warm and lets out heat when the air is cool thereby moderating the climate. The heat transfer within the ocean, through hot and cold currents, between the ocean and the atmosphere, and the latent heat release or evaporation is behind the dynamics of climate. The heat exchange also creates water vapour and chemical compounds that are released into the atmosphere. The energy is released through condensation driving much of the atmospheric circulation that redistributes heat and moisture throughout the planet. Ocean creates and maintains the climate. The warming up of climate as a global change by burning of the fossil fuel and felling of rain forests is contained to a great extent by the ocean. The ocean thus acts as a buffer to climate change.

The microorganisms that survive within the marine environment also contribute towards climate on Earth. Photosynthetic marine organisms remove carbon dioxide from atmosphere to build carbohydrates. Limestone and fossils that forms out of the remains of the microorganisms in the ocean remove carbon dioxide permanently from the atmosphere. Ocean water is a major sink for carbon dioxide. The water absorbs carbon dioxide 40 per cent more than the atmosphere. This decelerates climate change. The ocean thus keeps the climate balanced. Its ability to generate these balancing forces depends on the ocean environment, a constituent of ocean property.

The interaction of ocean with the land and atmosphere generates climate that makes life possible and survive. Changes in the distribution of water in the ocean at one place can have a ripple effect elsewhere. It can affect wind circulation, rainfall and nutrient distribution within the ocean. The ocean environment needs to be watched for changes that could harm the world. It has to be a global task. Climate, especially, is a global phenomenon. It has to be tackled under international regimes along with national governance.

Concept of Maritime Security—Change Forestalled?

The concept of the much spoken term "maritime security" settles within the terrain specificity of the ocean. Ocean has been considered a different domain and, thereby, another terrain for strategic and tactical manoeuvres. It is a geophysical terrain like the "ground" over land. But there is no term similar to maritime security that coins with manoeuvres over land. In strategic and tactical studies there is no term called ground security or land security. It also highlights the land based thinking driving the human system. Here manoeuvres can be any kind of strategic or tactical activity based on the specific terrain. There are other terrains too, other than land and ocean, where the games are played in national security governance. The problem is when the need for governing them arises. Has it to be done independently or in an integrated manner under the overall national security regime based on the end objective?

This study is about the ocean and examining whether there is a need for integrating maritime security with the overall national security. If that is so the entire system related to the ocean used for governance by national governments as well as international organisations has to change in a serious manner. It will be a major diversion in national governance on the Westphalian turnpike. This study does not indulge into other terrains under the terrain specificity of national security. It is about the ocean.

The subject matter is about integrated maritime security (IMS). Why integrate? With what? These two are the prominent questions.

The answer to the first question is that maritime security is a ghost protocol for governance by its association with the ocean in a landclasped world and, thereby, shows the tendencies to become a curious case. Isolated, insular , laid back or exclusive governance may not give it the desired identity for governance. Hence maritime security should be consciously integrated for governance and not dealt with as an exclusive domain for governance. At the macro level a nation or any geopolitical entity has to be governed to maximise the national security which ultimately maximises the wellbeing of the people. Hence the answer to the second question is that maritime security should be integrated with national security for governance. The conventional meaning of integration of maritime security, as envisaged in the world presently, deals with integrating the various aspects of ocean based security elements and agencies under a single forum by unification of sorts. The problem with such integration is that the ghost protocol will continue to remain elusive as a playful specter without yielding much result, though it has tremendous powers. These powers, this study finds, can be unleashed better by integrating it at the macro level with national security governance bearing on the unitary ocean property concept.

The study will be dealing with these two questions throughout the book.

Conclusions

For the human system, land is the abode where they seek their wellbeing. Ocean is a mysterious and perilous organic system that for the strategists is a terrain where nations can play the game of national security. Human beings clasp the land. Land is their security blanket.

Ocean is actually the flood waters over the land. Humans do not perceive the ocean that way. The tendency is to visualise the ocean different from the land. It is a perilous and unsafe terrain. This is so even for the people who live along the coastal areas. Under international law, ocean belongs to every nation including the landlocked and the geographically disadvantaged. They can take the benefit of the ocean depending on the ocean property availability and effective governance. It is not being done.

The landclasp syndrome presents itself strongly in national governance. The ocean is secondary and often isolated from the main theme except under certain selective approach. Maritime security is a term that is coined in many ways. Often it is expressed in military and other security perspectives. Maritime security is the wholesome complementary faction of national security. This idea is yet to sink in among governments seriously. Maximising the returns from the ocean property is the ultimate objective. It is possible only by integrating maritime security with national security in governance. This is what is being examined further in this book.

The next chapter looks at the ocean and the geopolitical entities more ornately as the stakeholders of the giant planet. In the meantime, the curious case of maritime security awaits further recognition.

NOTES

1 Gendered expressions are intentionally avoided.

2 Demarest, Geoff, *Geoproperty,* London: Frank Cass, 1998, p. 22. Geoproperty is a vital concept about the rights over property introduced by the author and scholar, Geoff Demarest. The concept is closely related to national security and national governance. The rights are not exclusively over land property but all the post-modern innovations, necessities, etc. In this study the concept is considered and modified to explain the yield from ocean as ocean property that includes its elements over which the nations can exercise their rights and put them to effective use from the perspective of maritime security.

3 Present day meaning of "no man's land" (*terra nomo*) is the land that is under dispute and not occupied under declared and accepted ownership. In military terms, it is a strip of land left between two opposing trench systems that act as a cushion along a disputed territory under mutual consent of the countries as a confident building measure. There is also "no man's land" between countries that are yet to be settled but may not be under dispute. The disputes may arise when the settlement process is on. Such an area may also have people inhabiting them under local ownership claimed by them. In comparison there is no "no man's sea." In rare cases there can be a strip of ocean left between the countries along their disputed maritime boundaries until the disputes are settled. But it will be an idling gap that converges into the high seas from the territorial sea. The left around part of the territorial sea at the notional boundary lines is free for navigation. Whereas over the land, any movement, even of nomadic grazers or hunters, is forbidden and can cause serious repercussion in geostrategic relationships if trespassed.

4 There are unresolved claims over Antarctica too.

5 en.wikipedia.org/wiki/Alfred_Wegener, accessed 12 March 2013. The book was first published in 1915. Wegener called it *Urkontinent.*

6 Paleri, Prabhakaran, *National Security: Imperatives and Challenges,* New Delhi: Tata McGraw-Hill Publishing Company Limited, 2008, p. 420. The ancient thought process in India, *Vasudeiva kudumbakam*—the whole world is a family, is a Sanskrit quote from the ancient Indian scriptures. Though quoted and spoken about widely, the concept is too idealistic to think of in the present day world where even the national security concept is yet to be accepted as the wholesome wellbeing of the people of a nation. The governance is aimed at selective welfare rather than wholesome wellbeing of all the people. *Vasudeiva kudumbakam* is about global security. It is a far cry from the present day collective security of the United Nations. However if optimism has a take, then the concept of national security can certainly

lead to global security one day.

7 Ibid., p.8, Law of invariance is a concept identified by the author, which states that *the changes in the core behaviour of a human system, while a reality, is too negligible to notice and, therefore, for a psychosomatic system application relative to humans, it is sufficient to presume the model applicable today will be constant in time whether it is past or future.* Under the law of invariance, according to the author, what human experiences in a life span will be more or less similar to what one would have faced and experienced earlier. Only the milieu will be different.

8 NASA Science, Science News, Continents in Collision: Pangaea Ultima, science1.nasa.gov/science-news/science-at-nasa/2000/ast06oct_1/, accessed 2 April 2012.

9 They Said It, "You are Indians, he is Pakistani, she is Chinese, they are Americans? Come on! We are all African Apes." *Times of India*, Kozhikode, 15 May 2013, p. 10, quoting Tasleema Nasreen, Writer, on race and ethnicity.

10 Human Migration, en.wikipedia.org/wiki/Human_migration, accessed 24 July 2012.

11 Ibid.

12 Sentinelese is a presumed language. The external world is not aware of the language since there is no contact with the people. Contact is hostile.

13 Paleri, n.6, p. 36,191, 214 and 232. Bio-model (also biomodel) is a concept by the author about modeling a system activity of human society including national governance at micro level or learning from a micro level reality model of human system about something similar but larger than it. A biomodel at micro level can help to understand the macro behaviour of the human system. Different from biomodels used in biological sciences.

14 As written on the banner displayed by the Chinese troops in Daulat Beg Oldie sector, Ladakh, India in the alleged border standoffs on 15 April 2013, www.tibetsun.com/news/2013/07/10/china-defends-its-latest-ladakh-incursion

15 Indian Coast Guard archives, Coast Guard Headquarters, New Delhi, 2006.

16 Explained later.

17 Human Domination of Earth's Ecosystems: www.lue.ethz.ch/education/Fowi/Ingbio/lubchenco_II.pdf, accessed 12 January 2013.

18 Ibid.

19 What percentage of land on earth is dominated by humans? wiki.answers.com/Q/What_percentage_ of_land _on_ earth_is_dominated_by_humans#, accessed 18 August 2013.

20 nationalgeographic.com/earthpulse/hu, accessed 22 August 2013.

21 Arnold J. Toynbee, *A Study of History, Vol. 1,* New York, Dell Publishing Co., Inc., 1978, p. 648.

22 Ibid., p. 648.

23 Ibid.

24 There are historians and writers of history who say that the word civilisation is used to depict many things. There are words like "uncivilised" to explain about societies that are inferior, normally by people who consider themselves as civilised. For this study, civilisation is taken as the process of growth by creative intellectual development towards increased comfort and the fact that, in a formal society, people may be at different levels of such advancement. The entire society, therefore, had to be seen as a civilisation with a lower and upper limit. This study propounds that principle sans a partisan attitude. Another aspect this book does not subscribe is to see the human system of a period the world over, especially under today's conditions of nation states, as different civilisations, but as people at different stages of development within a civilisation. Such understanding and perceptions are important for the study of national security as envisaged by the author.

25 Paleri, n.6, p. 4-5.

26 Paleri, n.6, p. 213.

27 Toynbee, n. 21, p. 398.

28 Carrying capacity is associated with a particular species relative to the environment. It is the number of individuals that the environment can support indefinitely to live without any decline in their given manner of living. It means if the population has to be sustainable it should be equal to or less than the carrying capacity. This was introduced by William Catton, an American sociologist in his 1980 book *Overshoot: The Ecological Basis of Revolutionary Change.* Carrying capacity is also emphasized by other ecologists through their studies.

29 Paleri, n.6, 205-220.

30 Harris, Gardner and Edward Wong, Where China Meets India in a High-Altitude Desert, Push Comes to Shove, www.nytimes.com/2013/05/03/world/asia/where-china-meets-india-push-comes-to-shove.html?emc=eta1, accessed 7 May 2013

31 Ibid

32 India China Sign Key Border Agreement, news.in.msn.com/national/india-china-sign-key-border-agreement, accessed 23 October 2013.

33 *Athirthi Bhoomi Bangladeshinnu: Rajya Sabhayil Kayyankali, Malayala Manorama,* (Malayalam), Kozhikode, 8 May 2013, p. 16.

34 Paleri, n.6, p. 24.

35 Ferguson, Niall, The Next War of the World, Foreign Affairs, Sep/Oct, 2006,

en.wikipedia. org/ wiki/ Human# cite _ref-139, accessed 6 February 2013.

36 Being examined separately in succeeding chapters.

37 *Rig Veda* (X, 121, 4-5)

38 Blainey, Geoffrey, *A Short History of the World,* New Delhi: Penguin Books, 2000, p. 24.

39 Ibid., p. 31.

40 Ibid., pp. 41-3.

41 Paleri, Prabhakaran, *Marine Environment: Management and People's Participation,* New Delhi: KW Publishers Private Limited, 2009, p. 2. According to another study the length is about 217,490 miles which is about 350,016 kilometers. uk.answers. yahoo.com /question/ index?qid=20090414075536 AAfHHk9. According to another study the length is 859,390 kilometers (2012), www.bigsiteofamazingfacts.com/what-is-the-maximum-total-coastline-on-earth-and-how-is-it-calculated-relative-to-current-sea-level, all accessed 14 February 2013.

42 Paleri, Prabhakaran, "Changing Concept of National Security and a Maritime Model for India," Ph.D. Thesis, Department of Defence and Strategic Studies, University of Madras, Chennai, February, 2002, p. 145

43 Ibid. p. 145-47.

44 Threat attraction is a terminology used in chaos theory, a field of study in mathematics. In the study of national security the author used the terminology to explain the relative characteristics of the chaotic attractor and the target. The threat causes chaos in the system of the target once it reaches it. The threat here is the chaotic attractor and will approach the target only if it can attract it (the threat). Every potential target, therefore, has certain degree of thereat attractiveness if the threat has to approach it. There are many ways the threat to target path can be managed in national security governance. One of them is reducing the threat attractiveness of the potential target. Often it is not possible.

45 Montgomery C. Meigs, *Slide Rules and Submarines,* Washington, D.C., National Defence University Press, 1990, p. 3.

46 A term used in this study to separate an island from a land that is linked to mainland through a land border but is also littoral.

47 The period taken is 1991, the year the civil war broke out to 2012, when the New Constitution was framed on 1st August.

48 Pati, Drubajyoti, Environmental Protection, *Employment News,* New Delhi, 9-15 December 2000, p. 1.

49 Beament, Emily, 'Act now' to Cut Ocean Damage Costs, www.independent.co.uk/environment/nature/act-now-to-cut-ocean-damage-costs-7579622.html, accessed 16 September 2013.

50 Subramanian, A.N., Introduction: Marine Environment, ocw.unu.edu/international-network-on-water-environment-and-health/unu-inweh-course-1-mangroves/Marine-Environment.pdf, accessed 16 September 2012.

Chapter 2

LAND, OCEAN AND GEOPOLITICAL ENTITIES

Defining "land" is tricky; perhaps, humans have taken it for granted. Land is more than they believe.

Land has different meanings. It can be dry land, the part of the earth that is not covered by water or wet land, mostly wet and partially under water at times. In common understanding, land is the solid ground on the earth. In economics, land is a factor of production comprising all naturally occurring resources. Humans, another factor of production as labour, appreciate their land as the dry ground on the earth or what an ancient ship's lookout sets sight and shouts when located after a long voyage, "land ahoy!" Ultimately dry land is the place on the earth where people like to stretch their lives peacefully. Still, these definitions shift the focus out of this study, which has to be precise on the relationship between land and ocean.

Land and ocean are seen as different entities since the days of yore. Scriptures, historical records and the associated human mindset while speak about the magnanimity of the ocean and its bounties, separate it from the land. Ocean had always been considered different from land. There is a disconnection. The entire idea about the ocean will change when it is seen as part of land similar to the inland seas, lakes, rivers, etc. In fact, the ocean covers a major part of the land with resources under water and drifts along with the continents as a whole, relative to Earth's motion.

There is, and will be, only one Ocean. Ocean is a great flood over land. This is the key statement of this study. Or, in other words, there is land under the ocean which is a part of the land that humans occupy above it presently. It will remain that way. The study is based on this factual statement.

Land and ocean along with the airspace or what is called the atmosphere in climatology define the planet in relation to life forms in its simple geometry. It is the combination of ground, water and air, among the elements of life in which the humans stand atop the evolutionary pyramid. Among the three, ocean is the least understood. Ocean remains a mystery. The mystery of ocean strengthens the landclasp syndrome. Nowhere is it more reflected than in national and international governance.

One of the common meanings of land is the earth above the mean sea level and also those below mean sea level whose geoproperty rights as land has already been established either by individuals or governments. It includes all parts of the earth submerged or surfaced that are owned by individuals or groups including governments and that may emerge from the ocean under various situations and are likely to be claimed and owned by individuals or groups including governments. Strategically this land could be extended to cover the entire bottom of the ocean that can be exploited. For that the ocean has to be understood.

Understanding Ocean

Understanding the ocean depends on the purpose. In all situations, the primary aspect is the fact that there is nothing mysterious about the ocean. It is the stealth element of ocean advantage along with a few other aspects of ocean property such as accessibility, perils of the sea, etc., that make the ocean look mysterious. Once the ocean property factor of a geopolitical entity or any other smaller entity such as a state, region or island within it, is examined and understood clearly, the ocean will cease to be mysterious. The attempt in governance, therefore, has to be to understand the ocean as a terrain for manoeuvres related to geopolitical governance by demystifying it. This is applicable to every geopolitical entity. It is not easy as it sounds. Humans know more about the outer space and the distant stars and planets than the ocean lapping on their backyards.

What exactly is the ocean? According to this study that recommends integration of the concept of maritime security with national security, ocean is a fundamental part of the land on which the humans survive. From this perception, ocean is strictly land inundated by saline water for a very long period.[1] This is from an entirely different perspective of strategic thinking. Though ocean is an extension of land masses, the rules related to the games to be played for national and international governance in and over it are different from those over the land. Therefore, ocean is a terrain different from the ground in strategic and tactical applications under the terrain specificity principle.

While this difference makes the ocean to be viewed differently from land, ocean governance comes under the much often used term maritime security whereas the landclasp syndrome makes governance to be viewed in a land-centric manner. This is where the perception of ocean as an extension of land justifies the governance of ocean based on land. It is paramount and ultimately justifies the need for integration of maritime security with national security. There are other reasons too. They are examined further.

Prior to that, it is important to appreciate the ocean and the geopolitical entities of the world in relation to it.

Ocean Divided

Ocean is a unitary entity. It is called the World Ocean or Global Ocean. It is a continuum of water that engulfs about 71 per cent of the solid crest of Earth. It is an expansive and uninterrupted waterworld seemingly restless in the attempt to swallow up the entire land to make the planet a perfect blue marble. The ocean is laced by the coastal interface of the land above it in a fractal form. The oceanographers and geographers have presently divided the ocean in parts at five geolocations. Closer to the land, the ocean is further divided into seas, bays, gulfs, archipelagos[2], straits and other sectors including navigable rivers that may even pass through various countries. The ocean divisions (oceanic divisions) are notified by the International Hydrographic Organisation (IHO). They are Arctic Ocean, Atlantic Ocean, Indian Ocean, Pacific Ocean and Southern Ocean. Each ocean division comprises various seas and other water bodies. Some geographers divide the oceans into three—Atlantic, Indian and Pacific. According to them the Arctic is the sea of Atlantic, and the Southern Ocean the southern end of all the three ocean divisions.

A summary of the geographical details of various ocean divisions is given in Table 2.1. This is based on the reports of the Central Intelligence Agency (CIA) of the United States of America (USA) in its World Fact Book 2012 and 2013. The details can change with respect to other reference publications.

Each part of the divided ocean is also changing constantly under the overall movement of drifting continents as well as other reasons. The importance of the ocean divisions depends on the geopolitical period through which they are moving, and the concerns of the natural rim countries and the owner countries of various territories associated with them.

The divisions of the World Ocean by IHO are for hydrographic convenience. It helps in identifying them from the standpoint of ocean governance. This study appreciates five divisions of the Global Ocean according to IHO notification from the strategic point of view, with a caveat. The caveat is that the ocean system can change in the long term. The overall impact of the changes will be visible only after a prolonged period. The parameters of the ocean divisions will change continuously. The caveat is important in the study of the ocean and its strategic appreciation. The five ocean divisions and their strategic aspects are briefly examined below.

Arctic Ocean

Arctic Ocean is the smallest and shallowest ocean division. It is in the northern hemisphere located largely north of the Arctic Circle around the North Pole submerged under. It is also called the Northern Ocean or the Northern Icy Ocean. The Arctic rim is covered by Eurasia and North America in parts and is largely covered by sea ice which is reportedly thinning and shrinking largely attributable to global warming.[3] It was noticed in 1980. There are many research stations over the hard sea ice of the Arctic. Studies have been carried out by select countries to examine the feasibility of seasonal sea route for ships, called the northern sea route, which is expected to cut down distance considerably to Europe and Far East or the west coast of North America. The Arctic Ocean holds large reserves of oil and gas.[4] It covers Baffin Bay, Barents Sea, Beaufort Sea, Chukchi Sea, East

Siberian Sea, Greenland Sea, Hudson Bay, Hudson Strait, Kara Sea, Laptev Sea, Northwest Passage, and other tributary water bodies with high potential for maritime activities.[5]

The Arctic may have a bigger role in future for many reasons. One of them is that it is a full ocean close to many countries on its perimeter unlike in the south. It is shallow compared to other ocean divisions. The Arctic was a mute witness of the half a century long Cold War. It was an undeclared theatre for many political game plans during the Cold War. Nuclear powered submarines moved under the Arctic at the highest degree of readiness. Many nuclear submarines met their graves under it by accidents. Arctic was also a secret dumping ground for nuclear and other hazardous wastes of the Cold War experiments far from the public eye.

The Arctic Ocean is slowly turning out to be a victim of climate change, provider for increased maritime transportation and a conflict zone with contradicting claims for legal continental shelf basin with the nations around placing claims on it. Under international law no state owns the North Pole. Everyone wants a share of the Arctic pie. The pending transnational issues in the Arctic are the division of Beaufort Sea between Canada and the United States and the status of the Northwest Passage. Denmark and Norway have made submissions on the limits of the Continental Shelf to the Commission on the Limits of Continental Shelf (CLCS). Russia is collecting additional data to augment its earlier submission (2001). Norway and Russia had signed a comprehensive maritime boundary agreement in 2010.[6] On 27 June 2007, Russia threatened to annex 460,000 sq mile chunk of frozen Arctic based on the claim that its northern Arctic region is directly linked to the North Pole via an underwater shelf. It is a direct claim.[7] Russian scientists visited Lomonsov Ridge in the Arctic which reportedly is a large reservoir of oil and gas. To extend a zone, the state has to show that the structure of the continental shelf is similar to the geological structure within its territory. Under the United Nations Convention on the Law of the Sea (UNCLOS), no country's shelves extend to North Pole, but there are claims. According to Russian scientists, Canada could also make a claim as it could say the ridge is part of its shelves. Some, like Denmark, can reach out with their claims through its territory, Greenland, in the Arctic. The Greenland, if becomes an independent country, can assert its claim too. It is a matter of reframing the claims.

The International Seabed Authority (ISA) administers the area as international.

Scientists believe Arctic meltdown will lead to economic disaster. Researchers from Cambridge and Rotterdam universities have concluded that the economic impact of melting Arctic could be nearly US$60 trillion which is equivalent of the world economy in 2012. Methane gas can emit from East Siberian Sea as a result of the meltdown which is only a fraction of the vast reservoirs of methane in the Arctic. They conclude that the economic impact of physical changes in the Arctic is serious.[8]

Atlantic Ocean

Atlantic Ocean is the second largest among the ocean divisions. It opens out about 20 per cent of the earth's surface. It is located between Africa, Europe, the Southern Ocean and the Western Hemisphere. The Mid-Atlantic Range (MAR) that runs north-south along the floor separates the Eurasian and North American tectonic plates in the North Atlantic and the African and the South American tectonic plates in the South Atlantic. The Atlantic covers Baltic Sea, Black Sea, Caribbean Sea, Davis Strait, Denmark Strait, part of the Drake Passage, Gulf of Mexico, Labrador Sea, Mediterranean Sea, North Sea, Norwegian Sea, almost all of the Scotia Sea, and other tributary water bodies including important strategic waterways such as the Kiel Canal (Germany), Oresund (Denmark-Sweden), Bosporus (Turkey), Strait of Gibraltar (Morocco-Spain) and the Saint Lawrence Seaway (Canada-US).

Atlantic Ocean is the only ocean division that is directly linked with all the other ocean divisions. There are overlapping claims for extended continental shelf in the Northeastern part of South America facing the Atlantic Ocean.

Indian Ocean

Indian Ocean is the third largest among the ocean divisions. It comprises four strategically important access waterways, otherwise known as choke points—Suez Canal (Egypt), Bab-el-Mandeb (Djibouti-Yemen), Strait of Hormuz (Iran-Oman), and Strait of Malacca

(Indonesia-Malaysia). It is located between Africa, Southern Ocean, Asia and Australia. Indian Ocean covers Andaman Sea, Arabian Sea, Bay of Bengal, Flores Sea, Great Australian Bight, Gulf of Aden, Gulf of Oman, Java Sea, Mozambique Channel, Persian Gulf, Red Sea, Savu Sea, Strait of Malacca, Timor Sea and other tributary water bodies.

Pacific Ocean

Pacific Ocean is the largest among the ocean divisions. It contains around 25,000 islands. It is more than the total oceanic islands of the rest of the world combined. Strategically important access waterways include the La Perouse, Tsugaru, Tsushima, Taiwan, Singapore, and Torres Straits. It lies between the Southern Ocean, Asia, Australia, and the Western Hemisphere. It covers Bali Sea, Bering Sea, Bering Strait, Coral Sea, East China Sea, Gulf of Alaska, Gulf of Tonkin, Philippine Sea, Sea of Japan, Sea of Okhotsk, South China Sea, Tasman Sea, and other tributary water bodies.

Southern Ocean

Southern Ocean surrounds Antarctica and extends to 60 degrees south. It was delimited by International Hydrographic Organisation in 2000. It is the fourth largest among the ocean divisions. It is located between 60 degrees south latitude and Antarctica. It is also known as Great Southern Ocean, Antarctic Ocean and South Polar Ocean. It lies in southern hemisphere encircling the continent of Antarctica. South Pole is located in Antarctica over land. Southern ocean fluctuates seasonally and forms from the convergence of two circumpolar currents, one easterly flowing and one westerly flowing. It covers Amundsen Sea, Bellingshausen Sea, part of the Drake Passage, Ross Sea, a small part of the Scotia Sea, Weddell Sea, and other tributary water bodies.

Table 2.1 Hydrographic Dimensions of Ocean Divisions

	Ocean Division	*Nominal Coordinates*	*Area (million sq km)*	*Depth at Lowest Point (m)*	*Coastline (km)*	*Direct Ocean Link*
1	Arctic Ocean	900 N, 0000 E	14.056	4,665 (Fram Basin)	45,390	Atlantic Pacific
2	Atlantic Ocean	000N,0250 W	76.762	8,605 (Milwaukee Deep—Puerto Rico Trench)	111,866	Arctic Pacific Indian Southern
3	Indian Ocean	200 S, 800 E	68.556	7,258 (Java Trench)	66,526	Atlantic Pacific Southern
4	Pacific Ocean	000 N, 1600 W	155.557	10,924 (Challenger Deep—Marianna Trench)	135,663	Arctic Atlantic Indian
5	Southern Ocean	600 S, 900 E	20.327	7,235 (Southern end—South Sandwich Trench)	17,968	Atlantic Indian Pacific

Ocean Governance

The great change in ocean governance towards maritime unification of the world came in 1982 when nations, responsible they were, capped their consensus and faith in the United Nations Convention on the Law of the Sea. The most significant among the provisions of the law of the sea (LoS), it could be said, was the limiting of waters and zones for jurisdiction and special rights. The Convention set the limits of various areas, measured from a carefully and precisely defined baseline calculated under varying situations and coastal profiles. Under the spirit of UNCLOS, the sea is the common property of humankind.

There are many geopolitical entities in the world that are landlocked or geographically disadvantaged with respect to the ocean.

The landlocked countries are those that have no direct access to the ocean. They are entirely enclosed by land, or whose coastlines lie on enclosed seas. Geographically disadvantaged nations are those that are coastal but not comfortable with their approach to sea in terms of exploitation of resources off their coasts. There is no exact definition. But the idea of geographically disadvantaged states is an achievement of UNCLOS among others relating to landlocked and coastal countries.

UNCLOS applies to all the nations of the world without discrimination. The Convention treated every state a "maritime nation."[9] The geographically disadvantaged and landlocked states also benefit from the ocean under the Convention. From this perspective, it will be in customary order to consider every nation as an entity that has an ocean element incorporated in it by international law. Every geopolitical entity thereby becomes a maritime entity. The land-locked and geographically disadvantaged nations are also beneficiaries of the oceans within their own rights specified in the UNCLOS. Beyond UNCLOS, even under the customary international law, a nation being an entity of the world is part of the world and its commons. The ocean is one such global commons. It influences even the nation that lie far in the hinterland by trade, commerce, economics, climate, environmental changes, etc. Even otherwise, irrespective of being non-littoral, a territorial entity could become a target for a sea-launched missile in a war or terror scenario or a victim of transnational ocean crimes. Every entity can access ocean based employment, lay vital pipeline or communication cables undersea or operate shipping lines as part of its trade practices. There could be many more activities with respect to ocean in future. Any such entity will have to have its eyes set to the sea far away and beyond its land horizon. From this point of view, a maritime entity has interests in the ocean in relation to its national security, whether landlocked or geographically disadvantaged. For these reasons, the maritime geostrategic affirmations should logically apply to every nation and other geopolitical entities of the world.

The UNCLOS articulates the rights and jurisdiction of nations within their maritime zones. But all is not well in a corrugated system that could put loopholes or exert pressure under the very law. There are arguments that UNCLOS and its appreciation of maritime zones makes international maritime disputes heavily anchored in permanency. Because, in any compromise over the ocean, nations stand to lose heavily in terms of ocean resources alone. This fact will seal every attempt to resolve conflicts over geoproperty rights[10] over the ocean territories. One of the ways to anvil the disputes, especially maritime disputes, are by mutual cooperation. The past attempts to resolve disputes were by aggressive political attitudes. Though wars were considered instruments of national policy, most of the victories (if not all) in war often outweighed the accrued benefits. To that extent every victory has been costly to the victor in a war. Today it is also a matter of reputation. The country may win but lose its face among the international public. Victory in war mostly turns out to be Pyrrhic by unleashing a chain of never ending political disputes into future, stifling generations. To that extent wars cannot be seen as an instrument of policy unless it is won without fighting. War is necessary and it should be won without fighting is the new commandment. Perhaps this is a fact the military scholars including Clausewitz had not enunciated.[11] It is based on such contemplations governance of the ocean and its entities is to be examined in strategic affairs. It could not only be prudent and tactful but also yielding high in the long run.

An attempt to examine the geostrategic context of the maritime world and its governance calls for a detailed investigation of many contributory parameters like those already mentioned, besides the correct appreciation of the term. It is important to establish the identity of the entity in a world heavily influenced by the ocean. The ocean will continue to remain decisive to the world of the future. It provides global access to interiors, extended territories, and for forward movement under the geostrategic context. Though the world is far more secure today than in the past, new regional problems are emerging within the geostrategic context for which the ocean will be another terrain-specific playing field. Besides, the ocean itself is flagging by damages caused to it; some of them are irreversible. The ocean can be governed in the national, bilateral, multilateral, regional, international and global context. The geopolitical entities irrespective of their relative geolocations automatically become stakeholders in ocean governance.

Beyond Ocean

Sans the ocean, the remaining part of the world that lies above the mean sea level in various undulations is much smaller. It covers about 29 per cent of the earth's surface and is the human habitat. It is occupied by recognised land habitats in a fragmented manner. They are exclusive as countries and other entities with geoproperty rights; quite a few are yet to be settled. Many such entities are still struggling for absolute identity. Within these issues the land entities fall under many categories. Identifying and listing out these entities are important for this study. A seemingly innocent and innocuous question, "*How many nations are there in the world or who owns a part of land?*" may bring different answers from different sources. In addition to countries there are also other entities. There are many areas in the world under varying forms of administration and governance where governments struggle to bring orderly governance.[12] The study becomes more complex when the perspectives of maritime strategy under asymmetrical situations are incorporated within the regimes.

The profiles of the ocean relative to the planet as a whole, and those of the land masses, especially, above it are important in such a study. It brings the term "maritime" in the open. The term is not rigidly bound within the meanings of "nautical" or "littoral." It is a wider terminology that indicates all matters related to the ocean. This connotation is important in the study of maritime affairs, or while discussing it. The concept of maritime security percolates from maritime affairs.

Expressions in maritime thinking could have their own connotations. Accordingly, definitions may vary based on the perception of the theorist and the strategist. In strategic thinking, the concept of maritime affairs has gone through a stream of metamorphosis based on national objectives, demands and understanding. Maritime strategy is within the ambit of maritime affairs, hence not an exception. The idea of the ocean and, accordingly, maritime affairs and strategy is not strictly that of the periods that belonged to daring explorers such as Christopher Columbus (1451-1506) or Vasco da Gama (1460-1524), or strategists who followed them in the realm of maritime security. Alfred Thayer Mahan (1840-1914), Kavalam Madhava Panikkar (1895-1963), Sergey Georgiyevich Gorshkov (1910-1988) or other scholars and strategic thinkers have placed their ideas straight and clear. The problem is in their universal admissibility over the period when national objectives and demands change or approaches towards them get modified along with intensified competition for survival.

The transformation in maritime strategic thinking came with the law of the sea in the 1980s. If anything, it has made the world understand that the ocean is not the terrain of the rich and powerful alone. It is for all. In fact a small country that did not even had a government, least an economy, could make the world's powerful watch dependently for quarter a century, by dominating their part of the ocean and even venturing beyond, exercising their rights as they felt right, in a way they could justify.[13] Others called it piracy. They too were right. But the interesting aspect is the way the Somalis linked the ocean for their lives over land and sustained their dealings over their part of the ocean to the extent that only they could bring an end to it. They reaped money from the ocean by keeping the ships of important but defenceless countries at the wave's edge. They called it the duty of the coast guard; others called it piracy. History does not repeat; law of invariance plays the game over and over. Both ways, the ocean advantage was at play.

Land and Geopolitical Entities

Land is not universally defined to suit all occasions. Hence it is important to define land for any discussions related to it. This is more so in strategic thinking. In this study land is argued as the earth's crest that contains life and resources required for life. Land is the abode of geopolitical entities as the world knows them. Major part of this land is covered by water—ocean, rivers, streams, lakes of all forms and sizes,[14] wetlands, etc. Here the first generated assumption is that ocean is part of the earth's crest hence a part or extension of land. This view augments the landclasp syndrome of humans to further this study. The second argument is that land in the perspective of geopolitical entities where human systems survive in an organised manner of their choice is the land on which individuals or governments claim geoproperty rights. There could be such land even under the ocean like those that will be covered under high water or sea level rise one day. Generally the land that projects above the mean sea level is the land that is occupied and owned by the human system as individuals or groups. But sea level is only a reference point. The land could be just below that also according to the way humans treat it. What is above mean sea level at a time could go underwater when the level rises. An interesting aspect that needs to be examined will be the geoproperty rights of such submerged lands that may not be just a property but an entire country.

To start with, this study looks at land as 1) the part of the world occupied or owned by people or governments, including Antarctica and has been termed as geopolitical entities, and 2) the part of the Earth' crest including the part that is covered by ocean that is available for exploitation now or in the future for resources. Here the ocean ceases to become a separate entity but a terrain.

The land is owned by the governments of the geopolitical entities and private. Identifying the land entities (as on 31 July 2013 for this study) is a straight task under serious research and cautious examination. This study identifies land in three divisions of geopolitical appreciation:

- countries that are members of United Nations,
- territories owned by some of these countries and
- other geopolitical entities.

Members of United Nations

United Nations (UN) has 193 members (31 July 2013). According to the Charter of the UN,[15] membership is open to all peace-loving states which accept the obligations contained in the present Charter and, in the judgment of the Organisation, are able and willing to carry out these obligations. The admission of any such state for membership in the United Nations will be effected by a decision of the General Assembly upon the recommendation of the Security Council. For the membership in the UN, the entity has to be a state that is peace-loving as appreciated by the international body. The membership will be processed through the bureaucratically political procedures of the UN in which the Security Council with its veto-powered members and the General Assembly on majority voting have to agree. The primary objective of the UN was to provide an alternative mechanism for collective security to those who are party to it—the members, under specific conditions. It was not exactly a substitute for the declining League of Nations when introduced immediately after the Second World War.[16] It was not meant to be the centre of global governance with authority for it. Geostrategically the tendency of the nations is more to break up into smaller nations than amalgamate or integrate into single unified nations.[17] The geopolitical gravity naturally pulls the nations down by disintegration. Holding against it has to be under tremendous pressure. That is why weak nations yield faster to geopolitical gravity. The process is expected to undergo many changes in future. The disintegration adds to the membership of the United Nations if the fragmented portions are accepted by the process under the Charter. An example is South Sudan which has been formed on 9 July 2011. It is the 193rd member of United Nations.

Territories

Seven members of United Nations own 73 territories in the world. All of them are either coastlands[18] or islands. This gives the holding countries geopolitical authority to claim their status as the rim country of that particular ocean division. However there are dissents from some of the rim countries in accepting the idea. The countries who own the 73 territories are Australia, China, Denmark, France, Netherlands, New Zealand, Norway, United Kingdom and United States. There are other claimants too in certain cases. These territories are briefly examined below.[19]

1. *Adélie Land*

   Adélie Land occupies a portion on the Antarctic coast considered as Territory of the French Southern and Antarctic Lands part (*Terres Australes et Antarctiques Françaises* (TAAF)). But certain nations including the United States have not accepted the entity as a French dependency. Under the Antarctic Treaty, the French claim to Adélie Land, like other claims to Antarctic territory, is neither recognised nor disputed by other signatories to the Treaty.

2. *Akrotiri*

   It is a small coastal locale in Cyprus in the Greek Cypriot area. It is a sovereign base area of the United Kingdom. Akrotiri is also known as the Western Sovereign Base Area.

3. *American Samoa*

   American Samoa is a territory of the United States. It comprises a group of islands in the Pacific Ocean between Hawaii and New Zealand.

4. *Anguilla*

   Anguilla is an overseas territory of the United Kingdom comprising a group of islands in the Caribbean Sea in the Atlantic Ocean.

5. *Aruba*

   Aruba is a separate, autonomous island in the Caribbean Sea in the Atlantic Ocean. It is a dependency of the Kingdom of the Netherlands.

6. *Ashmore and Cartier Islands*

   They are uninhabited islands in the Timor Sea in the Indian Ocean belonging to Australia.

7. *Baker Island*

   Baker Island is situated between Hawaii, US and Australia in the Pacific Ocean. It is a territory of the United States and part of the Pacific Remote Islands National Wildlife Refuges.

8. *Bassas da India*

   It is an atoll of volcanic rocks submerged during high tide in the Mozambique Channel in the Indian Ocean. The atoll is possessed by France as part of its Southern and Antarctic Lands.

9. *Bermuda*

   They are relatively large group of developed islands in the Atlantic Ocean on the east coast of the United States. Bermuda is an overseas territory of the United Kingdom.

10. *Bouvet Island*

    Bouvet Island is a glacier covered volcanic island in the Atlantic Ocean southwest of Cape of Good Hope towards Antarctica. The island is a territory of Norway.

11. *British Indian Ocean Territory*

    The island groups comprise the Chagos Archipelago of 55 islands south of India in the Indian Ocean. They are the overseas territory of the United Kingdom.

12. *British Virgin Islands*

    British Virgin Islands are the overseas territories of the United Kingdom situated in the Caribbean in the Atlantic Ocean.

13. *Cayman Islands*

Cayman Islands belong to the United Kingdom. They are situated in the Caribbean Sea in the Atlantic.

14. *Christmas Island*

Christmas Island is a territory of Australia. It is located south of Indonesia in the Indian Ocean.

15. *Clipperton Island*

Clipperton Island is an atoll southwest of Mexico in the Pacific Ocean. It is a territory of France.

16. *Cocos (Keeling) Island*

Cocos Island, also known as Keeling Island is a group of 27 coral islands southwest of Indonesia in the Indian Ocean. It is a territory of Australia.

17. *Cook Islands*

Cook Islands form a group of islands between Hawaii and New Zealand in the Pacific Ocean. They are under self governance in free association with New Zealand.

18. *Coral Sea Islands*

Coral Sea Islands comprise a group so islands scattered over a vast area across the Great Barrier Reef in the Coral Sea in the Pacific Ocean. It is a territory of Australia.

19. *Dhekelia*

Dhekelia is a small coastal area in the island of Cyprus in the Turkish Cypriot area. It is a sovereign Base Area of the United Kingdom. It is also called the Eastern Sovereign Base Area.

20. *Europa Island*

Europa Island is in the Mozambique Channel in Indian Ocean. It is an overseas territory belonging to the French Southern and Antarctic Lands.

21. *Falkland Islands*

The islands lie east of Argentina in the Atlantic Ocean as the overseas territory of the United Kingdom. They are also called *Islas Malvinas.* Argentina has a claim over these islands.

22. *Faroe Islands*

Faroe Islands are in the Norwegian Sea in the Atlantic Ocean. They are part of the Kingdom of Denmark.

23. *French Guiana*

French Guiana is a coastal area located on the north-eastern coast of South America. It is a territory of France as an overseas department (*department d'outre-mer, or DOM*)

24. *French Polynesia*

French Polynesia comprises archipelagos between South America and Australia in the Pacific Ocean. It belongs to the overseas lands of France.

25. *Glorioso Islands*

Glorioso Islands comprise an island group of two lushly vegetated coral islands (Ile Glorieuse and Ile du Lys) and three rock islets in the Mozambique Channel in the Indian Ocean. The island group is part of the French Southern and Antarctic Lands.

26. *Gibraltar*

Gibraltar is a small coastal area at the highly strategic point on the Strait of Gibraltar. It is the overseas territory of the United Kingdom.

27. *Greenland*

Greenland is world's largest island extending from the Atlantic Ocean to the Arctic Ocean. It is part of the Kingdom of Denmark.

28. *Guadeloupe*

Guadeloupe is an archipelago in the Caribbean Sea in the Atlantic Ocean. It is an overseas territory of France as part of the French Southern and Antarctic Islands.

29. *Guam*

Guam is an island close to the Philippines and a territory of the United States.

30. *Guantánamo Bay*

Guantánamo Bay is an enclave under the territorial control of the United States. It is at the south-eastern side of Cuba in the Guantánamo Province. The territory is under lease from Cuba.

31. *Guernsey*

Guernsey is an island in the English Channel in the Atlantic Ocean. It is a British crown dependency.

32. *Heard Island and McDonald Islands*

The islands are located between Madagascar and Antarctica in the Indian Ocean. The group is a territory of Australia.

33. *Hong Kong*

Hong Kong is a coastal island on the mainland China overlooking the South China Sea in the Pacific Ocean. It is a special administrative region of China.

34. *Howland Island*

Howland Island lies northeast of Kiribati in the Pacific Ocean. It is a territory of the United States and part of the Pacific Remote Islands National Wildlife Refuges.

35. *Ile Amsterdam et Saint Paul*

They are volcanic islands southeast of Madagascar in the Indian Ocean. The island group is an overseas territory of France as part of the French Southern and Antarctic Lands.

36. *Iles Crozet*

Iles Crozet is a large archipelago south of Madagascar in the Indian Ocean. It is an overseas territory of France as part of the French Southern and Antarctic Lands.

37. *Iles Kerguelan*

Iles Kerguelan is a large archipelago south of Madagascar in the Indian Ocean. It is an overseas territory of France Pas part of the French Southern and Antarctic Lands.

38. *Isle of Man*

Isle of Man is an island in the Irish Sea in the Atlantic Ocean. It is a British crown dependency.

39. *Jan Mayen*

Jan Mayen is an Island northeast of Iceland in the Arctic Ocean. It is a territory of Norway.

40. *Jarvis Island*

Jarvis Island is located between Hawaii and Cook Islands in the Pacific Ocean. It is a territory of the United States and part of the Pacific Remote Islands National Wildlife Refuges.

41. *Jersey*
Jersey is an island in the English Channel. It is a British crown dependency.

42. *Johnston Atoll*
Johnston Atoll is an island between Hawaii and Marshall Islands in the Pacific Ocean. It is a territory of the United States as part of the Pacific Remote Islands National Wildlife Refuges.

43. *Juan de Nova Island*
Juan de Nova Island is in the Mozambique Channel of the Indian Ocean. It is a territory of France.

44. *Kingman Reef*
Kingdom Reef is an island between Hawaii and American Samoa in the Pacific Ocean. It is a territory of the United States as part of the Pacific Remote Islands National Wildlife Refuges.

45. *Macau*
Macau is a coastal Island on the mainland China overlooking the South China Sea in the Pacific Ocean. It is a special administrative region of China.

46. *Martinique*
Martinique is an island in the Caribbean Sea in the Atlantic Ocean. It is an overseas territory of France.

47. *Mayotte*
Mayotte is an island in the Mozambique Channel of the Indian Ocean. It is an overseas collectivity of France.

48. *Midway Islands*
Midway Island is on the northwest of Hawaiian Archipelago. It is a territory of the United States as part of the Pacific Remote Islands National Wildlife Refuges.

49. *Montserrat*
Montserrat is an island in the Caribbean Sea in the Atlantic. It is an overseas territory of the United Kingdom.

50. *Navassa Island*

Navassa Island is in the Caribbean Sea in the Atlantic. It is a territory of the United States.

51. *Netherlands Antilles*

Netherlands Antilles is an Island group in the Caribbean Sea in the Atlantic Ocean. The group is part of the Kingdom of the Netherlands.

52. *New Caledonia*

New Caledonia is an island in the Coral Sea in the Pacific Ocean. It is a self governing territory of France.

53. *Niue*

Niue is an Island east of Tonga in the Pacific Ocean that is self governed in free association with New Zealand.

54. *Norfolk Island*

Norfolk Island lies east of Australia in the Pacific Ocean. It is a self governing territory of Australia.

55. *Northern Mariana Islands*

The islands belong to a group of 15 islands in the Marianas archipelago in the Pacific Ocean. It is part of the Commonwealth in political union with the United States.

56. *Palmyra Atoll*

Palmyra Atoll lies between Hawaii and American Samoa in the Pacific Ocean. It is a territory of the United States as part of the Pacific Remote Islands National Wildlife Refuges.

57. *Paracel Islands*

Paracel Islands are part of a group of about 130 small coral islands in the South China Sea in the Pacific Ocean. It is occupied by China since 1974 and also claimed by Taiwan and Vietnam.

58. *Pitcairn Islands*

Pitcairn Islands lie between Peru and New Zealand in the Pacific Ocean. The group is an overseas territory of the United Kingdom.

59. *Puerto Rico*

Puerto Rico is an Island territory in the Caribbean in the Atlantic Ocean. It is part of the territory of the United States with Commonwealth status.

60. *Reunion*
The island lies east of Madagascar in the Indian Ocean. It is one of the overseas departments of France.

61. *Saint Barthelemy*
The island is in the Caribbean in the Atlantic Ocean. It is an overseas territory of France.

62. *Saint Helena*
The Islands comprise Saint Helena, Ascension and the island group of Tristan da Cunha between South America and Africa in the Atlantic Ocean. The group is an overseas territory of the United Kingdom.

63. *Saint Martin (Sint Maarten)*
Saint Martin is an island in the Caribbean Sea in the Atlantic Ocean. It is a French overseas collectivity.

64. *Saint Pierre and Miquelon*
Saint Pierre and Miquelon Islands are close to Newfoundland, Canada in the Pacific Ocean. The group is a territorial overseas collectivity of France.

65. *South Georgia and the South Sandwich Islands*
The group of islands lies south of the tip of South America in the Atlantic Ocean. The group is an overseas territory of the United Kingdom.

66. *Spratly Islands*
Spratly Islands are a group of islands in the South China Sea in the Pacific Ocean. The group is claimed by China, Taiwan and Vietnam, and portions by Malaysia and the Philippines. Brunei established a fishing zone overlapping a southern reef, but has not made any formal claim.

67. *Svalbard*
Svalbard is a group of islands in the Arctic Ocean. It is a territory of Norway.

68. *Tokelau*

Tokelau is a group of atolls in the Pacific Ocean. The group is a territory of New Zealand.

69. *Tromelin Island*

Tromelin Island lies east of Madagascar in the Indian Ocean. It is an overseas territory of France. It is part of the French Southern and Antarctic Lands.

70. *Turks and Caicos Islands*

Turks and Caicos form a group of islands in the Caribbean Sea in the Atlantic Ocean. The group is an overseas territory of the United Kingdom.

71. *Virgin Islands*

Virgin Islands belong to an archipelago in the Caribbean Sea in the Atlantic Ocean. It is a territory of the United States.

72. *Wake Island*

Wake Islands forms an atoll between Hawaii and Northern Mariana Islands in the Pacific Ocean. The atoll is a territory of the United States.

73. *Wallis and Futuna*

Wallis and Futuna is a Group of islands between Hawaii and New Zealand in the Pacific. It is an overseas collectivity of France.

These entities are important for their holders in crafting their maritime strategies. Some of these territories are claimed by other nations. Some face protests and unrest. 63 of these territories are islands. The remaining 10 are coastlands (with links over land). Some of them are contiguous to their custodians as part of the state but under alternate governance by choice and consensus for long periods. Most of the islands were once unknown entities lost in the ocean. Some of them were located by pirates or smugglers in the past. They remained as hideouts or coves. With the advent of ocean exploration they were colonised and exploited for resources. They offered various resources. Among them were organic fertilisers like guanos (bird drops), phosphates, salt, etc. Strategically they offered vantage points and facilities for military staging, observation, weapon testing, target practice, etc. They were possessions of esteem for the kingdoms, royalties and the super rich. Some of the territories were used to keep convicts away from the mainland, interrogating hardcore criminal suspects, and other political extremes.

There were indigenous peoples in some of these territories. Many became extinct. Some merged with the settlers losing their indigenous identity.[20] Most of these territorial entities were carried forward from the past, some of them centuries before and some as regularised occupancies of World War II.

All these entities are geostrategically vital for their holders being situated at maritime vantage points and with valuable ocean property under the present day ocean regime. Most of the island protectorates and territories are officially converted into wildlife refuges including sea turtle parks, national parks, environmental habitats, strategic bases, etc. There are also territories that are financial havens with rules of convenience for trade and economics, and thereby thriving in tourism and financial holdings. France had reportedly carried out nearly 200 nuclear tests in the atolls Mururoa and Fangataufa in French Polynesia between 1966 and 1996. The tests invited severe opposition and protests in 1995.

These protectorates and territories vary in size and area from submerged tidal flats to tiny foothold islands to those larger than some of the independent states of the world. Some of them are inaccessible at times or are generally difficult to get into from the sea. Their roles changed with changing times and situations, and are now poised for great advantage to their holders in terms of ocean area, resources, and strategic advantage. The territories turned out to be great investments for their holders in the long term to enhance their ocean property. There are huge areas around tiny islands and even the submerged ones that the holders can claim under UNCLOS. For example, the Coral Sea islands give about a million square kilometres to Australia whose marine territory is huge. The countries who own such ocean property should be powerful maritime states provided they have the capacity to govern integrated maritime security with national security.

Among them, the Falkland Islands (*Islas Malvinas* for Argentina) had to weather a war between Britain and Argentina in 1982. Though Britain retained ownership, the claim of Argentina still holds. The island was first sighted by a British navigator in 1592.

Every one of these territories like most of the independent nation states is draped in history of violence and suppression.

The 73 protectorates and territorial entities are extended to all the five ocean divisions as given in Table 2.2. Greenland overlaps Arctic and Atlantic oceans.

Table 2.2 Territories and Ocean Divisions

	Ocean Division	*Territories*	
1	Arctic	3	Includes part of Greenland
2	Atlantic	30	Includes part of Greenland
3	Indian	14	
4	Pacific	26	
5	Southern	1	Adélie Land, French claim

Table 2.3 gives the holding position of the territories.

Table 2.3 Holding Countries, Territories and Ocean Links

	Countries	*Number of Territorial Entities*	*Ocean Links (through Entities*
1	Australia	6	Indian Ocean (3) Pacific Ocean (3)
2	China	4 (including claim on Spratly islands along with Vietnam)	Pacific Ocean
3	Denmark	2	Arctic (1) Atlantic (2)
4	France	21	Atlantic Ocean (4) Indian Ocean (11) Pacific Ocean (5) Southern Ocean (1)
5	Netherlands	2	Atlantic
6	New Zealand	3	Pacific (3)
7	Norway	3	Arctic ocean (2) Atlantic (1)
8	United Kingdom	16	Atlantic Ocean (14) Indian Ocean (1) Pacific Ocean (1)
9	United States of America	16	Atlantic Ocean (5) Pacific Ocean (11)

Three countries among the holders—Denmark, France and the United Kingdom—can claim extra ocean link as they have possessions beyond their mainland ocean divisions

Other Geopolitical Entities

There are 12 other geopolitical entities identified exclusively for this study (2013). They are,

1. Abkhazia,
2. Antarctica,
3. European Union,
4. Gaza Strip and West Bank,
5. Kosovo,
6. Nagorno-Karabakh,
7. Palestine,
8. Taiwan,
9. Transnistria,
10. Vatican City,
11. Western Ossetia and
12. Western Sahara.

They are briefly examined below.

Abkhazia

Abkhazia is a self declared independent state in the Caucuses under limited recognition. Georgian government and many others who support them consider Abkhazia as part of Georgia. This results in Georgia-Abkhazia conflict frequently.

Antarctica

Antarctica is a unique region. It is a land still anchored at the South Pole in the churning of global landmasses under the continental drift. Why was it not inhabited by the humans? Perhaps the answer lies in the fact of inaccessibility and adverse weather conditions. Considering the world's interest in Antarctica as a global commons and the activities in and around it in Southern Ocean, it is considered a territorial entity for this study.

European Union

European Union (EU) is an amazingly new concept in nation building of the advancing world. It is macronisation of a different kind. The creation of European Union added a new dimension to international law in real statehood by moderate deviation from Westphalian conformity. International law in its basic structure binds the nations together. It was amazing the way the independent nations agreed to cede their national jurisdiction to an overarching entity in the form of a Union when nation states are naturally disintegrating. European Union as a supranation frowns nationalism within the pool of security by economics and strength. The concept of European Union could not be brought under the two divisions of international law—public international law and private international law. The idea is within the supranational law. Individual national laws of the constituent states become inapplicable when conflicting with the supranational legal system.

This study considers European Union as a separate entity also giving entity status to all its members. The membership of the European Union grew to 28 from the original six founding states—Belgium, France, West Germany, Italy, Luxemburg and Netherlands as on November 2013. Chances are that there will be more members. There are also chances some members may leave. European Union has the characteristics of a national entity with its own anthem, flag, currency and founding date. It has special policy in its joint dealings in international affairs. The European Commission (EC), the executive branch of the European Union is a powerful body in supranational affairs. There is also the possibility of expansion of nation state characteristics within the Union. After all, the nation states originated from the European model.[21] European Union, as an exclusive entity, could influence strategic maritime decisions.

There are also problems within the supranational system. Members with debt loads will make it difficult to generate satisfactory economic growth. The complaints that European Union is not an economically viable statehood is slowly gaining ground. According to the television channel, Russia today (22 May 2013), titled "Portugal goes back to land; EU leaves them empty hand" many countries are expected to leave the European Union under financial crisis. The title is also interesting to this study's basic concept. Land is till prominent in the statement when a country is concerned about its national security matters. It is so even for Portugal who was a maritime force to be reckoned with just a century back. The land certainly is taking over the ocean in survival instinct of humans more today than in the past even while the ocean is rising over the land with the melting of ice under global warming.

Gaza Strip and West Bank

Among other entities are the Gaza Strip and the West Bank, in two different geolocations, which are ultimately expected to be the absolute Palestinian State, mentioned as another entity in this study.[22] While West Bank is landlocked between Israel and Jordan, Gaza Strip has 40 km long coastline on the Mediterranean Sea. Access is controlled by Israel under continuing volatility of situation. Both these entities have to be seen together under maritime studies if they are heading towards a common objective of an independent recognised entity. But before that it is necessary to examine the riddle of the bygone years.

Kosovo

Kosovo comes out of the unsettled Yugoslavian imbroglio which had its beginning, as one could extend in history, as early as the seventh century if viewed from the Kosovo-centric meridian. It was followed by the Ottoman rule of four centuries—from late 14th century to the full 19th century. The stage was perfectly set for brewing the ethnic stew with the end of the Ottoman Empire (1299-1923) followed by World War II. The Ottomans were formidable in the maritime scenario also. They were the first to use cannons and fire torpedoes from submarines in naval warfare. In the sliding avalanche of political uncertainty of the periods, Kosovo now stands broken away from Serbia but unrecognised by Serbia and UN. Kosovo assembly declared independence from Serbia on 17 February 2008. Serbia considers it a UN governed entity within its sovereign territory. A number of other countries support this position. It is another entity listed out in this study for the reasons mentioned. Kosovo is a landlocked entity.

Nagorno-Karabakh

Nagorno-Karabakh is a *de facto* republic in the caucuses. It is landlocked. The republic is unrecognised. It is an autonomous oblast[23] of the Soviet era. There is an ongoing conflict between Armenia and

Azerbaijan. Majority of the population is Armenian (2013). The unrest continues with many displaced persons. Meanwhile the entity creeps ahead reliving its past, not the future, mostly.

Palestine

Does Palestine exist as a geostrategic entity? It does. If so where? With political connotation the area has to be seen based on the Israel—Palestine conflict. Here is a territorial entity or an area without defined borders whose existence is recognised by a vast number of countries. It is emerging out of its virtual state. Roughly the Gaza Strip, the Golan Heights and the West Bank come within its purview. It is a proposed "site"' of a country. Gaza Strip and West Bank are currently taken for this study separately. Golan Heights is excluded from this study. In spite of its virtual status, Palestine is one of the key players in maritime studies.

Palestine is not a recent idea. It is a sovereign state proclaimed independence by the Palestine Liberation Organisation (PLO) on 15 November 1988. The Palestine Declaration of Independence claimed the borders as existed and occupied by Israel since 1967. PLO is the sole legitimate representative of Palestine at UN General Assembly as observer as a non-state entity since November 1974. The UN General Assembly officially acknowledged the proclamation and voted to use the designation "Palestine" instead of Palestine Liberation Organisation. UN General Assembly passed resolution on 29 November 2012 recognising Palestine as a non-member observer state within the United Nation's system. Majority of the member states of United Nations recognise the State of Palestine.

Taiwan

Taiwan is called the Republic of China (ROC). It was established on the island of Taiwan since 1949. The Peoples Republic of China (PRC) claims Taiwan as one of its provinces. The world follows one china policy. Taiwan is yet to undergo full transformation as a nation state or part of one. Perhaps it may not, in the near future at least. Taiwan has a claim that the entity was a founder member of the United Nations in 1945 as the sole representative of China. In 1971 it withdrew from the United Nations after a resolution.[24] Subsequent applications were rejected as the world had changed its opinion. Taiwan still continues to assert for its rights over certain islands in South China Sea and the East China Sea along with the Peoples Republic of China and other littorals. It has participated in the Olympic Games including the 2008 Beijing Olympics as an independent entity.[25] It has a coast guard and other forces. There were international maritime incidents at sea (INCSEA) between the maritime forces of Japan and Taiwan on maritime claims.[26] Notwithstanding such conflicts and lack of identity in international affairs as a recognised nation, Taiwan thrives with hope and even has objectives of improving ties with China in economic relations. Taiwan believes international space and peace accord will be a possibility once economic relations with China are established.[27] While China is often contemplating the use of force for reunification, Taiwan is busy assuming situation will transform by change of name like Chinese Taipei or other hopefully acceptable names to join the international organisation. While there are many solutions, it is a long way to Taiwan's resurrection or mortification as an independent entity. Till then Taiwan has to be considered as a separate geostrategic entity for strategic studies, especially on maritime affairs.

South Ossetia

South Ossetia, in the Caucuses, is a partly recognised state. It is Soviet era Oblast. The entity declared independence from Georgia on 1990 as the Republic of South Ossetia. Georgia used force to control it in1991-92. Subsequently in 2004-2008 the situation became worse leading to Russia-Georgia war. South Ossetia established de facto control of the territory with Russian support. The entity is landlocked.

Transnistria

Transnistria is a breakaway unrecognised territory on the eastern Moldovan border with Ukraine. The entity declared independence in 1990. After the War of Transnistria in 1992 the entity became independent as the Pridnestovian Moldavian Republic (PMR) with limited recognition.

Vatican City

Vatican City is also called the State of Vatican City. It is an independent and recognised state. Vatican City came into existence in 1929 under the Lateran Treaty. It is a recognised national territory under international law. Often Vatican City is referred to as Holy See by authorities. The state identified as a geopolitical entity controls more than a billion Roman Catholics, the largest adherents of the Christian faith, worldwide, who live in various other states and other geopolitical entities of the world.[28] Vatican City on its own has a recorded population of 828 (2008). If that is to be taken as an entity with sublime control over the Catholics it will become perhaps the world's third populated geopolitical entity, if not larger, occupying extensive maritime domain.

Western Sahara

Western Sahara is another territorial entity. It is on the Atlantic in Africa. The major portion of the entity was formerly Spanish Sahara that was annexed by Morocco in 1976. Subsequently guerrilla war erupted with the Polisario Front (Popular front for the Liberation of the Saguia el Hamra and Rio de Oro) that ended in a UN-brokered ceasefire. While negotiations are on, the legal status of the territory and issue of sovereignty remain unresolved.

Geopolitical Entities and Ocean Dependency

The study identifies 278 geopolitical land entities besides five divisions of the World Ocean (2013). The land entities are identified as landlocked, coastland and island categories. All these entities are constantly changing in their geoprofiles, though the changes are not normally visible in day today life at the pace of life.

The situation can change in their identities by the process of micronisation or macronisation in the course of socio-political developments.

The identified entities are exclusive to this study to examine the world from the assumed maritime security perspective. All these entities are interactive in this matter as the ocean beyond the sovereign territory of a country is common to all as global commons except for resource exploitation limited by law of the sea and where national laws exist in support of a country's claim. Among the 278 entities 48 are landlocked, 129 are coastlands and 101 islands. All the remaining entities have direct access to sea. They are either coastlands or islands. An interesting aspect is that many among today's landlocked entities had maritime histories or direct maritime links in the past. They are anyway not strangers to the sea.

The list of identified land entities of the world according to this study as in November 2013 is placed at Appendix A along with their status as landlocked, coastal or island and length of land and coastal boundaries and ocean link.[29]

It is exciting how these land entities originated as nations and other territories of ownership and remained interfaced in a world where the ocean is dominant. It also explains the high density of coastal population and the importance of island territories in the world. The 73 entities identified as territories of nine other states are all ocean linked with 10 of them contiguous to mainland and the rest as oceanic islands. Every entity has its own geostrategic fingerprint with respect to its proximity to the ocean, land borders, border mapping and geoproperty rights and disputes. The overall geometrics of all these geopolitical entities are dissimilar. No entity is identical. Within this geopolitical system profile, the entities have to manage their geostrategy and face the challenges related to their rights and aspirations under the landclasp syndrome. The geometric identity is asymmetrical for each entity. The asymmetry of this identity is reflected in their interactive dynamics in international relations. There are also hidden symmetries in relation to aspirations, sustainable wellbeing of people, apprehensions related to common threats, etc. that could be used to resolve common issues—disputes, transnational threats, other unlawful activities, disasters, environmental damages, etc. if the governments, thereby, the people are willing.

The geostrategic entities are distributed in different ways. This distribution can change in the evolutionary process of these entities. The distribution is as given in Table 2.4 (November 2013).

Table 2.4 Entity Distribution in Relation to Land-Ocean Links

	Distribution of Geostrategic entities	*Numbers*
1	Ocean divisions	5
2	Member States of the United Nations	193
3	External territories of nine member States of the UN	73
4	Others	12
	Total	**278**
5	Landlocked	48
6	Coastlands	129
7	Islands	101
	Total	278
10	Entities with single ocean link	211
12	Entities with multi-ocean link	19
13	Entities with Arctic Ocean link	9
14	Ent ties with Atlantic Ocean link	127
15	Ent ties with Indian ocean link	49
16	Entitles with Pacific Ocean Link	65
17	Entitles with Southern Ocean link	2

Among the 48 landlocked entities 43 are members of UN. Others are Vatican City, a recognised state, and Kosovo, Nagorno-Karabakh, South Ossetia and Transnistria that claims to be independent but not recognised under international law.

Another way to look at the status of entities is in relation to their maritime affiliation as members of International Maritime Organisation (IMO), the primary body of the United Nations for ocean governance in maritime transportation. There are 170 members and three associate members, including landlocked countries in IMO (Appendix B) (2013).

The finding shows the dependency of world population on the ocean. The entities that have links with the ocean either as land based nations or island nations have many smaller nearshore and offshore islands. None of the landlocked states have island territories in the ocean. An island territory enhances ocean property rights of a nation besides providing strategic advantage in geostrategically adverse situations. The landlocked states stand to lose this advantage.

The world is vibrant and continuously evolving with its dependency over the ocean becoming more and more pronounced with the passage of time. No nation, including those that are landlocked is free from ocean dependency. Besides recognised nation states there are many other territorial entities that will be influenced by the ocean. The purpose of this chapter is to highlight this fact. The world is a dynamic entity as a whole with a small land space available for habitation for people with a supporting oceanic environment which by itself is an expansive and multidimensional terrain. It has been regulated by UNCLOS regime to avoid trespassers. But maintaining the ocean from the existing and emerging threats has to be done with the support of everybody who is benefited by it as a global common. These entities are also constantly changing in the dynamism of demographic and political shifts.

Chase for Land—Disputes Worldwide

No geopolitical entity could ever satisfy with the land it owned; land was a security symbol. Every entity engaged in acquiring land within their power. The modes of gathering more and more land were direct acquisition, annexation, coercion, conflicts, war or a combination of all. None of these methods are easily possible today. But the claims over land still prevail in the form of unresolved disputes. The possible means of resolving disputes between entities over land today are by negotiation or legal action under international law. Many territories are under disputes. They were carried forward since historical times—end of geopolitical wars and conflicts or beginning of independent governance.

There are also examples of amicable geostrategic solutions. India's agreement with Sri Lanka on *Katchativu* that lie north of *Ram Setu* (Adam's Bridge as referred by British cartographers), and with Burma (Myanmar) on *Coco Islands* of the Andaman group of islands, Sino-Russian demarcation of islands at the Amur and Ussuri confluence and in the Argun River, etc. are examples of pragmatic diplomacy in a world of fanatic nationalism or economic nationalism.[30] But in the post-UNCLOS world, a country stand to lose considerably in terms of legal continental shelf, exclusive economic zone, territorial sea and associated loss of resources, especially oil and gas buried underground, if it has to give away even an island that is microscopically tiny or submerged during the high tides. Many islands are of great strategic importance to a state in controlling the waterways around them. No country will be willing to walk the line of negotiation unless the compensations in terms of geostrategic advantage are sufficiently high. Negotiations on such issues have to be on a win-win game strategy with the involvement of people through their political establishments. Often it is not possible. This is evident when some of the establishments in India complain on the past decisions of the government in relation to *Coco Islands* or *Katchativu*.

Solving territorial disputes permanently will require extraordinary understanding and intuitive capability for governments. In their absence the disputes will remain and hinder global progress and mutual confidence. Adversaries can take advantage of such situation.

The territories under disputes between two or more geopolitical entities are of very special nature and are not seen exclusively for this study because they are partially referred to as examples in this chapter besides being inclusive of identified entities based on the holders' regime. The holders or the claimants of these territories have independent or joint responsibility towards international community to see that these terrains are safe and sound and not detrimental to international peace and wellbeing.

There is a tendency among scholars to depict countries as sea power and land power. For example some consider India as a land power and Japan as a sea power. It perhaps may not be appropriate to think that way as the very concept of national power itself can be questioned. For example a nuclear power can be understood but the terms like "soft power" cannot be validated critically unless "hard power" is defined along with it and categorically established. National security governance should be devoid of terms that cannot be defined firmly, including the word "peace." Abstractness looks and sounds better in art, literature and philosophical discourses; it is dangerous in governance.

Conclusions

Ocean, land and geopolitical entities are the trident of human system environment. They are not only interrelated but, in a deeper perspective, are unified in singular appreciation as land everywhere. Ocean is nothing but a vast and expansive flood over land. Under these conditions and by design, it is natural that the survival of human systems is exclusively land based.

The need for understanding the ocean and beyond originates from this appreciation—its nature as a great flood over land and the exclusivity of land based governance for human survival. The understanding develops the idea of ocean property that also unifies the concept of ocean wealth and much more.

Within this scenario the human system perches in their little abodes, the geopolitical entities. Majority of them are recognised by all, some partially recognised and a few unrecognised. Every entity has its extension into the ocean, directly or indirectly like the telomere of the mitochondria in their cells. Any damage to it will sound disaster.

The ocean is single with five divisions. These divisions can increase or decrease in area according to the geopolitical outlook of the world. They are also subject to the perennial movement of the continents.

The land and geopolitical entities are symbiotic. In this relationship the ocean is not seen as a party primarily by the hardcore landclasp syndrome. It is primarily the expansiveness and inaccessible depth that make the ocean look mysteriously different from land. The inscrutability in perception rings in maritime security as a ghost protocol. The concept starts hunting like an unsettled gyroscope to find the true direction as a ghost protocol. In the bargain, the governments lose direction in governance. This is in spite of the fact that even landlocked states are considered maritime states under various compulsions and actions

NOTES

1 Not exactly! There is also fresh water in ocean and ocean is considered a good reservoir for fresh water in the future. Fresh water enters ocean through underground and submarine fresh water river outlets. These are called fresh water springs as the water rises above the denser saline water. Water also rises from submarine artesian wells. Fresh water is one of the ocean resources as part of ocean property.

2 Archipelago contain large group of islands. It is a chain or cluster of islands.

3 news.bbc.co.uk/cbbcnews/hi/newsid_7460000/newsid_7462800/7462806.stm, Arctic Ice 'Melting even Faster,' accessed 12 July 2008.

4 Mouawad, J, Arctic may Hold as much as a Fifth of Undiscovered Oil and Gases, *International Herald and Tribune, Tokyo, 25 July 2008, p. 10.*

5 Central Intelligence Agency, *The World Fact Book 2012*, www.cia.gov/library/publications/the-world-factbook/geos/xq.html, accessed 20 April 2013.

6 Ibid.

7 Kremlin Lays Claim to Huge Chunk of Oil-rich North Pole. www.guardian.co.uk/world/2007/jun/28/russia.oil, accessed 20 April 2013, Russia had taken its case in 2002 to the UN with geological data backing the claim that was rejected. Since then it is accumulating evidence to press its claim gain.

8 Sinha, Kounteya, Arctic Meltdown to Cost Global Economy $60tn, *The Times of India, Bangalore*, 26 July 2013, p. 17.

9 Strictly the status of landlocked countries changed to that of maritime nations with a declaration in 1921. The Declaration recognising the Right to a Flag of States Having no Sea-coast was passed in 1921. The declaration legally recognised the right for a landlocked state to become a maritime flag state and register ships and sail them on the sea under its flag. It was a great development in the history of ocean governance more than half a century before UNCLOS which perhaps is long forgotten in the hype created by UNCLOS. The debates whether they could do it was blocked by France, the United Kingdom and Prussia on the argument that the landlocked states would not be able to manage their ships as they had no access to ports.

10 Used in place of property rights as well as jurisdictional rights under the term geoproperty.

11 There was a reference to winning war without fighting by Sun-Tzu. He quoted in his *Art of War, "The supreme art of war is to subdue the enemy without fighting."*

12 Shah, Pir Subair and Jane Perlez, Taliban Fill a Political Void in Pakistan, *International Herald and Tribune*, Tokyo, 15 July 2008, p. 1-4. There are

examples where national governments are fighting continuous wars within their own countries against unlawful combatants who establish regimes within and collect taxes and enforce local laws over the people. An example is that of Taliban who has become a strong force in Pakistan and Afghanistan. They settle feuds between the tribes in Pakistan's tribal areas faster and better than the governments for a price. They become self sustaining by their self rule. Virtually they are ruling the Federally Administered Tribal Areas (FADA) of Pakistan. They net where authorities fail.

13 Somali pirates argue that they are preventing alien poaching in their waters acting like the coast guard. The country did not have a recognised government between 1991 and end 2012 though it remained a member of the United Nations. An important question that arises from here is "Can a country without a government remain recognised as a member state?" It is time to examine this aspect as history will repeat under the law of invariance. It also throws light into the fact that one of the major hurdles in handling Somali piracy by the international community was its membership in the UN in absentia of a recognised government.

14 Some such lakes are so large they are called seas—examples are the shrinking Aral Sea shared by Kazakhstan and Uzbekistan and, the largest of all, Caspian Sea shared by Iran, Kazakhstan, Russia, Turkmenistan and Azerbaijan. Such seas are large enclosed inland water bodies.

15 Article 4, Chapter 2.

16 The League of Nations was still in existence when the United Nations was formed.

17 This is further amplified by using the term "micronisation" by the author in his book, Paleri, Prabhakaran, *National Security: Imperatives and Challenges, New Delhi, Tata McGraw-Hill Publishing Limited, 2008, p.193.*

18 Coastland is a term used by the author to explain a littoral that is not an island but has part of it linked to other land bodies.

19 Also see, Paleri, Prabhakaran, *Coast Guards of the World and Emerging Maritime Threats*, Tokyo, Ocean Policy Research Foundation, 2009, pp. 11-23.

20 Examples are the Manx of the Isle of Man and their Celtic language, and the indigenous people of Puerto Rico. There are parts in the world where indigenous people are still thriving either in primitive identity or modern. The indigenous islanders of Andaman and Nicobar in India are looked after by the government in their primitive habitats, and agencies protect them. The Government of Japan recognised the indigenous identity of the Ainu population of Hokkaido Prefecture.

21 The Treaty of Westphalia and French Revolution where considered the catalysts for the formation of sovereign states.

22 Under the 1993 Oslo Accords, parts of the territories politically came under the jurisdiction of the Palestinian National Authority.

23 Oblast is an administrative division of Slavic countries. An oblast is often translated as area, region zone, province, etc. depending on the context. Some uses it as a cognate of the Russian term voblast (roughly translated as province).

24 General Assembly Resolution 2758 replaced ROC with PRC.

25 76 athletes from Taiwan participated in the Beijing Olympics, 2008.

26 Taiwan Vessels Intrude, Japan Says, *International Herald Tribune*, Tokyo, 17 June 2008, p. 3.

27 Bradsher, K. and E. Wong, *Taiwan is Pressing to Improve China Links,* International Herald Tribune, Tokyo, 19 June 2008, p.1, 8.

28 According to Vatican figures as reported in BBC World News, there were 1.2 billion Roman Catholics in the world out of which more than 40 per cent reside in Latin American countries. www.bbc.co.uk/news/world-21443313, 14 March 2013, accessed 22 March 2013.

29 Collated from various sources including the CIA Fact Book, 2008, Wikipedia, Indian Coast Guard Sources and others. The information is likely to have variations with respect to available sources as well as in the records of individual states and other entity authorities. The details collated in the table are for comparative assessment to highlight as well as to assert the importance of each entity with respect to the World Ocean. The territorial dimensions of all these entities shown in the table are taken after comparison with the available resources or interpolated where necessary and are not precisely accurate. The dimensions will vary because they are fractals and countries and associated entities will have their own view points. Their use in this study is for comparative analysis and in understanding the dimension of the geoproperty and ocean property advantages. The maritime finger prints or the geometrics of these entities other than the ocean entities depend on their status as a coastal area relative to the land border. For a territorial entity, maximum maritime exposure is when it is an island. It is a bench mark. The maritime vulnerability and maritime advantage varies accordingly. But it is not proportionate because no entity is identical. The asymmetries between each entity add additional variables to the strategic games.

30 But these issues do not advocate nations should settle disputes by means following these examples. There are many contentious views that have been raised subsequently in the respective nations.

Chapter 3

EMERGENCE OF NATIONS AND EVOLUTION OF NATIONAL SECURITY CONCEPT

National security is not just about the physical security of a nation; it is about the wellbeing of its people.

The striking fact is that the much spoken about term "national security,"considered to be a modern concept originated subsequent to the formation of sovereign states under the European model of Westphalia, can be traced back to a period much earlier than the emergence of nations in the rudimentary form of its evolution within the human system.

In the early periods, especially when human systems were territorially contented without thinking of formal ruling or governance, existentialism was all about physical security. But with the advent of sovereign aspirations and related essentials of statehood, nationalism and national governance, the concept is turning leisurely towards existentialistic wellbeing of humans. The security concept slowly evolved into national security. This is seen at least in some thought processes of governments but no nation has yet accepted it solely. The concept is still evolving with primordial physical security apprehensions still dominant in its perception. This aspect is what makes the governments think of national security as a part of national governance and not as the sole objective of national governance.

This is a finding of this study.

In the progressive study of national security, the foremost question is not about the concept as it is, but the meaning of nation in the term "national security."

There are other terminologies too in frequent usage. Among them, the terms "country,""state" and "nation"employed generously during interactive communications. "Nation," as a term in usage, figures frequently in geostrategic applications and considerations. For example, national security as a keyword has much more prominence in its application than "country security" or "state security." It also points out that national security,as an expression of substance, is not merely about the security of a country or a state alone. The connotation of national security breaches the boundaries of mere physical security.

A statement of facts or hypothesis of the nature of the above paragraph throws out challenges in defining the terms or expressions appearing as key words. These challenges demand appropriate definitions of the words of key expressions for clarity of perception. Often the attempt to induce clarity can invite further challenges. The reason for such challenges is that these keywords are not proprietary to the scholars or any other exclusive group of discussants who use them frequently. They are common terms of usage in a responsible human system concerned about the wellbeing of its members. A geopolitical entity is a macro human system. The key words are in usage by its citizens at one time or the other. Hence the keywords need to have universal clarity in expression. But achieving such a state by sheer definition is an impossible task as the appreciation of the concept by affirmed perception will be different for people. This trend is very visible even in modern times in the study of national security. This is examined and founded progressively in this study based on previous studies on the subject.

The first attempt is to examine the meanings of the terms "country,""state"and "nation" along with another frequently used term, "nation state"in relation to national security. This is important since all these terms carry different meanings based on the context of expression. One of the rationales for identifying the geopolitical entities of different kinds that exists as on the time of study was primarily to draw attention towards definitions of the key words expressed here. It is another aspect that these entities, as human systems, keep evolving and changing as time progresses.

Country, State, Nation and Nation State

A country, by one definition, is a territory of the people of a state or a nation. It is a tract of human compatible land. Humans live in this track of land as its citizens. A country, by this definition, is also a state as well as a nation. But this aspect needs to be examined seriously. A country also has legal identity as a distinct entity of a human system. But it is seen in the earlier chapter that there are geopolitical entities other than a country. For example, Antarctica or Western Sahara is not a country per se, though in certain cases they are listed as countries.[1] What about Palestine or Taiwan? Are they also countries and thereby states or nations? Which way Transnistria will turn out after a century or so?

Further ahead in its definition, a country may be an independent sovereign state, or one that is occupied by another state, as a non-sovereign or formerly sovereign political division, or a geographic region associated with sets of previously independent or differently associated peoples with distinct political characteristics.[2] Sometimes the word "country" refers to both sovereign states and to other political entities while other times it refers only to states. The term country represents a wide variety of dependencies, areas of special sovereignty, uninhabited islands and other entities in addition to traditional countries or independent states as the people know. Under this principle, the entire geopolitical entities can be referred to as countries according to this study. This is especially so since the subject matter is about the study of maritime security that delves in national security when related to geopolitical entities. Every geopolitical entity examined in the previous chapter is also related to the ocean directly or indirectly and is influenced by it.

The term"state"explains a body politic, especially one constituting a nation.[3] It has a deeper, wider and more comprehensive, if somewhat conceptual, meaning in political philosophy. The government is implicated continuously in the life of the community as the operating agency. A state is the supreme public power within a sovereign political entity. A state gives political identity to its citizens which will be dominant over other forms of individual identities. The state exercises power over its people through the government.

The role of the government is to govern the nation. It is expressed in many ways by scholars. For example, William E. Gladstone pronounces the duty of the government is to make it difficult for people to do wrong, easy to do right.[4] The first part of the statement can be seen as establishing rule of law whereas the second part is not clearly appreciable until what is right is defined. The role of the government needs to be defined clearly within the constitutional requirement and acceptable to the public. Defining such a role is easy and definite under national security governance once the concept is understood and defined.

State is a political system or arrangement based on law. Law is both primary and secondary. Primary law is the constitution. Secondary law is by which the state is governed. The system of a state is protected by the military and other forces both armed and unarmed. Here the state becomes a nation, which is a state in governance. It also implies that there is rule of law under the constitution in a state. It may also be seen that there could be states where the enforcing agencies are government-approved militia. In such case the applicability of rule of law will deviate from the constitutional charter.

A nation is defined as a relatively large group of people organised under a single government. Here, nation attains a meaning—a large human group governed by a government. A nation is a country by the definition of a country; it is a state because it is a body politic. The nation becomes a superior human system that is orderly under governance as a single body. It is expected to be dynamic and progressively moving in time. There are contradictions to these statements. How does Somalia figure in here between 1991 and 2012, when it did not have a formal and recognised government? Is a country a nation when it is not governed by a formal or recognised government? Somalia was still a member of United Nations during the period when it did not have a government. It was a member before that period as a responsibly governed nation like many others. Its membership was not revoked by any resolution during the period under reference. A member in UN is a recognised and responsible country, state and nation. Recognition also means being governed by an acknowledged government. But Somalia continued as a member in spite of not being governed by a recognised and formal government. All these summations and more, call for a serious look at the concept of nations and national security.

A nation like a country or a state is a common territorial entity for its people or inhabitants who share many things in common. The most essential of them all is the government. Without government, the system cannot become a nation as per this definition. A government is the common arrangement for collective governance of the inhabitants of the identified territory. A nation gets upgraded to a nation state when the commonality principles nudge beyond differences caused by any kind of ethnic[5] makeup in every respect. The idea of a nation state is a modern social reality. For some authors, nation is an imagined political community.[6] It is not exactly so in this study, especially in the case of nation state. Nation state is a real community thriving under formal governance. The governance here can be identified under realpolitik sans any of its pejorative assumptions and appendages. Here realpolitik turns out to be politics based upon practical and pragmatic considerations of governance. Realism and pragmatism along with naturalness of wellbeing of the citizens hold the key.

As mentioned earlier there are many unconventional uses of these terms in English language. All of them have evolved over time. The usage of nation state should fundamentally be for a nation that is not based on ethnic experience or shared beliefs alone. Definitions change over time. The strongest of all survives the period. But for the moment in time, multi-definitions and appreciations make the perceptions complex.

The term national, associated with national security in this study will be clearer when the concept of national security is examined. But for all purposes, as it stands now in this study, it is about the people of a geopolitical entity, a country, as used in some terms, who are under governance of some form. It also applies to a state. Nation, in its overall concept applies to the territorial entity where there are people as a collective human system under some kind of governance. To that extent, every geopolitical entity mentioned in this study comprises people who are under some form of governance. They are subjects of national security as perceived by them. The caveat is that national security is also not nation state security or about the security of a nation state. It is about the wellbeing of the people of a nation.

In one of its definitions, a nation state is a sovereign state of which most of the citizens or subjects are united also by factors which defined a nation such as language or common descent. In another study, nation state implies that a state and nation coincide. The nation state thereby projects the characteristics of a nation and a state. All these are applicable within the context of the idea of modern state which is relatively new to the age old human system.

The study of state, its functions under a government and associated organs, and statecraft come within the purview of political science. Political science took a wider turn since Peace of Westphalia which declared a series of peace treaties in 1648. Signing of the treaties of Westphalia by the parties to it led to the concept of sovereignty of statehood in Europe by ending the "Eighty Years' War" (1568-1648) between Spain and the Dutch Republic with Spain formally recognising the existence of Dutch Republic, and the German phase of the "Thirty Years' War." The Spanish-Dutch treaty was signed on 30 January 1648. The treaty of 24 October 1648, comprehended the Holy Roman Emperor Ferdinand III, the other German princes, France and Sweden.[7] The treaties paved way to a new political order in Europe. It came to be known as the Westphalian sovereignty. It was based upon the concept of sovereign state. Attacking a sovereign state by another became a matter of prejudice under the system. This prejudice still exists and is getting transformed seriously making it impossible to wage wars at will as in the pre-Westphalian days. It also implies that the treaties did not eliminate wars. Wars are still fought in many different ways of human ingenuity in surmounting prohibitory homilies especially about war and conflict. The common purpose of the treaties was to recognise the right of another state to exist as an independent entity.

National Security

"National security," as an expression in English language is a compound word, comprising the words "national" and "security" where national means belonging to a nation. Nation, as seen, is a term applicable to a country or a geopolitical entity as accepted by people living in it as a collective system. The nation has an exclusive identity as a human habitat under unified governance, even if opposed, at any given time. Existence of a nation is a function of time. A nation is dynamic as well as organic—dynamic, because it contains a vibrant and clamorous human system; organic, because it is a living entity. To that extent, it is a reiteration that every geopolitical land entity identified in this study, occupied by people as a separate habitat of exclusive governance, is a nation for the purpose of this study. Further, this appreciation is expected to apply to every human habitat of exclusive governance that may come up in future by integration or disintegration of existing entities explained by the terms macronisation and micronisation respectively by the author in a previous study.[8] National security, thereby, becomes the security of a nation, as identified in this study, subject to the definition of "security" considered for governance by the government of the particular nation. Within this context it is the definition of security amplified by the adjective "national" that requires careful attention when it is about governance.

Within the concept of national security, and according to a researched study of the author, security, as envisaged in the combined term, is about the wellbeing of the people of a nation under governance, not just their physical security.[9] The purpose of national governance, therefore, is ideally to maximise the wellbeing of the people, the national security, of the concerned nation.[10]

To begin with, it is considered that security is the primary human need as the way people perceive it. It is by origin. It is an old term. Whereas, nation is an idea that is very recent. The term can be traced to the Peace of Westphalia. The idea of a nation was further sharpened and reaffirmed with French Revolution (1789-1799) transforming on the way to the present. It may transform further. French Revolution created a never-before-seen radical and political upheaval in France that had a lasting impact not only in Europe but also in the world. The underlying principles were liberty, equality and fraternity in the human quest for survival. Nations in today's sense are based on them and more. It is a European idea. It remains so.

If security is the primary need by origin, then amplifying adjective "national" is very modern as the concept of nations is relatively recent. The first reference to the term "national security" appeared in 1790 when a group of Yale undergraduates debated the question whether national security depended on fostering domestic industries.[11] Martin Walker's postulation of the Cold War[12] may leave an impression that the term "national security"would have emerged from the dark abyss of the Cold War and the Freudian mindset of the totalitarian forces in a democracy.[13] However if the proposition of the Yale University students in 1790 is acceptable, the original approach to national security was much earlier than the Cold War period. The Cold War was just another global conflict between the two sides[14] that perhaps stressed the importance of deterrent military power in national security. Since then, it became hard to conceive national security beyond military power, though the original concept had a much wider connotation.

An exciting trend is visible here. The concept of national security shifts and converges towards military security or, rather, physical security of the nation and its people during the days of impending destruction by extreme physical forces. Thereafter, when the threat subsides, the various other factors of human wellbeing additional to security from external or internal physical threats come into view. In other words, the concept of national security is still very much momentary and is based on immediate situational demands instead of being pervasively enlarged to envelop the entire aspect of human wellbeing. The governments haplessly become short sighted under the blinding forces of physical threats. Any country that governs a nation in this manner should be under the perceived physical threats internally or externally all time along. Such countries or its governments may not do justice to the overall national security governance. Under such situations the overall wellbeing of the people becomes a far cry.

Author and scholar Joseph J. Romm traces the modern etymology of the phrase national security to August 1945 when in the US Senate hearing, James Forestall, the secretary of the navy, expressed that national security was a broad and comprehensive front.[15] Senator Edwin Johnson confirmed his appreciation for the terminology—national security. Forestall emphasised that the concept of national security was not merely a question of the army and the navy. It comprised the whole potential for war, mining, industry, manpower, research and all the activities that went into normal civilian life.[16] Here there is an implied extension of the concept of national security beyond the military and other physical security aspects. It involved all the activities that go into the normal life of the people of a country. The concept of national security was coming out in application.

The phrase received wider circulation in the United States with the National Security Act 1947. The National Security Council (NSC) of the United States was formed under the Act. United States was the first country in the world to have a formal national security council. The term "national security"was not defined in the Act, but was left flexible for wider use. According to the Act, the function of the national security council was to offer advice to the president with respect to the integration of domestic, foreign and military policies relating to the national security...."[17] It also meant the concept of national security extended to various other policies of the government leading to the overall wellbeing of its people. The word is "wellbeing."

As the world progresses, nations face comparatively reduced physical threat from each other. They are in a position to address domestic issues more comfortably. It is only an understanding as nations still prepare their combat and enforcement outfits to face external and internal physical threats. The term, national security, is often mentioned in various forums today. The concept, therefore, calls for an appropriate definition to understand and analyse at least with the changing trends in national governance.

The concept is set to go through major changes with the importance of states gradually eroding under the global outlook. National security as a concept can dictate decisions in the international playing field. Under the emerging international system,economic interdependence and heightened awareness of global effects of cultural, social and environmental challenges are narrowing down insular national perspectives, though very slowly. Here it is important to understand the role of state in national security.

State and National Security

National security undoubtedly is the responsibility of the state. Many theories and practices purport the role of the state in making the people feel good.

One of the earliest theories belongs to Adam Smith (1723-1790).[18] Under his theory of atomic capitalism, the role of the state included defending from external aggression, maintenance of law and order, enforcement of sanctity of contract entered between different individuals for commercial transactions and providing infrastructure, education and assistance to the poor. In socialistic approach, privatisation was abolished under the stated purpose of removing inequality among people. State, should on the forefront to develop fresh social order based on equity. Keynes (1883-1946)[19] exposed the basic weakness of capitalism and called for an end of *laissez faire*. His statements were on economic security in macroeconomic conditions to maintain equilibrium. The role of the state was to promote public participation in economic welfare. But in an underdeveloped country,changes in market mechanisms will not change the wellbeing of people in a serious way. This is because of predominant poverty. Poverty can be resolved only if the state is concerned about employment generation for the poor and promoting social welfare.[20]

Ancient Indian scholar and revered teacher of political science at Takshashila, Kautilya,[21]suggested to the rulers to be ruthless against anti-socials, criminals and others not obeying the state. He was advocating firm handling to establish rule of law for orderliness in the governance of the state. Years later again in India, Gandhi (1869-1948) told the people, *"Whenever you are in doubt, or when the self becomes too much with you, recall the face of the poorest and the weakest man whom you may have seen and ask for yourself if the step you are going to contemplate is going to be useful to him. Will he gain anything by it?*[22] For Gandhi it was compassion that would lead to fair governance. In both the advocacies the public were at the centre of governance.

According to the World Development Report, 1999-2000, "governments play a vital role in the development, but there is no simple set of rules that tells them what to do."[23] This statement can prompt studies on the government's role in governance as well as the purpose of governance. Another vague area lies between the terms external security and internal security. These terms are often considered mutually exclusive. In India, according to author, Varghese Koithara, the state and the influential public tend to view external security through a politico-military prism, and not through an economic one. Internal security is considered state-centric.[24] Though these concepts are changing with the advent of militant activism, proxy wars and globalisation process, concern for human security is still expressed in abstract manner.

The Supreme Court of India ruled in 2001 that the government, having failed a licit promise cannot claim impunity on doctrine of promissory estoppel, and is bound by consideration of honesty and good faith. On the contrary, the government should be held at high degree of rectangular rectitude while dealing with the citizens.[25] The role of the state is formidably expressed in this ruling.

All these are ideas based on judgments and scholarly wisdom on social governance. They lead to national security in its conceptual form. National security is not an end by itself. It is an approach goal. If the assumption is correct and acceptable, then the role of the state, irrespective of its basic structure and form is to go for it by measures that indicate the process status at any given time or period. This is done by defending the state, providing law and order, producing goods and services, regulating the system and supplying "public goods" such as education, health, infrastructure, drinking water, etc. There are many activities in governing for national security. In this role, the state has to understand that national security is a process, not an end. It needs the participation and concern of the citizens who are the end beneficiaries.

According to American sociologist, Robert A Dahl, there is no definite study on the behaviour of the people in their attitude towards national security and definition of a leader who is responsible for the governance of a nation towards it.[26] But a society cannot manage without having a system of governance. Governance is the role of the government. It is a collective process that will also include the people who are governed. The form of government doesn't matter. It is the wellbeing of the people that matters ultimately in national security.

Before debating on the role of the state in national security, it is imperative to define the concept in a universally acceptable mode and then craft strategies for achieving it through governance in the national perspective. The concept has to be unitary though the national perspectives according to it can change with respect to situations. Here the problem is in defining national security in an acceptable mode. Such a definition eluded the concept all the time, even after it was expressed in 1790 for the first time.

Defining National Security

National security as a concept, sans a definite description, was perceived all the time. The term, as mentioned, was coined in 1790. Thereafter the expression went through various adaptations. The countries appreciated the concept relative to their perceptions and issues. An interesting point was that national security was never practised in governance consciously and seriously. It was practised in a selective mode by governments, all the time speaking loud. Clarity of purpose was absent or inconspicuous. The primary reason was the dearth of a definition to perceive the concept correctly and universally.

The author, in his studies on national security, referring to various scholars on the subject, had made an attempt to define national security prospectively. It was brought out in his primary thesis and subsequently in his book *National Security: Imperatives and Challenges*.[27] It was more a desirable definition than what the governments or scholars may agree instantly. Arriving at such a definition had gone through serious survey and examination to understand "what people want" and "what they need" starting with the theories propagated by the early psychologists and sociologists besides others in the field of human studies.

The study was based on the assumption that governance in any geopolitical system was singularly aimed at the ultimate wellbeing of the people. The people were at the centre in any form of governance. The role of a government was to perform governance for the wellbeing of the people of the entity. Maximising the wellbeing of the people was the sole objective of governance in the modern world. Hence, "what people need" and "what people want" becomes two of the imperatives for the study before attempting to examine the "who will do it " and "how will they do it" challenges.

The study led to the fact that people were subconsciously chasing perceived security all the time and indecisively most of the time. People were not conscious about apparent security, what they actually needed. What the governments could attempt to provide the people by governance par excellence was only apparent security. Another serious finding of the study was that the concept eluded a definition not because the subject was hard to appreciate or unfeasible to introduce and practice in national governance, but because the dynamic inertia of the changing social arrangements caused by the evolving human system and difficulties experienced by governments in governing such a system under limited experience and foresight. The causes were natural.

There is yet another point of interest in studying national security—the governments are seemingly unable or hapless in governing true to the principles of the concept. Does it make national security an unreal or idealist concept? It should not. The evidence lies in the progress of governance in the human system. The process of governance has always been evolving for the better. National security, as mentioned earlier, is not an end by itself; it is also an evolving concept. The concept is real and present. It is also the basic driver of human development.

The governments always project unforeseen urgency in dealing with national security issues. It was based on situational demand.

Does this mean that governments will find it difficult to govern their nations to the extent demanded by the changing principles of national security? Yes, very much so, unless they upgrade their capabilities and change priorities towards national security.

The argument is to establish that the concept of national security is not a ghost protocol. It is the sole object of governance whether national or global. Its principles can also apply in micro human systems. It can provide benchmarks for governance and yardsticks for measuring its effectiveness in various ways. Here, the most important question, perhaps could be, "What is it by itself?"

The national security acts of various countries are also devoid of an answer to this question. Among the 278 identified geopolitical entities only less than a handful ever thought of it seriously or has enacted legislations on it. The acts too do not define national security. The points raised above are visible. Most of the acts are recent, the earliest being the one introduced in the United States in 1947. The National Security Act 1947 of the United States was signed by the then president Harry S. Truman (1884-1972) on 26 July 1947. The Act came in the aftermath of World War II. The purpose of the Act was to align the armed forces, foreign policy and intelligence community apparatus of the country. This, the Act did well. James Forestall, quoted earlier, was the first secretary of defence. He had a serious role in extending the realm of national security beyond the military aspects in the United States. Forestall could hike his authority towards national defence through the Act, by amending it in 1949.[28] His intention was to integrate the armed forces and all the agencies related to the Act under the Department of Defence.[29] The Act did not define national security, instead integrated defence.

India introduced National Security Act in 1980 after too many deliberations as demanded by situations related to terrorism and conflicts induced by external agencies. The purpose, as given in the act, was to provide for preventive detention in certain cases and for matters connected there with.[30] The act extends to the whole of India except the state of Jammu and Kashmir. In the overall, it is a criminal law for preventive detention of suspects who threaten the physical security of the people of India except those in Jammu and Kashmir. It has all that is necessary for such predicaments except the concept of national security in its real perspective. It is vague about national security as a concept. It is not defined. Such an act could have been in any other name. Critics to the Act are apprehensive that it can be misused along with other laws allowing preventive detention. They are also wary of excluding Jammu and Kashmir as a central law should apply to the entire country. The Act's constitutional validity even during peacetime has been described by some sections as an anachronism.[31]

The Himalayan country of Bhutan introduced a National Security Act 1992, which, according to legal pundits was one of the three most comprehensive legislations of the country.[32] The act actually codified the Criminal Procedure Code 2001 of Bhutan. The purpose of National Security Act of Bhutan was to establish action against treason and related activities—speech crimes, unlawful assembly, etc. It did not provide a definition for national security.

Sri Lanka, which has been burning under insurgencies for a very long time, has various laws on matters related to national security as perceived by its governments. Often these laws are said to trespass the thin line of human rights and humanitarian law according to some among the observers of socio-political systems. They also complain that frequent emergency rules existed in Sri Lanka since 1958 empowered governments to override, amend or suspend any legislation. The declaration of emergency cannot be challenged in any court of law. The principle law related to national security isthe Emergency Regulations and the Protection of Terrorism Act 1979 (ER&TRP Act 1979) of Sri Lanka. The law is draconian according to the critics.

Pakistan created a national security council as an institutional and consultative body in 1969 under a presidential decree. There was no national security act. It was mandated for considering national security and foreign policy matters. In this presumption foreign policy becomes external to national security for Pakistan. Criticism arose that national Security Council provided for the expansion of military domination over political affairs.[33] It became very unpopular with the public. It was recreated in 2004 under the National Security Council Act. It is not active since 2008. It was also said to be the fallout of the terrorist attack in Mumbai, India on 26 November 2008 by militants of Pakistani nationality trained in Pakistan.

In all these examinations it is clear that national security for a geopolitical entity, however advanced it may be, is about the way the government of the entity perceives its physical security (alone) and managing it under political governance. Here lies the basic flaw. The blemish of misconception makes even the most advanced governments steer haphazardly in national governance.

National security is about the people, their present and future. It is not about governments. Therefore it has to have universal acceptance. It also has to be quantitative and thereby measurable and amenable to calibration and audit.

National security is a much larger concept in its macro sense than what the governments perceive today. It has to be universal in meaning and sense for effective application in national governance. To sum up, the missing aspects of the concept are:

- a universally acceptable definition and
- macro-social appreciation of the concept for national governance.

While appreciation of the concept for national governance is entirely the prerogative of national governments, a research attempt to find a universal definition for the concept need not be elusive. This study examines the author's definition based on his work towards this objective mentioned earlier. The approach was initiated with the question "What people need and what they want?"

It was found that the concept of national security was driven by the fact that people thrive for perceived security in their lives which is much beyond what they need in the form of apparent security that the governance can provide at the maximum. The apparent security that the government can provide is national security. The quality of life depends on it. The concept of security and appropriate behaviour modification has been evolutionary aspects in human lives. Under such conditions, the quest for a definition that will still be time bound, and subject to changes in future, starts and ends with the concept itself. Security is derived from safety, the primordial requirement for life to sustain itself on the earth. For every form of life, existence on the planet was based on its physical safety. What was not physically safe did not survive. The concept of security changed with the developing brain and, along with it, the intellect. The concept of security went beyond physical safety.

On the way to a definition the study has to proceed through various stages of its evolution, a kind of Greek odyssey, satisfying at the end.

It could start anywhere. The study preferred to have a look from where it left James Forestall and Edwin Johnson, the US senator, who responded to the former stating,"I like your words...national security."[34] That was in 1945. The US National Security Act appeared two years later. It was the foremost Act in the name of national security in the world. The term slowly broke into serious forums of national governance in the United States. The rest of the world was yet to wake take notice. The words "national" and "security" gave it a meaning that is too serious for governments around the world to appreciate even today. Individually the words stand for different meanings. National security is a term that can invoke endless interpretations, because the concept varies in individual perceptions. Whatever may be the interpretation ultimately, national security is the matter of the people and their wellbeing. It is a field for the strategists more than the politicians in governments. A strategist cannot afford to underestimate the power of a word or term like national security. It has to be precise and well meaning with local knowledge incorporated. Imprecise vocabulary can turn the concept around. Perceived definitions of a single term can be different. Therefore, each term has to be defined precisely even if such definitions are relative expressions. A concept will be abstract when it is not defined, and worse when defined incorrectly. National security is one such concept. At least the strategists should appreciate it precisely.

Confucius (551-479B.C.), Chinese political theorist and philosopher is quoted for the statement, *"The beginning of wisdom is calling things by their right name."* They were great words of wisdom. It is very apposite in the case of national security. Wrong appreciations can result in strategic blunders. Many nations have experienced it in the past. Many will follow.

But there are serious limitations in defining and appreciating national security. The biggest limitation is that the world is premeditated with war and conflicts. This leads to aiming more at national power[35] in whatever form it may be than thinking of the wellbeing of the people

Shortly after the 1965 War with India, Zulfiqar Ali Bhutto, the foreign minister of Pakistan, a great country of historic nobility, famously declared in an interview with Manchester Guardian in 1965, *"we will eat grass, even go hungry, but we will get one of our own* (nuclear bomb)."[36] And he did it as the popular leader of the country. But what he didn't probably understand was that a country can make nuclear bombs without forcing itself to eat grass. All what the governments have to do is to be conscious about the concept of national security in its clear perspective. Bhutto's statement also emphasises the fixation of the countries obsessed with military aspects of national power. But a leader like Bhutto can't be naïve. He would have understood that the need of the hour was to get the people moving ahead with hope after a war that was a miscarriage in governance for Pakistan. That is how mostly nations are governed in the traditional sense—through decibels of rhetoric and mass hypnosis.

The phrase "national security" was not widely used until World War II. In a world premeditated with war, the concept continued to be associated with or perceived as "military security."War is a primitive behaviour of conflict resolution. The more powerful invades the less powerful. Any situation will be used as a rationale. Conquest to annex land or bring the victim to the terms of negotiation becomes the prime purpose. But the surprising fact is that in spite of this predisposition of governments, there are evidences that the importance of national security beyond war was recognised even in the early days, though not practised. Somewhere in the course of the conflict-ridden world, the idea of national security was restlessly transforming. Temporarily the concept got diluted by its preoccupation with expressionism related to war, though war was the underlying concern. Other areas were neither studied nor easily understood since war was a serious affair that occurred throughout these epochs at regular intervals and lasted for long periods. More than the development of intellect on advanced and secured human life, competitive advancement in technological and scientific aspects depended on it. The intellect developed, but was directed towards destruction. The psychology of invention was rooted in destruction. National security was closely associated with this intellect and thereby became an issue related to defending a nation from external aggression.

Unlike nation states, which are based on the European model, the concept of national security, though originated in the United States, is yet to follow a form since the world is very much behind in adopting a governance system that would impeccably incorporate the elements of national security in their mutually inclusive form. The nations that practice national security follow their own models guided by situational demands and political considerations. Nations are yet to follow a governance system absolutely based on the national security model. It will take time. The reason for that is the urgency of situational demands of the moment and political survivability of governments. The concept of national security as a holistic system of governance is yet to take shape. It will even require constitutional amendments. Many of the constitutions of the world narrowly follow the national security principles identified in this study.

The case of Bhutan is interesting. The constitution of Bhutan highlights the importance of gross national happiness (GNH) in national governance. The term coined by the fourth Dragon King Jigme Singye Wangchuck defines the indicator of quality of life or social progress measured in more holistic and psychological terms than only the economic indicator of gross domestic product (GDP). It is the GNH that matters, not the GDP in Bhutan's governance according to the King who had opened Bhutan to the age of modernisation. It suits Bhutan. The term that levels ultimately with the wellbeing of the people is the first statement of national security in a value based manner. Perhaps it is also the first statement, though indirectly, about national security that deviates exclusively from the physical security fixation of any country. Bhutan's unique cultural and religious values reflect in the statement. The problem with GNH is that, like many other social indicators, happiness cannot be measured mathematically under precision. Besides, according to this study, happiness cannot be the ultimate indicator of expected wellbeing of a human system. Happiness is an individual prerogative. It is not a measure of wellbeing in a security syndrome. But Bhutan's ideology certainly leads to the principles of national security, as envisaged in this study, if taken in the larger perspective of human wellbeing within the social system. Nevertheless gross national happiness, according to the author, guides Bhutan better than any other country in leading a value-based path in national governance with a sense of purpose that is beyond political compulsions. That is, provided Bhutan understands its value under the situations that are speeding up in the country post devolution of the power of the monarchy. Bhutan has many challenges ahead. One among them is demarcation of its long border with China. Here is where the GNH may take a beating. Land is too precious for Bhutan; and also for China.

But the ultimate concept of national security and governance by it is a far cry from all these.

Strategic thinking and crafting strategies will not yield immediate results. Strategy is about the future; hence cannot be depended upon short term political objectives. Until national governance boldly cracks the inertia of long-term confidence, the idea of national security as the only panacea for long-term problems of human survival will not take shape. Today governance packages future to showcase the present in a deceptive mode. It also includes self deception. Governments showcase future to the people without it happening in reality. This statement can be better emphasised in a quote by the entrepreneur environmentalist Paul Hawken according to whom, *"At present, we are stealing the future, selling it in the present, and calling it GDP."* More than the issue of GDP the phrase "stealing the future, seeing it in the present" when applied to national governance speaks volumes about non-implementation of governance by national security and the resultant lag in appreciating the concept. Commercial slogans like"make-believe," "everyone's envy," etc., will become a nemesis to the companies when their customer relations are at the rock bottom. Make-believe is what the countries follow in today's governance to appease their own citizens. This is what prevents governments from thinking seriously about the concept of national security in its clear perspective.

Any nation including a supranation that can adopt model governance by national security principles, as envisaged in this study, for the wellbeing of its people rather than focusing on the security element alone, will be a reformer and role model for others in the world.

All these statements show that, in spite of advancements in the world, the concept of national security in a wider facet is yet to gain momentum. It is still in infancy. Everything and anything related to national security, even in today's developed world, gets into the military and legal aspects of national security. Therefore, defining national security as a concept beyond defending a nation from external aggression and protecting it from internal disturbances is bound to be unresponsive, especially from governments. The attempt for a definition in this study and earlier arises from the earnest conviction that the basic centre of gravity of the concept of national security lies outside the military aspects of national defence or aggressive combats for envisaged gain.[37]

Under these conditions, defining national security demands a cautious approach. There are scholars and authors who argue that the term has been overstretched both objectively and subjectively to fit into the context. Most of them call for the distinct need to define or re-define national security.[38] Some of them have been already examined. There are studies that point out national security centricity with military security shifted after World War II and the earlier decades of the Cold War.[39] Thereafter there is a visible shift in thinking, though wars and conflicts continue. Various authors identified national security with a host of variables and unknowns in an effort to model it. Some devised periods as variables that changed the concept of national security in the path of its evolution. The parameters included military power, economic conditions, global alliances, support from international organisations, etc. The periods identified were that of the world wars, Cold War and other factors that affected global stability.[40] The recipes varied in relation to space (geographical location), time (whether there was stability in the region during the period), attitudes of superpowers towards the countries concerned, hostility of neighbours (or otherwise), the internal security situation, economic vulnerability, social equilibrium and a host of other factors.[41]

Defining the concept of national security has to be seen against all these and beyond. The existing definitions, occasions of usage, collective acceptance of the term, activities related to the execution and governance of national security, ongoing debates and, above all, the objectives and the ultimate goal of national security need to be examined. In an exploratory mode, it is best achieved by examining the definitions of the concept over the period based on its evolution.

The search for definitions of national security will lead to the exploration of the evolution of human systems in course of time. It is a function of time. To understand the perceived meaning of national security, it is necessary to sift through the existing and now discarded terminologies, expressions and analogies. The perceived meaning needs refinement to get to the actual meaning, especially in a situation where strategists hold the opinion that national security does not have a clear definition.

The author's earlier and ongoing studies in this direction reflect several expressions from authorities and scholars to include other elements in the concept of national security along with military aspects. These elements included environment, foreign policy, information, economics, etc. A brief chronological summation of the findings is appended below.[42]

- 1790

  Mention of national security in the United States at the Yale University about its extension beyond military concepts. It was the earliest recorded reference to national security. The deliberations referred to fostering domestic industries along with military aspects. It was the first time as known to scholars that any reference has been made to the term "national security."

- War and Interwar Period

  Preoccupation and fixation with war and military matters in human systems were reemphasised throughout the period, irrespective of the interruption between the first and the second global wars.

- 1943

  There was a reversal to this fixation when the American political commentator Walter Lippmann (1889-1974) mentioned that national security prevented the need to fight a war and assured victory if one has to fight. According to him national security was the ability of a nation to retain its legitimate interests without a war, and if challenged, to maintain them by war. It was a great statement on the ideology of winning a war without fighting. But war and military still remained at the centre of national security at least in the United States. This definition emphasised military strength would continue to be vital to establish national security. And the countries that are going to harp on war for their survival will be just the one on the top.

- 1945

  There was a reference in the US Senate during a hearing that national security was a concept beyond the navy and the army. Inclusion of nonmilitary security aspects were called for. It was a wide angle view of the concept.

- 1947

There were comments in the National Security Council (NSC) of the United States about flexibility of the term for wider use inclusive of nonmilitary security aspects. It was the practical body to advise the president on the integration of domestic, foreign and military policies relating to national security.

- 1950

The NSC advocated the concept of national security for preserving the United States a free nation with their fundamental institutions and values intact.

Harold Lasswell (1902-1978), American political scientist and communications theorist commented that national security was about balancing instruments of foreign policy, coordinated handling of arms, diplomacy, information and economics and proper correlation of all measures of foreign and domestic policy.

- 1962

American political scientist and author, Arnold Wolfers stated that security, in an objective sense measured the absence of threats to acquired values, in subjective sense, the absence of fear that such values will be attacked. For him national security was an ambiguous symbol under a deceptive name. It was an abstract concept.

- 1965

In the statement of India's Institute of Defence and Strategic Analyses, its purpose was to carry out studies in defence and national security. National security here stands apart from national defence.[43] It was seemingly an original idea. The only other mention of the term officially in a formal document in India is in the National Security Act 1980; the purpose in its preamble has been already mentioned. There are differences in appreciation.

- 1968

International Encyclopedia of Social Sciences defines national security as the ability of a nation to protect its internal values from external threats.[44] The threat is seemingly vague. The threat dimension is singular—external. It could be internal too. It is a case that is applicable in a limited sense. Threat is multifaceted and multidimensional.

- 1972

  According to William Blair, the then American deputy assistant secretary of state for public affairs, national security of the United States depended on many elements that included balance of payment, economic affairs and foreign assistance.[45]

- 1973

  John E. Moss, representative and chairman of the House subcommittee of the US Senate that considered the original 1967 Freedom of Information Act (FOIA)came with a path breaking finding that national security was still an undefined or rather ill-defined word. He emphasised freedom of information to people in national security. It pointed towards information and people's right to know in national governance.

- 1976

  William Blair's statement in 1972 was concurred by the Yale Review that national security was an ambiguous and ill-defined phrase as it stood at that time.[46]

- 1974

  Maxwell Taylor (1901-1987) the American soldier and envoy states the most formidable threat for the US is in the nonmilitary field.

- 1976

  Yale Law Review stated about military security in a high defined manner turning national security into military security

- 1977

  Lester Brown, the then president of the World Watch Institute brings out various nonmilitary issues that determine the state of the world. They included energy, environment, climate,economy, immigration, food insecurity, deforestation, soil erosion, climate modification, greenhouse effect, etc., should be part of national security.[47] The list of concerns of national security was lengthening.

- 1979

Maxwell Taylor talks about energy, population, economy, international trade and inflation as part of national security pointers.

- 1981

American Congressman William Taylor (1788-1846) expresses large scope in nonmilitary aspects since they are vital for people's wellbeing along with physical security.[48] It is also implied protection through a variety of means of vital and economic interests, the loss of which could threaten fundamental values and vitality of the state.

- 1983

Richard Ullman, professor of international affairs at Princeton, narrows down the concept of national security to quality of life of the people and the range of policy choices available to the governments or private nongovernmental entities. Ullman mentions about threat based perception of power where power is within the political as well as military concepts.

According to Barry Buzan, author and scholar in international relations,the term, national security, as a concept is weak and ill defined, at the same time strong and powerful politically. He attributes the ambiguity to "power-maximising" strategies of political and military elites for leverage over domestic affairs invoking it. It can bring in the contention that the ambiguity results fromthe power maximisation games the authorities play.

- 1989

According to Jessica Mathews, vice president of the World Resources Institute, global developments suggested the need for broadening the definition of national security to include resource, environmental and demographic issues.[49]

- 1990

Charles Maier of Harvard University defined national security in 1990 "as the capacity to control those domestic and foreign conditions that the public opinion of a given community believes necessary to enjoy its own self-determination or autonomy, prosperity and wellbeing."[50]

- 1991

Theodore Moran, Director of the programme in international business diplomacy at George Town University's School of Foreign Service mentioned six points to enhance the national security of America. They were 1) to encourage stability and reform in Soviet Union, 2) maintaining a cooperative US-Japanese relationship, 3) avoiding vulnerabilities from the globalisation of America's defence industrial base, 4) reducing dependence on oil from the Persian Gulf, 5) moderating the impact on the Third World of the prolonged debt crisis and 6) limiting damage from narcotics trade.[51] They were the primary issues of America in 1991 according to Moran who, perhaps did not anticipate the total disintegration of Soviet Union in the same year.

- Cold War (1948-1991)

The world turned around on a bipolar symmetry similar to a world war with conflicting ideologies and the subsequent containment policy of the United States against the Soviet Union and its supporters. The scenario was that of a war of sorts. The Cold War on a bipolar front was fought on political, economic and informational (propaganda) fronts, though recourse to weapons was limited.

- 1993

Walter Lippmann advocates on national military capability to protect various "other interests."

- 1994

The National Defence College, New Delhi, India, declared national security as a multidimensional field that includes politics, environment, economics, defence, culture, technology, resources, military, etc. in a seminar.

- 1996

The proceedings of the Seminar on "*A Maritime Strategy for*

India" of the National Defence College, New Delhi, India states, "a nation's security flows from an appropriate and aggressive blend of its political resilience and maturity, human resources, economic structure and capacity, technological competence, industrial base and availability of natural resources and finally its military might."[52]

On the other hand, the previously mentioned seminar in the National Defence College, New Delhi, observed the idea of national security as military oriented. The speakers stated that when it came to planning, the tendency was to focus on clearly identifiable military threats to territorial integrity alone.[53]

In a seminar at the Defence Institute of Psychological Research, New Delhi, India R. Gopalaswamy and others acknowledged that national security implied far more than the traditional concept of pure military power with its supporting hardware. It encompassed all the major elements affecting the development of a free nation state: geopolitical, economic, technological, ecological and demographic. Nonmilitary factors could impact the progress of a nation in very significant manner demanding a holistic approach.[54] All such statements show the projection and influence of the term "national security" in today's strategic psyche. Such thinking invalidates the military theory as the sole element of national security.

- 1999

Former director of India's Institute for Defence and Strategic Studies K. Subrahmaniam in his introduction to author Jaswant Singh's book *Defending India* (1999) supports the latter's conceptualisation of national security in broader terms encompassing economic development, food security, energy security, environment, etc., including evolving threats.[55] His findings broaden the concept of national security beyond military affairs.

- 2000

According to author Anuradha M. Chinoy state security (rarely used term, not national security)meant maintaining political and other structures of military might delved much more into military security aspects as the sole power for anation.

Accordingly the author states that it is time to decide whether to retain the traditional notion of national security or to think an alternative.[56] The author also states that, for national security, the state combines force through its military power and consent in these exercises.[57] Neo-realist (and realist) theories that provide the theoretical foundation for this argue that the security of individuals is linked with the state that preserves the special order and protects them from invasion by aliens and from injuries to one another. In the national security discourses, the state has shown masculine and virile only when it has adequate force (and nuclear capacity) and is seen as emasculated and categorised as a eunuch without it.[58]

Author Vinod Saighal finds national security an overstretched term. It includes military, economics, global institutions, UN and unidentified factors in a security model. In the nonsecurity model he emphasises chaotic situations edging towards insecurity which dealt with economic insecurity, reduced military might, political unrest, social unrest, etc. His observation of India is quote, *"If India's national security aim for the second half of the 20th century could have been succinctly defined as the preservation of India's unity, the country's aim for the first half of the 21st century could equally succinctly be defined as the preservation of the integrity of the subcontinent, as an essential prerequisite for the global equipoise for the third millennium"*[59] unquote. His perception is in a subjective mode, as an entity that needs to have an aim that changes with time.

- 2001

In the seminar of the Indian Navyon 16 February 2001, in Mumbai, India,the naval strategists were unanimous in their observation that national security is a multidimensional concept comprising political, environmental, economic, defence and cultural aspects.

Seven months later an unsuspecting United States was shaken by the deceptive and extreme terrorist attack on 11 September 2001. The country got into war as in the past when the Japanese jolted Pearl Harbor deceptively on 7 December 1941. This time it was war on terror and as a matter of homeland security—a new terminology that is not used by any other geopolitical entities so far. But for a close observer the situation and response were identical to what happened to the nation sixty years back. Where is the change? The concept of national security was totally absent or rather it was very much in military security as it was in 1941. The subsequent change was to homeland security which is different from the concept of national security debated for half a century by then. There was no new policy. The option available for the US Government was what they used 60 years back.

A conflict in Kargil, India in 1999 on the line of control brought India's national security interests across the discussion table. The conflict was attributed to intelligence failure by the pundits in India. A report prepared by the group of ministers (GoM) in 2001[60] stated national security "as a function of a country's external environment and the internal situation, as well as their interplay with each other."[61] The former is influenced by the features of the prevailing international order, the position of its immediate and extended neighbours, and the major powers. The report was primarily aimed at military security, safeguarding the interests of the nation from external aggressors. The recommendations included creating a National Security Council, joint command concept, nuclear doctrine and other subjects related to military strategy rather than an overall national security strategy involving nonmilitary aspects. Therefore, there is the possibility of the National Security Agency of India being preoccupied with military security since its genesis is derived from the post-Kargil India. The extensive Kargil Committee Report of India did not define national security holistically.[62]

Joseph J. Romm[63] whose authentic findings have been mostly examined so far preferred to turn out to the definition given by Richard Ullman in 1983 on national security. According to this definition, a threat to national security is an action or sequence of events that threatens drastically and over a relatively brief span of time to degrade the quality of life for the inhabitants of a state, or threatens significantly to narrow the range of policy choices available to the government of a state or to private nongovernmental entities (persons, groups, corporations) within the state. Here the affirmation is on "quality of life" and the factors that threaten it. Next the interpretation focuses on the nature of government—the process of governance itself. It is the finding of the author that Romm's adaptation of Ullman is an excellent way of concluding an evasive concept with prospect of further research in finding a definition.

That was the attempt.

The idea of national security kept evolving as nations faced many challenges. Defeats in war and conflicts, demographic imbalances, economic declines, oil shock and energy crisis, environmental damages, deficits in international payments, ethnic issues and various other challenges made governments think of nonmilitary aspects of national governance.[64]

Appendix C reproduces[65] the evolution of the concept of national security through ages from the author's research studies.

These findings and observations suggest that the concept gradually evolved to include nonmilitary components in its domain. It is also clear that the phrase was never been defined properly. Those engaged in national security issues should, therefore, include not only those concerned with the military and associated matters, but also experts on nonmilitary aspects of national security. There is no singular expertise in national security governance. It is a multidimensional reality concept. It cannot function under a single advisor or executive. But every advisor and executive can adapt to its multidimensionality in national governance.It is the basic need. Otherwise governance will turn to be selective. In the concept of a state, nothing defines the concern for its people better than its constitution. The constitutions generally affirm the basic concern for humanity. The United Nations Development Programme (UNDP) articulates the basic concerns as justice, liberty, equality, fraternity, unity and integrity, welfare, and freedom.

All these leads to the ultimate objective—the wellbeing of people, under the principles of equality for the unity and integrity of the nation state. It is different from human development, improving quality of life or finding happiness. National security provides for apparent security, which is for everybody; human development and quality of life are included in the process. The examinations lead to various findings given below.[66]

- National security is a realistic concept that relates to the wellbeing of the people of a country.
- It is not about physical security from external and internal threats but also by all other parameters integral to its evolution that will constitute as elements of national security as functions of time.
- This indicates that there could be elements that were prominent in the past and lost importance subsequently and also chances for new elements to come up in future.
- The concept, therefore, is definable.
- Once defined, it could be measurable with respect to time.
- If measurable it could be capable of modeling.
- If national security is about the wellbeing of people, then it cannot have a specific goal quantifying the wellbeing at a particular limit, but an objective to maximise it.

Defining national security for universal acceptability is a challenge. The concept is yet to gain universal recognition. All the existing definitions of the concept project its significance and relevance in relation to national policy. They are appropriate to the situation though seemingly not in consonance with the developments of the world. An attempt to define the concept, therefore, may not be the end in itself as situation can change drastically. Reaching out for a definition involves careful examination of applicable factors.

One of the ways to minimise ambiguity in a definition is to formulate a complementary statement. It is possible by introducing a mathematical variable. But such a variable has to be precise and accurately defined. A suitable variable as a function of time will be an index for national security. Once the national security index (NSI) is introduced, the concept can be explained as a measurable entity: *"The state of apparent wellbeing of the people of a nation based on the aspirations of the ordinary people of that nation."* This is not the definition, but the perception of the concept. The state of wellbeing should be indexed within acceptable parameters particular to each nation. Here it is necessary to elaborate on a nation, its people, the meaning of the term "ordinary people," and their aspirations in understanding the process of approach to a definition. The people are central to it. They aspire for perceived security within their own limitations. It is applicable to the entire people of a nation including the ordinary people who may be ultra rich, super rich, rich, lower rich, middle, lower middle, poor or below it—the eight class generalisation in terms of wealth and purchasing power.[67] The ordinary, therefore, is the ideally balanced human—the standard for the study, who could belong to any of the classes and requires the feel of wellbeing under national governance. The difference is that the aspirations of the ordinary human are close to apparent security and the willingness to work for it by participation in national governance.

The author in his study had considered all these factors mentioned above besides additional factors and parameters to define the concept of national security as,

"the measurable state of the capability of a nation to overcome the multidimensional threats to the apparent wellbeing of its people and its survival as a nation state at any given time, by balancing all instruments of state policy through governance that can be indexed by computation, empirically or otherwise, and is extendable to global security by variables external to it."[68]

Mathematically, wellbeing is about the entire population of the country getting elevated by the fulfillment of their hierarchical needs to the conditional state of self-actualisation, the highest level in Maslow's hierarchy of needs. It is the transcendence to self-actualisation within apparent security. Such self-actualisation is an indication that governance is effective. From another examination point of view, it can be said that *"it is the state when the survival instinct does not affect the individual motive of self-actualisation and thereby creativity."* This sums up the definition of national security as a concept that denotes the wellbeing of the populace of a nation that includes its domestic and geo-strategic prosperity, in which the strength of that nation is seen against the multidimensional threats faced by it at any given time. There is an acceptable deviation here from the perceptions so far on the subject.

Once the concept of national security is identified as a measurable quantity and a function of time, it could very well be indexed. Such indexing will give rise to the NSI. The NSI will be a sliding index with respect to time and will need serious research for indexing and identifying appropriate parameters for accuracy. Once the NSI is assessed it will be easy for comparative analysis of nation states in the world and for internal evaluation related to progress of a particular nation state that could be audited by the people themselves. The NSI could be far more important in assessing the state of a nation than the current methods of evaluation by various indices.

From the exploratory examination of the concept, it could be visualised progressively in human history starting with the basic physical needs of security of the human being. The word "nation" may be a misnomer in its early evolutionary stages but when conjoined with security, the meaning ends up with the wellbeing of a human system that today is in the form of a nation as the largest formal unit. The concept is applicable to any human group, since it is the measurable state of the capability of a nation (a formal group) to overcome threats to provide apparent security—the wellbeing—to its people. In this book, though, the concept relates to the human systems exemplified as nation states.

A word of caution here. National security is an English word, the meaning of which is different from the independent constituent words—nation and security. This will have to be seen when the term is interpreted in any other language. A literary translation of the independent words may sound a different meaning, especially the word "security." The appropriate word has to be identified afresh; it should not be the direct translation. The term can be identified from the definition.

Elements of National Security

Author's studies earlier on matters related to the elements of national security, including the elements themselves, pointed out to an interesting aspect: the elements are interactive and their interactive matrix could decide the centre of gravity of national security.[69] The centre of gravity of national security lay on the configuration of the elements while they were interactive. The configuration of elements is also a time function. The positioning of elements can change with respect to time in a nation's life.[70] The centre of gravity is the Achilles heel of any system. If it is hit, the entire concept will be jeopardized. The governance of a nation can go berserk if its national security configuration is hit at the centre of gravity. It could also happen without any external threat. Sheer misgovernance or wrong prioritisation of elements in national governance can damage governments and national security. Similarly external threats, if aimed, at the centre of gravity can be quite serious. The configuration can change with respect to time. What is important is to appreciate the elements of national security and their restrictive aspects. Integrating maritime security with national security, the objective of this study, is to strengthen the centre of gravity of national security. Effective integration of subsystems strengthens the centre of gravity of the system itself.

In this study, national security is identified as a concept that has been evolving for a very long period. The concept is identified as a suitable destination for the best in national governance. The best that can happen in national governance under the notion of a nation and nation state is maximising the wellbeing of the people. The primary goal of governance, thereby, becomes maximising national security.

In a system approach, an element is a fundamental and very essential part of the total concept. The concept may comprise one or more such elements. The element, therefore, has to have an independent identify and an interactive geometry of mutual inclusiveness with other elements of the concept. It is important to understand that the elements are not mutually exclusive or standalone parts in the total system concept of national security. National security is a multi-elemental and multi-terrain concept. Elements can be under various threats. Threat to the elements cannot be observed easily since it is symptomatic. The symptoms are those that lead the attention of a strategist towards the concerned elements of national security indicating that something is wrong with its governance and management. Capability for proper diagnostics is vital in identifying and analysing elements.

Prior to examining the elements it was felt necessary to appreciate the threats they can face. Threats can be expressed in many ways. Specific threats in terms of appreciation, threats by intensity, collateral threats, threats based on attractiveness (threat attraction), threat to target approach based on time, etc., could form part of the approach. But for a study at macro level, such as the study of national security, the threat analysis is also preferred to be macroinstructional.[71] The threats thus examined under the macroinstructional means are generalised under which each appreciated threat can be placed. This has been achieved by a simple threat matrix cube.[72]

Threat Matrix Cube—Modeling Threat Perception

Threat perception at macro level can be applied to any system or concept. This is especially so in the context of the human system. National security is about the wellbeing of people in a human system. Wellbeing is a "threat attractor."

At the macro level perception, threat is a forewarning. Threat warns danger or harm to the "target." Threat is multi dimensional, a sort of multi-headed mythical Hydra. Threat can be invisible and abstract. But it has to be identified if the target has to be saved and secured. Analysis of threat perception related to various situations can lead to a matrix at the macro level. It will apply to everything that is a threat attractor. And everything that a human deals with, including self, is a threat attractor; well, almost.

The macro level threats can be classified in a three dimensional manner as part of a cube called the thereat matrix cube (TMC) shown at Figure 3.1. The threats represented by the cube are direct or indirect, external or internal and covert or overt. The intensity and degree may vary for the same threat with respect to the time. At any point in time the threat may be intensifying or attenuating. In some cases the threat may remain without any appreciable change. This too is three dimensional— increasing, decreasing or remaining unchanged. The threat perception is a variable and a function of time and situation.[73]

Figure 3.1 The Threat Matrx Cube (TMC)

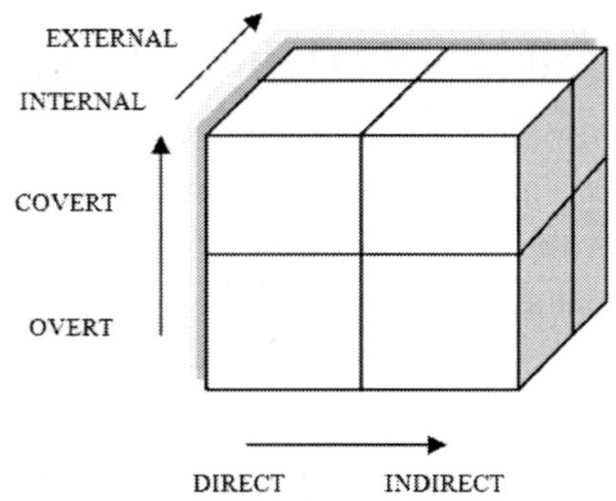

According to the threat perception matrix, the multidimensional threats that a threat attactor can expect will fall under eight categories and sometimes in combinations of them. They are,

a. Direct-Overt-Internal (DOI)
b. Indirect-Overt-Internal (IOI)
c. Direct-Overt-External (DOE)
d. Indirect-Overt-External (IOE)
e. Direct-Covert-Internal (DCI)
f. Indirect-Covert-External (ICE)
g. Direct-Covert-External (DCE)
h. Indirect-Covert-Internal (ICI)

Threat can be analysed in many different ways. Sometimes threats can also be termed as risks involved depending on the situation. The TMC can be a handy tool not only in threat analysis but also in shadowing the threat thus identified in national security governnce.

In modern times there are attemtps to replace the term "threat" with "challenge." While it may be appropriate as long as the meaning is understood, the study of national security may do well with the usage of the term "threat" as it reflects something that has to be prevented or preempted by every possible means in the quest for human wellbeing. A "challenge" is perceptionally milder than a threat giving a feeling that one can live with it if the situation so demands. A challenge has to be overcome; a threat has to be prevented or preempted before it hits the target.

Identifying Elements

The elements of national security are identified by examining their fundamental nature and characteristics in support to the vitality of national security governance. The elements have certain properties and periodicity. The conceptual elements have an informal hierarchy, especially with respect to their period of identified origin. The elements develop, and may even disappear as an independent entity by integration or disintegration on a larger time scale. New elements may come up. Therefore, periodicity is a constant property of elements. The hierarchy of the elements can be determined by the period in which they were identified or with respect to their interactive superiority in a matrix. The choice can vary. The art of distinguishing various elements of national security is based on their contribution towards national security singularly and jointly by interaction. The characteristics of the elements can be identified from this lemma.

15 elements have been identified by a research study as the fundamental constituents of national security as defined earlier.[74] The properties of these elements reflect the properties of the period of their origin. The elements develop over a period and not at a particular time or date. They may also vanish; it is still a hypothesis. There are no examples.

Elements of national security enhanced the concept as and when attempts to define it progressed through the period of its evolution. The elements are mutually inclusive and thereby interactive. Hierarchy of elements is with respect to situational parameters since they cannot be expressed in relative importance. The findings show military security as one of the elements and not national security by itself. Besides, like any other element, military security has to be seen along with other elements in national governance because of their interactive nature and affinity with each other. Fixation with a particular element should be avoided in national security governance for this reason.

Qualifying Characteristics of Elements

The considered qualifying characteristics of an element of national security were as given below.[75]

- Directly influences human life—as a system entity within its own boundaries.

- Fundamental whole of the concept—definable and appreciable within a system boundary.
- Independent threat attractor—should have affinity to threat.
- Periodic in origin—appeared in different periods of time in the evolution of the concept.
- Continuous and uninterrupted since origin—the element should be ongoing since its origin. An element interrupted in between will be a new element when it reenters the chain.
- Independent variable with a profile—so that the indicators of the element can be ranged on a minimum-maximum scale.
- Interactive with other elements—mutually interactive and well interfaced with each other for effective integration in the national security matrix.
- In vogue in its usage in national security—should be known and easily comprehensible to the people, not a select few. National security is a people oriented subject.
- Likely to remain in future as an element—a desirable characteristic. The element should not be in a stage of decline or rather, dissolution at the time of identification. In such case it has to be handled separately because it would have lost luster in other desired characteristics, especially in interactive capabilities.
- Macro level social impact—the concept of national security is seen at macro level. Therefore, the element should be acceptable at the same level.
- Terrain specific—the element should be identifiable with one or more terrains.
- Can maximise national security—It should be governance friendly with the capability to maximise national security.
- Universal in character—national security is a global entity though applicable to a nation. Therefore, the element has to have universal characteristics applicable to every nation.
- Capable of modeling—the elements should be definable and capable for quantitative alteration in values for scientific modeling.

An element has to be definite as an integral part of national security. The effect within an element directly impacts national security, whereas, a condition or a threat impacts an element. A condition or a threat should not be misconstrued as an element for national governance. It is often the case. It is a blunder the governments make like inadvertently or impatiently pressing the system knobs without knowing them. Conditions and threats are mere symptoms for diagnostics. Access to wellbeing is through maximising the elements of national security, not conditions or threats. Governments put up considerable amount of efforts and incur heavy expenditure in treating symptoms that may be mere conditions or threats instead of elements of national security. One of the reasons for identifying elements of national security is to avoid this mishap.

The 15 elements identified qualify under the prescribed characteristics. They are listed below in their appreciated hierarchical order by evolution and usage.

1. Military security
2. Economic security
3. Resource security
4. Border security
5. Demographic security
6. Disaster security
7. Energy security
8. Geostrategic security
9. Informational security
10. Food security
11. Health security
12. Ethnic security
13. Environmental security
14. Cyber security
15. Genomic security

The hierarchical order of the elements is not from the date of the Westphalian (European)[76] sovereignty, but the time since the humans were seriously involved in their struggle to survive under the existential urge.

The elements are briefly examined below.[77]

Military Security (Element #1)

National security is perceived to be military security until the thought process developed with the remarks of the undergraduates at the Yale University in 1790. To begin with, military security was involved in physically protecting a collective human system from the invading another. With the advent of sovereign nations, military security became protecting a nation from invaders who challenged its sovereignty. The invaders were primarily external to the nation. It also involved aggressors who questioned the sovereign status. Today, almost every nation has invaders from within. In military security, force and law are used to handle a situation that will impact on it and thereby on national security. The term military security is associated with the use of military in preventing or preempting threats to the sovereignty of a nation and the physical security of the people of the nation. It is the earliest element of national security. It is continuous and will lose importance only if wars are eliminated once for all. It is not likely. War and conflicts are conditioned behavioral characteristics of humans for survival. They may change forms but will never get eliminated in human system.

Jaswant Singh, India's author politician, in his book *Defending India* states that during the first centuries of the nation-state system, economic welfare was thought to be advanced by extension of national territory in the interests of trade and investment. Thus the requirements of military security were closely allied to economic self-interest. During the latter decades of the 20th century, this linkage was largely destroyed by the universal belief that prosperity derived from, not by extension of territory by military aggression, but free trade global markets. Some began to regard policies to improve national economic competitiveness as an equal, if not more important, contribution to national security.[78] In this statement, national security takes turn to depart from military security and visualise economics as a unique part of it, at the same time interactive with military security.

This is also indicative of the two elements of national security and their inclusiveness—military security and economic security.

Economic Security (Element #2)

Economic security is decided based on the economic power of a nation. Nations invaded others in the past to boost their national income by plundering or dominating. It is necessary to see such invasions with military security on one hand and the economic rating of a nation on the other. An economically weak nation cannot protect its territories and interests militarily. In such cases, it feels weak and threatened. Vulnerability forces the country to spend on military equipment for defence that further reduces the economic standards. Though hypothetical, it is an interesting supposition in the concept of national security. Military expenditure is spending based on feelings of vulnerability. The other aspect of interest is that the richer a country is the more it feels vulnerable. It is visible in individual behaviour too. Nations are nothing but collective sovereign human systems.

This leads to a hypothesis: *"In the diminishing correlation between economic security and military security, there is an optimum point that could be termed as economic defence spending (EDS) which is the optimum balanced spending for military security for a particular nation, variable in time."*[79] Considering that any country will spend on military and armed forces,under this hypothesis, ideally a government can arrive at a figure that will be optimum expenditure for its military security. The assumption behind this hypothesis is that war and conflicts are acceptable realties that may impact economic security unless they yield return on investment (RoI). In a world where entering into a war at will is becoming progressively inflexible, the return on military investment will have to be in nonmonetary terms. The optimum expenditure for maintaining military security is the point at which the economic security is balanced to the optimum—the point at which the spending stops. It is a variable since economic standards of nations can vary.

But military spending is not on defence alone. There are nations that spend heavily on dubious offensive objectives as a matter of policy. Offensive activities include limited wars, preemptive strikes, surgical strikes, state sponsored proxy wars, insurgency supports, etc. In such cases the economics takes a different turn, with money accounted from some other sources—secret spending, black budget for nefarious activities including espionage, secret borrowings, dirty laundering, drug sales, arms trafficking, hidden energy futures, dirty tricks business, etc. Economic security was focused through various ideologies in the past and the pattern still continues. The theories of political philosophy—liberalism, communitarianism, capitalism, communism and socialism[80] were all based on economics. Economically weaker nations counted on military security either directly or by submitting to the more powerful by direct or indirect protectionism as a continuing trend.

Destroying a country economically is called, in simple sense, "economic warfare." In one of the definitions, that too very conservative, it is about taking economic policies followed as part of military operations and covert operations during war situation. But it is a subject that can be extended beyond war to other-than-war situations with an objective of destroying another country's economy by changing the economic and other policies of the attacking party or parties. Aids, assistances, sanctions, pumping money from central banks, protectionism and other trade barriers, speeding up recovery of funds from other countries without allowing them to plan return at their pace,[81] pumping from reserve..., there are a host of such economic warfare techniques in a leveled up country's quiver. Here there is a question, still at the level of hypothesis: "Is it possible for an economically weaker country to wage an economic war over another that is economically superior?" It is seemingly a positive hypothesis, though untested at this stage.

Resource Security (Element #3)

Wars and conflicts had direct relationship with resources. In the prehistoric days the most important resource was fire. Fire is replaced by the term"energy" today. It is the oldest resource on which human life thrived all along and developed. Though energy has become a separate entity today, generating energy needs energy resources. Strategic control of resources, including global commons, is an important agenda for many global players. Resource colonisation is an attempted practice. All these are expected to continue in spite of global reforms and awareness. Scarcity of resources makes nations take adversarial positions. Water, energy resources, food, etc., can cause conflicts among human groups including nations. The United Nations estimate is that there are about 300 potential conflicts over river borders and drawing water from shared lakes and aquifers all over the world.[82] Water scarcity and the need for sharing river waters cause serious internal conflicts within a nation.

Resources are not restricted to water alone. It includes all such resources that are required for human existence including strategic metals and minerals. Resource demanding nation state has to have access to it for resource security. Often the urge to gather resources makes nations to enter into the global commons and deny resources to the opponents. Rightful allocation of resources in a sustainable manner among and within the geopolitical entities, thereby, becomes an emerging idea.

Border Security (Element #4)

Borders in the concept of national security are the boundaries identified by the respective entities and established or lie disputed with the adjacent countries. The concept of borders as a symbol of security and possessiveness is prominent in human systems. The boundaries for all purposes are recognised internationally. But there can be disputes between two entities. The boundaries still exist as a cause of dispute in such case. Protecting the borders, especially from cross border human movement is a serious concern to a nation-state. The nations are actively engaged in defending their borders to prevent or preempt a breach in every possible way in every terrain — geophysical or otherwise.

People cross borders into alien terrains for various reasons. Protecting them with its associated disputes and all, at the outer perimeter or within the state at the entry points is essential for national security.

Demographic Security (Element #5)

Population can be a boon or a bane for a country. Population explosion can impact on the overall wellbeing of the people. It has to be governed effectively. Under effective governance,population can be a boon. This raises a chain of questions. "Is there an optimum population for a particular nation in relation to its demographic security governance towards national security maximisation?" "If so, how to arrive at it?""How to balance the optimum population for best results?"But demographic security is not about population growth concerns alone. There are many other factors such as migration, trafficking, socio-economic issues, etc. associated with demographic security. Demographic movements can affect national security if not monitored and governed effectively.

Another serious issue is dehumanisation of a population under various threats. It is against the principles of national security. The victims of dehumanisation, like anybody else, are individuals looking for avenues to steer their lives towards a better future. Dehumanisation is a term used to explain people who face physical, mental and emotional threats. They get exploited. Sheer powerlessness of the victims arising out of various situations including lack of economic choices fails a society and a nation and deprives its wellbeing.

Disaster Security (Element #6)

Disasters are packed with powers of destruction. A disaster is an incident that causes loss of life and property in human life. An incident is not a disaster unless it has a negative impact on human life. Natural disasters are part of the human system. Disasters are also human induced—direct as well as collateral. The worst human induced disaster, perhaps, is yet to come. Disasters can induce deep trauma and anguish among people. The agony would be reduced if the tragedies can be contained. It is a daunting task to find sustainable mechanisms to meet the humanitarian needs during disaster situations. The difference between natural and human induced disasters is marginal. There is no official definition for a disaster. But, it is easily understood and often classified in accordance with their nature.

No part of the world is free from disasters of some sort. The collateral damages of disasters can be equally serious and cascade into the social system. Economic growth, health, development and resource will be victims of disasters. Disasters, like environmental issues, can also be cross border. The impact may even affect geostrategic environment and change the maps of nations. The loss due to a disaster is socio-economic and generally irreversible.

Energy Security (Element #7)

The background of energy security as an element of national security can be traced to the 1973 oil shock that jolted the United States.[83]

According to Joseph J Romm,the underlying concept in any security analysis of energy has been vulnerability that exists if there are plausible scenarios of resource and trade disruptions, which could be overcome only at high economical and social costs.[84] The importance of energy security as an exclusive element of national security cannot be underestimated. Today energy means primarily oil and gas. There are other prospective energy resources that are being tried out on the side.

Those who are concerned, look at various sources of energy including nuclear power and new generations of fail-safe nuclear reactors. According to the US Strategic Assessment 1999, globalisation is the key trend affecting energy, resources and the environment. Global market demand controls it.[85] Security for energy production, ownership rights of energy resources and production of clean energy are among the major challenges that nations face. World's outlook for cleaner energy sources is focused on biomass, hydropower, nuclear power, hydrogen fuel and natural forces: wind, solar power, thermal energy, etc.

Geostrategic Security (Element #8)

Geostrategic security is about the bargaining power and goodwill a nation enjoys among the global community. Invaders and colonial empires were not serious about this element. War was the only means to meet the end for them. It proved right literally; the world has understood it by now. But this ideology and revelation gave way to many unmindful invasions in the past and still continues though less in number and higher in intensity. The new policy resides within the geostrategic context. The result is visible in the changing international affairs today.

Geostrategic security is entirely different from military security as an independent element of national security though, as in all other cases related to elements of national security, interrelated inclusively. This could be amplified in today's scenario with respect to the position of a nation and its image among the world community. Every nation has to safeguard its geostrategic security towards maximising goodwill and strength of international relations. Image building is not an easy exercise in geostrategic context. It is also not part of power projection. Carefully cultivated image helps in geostrategy.

Geostrategic security cannot be achieved only through power. Goodwill rides national power towards geostrategic security. Deception in diplomacy damages it sometimes permanently causing suspicion and lack of faith. The world is fast advancing not only technologically, economically or socially but also emotionally. It is the combination of power diplomacy and communication in a timely and sagacious form that will ensure geostrategic security for a nation.

Informational Security (Element #9)

Information in a human system is based on direct and indirect communication. Information gathering through espionage and other means of intelligence were accepted norms according to ancient strategists for a human system. But information is not intelligence. Intelligence is intention derived by processing information. Information and information sharing without distortion is vital for national governance.

Information that affects sovereignty, integrity and elements of national security are to be accessed and secured for appropriate analysis as an ongoing process in a nation's governance. Citizen's rights for disclosure of information become part of informational security as an element. These rights may seemingly strike a discord with national security objectives but can be balanced effectively. Balancing information is an important aspect of national security. Keeping the people in dark about information will be counterproductive. The situation can be damaging if people lose faith in the government. That happens when information crash. Media, right to information policies, intelligence organisations, public information offices, etc., play major part in informational security.

People want to be informed.[86] They voice on this topic frequently everywhere in the world. People are very much interested in public affairs and governments are required to balance the process of information release and containment carefully at all times while governing informational security. Informational security is not about the security of information but about governance of information as an element of national security.

There is growing gap between the information rich and the information poor. Information rich have access to "correct" information. Information poor are those with less access to information or ill-informed. Wrong information is a kind of dark knowledge, the knowledge that is not just untrue but also mostly non-existent. Information in any form spreads once released through grapevine and other sources or media. Spread of wrong information can be damaging. Gap in information causes information inequalities in society leading to negative consequences. The overall strategy should see through this gap. Another disturbing aspect of informational security is information trafficking. It is a serious matter that deals with free travel of information that can cause damage to vital interests of a nation and its people. Containment of information trafficking is as crucial as controlling other criminal traffics.

Food Security (Element #10)

Food security is defined in many ways. The UN Food and Agricultural Organisation (FAO) define it as "ensuring that all people at all times have both physical and economic access to the basic food they need" (1983). The World Development Report (1986) defines food security as "access to all people at all times to enough food for an active, healthy life." Another definition (Staatz—1990) is that food security is "the ability to assure, on a long term basis, that the food system provides the total population access to a timely, reliable and nutritionally adequate supply of food."[87] According to Rome Declaration on world food security, poverty is a major cause of food insecurity and sustainable progress in poverty eradication is critical to improve access to food.[88] More than 800 million people in the world, particularly in developing countries, do not have enough food to meet their basic nutritional needs. The cause is not shortage of food but lack of access to it for the needy. Supply and distribution constraints, continuing inadequacy of household incomes to purchase food, instability of supply and demand, and natural and human-induced disasters contribute to it. According to the FAO, the problems of food insecurity in its global dimensions are likely to persist and even increase dramatically in some regions.[89] The FAO has taken up the pledge to reduce the number of undernourished people by half in the world through articulated commitments and action plans by 2015.[90]

Food is not just a matter of existence in the modern world. It is also philosophically inclined cultural embodiment of the human system.

Food security from such viewpoint has to be seen not only a physical need, but also psychological in most of the civilised world.

Health Security (Element #11)

Health is a sensitive matter in national governance. It also means productivity. The people of a nation have to be healthy. Public health is a matter of great importance. There is a great need to eliminate diseases and disability. Public health concerns existed in the early days too. Public health was a special area of activity in Europe in the mid 19th century. Health consciousness arose in industrialised locations with the realisation that the health of one particular section of society was closely bound to that of the other, and that of each section was determined by its conditions of life. Improving the abysmal living and working conditions of the poor was undertaken, realising that these lead to rampant malnutrition and communicable diseases and also posed a threat to the health of the better-off through epidemics and social delinquency. Quality of life became a serious quest within the society and everything related to the human development.

Ethnic Security (Element #12)

The term ethnic, in the study of national security by the author has been viewed in the larger perspective as all matters of disparity that could be identified among people and usually used in comparison, often in relative terms of superiority—nationality, community, culture, religion, race, tribe, caste, gender, origin, age, colour, sex, sexual preferences...[91] Ethnicity differentiates[92] one individual from another and, therefore, their wellbeing under the national security principles should be seen differently. Mathematically, integration is not possible within differentiation. Hence ethnicity, which is a differentiation, cannot be conjoined to form a force in collective living. Society breaks at the seams of ethnicity. The much talked about secularism, nationalism and other social forces are strictly non-existent where ethnicity rules the roost. To a great extent they are mirages. But they can be kindled under the primitive forces of security and social wellbeing that drives people subliminally towards security. Everyone joins when the effect they desire is same. Besides, humans are social animals. They also have an inherent need to be together; but ethnicity pulls them apart. And it does all the time from the simple gender bias or sexual preferences to the deadly rigours of religious or political fundamentalism. Governance has to balance them. Governance has the power. It is possible if governance is aimed at national security maximisation.

The element of ethnic security is meant to cover these aspects in national security governance. According to the Genocide Convention and in general lexicography, ethnic groups are considered separate from three other identified groups—national, racial, and religious.[93] As an element of national security, the expression covers all differences under which the humans are classified or perceived. When there is an identified difference between one and another, the ground for ethnic breeding is ready.

The contemporary world is witnessing ethnic campaigns of different kinds. These conflicts have been attributed to lack of statesmanship and governance, paucity of reasonable leadership among various ethnic sections of society and the persistence of inappropriate military bureaucracy. It is a cruel predicament to the world. The end of the road in ethnic conflict is breakup of the nation state. It doesn't end there. In a world that is misguided, ethnic issues inverse development stunningly.

Ethno-nationalism, fundamentalism, militant secessionism, militarism, territorial disputes, national chauvinism, economic deprivation and gender-bias leading to insecurity are all factors that affect ethnic security. There are millions of victims of such conflicts all over the world including women and children. The result of xenophobic nationalism that breaks into ethnic security is militarism and suppression. A gendered human security would go further and broaden the value of security to privilege the marginalised communities, women, children, minorities and others.

Environmental Security (Element #13)

Environment sustains life. Joseph J Romm[94] divides environmental security into two categories: 1) transnational environmental problems that threaten a nation's security, and 2) transnational environmental or resource problems that threaten a nation's security. In the first case the issues involve the ongoing concerns such as global warming that can affect the quality of life for the inhabitants of a state. In the second case the issues are those that affect the territorial integrity or political stability of a nation such as disputes over scarce water problems or the question of environmental refugees and the resulting demographic imbalance.[95] In the authors study, resource security is separated from environmental security for a better understanding and convenience of governance. The study is focused on governance. However it is important to reiterate that all the elements are interactive and mutually inclusive.

Since 1985, global climate change became one of the major issues related to environmental security[96] Thehuman-induced changes to the global environmental system became the highlight of the period. The year 1988 witnessed unprecedented heat waves, fires, floods, drought and super cyclones. The greenhouse effect was said to be responsible for the warming trend.

Environment is transnational; hence environmental security is also a global issue. Environmental security has been an important agenda for the UN that encouraged collective cooperation through world environmental initiatives. The governments and non-governmental agencies are focused in various environmental projects and activities for this reason.

Cyber Security (Element # 14)

Cyberspace is the fifth identified terrain in national security governance. It is well populated today in matters related to national security. The security of the cyber terrain has become an alarmingly reported topic in the 21st century. Cyber world controls the information-matrix which is vital for a nation. Panic buttons on the computer can upgrade to cyber terrorism or take possession of information warfare. The cyber world has the potential to be fatal. Today's terrorists may look primitive when compared with the cyber terrorists of tomorrow according to scholars.[97] Cyber specialists are equivocal that terrorism may spread into the cyber world as it is much easier and more comfortable than blowing up people to induce policy changes. For these reasons cyber security is considered an evolving element of national security that needs to be studied carefully as a separate entity.

According to the US Central Intelligence Agency (CIA), computer-generated terrorism is the "ultimate precision-guided weapon," and this capability already exists with a number of terrorist organisations.[98]

These threats are considered to be real. Experts say that computer-generated attacks are much easier to carry out than other terrorist activities. It is also true that cyber insecurity can jeopardise other elements of national security. Already military security, economic security and informational security are within its reach. The reality is that while the computers have changed the life style worldwide, the security aspects have not caught up yet to face the threats.

The Internet is not regulated. It does not come under serious laws, government, and geographical boundaries. According to many panelists in various seminars for Internet security, the unanimous opinion is to regulate it by laws.[99] While the panelists agree that such an issue is riddled with problems because of the universality of the Internet and issues related to privacy, the urgency and the need to circumvent such problems cannot be overlooked any more. Cyber security is the modern age element of any intricate national security system. The damage it can cause is serious. One of the major cyber attacks that put a nation's public systems in jeopardy was the series of strikes on Estonian organisations that commenced on 27 April 2007. The attacks brought attention of the world on the importance of cyber protection and Estonia as one of the countries on the forefront of cyber security.

The world is witnessing whistle blowers audaciously bringing out government efforts to snoop on citizens standing on the cyber space. These and similar issues in a reverse process means the governments have to take cyber security seriously lest their informational security should collapse.

Genomic Security (Element #15)

Genomeis considered a terrain by itself. It is the genetic space that governs every individual life and life form. In 1953, the world woke up to the helix of life that showcased the secrets of the beginning and end of it. Today the world is quite advanced compared to the initial days of genomic understanding. It is with this concern the new and latest element of genomic security is added to national security concept. It is an entirely different terrain unfolding in its own pace in front of a bemused world.

Ethics and ethicality governs research in genetics today. It is the early stage that may find more complex movements much later.

Genomicstudies deal with advancement in biological sciences related to biogenetics, bioinformatics and genomic research. The world does not seem to be in a hurry to estimate its security aspects. But it is only a forewarning at this stage that a silent revolution like genomic research also has to have its darker elements that can smother humanity. It has opened up all sorts of possibilities. Biotechnology is an instrument of development that can improve the quality and quantity of plants and animals quickly and effectively. In the reverse, these alterations can cause havoc among forces that balance nature. Killer algae created with bio modifications can wipe out fisheries sources at sea by asphyxiation. Gnomically created transgenic weeds can obliterate food stock. The scientific community has reasons to worry about "super weeds" and "super viruses." There are protests around the world on ethical and ecological grounds. The safety, effectiveness and necessity of biologically modified (BM) food, which may find its way into the supermarkets of the future is questioned now.[100] The world is cautious on the genomic front.

The issues of genomic security are also of biopiracy and allied subjects including patenting versus common wealth. Strategists and policy makers will have to tread carefully on genomic security, the newest element of national security.

Factors Considered but not Accepted as Elements of National Security

There are many other factors often considered to be elements of national security by various governments and agencies in the process of governance. None of them qualify for consideration as elements of national security as they do not satisfy the identified characteristics. They are conditional to the concept. Some such factors in frequent use are given below.

- Governmental system

  Governmental system is a choice factor. Any governmental system is suitable if it appreciates the concept of national security. Ultimately it is the governance that matters.

- Political stability

  Political stability is a desired condition; it is not appropriate as an element. Political stability can be achieved through effective national security governance

- Unlawful acts

  Crime and criminal activities and various other unlawful acts are law enforcement issues and, thereby,constitutional aspects for establishment of rule of law. Good governance results in rule of law.

- Social security measures

  It is a matter of governance related to welfare.

- Weapons of mass destruction and proliferation

  These are threats and a matter for consideration in national governance.

- Education

  Education is part of governance being a concern of the constitution and policy issues.

- Terrorism and insurgency

  They are law enforcement issues and also threats to elements of national security.

- Homeland security

  Homeland security is a North American concept against the background of multiple terrorist attacks on 11 September 2001 in the USA. It is more a planned and organised approach in dealing with physicalsecurity challenges than an exclusive element of national security.

- Internal security

  Conceptually and operationally similar to homeland security within the limitations that a nation feels in other-than-war situations.

- Judicial security

  Basically about the functioning of the judicial system and its impact on people. It is a matter of constitutional governance.

There could be many such issues that will be conditional in

governance as part of one or more identified and qualified national security elements. They should not be misconstrued for exclusive national security elements. Otherwise the direction of national governance will change. The final destination will be what one has not foreseen. National security is best governed with specific attention to the elements and not conditions.

Chronological Hierarchy of Elements

Allocating hierarchical status to identified elements is another matter for consideration in the study of national security. Formally, the elements do not have a hierarchical system of priority. Chronologically they can be brought under a hierarchical system. But in reality each element is equally important for national security and they are not only highly interactive but also self effacing at the expense of another. The importance of a particular element depends on the situation and period through which a nation moves.

In this analysis, the element of military security qualifies for the first place being a wide derivative of physical security. It is the oldest. At the bottom of the hierarchy, based on the period, the latest addition is the developing element of genomic security. The listing of national security elements in this chapter is in the chronological hierarchal order.

Another way of examining the hierarchy of elements is based on their interactive preferences. Interaction between elements will be based on situations. Situations will prioritise elements. Every element of security will be on high priority during war situations. In other-than-war situations they will be prioritised by situations. Governments may prioritise food security in a famine or the period close to general elections. Disaster security governance may be prioritised during a disaster scenario.

That is the ideal form of governance—decision making based on the situational hierarchy of the elements of national security.

Therefore, the choice of a hierarchy is best left to the governments interested in managing national security. The government can decide on the priorities with respect to the situation. This study examines a general way of arrangement by attempting to chronologically sequence them.

1. *Military Security* (the earliest known period).

   War is organised and planned conflict. It has been associated with the human systems since they were collectively driven by the primordial instincts for survival. Military security, therefore, is dated as the earliest element for governing the human system wellbeing. This was, perhaps, the only element the human system was concerned about until modernisation dawned. The reason is that war is not just an instrument for straight line physical survival but a kind of fiery journey towards perceived security. It is the most amazing human behaviour primordially conditioned. The human system has not still understood the psychology of war and conflicts though there are many treatises on the art, science and politics of war since the earliest times. But it is important to understand that military security is not just about war but every conflict the human systems indulge in their search for perceived security. The human systems that could not physically secure themselves perished without trace. There is no serious change in this reality factor today and not going to be in many years to come. Military security is etched in the human psyche as the primary form of national security and it appears in different forms today. Though oldest, this element may not leave the national security configuration. The affinity to war as the survival tool burns in every mind that is conditioned or survival by destruction. Everything starts with this element in national security governance. It is so strong that people and their governments continue to believe national security is all about military security.

2. *Economic Security* (next and close in hierarchy—the early days).

   While money has been a record or object of payment for purchase of what one felt needed in a strictly individualistic perception, the need existed even before money was invented. Today money also buys money as a commodity in the exchange market. Money induces a feeling of security in the perceived form. The need for money became never ended. Money or its equivalent before it arrived on scene decided the perception of security in the human psyche. Today it is the"hard currency" that rules the scenario where one vies with the other for supremacy. The world is still struggling to understand the intricacies of economics and its impact (including limitations) on human lives. Economic security as an element, therefore,is leveled up in the hierarchy since purchasing parity is close to military security in evolution. Economics have a lot to do with individual psychology which the author prefers to call psychonomics.[101] The way an individual generates, saves, spends and regenerates money or equivalent have a lot to do with psychonomics. Psychonomics rules economics in every individual way. Economics is not a self administering word. It also means that every theory in economics could be psychonomics oriented. It is an area for further study. The physique (body) and the psyche (mind) are symbiotically implicated so is the element of military security with economic security. Hence economic security is dated close to military security.

3. *Resource Security* (next in hierarchy—the early days).
   Humans knew the importance of resources very early. Resources formed the implied signatures of military and economic elements. Adventurers and explorers went in search of resources to meet the perceived needs of the world. The importance of resources for quality life was highlighted by war and economics. Hence it is given chronological priority after economic security.

4. *Border Security* (1648).
   It is the concept of nation states (1648 model) that affirmed the borders more seriously than it was before. Sovereign rights brought the idea of secured borders to the forefront. Since the formation of sovereign states, the idea of border has been evolving in national governance. The idea of borders in the ocean is relatively new and has assumed a definite profile after UNCLOS with variations from borders over the land. The idea is yet to be appreciated by the world seriously, primarily because of the landclasp perception and behaviour of the human system.

5. *Demographic Security* (post 1648).
   Along with the borders, people divided nations. A nation can contract or expand by micronisation or macronisation respectively. There are many examples in history. The idea of demographic security comes from the perception of a settled nation-state as long as it is stable. Demography became the key word after nation states were formed. The dynamics of demography persistently attempt to breach the borders. The chronological hierarchy of the element, therefore, has been placed immediately after border security.

6. *Disaster Security* (next in hierarchy—post 1648).
   Disaster is not the incident per se but the occurrence of destruction and damage to human life and property directly or indirectly because of the incident. Disasters were experienced from the time humans began life on the earth. They were accepted then. The views changed since the formation of stabilised nation-states. It became part of governance. Disaster is placed after demographic security.

7. *Energy Security* (End 18th century).
   Since the dawn of inventions, the world entered an era of essentials for improving the quality of life. It needed energy. The change began in England in the later part of 18th century. Human dependence on external energy has been escalating since then.

8. *Geostrategic Security* (1919).
   Geostrategic security is not about diplomacy or foreign affairs. They are part of it. It is a question of national existence in a world that is global. The idea came in the aftermath of the First World War. The victorious allied powers established the League of Nations (1919) to encourage international cooperation and avoid another total war. It did not succeed because the power of rational thinking still eluded humans. It was too early. But this study considers the origin of the concept of geostrategic security since that date. The concept and ideology behind the League of Nations reflected in the United Nations (1945) though there are no similarities in visible projections of both. Besides, the League of Nations

continued along with the United Nations for some time. The UN today stands for collective security and the nations will have to work for it developing geostrategic security and governing it as a continuous process.

9. *Informational Security(1927).*
   Dating informational security for its chronological order in the list of national security element was found difficult. It is an old concept related to war and intelligence when it started figuring out in strategic conversations. The element informational security referred to in this study is not based on the military aspects. It is a part of it. It is a standalone but interactive element of the national security concept. It involves, among others, information management and information sharing. Under formal governance, people have the right to know about the way they are governed. It began with the advent of the newspapers and the radio. The chronological hierarchy is chosen with the date when the British Broadcasting Corporation (BBC) was established (1927). There were also records of broadcasting earlier. But it was the BBC that initiated the key role of information through public broadcasting. Information for the people, as a concept, developed fast since then. Today the world is flooded with information through media. Managing information has shifted to governing information for maximising national security.

10. *Food Security* (1945).
    Food security is dated to the world food programme of the UN in this study. The Food and Agricultural Organisation (FAO), established by the UN in 1945, has the mandate of eliminating hunger from the world, increasing nutrition and improving agricultural productivity. Serious thought on food security originated from this regime.

11. *Health Security* (1948).
    The UN established the World Health Organisation (WHO) in 1948 to consider matters related to improving the health of the people by international cooperation. Health security at

international level has been under a global umbrella since the formation of WHO.

12. *Ethnic Security* (1949).
    This study places ethnic security as a serious fallout of the World War II genocide and the subsequent activities that resulted in the Holocaust and Genocide Convention—1948, adopted in 1949. Though it has followed the League of Nations' specific health concerns, it is dated on the formation of the WHO since when it gained the momentum with results as seen today. But it is reiterated that the theme ethnicity for the study and practise of national security goes to everything that separates one human from the other and not just limited to race or colour.

13. *Environmental Security* (1972).
    Environmental security is dated to the formation of the United Nations' Environment Programme (UNEP) in 1972. UNEP guides and coordinates environmental activities within the UN system. It is subsequent to the formation of the UNEP the world awareness towards environment was focused.

14. *Cyber Security (1990).*
    The earliest known computer was the abacus invented in 1100 B.C. It is still in use. The cyber world originated much later supported by the information technology revolution. While the early cyber computers are dated to 1943, cyber security as a serious subject is far more recent and could be taken at the beginning of information technology boost that revved up in the last decade and, therefore, taken as a fairly recent induction with the advent of microprocessors and personnel computer. The sudden shift came with the Internet. The computer revolution is just beginning and along with it the associated security issues. Strictly, the importance of the element in national security can be dated to the beginning of the 21st century and just above the new concept that has the power to change the human system in future—genomic security.

15. *Genomic Security* (2000).
    Genomic security is associated with the DNA (Deoxyribonucleic acid), first discovered as a chemical in 1869, but identified in the

role as the miracle helix of biology carrying genetic inheritance much later. With it the scientists introduced a new terrain, strictly biological, in matters of human system governance. In 1953, James Watson and Francis Crick determined the structure of the DNA when they found it a double-helix polymer. The element has tremendous potential for the future of humankind and also associated risks. Its growth is dated in this study with the beginning of the new century.

The chronological hierarchy, thus explained, is for the convenience of appreciation and also to examine the redundancy of identified national security elements in future. The elements have evolved considerably since they are dated. In reality,governance is based on situations especially related to future. The importance of a particular element will be decided depending upon the situation of governance. All the elements of national security are interdependent. They are not mutually exclusive. Interdependency is one of the essential characteristics of an element of national security. A change in one element induces a change in another resulting in an incremental or declining effect in the overall national security. This is an area that needs to be understood seriously and also calls for serious research.

National Security and Governance

Governing national security is about governing the elements for maximisation of national security. No government has made such an attempt so far in a holistic manner. The idea of national security, its elements and the process explained in this study are yet to be accepted universally for various reasons. The inertia is extremely strong making the evolutionary process slow, almost unnoticeable under the law of invariance. Hence acceptance and execution will have to be naturally at an unnoticeably slow pace.

There is time to develop the national security concept. The first step towards this objective is to model the elements in a matrix. One of the requirements of an element of national security is its flexibility for modeling.

National security as defined is a variable and a measurable quantity. It is a function of time. Modeling national security starts with it. The model visualises the subject as a function of time because the process is a vector, not a scalar for explanation. It has a direction into time. Once released from its static inertia, it moves forward and backward oscillating dynamically (surging) depending upon the national security index in time, which is irreversible. Today the concept of national security is in a state of static inertia (called a limbo at times, though not exactly the same) in many nations of the world. The concept has no momentum in such state. Wherever introduced in a limited fashion, the subject is gaining momentum, thereby breaking the static inertia and getting on with the dynamic inertia.

The lemma here is that the concept of national security is a dynamic vector in motion. Hence the concept when integrated from zero to infinity will aim at maximisation of national security in a country. The ultimate objective for a government thereby becomes maximisation of national security. The target could be depicted by a symbol. For the sake of convenience, and to avoid complications in its comprehension, it is symbolised in a non-mathematical form in this study as,

$$NS_{max}$$

Here the objective of a nation is to achieve $NS_{max.}$ It can be integrated as,

$$\int_{0}^{\infty} NS\ d_{ns}$$

It is further equal to the sum total of the optimised value of each element. It is necessary to know that the optimised value of an element is different from its maximal value. It has to be arrived at taking into consideration the gain in the interactive value of each element with another. Because, an incremental increase in one can cause a decline in another in some interaction. Efforts to maximise an element (say, military security) did not cause a change in another element (say, in economic security) by decline larger than the former means that the total change in NS_{max} is positive (incremental). It is the total make up of national security factor that has to be prevented from decline by the interactive gains and losses of elements. In such case the quantum of national security is equal to,

$$NS = \sum NS_{elements}$$

Whereas,

$$NS_{max} \text{ need not be equal to } (\sum NS_{elements})_{max,}$$

Unless all the elements are positively changed by an incremental change in their interactive element. The change in the quantum of national security will be the resultant of changes in the interactive elemental matrix. This is an important aspect of governing for maximising national security.

A slightly modified explanation, under such circumstances, is to identify value of the elements at a particular stage through which the national security matrix of a country at that stage can be derived. This can be achieved by giving the elements certain values before calculation. To give them values is not possible unless specific studies are undertaken. The elements can be symbolised alphabetically. A symbolic assessment of currently identified national security elements is given in Table. 3.1. Symbols are allocated to the elements for identity while assessing their quantum in mathematical modeling and calculation of national security index at any given time. They are variables. Values can be assigned to them based on situation appreciation.

Table 3.1. Symbolic Representation of National Security Elements[102]

	Elements of National Security	*Symbol*
1	Military security	m_s
2	Economic security	e_{s1}
4	Resource security	r_s
5	Border security	b_s
5	Demographic security	d_{s1}
6	Disaster security	d_{s2}
7	Energy security	e_{s2}
8	Geostrategic security	g_{s1}
9	Informational security	i_s
10	Food security	f_s

11	Health security	h_s
12	Ethnic security	e_{s3}
13	Environmental security	e_{s4}
14	Cyber security	c_s
15	Genomic security	g_{s2}

The "quantum" value of the 15 identified elements will be the prime parameter in decision making in national security matters. National security of a nation can be enhanced effectively by managing its elements with due consideration to its effects on other elements. These elements can be brought under a matrix to project the national security matrix for decision making. It will be then:

$$NS = \begin{vmatrix} m_s & e_{s1} & r_s & b_s & d_{s1} \\ d_{s2} & e_{s2} & g_{s1} & i_s & f_s \\ h_s & e_{s3} & e_{s4} & c_s & g_{s2} \end{vmatrix}$$

Symbols representing the 15 elements of national security are arranged in a rectangular 3 x 5 matrix (three rows and five columns), which could be compared with other matrices in a finer assessment of interactive dynamics. Such matrices could be either that of terrain based security matrices or elemental matrices as required. For example, a holistic view of maritime security matrix, a constituent part of national security, could be analysed with respect to the national security strategy in a model exercise. This concept, it is believed, can lead to models based on mathematical design that can support the calculation of the national security index. The elements can be a set of natural numbers (N), integers (Z), real numbers (R) or complex numbers (C) according to calculation for the purpose of modeling.

The matrix of 15 elements could also be arranged in five rows and three columns. But an array with fewer rows, unless equal, is preferred. When there are additions or deletions—whenever a new element comes up, or an existing one disintegrates or does not have subsequent value any more, the number may change. For example, if the world one day decides that the concept of military campaigns is outdated, there will be no more wars. The military security element may either disappear or disintegrate into more than one, making it difficult to make a geometric array.[103] If the element fades away, the number will be reduced to 14. In such case the matrix could still incorporate the element of military security as in the past, but its value will be null for calculations. Such arrangements provide flexibility. The rows and columns may have extra elemental space(s) filled by null elements that are dummies. It will be advisable to place minimum dummy elements for a comfortable matrix for calculations. The matrix set up with 15 elements for national security is not expected to change in the near future.

The interactive arrangement of the identified elements of national security has been made in arrays (horizontally in rows) in sequence of their assumed hierarchy. It is only for the sake of convenience of model building. The hierarchical qualities with respect to the presumed time of introduction of these elements have no (serious) significance in NS_{max}.[104] It is the interactive geometry that is important. The elements, therefore, can be arranged in arrays as convenient. It is entirely at the discretion of the planners.

An array in the form of a table of 15 identified elements and their accepted symbols are given in Figure 3.1. The array is made according to their appreciated chronological hierarchy. It is not necessary to follow such an order; it is preferable since no new element is likely to come up in between chronologically. Any new element that will come up in future will lineup after the last element in the table. Any element that is disappearing (if such a thing happens) will be in between.

The objective in national security is achieving NS_{max}. Hypothetically it means maximising each of its elements. But there will be situations when maximising one can bring a reduction in another. In such cases the objective will be optimising both. It is very intricate, especially when more than one element is involved in the combination game. It is the most difficult part of managing national security and often riddled with political and bureaucratic conflicts in governance. In a hypothetical situation statement, an incremental change in military security (m_s) may,

- Either increase or decrease economic security (e_{s1}), energy security (e_{s2}), ethnic security (e_{s3})...

- Decrease environmental security (e_{s4}), resource security (r_s), demographic security (d_{s1}), health security (h_s), disaster security (d_{s2}), food security (f_s), geostrategic security (g_{s1})...
- Increase border security (b_s), informational security (i_s), cyber security (c_s)...
- Have null[105] effect in genomic security (g_{s2})...

The first step in understanding the interactive matrix of elements is to appreciate that an increment in one element may produce one of the four strategic application points as per situation:

a. A duality situation in which there is a probability for an improvement in one case and a decline in another in the same element.
b. A singular situation where the probability is only for a decline.
c. A singular situation where the probability is only for improvement.
d. A null situation where, seemingly, there is no effect.

In the above case, m_s is the primary element whose incremental change is compared with the corresponding effect in another element—the secondary element. The reaction can be in four different ways. It is important to know that it is not reciprocal—that is when the role is reversed. When the secondary element becomes the primary element and an incremental change in it is considered and examined with the corresponding change in others, the result need not be exactly the same as what it had when the elements were reversed. For example, when an incremental change in m_s brings a corresponding proportional decline in economic security, in the opposite case, an incremental change in economic security may have an effect on m_s that may be progressive. Therefore, each element has to be seen as primary as well as secondary at different times for different applications of strategy. In this way each element will have 14 different interactions in their primary roles with other elements for every task in strategic application. There could be thousands of tasks in strategic application that has an impact on each element in its primary capacity and a corresponding four ways change in each other element in secondary capacity. It means there will be 210 possible interactions (14 times 15) among elements at the minimum for each task. It is considered minimum since there are more interactions of primary elements with secondary elements in more than one combination.

For example, an incremental change in military security (m_s)can affect economic security (e_{s1}) and geostrategic security (g_{s1}) together negatively. An example is a nuclear intention by an underdeveloped country. The decision has to be weighed accordingly. It is important to understand here that it is the incremental change that matters in NS_{max} and not decline since the objective is the process of maximisation, not minimisation.

The interactive matrix of national security elements is a complex game. The complexity keeps the practitioners of governance away because it needs the highest degree of coordination and understanding, which is not easy to come by under bureaucratic conflicts. The usual way national security governance is carried out is by following the path of least effort.[106] Today's political scenario anywhere in the world is not conducive to the hard work required in establishing national security governance. The beaten track of yesteryears will lead the way for many years to come. It also validates the law of invariance besides following the theory of isomorphism[107] in governance at the mediocre level.

But if desired and determined to face challenges there are many approach paths—politically oriented (as in political party manifest), bureaucratic (based on bureaucratic demand), terrain based (such as ocean policy), doctrine of the agency based (e.g. research doctrine), internationally oriented (based on law and treaty agreements), directives (e.g. the superpower dictum), globalised (as UN mandates), integrated (similar to military armed forces joint doctrine), etc. Managing national security governance by elemental interactive matrix is complicated and needs highest degree of professional competence. Once mastered and implemented, it could be the easy way to NS_{max}.[108]

The net result in the process of maximisation of national security will be the sum of increments and decline in each of the elements in its primary and secondary role for every task of strategic application. The results consequent to the application of strategic tasks may not stop at the four points already identified. It can be more. Each of these elements when they increase in their status can cause another four situation application points. This means 15 elements can ultimately cause a maximum of 60 application points in their interactive geometry. Out of these, many may seem to be common for one application and uncommon for another. In practice, it may not be so. That means for each action with respect to a particular element, there could be four more application points. Here the application of the task related to improvement of a particular element is important. Each task, therefore, has to be seen as with four application points in each element. The case that an incremental change in military security (m_s) brings an incremental change in economic security (e_{s1}) is different from an incremental change in economic security (e_{s1}) brings and incremental change in military security (m_s). These combinations, therefore, has to be examined very carefully by the planners of national security. And such planning has to be done before the application of a particular task for maximising the element. Often, it is a difficult. Therefore, the planners will have to depend upon national security strategists who, in turn, have to depend upon model-based calculations. Fortunately the most cost effective and live modeling can be done using biomodels in live situations in many parts of the world as and when such models unfold. The bad news is that, in national security, many insomniacs are somnambulism; they sleepwalk while awake.

Defining the problem related to national security involves identifying the concerned elements and associated deficiency in it. It is better done by considering each element as a system and then configuring the systems effectively. Problems will appear in imprecise manner initially. Refining the problems to arrive at the actual issues is the process of diagnostics that separate the symptoms from the syndrome. Otherwise the planners and strategists will end up finding a solution for a wrong problem. It often happens. The result will be more damaging to the objective of NS_{max}.

Conclusions

National security is a wholesome concept. Understanding the concept along with its elements and threat attractiveness is important for national planning for governance. This study examined the previously identified elements of national security against the background of the evolution of the concept through the ages. The elements are threat attractors, one of the conditions for acceptance. Threat appears any time in one of the eight different dimensions or combinations as identified in the threat matrix cube. The idea of national security has been evolving throughout. National governance is a concept originated with the evolution of nation states under the Westphalian principle followed by French Revolution as a European model. The concept of national security had also been spoken about around this period in Yale University. The idea as examined in this study is still in the shade of geopolitics of survival of governments. The reality perception of national security originates from the idea of human survival and wellbeing. There are nations that understand this principle and accordingly modify governance.

The study defines national security as a measurable concept aimed at the wellbeing of the people of a nation with respect to time at macro level. Under this finding, it is possible to index national security of a nation at a given time. It necessitates further research on the subject to arrive at a universally acceptable index. Careful analysis identifies 15 elements that are currently integral to national security. These elements are interactive with each other at varying degrees with respect to situation and, under expert governance, are expected to contribute towards maximisation of national security. A rise or decline in the elemental security will impact the overall national security. In such cases the resultant has to be seen. Maximisation of an element has to be achieved very carefully under such conditions. Mostly, the preferred objective of governance is the optimisation of an element within the interactive geometry of elements. Often, maximisation of an element is not the objective, since the net resultant in national security maximisation may be affected. In many cases of interaction an incremental change in one element may bring a corresponding decline in another. This tendency has to be carefully balanced in national security governance.

This chapter also points out many conditional factors that are often mistaken for elements of national security. They could be symptoms, threats, conditions, procedures or modes of governance that are viewed by the public and government equally as elements. They are all related to national security. Though the elements may not form part of any hierarchical order, it is comfortable to place them in an order of the period of their origin. These periods have to be hypothetically established. In spite of the presumed hierarchy, each element is equally important in modeling national security.

National security is a reality concept in this study with a definition that is different from the definitions in vogue. The definition could change as the concept evolves further. Within the definition, national security is measurable and can be indexed for comparison internally and externally. National security is about the apparent wellbeing of the people, not the perceived wellbeing they endlessly desire. It is the sole function of a government. The principles are compatible with any human system where governance is a process. It can also be extended to global security under international governance. The concept, however, will take a long time to break the inertia of geopolitical governance among plenty. A shift is probable when human systems get constrained from every aspect of apparent security.

In the next chapter the concept of maritime security is revisited for examining the parameters for integration with the concept of national security in governance.

NOTES

1 For example, the World fact Book, published annually by the Central Intelligence Agencies, lists them under the heading of countries.

2 en.wikipedia.org/wiki/Country, accessed 26 May 2013.

3 Ayoto, John, Bloomsbury Dictionary of Word Origins, p. 499

4 Thought of the Day, The Times of India, Kozhikode, 25 June 2013, p. 12.

5 Paleri, Prabhakaran, *National Security: Imperatives and Challenges*, New Delhi, Tata McGraw-Hill Publishing Limited, 2008, pp. 328-342. According to the author, ethnicity is everything about the humans that make one different from another in group living in a human system.

6 Anderson, Benedict R. (1991),*Imagined Communities: Reflections on the Origin and Spread of Nationalism* (Revised and extended. ed.), London, Verso, p. 224.The argument here is not incontrast to Anderson's statement but amplifies the fact that realism is the key and not imaginary assumptions. People interact with each other through the process of governance and associated means in a community that is meant to work together for a common cause—survival by existence..

7 Encyclopaedia Britannica, CD-ROM, 2001. Count Maximilian von Trautmansdorff represented the Holy Roman emperor. The successful conclusion of the peace process was attributed to his sagacity. The French envoys were nominally under Henri d'Orléans, Duke de Longueville, but the Marquis de Sablé and the Count d'Avaux were the real agents of France. Sweden was represented by John Oxenstierna, son of the chancellor of that name, and by John Adler Salvius who had previously acted for Sweden at Hamburg. The papal nuncio was Fabio Chigi, later Pope Alexander VII. Brandenburg, represented by Count Johann von Sayn-Wittgenstein, played the foremost part among the Protestant states of the empire. On 1 June 1645, France and Sweden brought forward propositions of peace, which were discussed by the estates of the empire from October 1645 to April 1646. The settlement of religious matters was effected between February 1646 and March 1648. The war continued during the deliberations. These people are responsible for the concept of nation states, perhaps the most important turning point in human history of collective living.

8 Two new words used in a previous research study to explain the strategic derivatives of integration (amalgamation) and disintegration (break up) of nations after a serious and chaotic disquiet like war, political turmoil, etc. More so in the background of the breakup of the erstwhile Soviet Union. In the future world, the chances or micronisation are more as seen in the post Soviet era. The latest is South Sudan. Supranational formation (under supra

national law) such as the European Union does not fall under this category of nation formation.

9 Paleri, Prabhakaran, "The Concept of National Security and a Maritime Model for India," doctoral dissertation, Department of Defence and Strategic Studies, University of madras, Chennai, February 2002.

10 The term "ideal" here is not because of absence of pragmatism in governance, but the constraints associated with it.

11 Romm, Joseph J., *Defining National Security: The Non-military Aspects*, New York, n. 50, p. 2.

12 Walker, Martin, *The Cold War and the Making of the Modern World*, London, Vintage, 1993. A researcher of national security may assume that the very concept of national security originated from the abyss of the Cold War unless explored further backward in time.

13 Paleri, n.5, p.33.

14 Ibid. According to the author, if the best way to win a war is by not fighting as proclaimed by the strategists, then the war that is not fought and won becomes a war by itself. Cold War should, therefore, be treated as a war, at least by the victors. The entire world participated in it; hence taken as the third world war.

15 Romm, n. 11, p. 2.

16 Ibid, pp. 2-3.

17 Encyclopaedia Britannica, n. 7.

18 Scottish economist and philosopher. In "atomic capitalism" every individual is considered to be the best judge of welfare. Social welfare was the sum total of the welfare of the individuals.

19 John Maynard Keynes was an English economist, journalist and financier best known for his economic theory on the causes of prolonged unemployment.

20 Datt, Ruddar and K. P. M. Sundaram *Indian Economy*, New Delhi, S. Chand and Company Limited, 2001, p. 214.

21 (350 B.C.). Author of Arthasasthra, ancient Indian treatise on state and governance dealing with property, economics, society and strategy.

22 Paleri, n.9, p. 35.

23 Datt, n. 20, p. 216.

24 Koithara, Verghese, *Society, State and Security*, New Delhi, Sage Publications, 1999, pp. 36-38.

25 PTI News Scan, 5 December 2001.

26 Paleri, n.5, p. 36.

27 Paleri, n.5.

28 National Security Act 1947, en.wikipedia.org/wiki/National_Security_Act_of_1947, accessed 21 January 2013. Also see, United States Government online public access at research.archives.gov/description/299856, accessed 21 January 2013.The preamble states, " Act of July 26, 1947 ("National Security Act"), Public Law 80-253, 61 STAT 495, "to promote the national security by providing for a Secretary of Defence; for a National Military Establishment; for a Department of the Army, a Department of the Navy, a Department of the Air Force; and for the coordination of the activities of the National Military Establishment with other departments and agencies of the Government concerned with the national security., 07/26/1947. There is a mention of national security but it is not defined.

29 n.28. Section 308 (b).

30 Government of India, The Ministry of Law, Justice and Company Affairs, The National Security Act 1980, Preamble, 27 December 1980.

31 en.wikipedia.org/wiki/National_Security_Act_(India), accessed 3 January 2013.

32 The others are the Civil and Criminal Procedure Code 2001, and the Penal Code of 2004.

33 en.wikipedia.org/wiki/National_Security_Council_of_Pakistan, accessed 3 January 2013.

34 Romm, n.11, p. 2.

35 National power is another concept widely in circulation that lacks a critical definition.

36 www.sunday-guardian.com/analysis/well-eat-grass-but-build-the-bomb, accessed 12 July 2013.

37 Paleri, n.9.

38 Saighal, Vinod, *Restructuring South Asian Security*, New Delhi, Manas Publications, 2000, p. 36.

39 Ibid.

40 Ibid., p. 37.

41 Ibid., pp. 37-39.

42 Paleri, n.9.

43 Paleri, n.5, p.44.

44 Ibid. p.45.

45 Romm, n. 11, p. 7.

46 Ibid.

47 Ibid., p. 7, Lester Brown mentioned it in his paper "Redefining National Security."

48 Ibid., pp. 5-6.

49 Ibid.

50 Ibid., p. 6.

51 Ibid.

52 National Defence College, Proceedings of Seminar on "A Maritime Strategy for India," New Delhi, 1996, p. 22.

53 Ibid, n. 25, p. (i).

54 Gopalaswamy, R., et al., *A Strategic Framework for National Security in Battle Scene in Year 2020*, edited by P. N. Chaudhary and W. Selvamurthy, New Delhi, Defence Institute of Psychological Research, Year not mentioned., p. 16.

55 Singh, Jaswant, *Defending India*, Bangalore: Macmillan India, 1999, p. xxi.

56 Chenoy, Anuradha M., Peace Process: Towards a Gendered Human Security, The Times of India, Mumbai,20 December 2000, p. 10.

57 Ibid.

58 Ibid.

59 Saighal, Vinod, Remoulding the Subcontinent, Part II, United Service Institute of India Journal, New Delhi, October-December, 1999: 526-34.

60 Reforming the National Security System, Recommendations of the Group of Ministers, New Delhi, February 2001, (Unclassified).

61 Ibid., (Unclassified), p. 6.

62 The Kargil Committee Report in its unclassified form was published in paperback under the title: "From Surprise to Reckoning" by Sage Publications, New Delhi in 1999. The terms of Reference of the Committee was to review the events that led to the Pakistani aggression at Kargil, India and to recommend measures to safeguard national security against such armed intrusions. p. 25.

63 Romm, n. 11, p . 6.

64 Ibid.

65 Paleri, n.5, p.58.

66 lid.

67 According to Indian system there are nine economic classes—param samridha, samridha, sampanna, siddha, unmukh, samanya, sangharshi, garib, and nirdhan. See Consumers and the Market, bijapurkar.com/demanddrivers/dsds_indianconsumers1.php.Accessed 16 July 2013.Super rich, *garib* and *param samridha* are author's findings.The idea is to classify people according to their purchasing power status in relation to business environment. But in relation to the aspirations of national security all of

them are "ordinary people" from the point of view of governance. There is no discrimination in relation to apparent security.

68 Paleri, n.9, p. 57.

69 Ibid.

70 A new concept originates here. Like anything organic, does a nation also go through birth, growth, decline and death? It happens in the process of an organisation, business or otherwise. If so every nation can expect an end. Many nations have died. The role of governance is not only to see the wellbeing of people but also extend the life span, disability included. However this aspect is not examined in this study.

71 Macroinstructional is an idea from programming language. A group of programming instructions compressed into a simpler form and appear as a single instruction. When used a macro expands from the compressed form into its actual instruction details. Both the name of the macro definition and other variable parameter attributes are included within the macro statement. First used in assembler language rather than a higher level programming language. www.techopedia.com/definition/24802/macro-instruction, accessed 26 July 2012. Like in assembler language, in strategic studies threats can be made simpler by compressing them intosimpler models for handling. The TMC can be used for identifying and enumerating them under various classifications.

72 Paleri, Prabhakaran, *Role of the Coast Guard in the Maritime Security of India*, New Delhi: Knowledge World, 2007, p.25-26.

73 Paleri, n.9, p. 61.

74 Ibid.

75 Ibid.

76 There are opinions among authors and scholars that nationalism is a European creation as a precursor concept of sovereign nation states. The concept of nation states, according to them, was transported by European colonial empires to various parts of the world. Anti-colonial movements in various parts of the world embraced the "colonial" concept of nationalism to fight against them. This is an interesting viewpoint.

77 The elements are further amplified in exclusive chapters. See Paleri, n.5.

78 Singh,n.54, p. xxiv-xxv.

79 Paleri, n.5, pp.154-5.

80 Audi, Robert (ed.), *The Cambridge Dictionary of Philosophy*, Cambridge, Cambridge University Press, 1999, pp. 718-20.

81 Threats of Stimulus Withdrawal Hurting Emerging Economies: PM, Times of India, Kozhikode, 5 September 2013, p.1.

82 Romm, n. 11, p. 21.

83 Ibid, p. 37.

84 Ibid.

85 Institute for National Strategic Studies, Strategic Assessment 1999, Washington, D.C., National Defence University, 2000, p. 39.

86 Khandeparker, B. G., Keeping the People Informed, Letter to Editor, The Navhind Times, Goa, 24 August 2001, p. 8.

87 Datt, n.20, p. 490.

88 Rome Declaration on World Food Security, World Food Summit, 13-17 November, 1996, Rome-Italy, www.fao.org, accessed 23 July 2012.

89 Ibid.

90 Ibid.

91 Human Development Report 2000, United Nations Development Programme, New Delhi, Oxford University Press, 2000, p. 1. According to the report one of the seven freedoms is "Freedom from Discrimination—by gender, race, ethnicity, national origin or religion. In this book, the author chooses to confer discrimination by all means to one term: ethnicity, the underlying basis of ethnic security. Gender, race, origin, religion and all other forms of human differences are included in the term ethnicity.

92 It is different from biometric separations, where one individual is entirely different from the other even when cloned.

93 Roberts, Adam and Richard Guellf, (eds.), *Documents on the Laws of War*, Oxford, Clarendon Press, 1989, p. 158.

94 Romm, n.11, p. 15.

95 Ibid.

96 With the discovery of the ozone hole over Antarctica.

97 Nando.net and The Sacramento Bee, New Security Threats Rest in Cyber Terrorism, infowar.com, 12 February 1997.

98 Ibid.

99 Molloy, Tim, Virus Hacker Fears Prompt Cyber Security Summit, www.post-gazette.com, 15 July 2000.

100 Insight, Concept of Genetically Modified Food, The Navhind Times, Goa, 24 August 2001, p. 10.

101 Paleri, n. 5, pp.154-73, Psychonomics is a term used in experimental psychology. The author uses the term in economic security to draw the attention of scholars on the subject the way human psychology influences earning, spending and saving money. It is the basis of economics where human psychology impacts with the theories causing uncertainties in every decision.

102 The symbols given in this table have been modified from the original. Such modification is convenient for modeling by nations the way they appreciate as many may like to keep them classified.

103 This is a mere hypothetical situation. The opposite that wars or the fear of war will continue is more hypothetically valid for research.

104 The period of introduction of the element could find some importance with respect to method inertia. The earlier the introduction, the more the method inertia. Method inertia prevents implementation of new thoughts and ideas and resists change. That is why military security, the earliest known element, is hard and bonded with national security. Recommendations to dilute its importance will be vehemently opposed.

105 Considering the characteristics of elements, a null effect is impossible. A change in one will have its impact on another. The nullity is from hypothetical point of view as well as for reasons that a change that is negligible could be considered as null in mathematical application.

106 Paleri, n.5. The word effort is preferred for the usual term "resistance." There is a difference.

107 Isomorphism is an interesting aspect of organisational management and governance. A new system will always have the tendency to follow an already existing system in any of the three ways—normative, mimetic or coercive. Isomorphism prevents bold change. It can happen to any human system—a new department in a university, an organisation, a new governmental system, a new born nation, new governmental system, etc. They can be gravitated towards an existing one instead of becoming a model for other parallel systems to follow.

108 Paleri, n.5. p. 176.

Chapter 4

REVISITING MARITIME SECURITY: GHOST PROTOCOL IN ISOLATION

Exorcism (ék sawr sìzzəm) ***n.*** *Expelling the spirit from the human body that it has got into.*

Ghost (gōst) ***n.1.*** *A faint trace of something that is believed to exist.* ***2.*** *The spirit of a dead person that, it is believed can get into a living human body and gain identity.* ***3.*** *What the believers think exists in that netherworld between the living and the dead.*

Ghost Protocol (gōst protə kàwl) n. A procedure that refers to a mission without proper backup and support.

Protocol ***(protə kàwl)*** ***n.1.a.*** *Etiquette observed in social conduct.* ***b.*** *A code of correct conduct.* ***2.*** *Draft international agreement before ratification.* ***3.*** *The plan for a course of action.*

Reverse (ri vúrss) ***v.1.*** *Change order to opposite.* ***2.*** *Turn something inside out.* ***3.*** *Go in the backward direction.*

Reverse exorcism *(ri vúrss ék sawr sìzzəm)* **(in this study)** ***n. 1.a.*** *Giving a body to a spirit to gain identity.* ***b.*** *Invoking a spirit into a body by conjuration.* ***2. In strategic sense (for this study). Intentionally backing and supporting a ghost protocol into a protocol for definite action by planning. 3.*** *Possession.*

Looking at the definition of national security in this study, it is nearly impossible to refer to maritime security in similar definite terms. First, it cannot be measured; whereas national security as defined is a measurable index. Second, any definition of it will be within the realm of abstractionism. Even its meaning as a protocol needs to be exactly distinct. The term, maritime security, itself gets embroiled in a range of issues and activities—from military aspects of the ocean governance to traditional fishing or further down towards activities at the lowermost end. This is what is elaborated in this chapter, where maritime security leads to a perfect ghost protocol that has to be brought under governance. It is difficult to craft a strategy for governing a ghost protocol in isolation. It needs a body for an action plan. The body for maritime security is national security. Maritime security can best be managed if integrated with national security. It is a kind of reverse exorcism for providing identity to a ghost protocol for deliberate and intended action.

Just before entering the realm of the unknown and, if the explanations so far grope in a kind of inadequacy to highlight the curious case of maritime security, it may do well for the still uninitiated to know that there is nothing similar on land to maritime security—there is no term called "terrestrial security." This adds to the curiosity in the case of maritime security.

Examining Maritime Security

Maritime security is a term used to explain the ocean relations of a geopolitical entity. It applies to the entire world in the global perspective. The world presently does not have an exclusive global regime for governing maritime security in totality. The International Maritime Organisation (IMO), the specialised agency of the United Nations, is for ensuring safety and security of ships and preventing marine pollution by ships.[1] The IMO could be helpless in other matters, especially in suppression of unlawful activities at and from the sea. IMO's helplessness was very visible in controlling Malacca Strait and Somali piratical attacks against ill-fated merchant vessels. Maritime security is much wider in scope and applicability. Therefore, the geopolitical entities will have to craft strategies for maximising maritime security. It is best done with integrated maritime security.

The term, as perceived, explains the relationship between the ocean and a geopolitical entity in a situation that is bilateral, trilateral,[2] multilateral, regional or global itself as per the geostrategic scenario. Maritime security is linked with every geopolitical entity of the world. This becomes more vital when an entity has to deal with it in the absence of a holistic international regime on the subject. IMO intervenes and supports nations to decide on maritime transportation for carriage of goods and people. But there are various other aspects about maritime security.

The definition of the term also goes through variations. One of the definitions is maritime security *"comprises the issues that pertain to the sea and have a critical bearing on the country's security."* The critical bearing of the issues of the sea is what guides this definition towards integrating maritime security with national security. The definition includes sea borne trade and commerce in energy resources, management of living and non-living marine resources, delimitation of international seaward boundaries and deployment and employment of naval and military forces in the ocean as the components of maritime security.[3] Another comment was *"the term maritime security represents the broadest approach to issues and aspects, which pertain to the sea and have an important bearing on the country's security."*[4] The bearing mentioned is on country's security. It goes beyond military aspects, although military security remains the final arbiter of national security that is perceived to protect and sustain the core values and vital national interests today. This aspect is already examined in the attempt to recognise and define the concept of national security. This statement too proposes the integration of maritime security with national security.

According to author and India's eminent naval strategist Mihir K. Roy (1926-2013), "maritime illiteracy" causes "sea-blindness" to a nation's people. He refers to the United Nation's Educational Scientific and Cultural Oraganisation's (UNESCO) Report in 1988, calling for development and application of maritime knowledge.[5] According to him, such illiteracy about maritime affairs is common. He recommends proactive literacy measures to eradicate the "blindness." Such measures call for identity of mind as a prerequisite in defining appropriate terms for clear perception of the issues that may relate to policies on maritime security.

This research looks deeper into the excellent find of Mihir Roy about illiteracy of maritime affairs. But the study leads to a different opinion. It is very evident that the people at the helm of affairs related to policy and plans in every nation are aware of the importance of the ocean in a nation's affairs and the world in general, but projects a concealed ignorance or indifference in their policy decisions that often gets limited to land-based activities having a shore view of the ocean instead of an ocean view of the shore. But the world is undoubtedly maritime literate. The proof is in the UNCLOS (United Nations Convention on the Law of the Sea).[6] UNCLOS would not have been there if the world was ocean illiterate. This study examines the perception of ocean illiteracy and sea-blindness, which are seemingly real for a keen observer like Mihir Roy, and attributes it to the landclasp syndrome of human beings who, in spite of their awareness of the ocean, are unable to see the land from the perspective of the ocean, thereby leaving it as a ghost protocol. Maritime security has been thus wandering within the perimeters of the ocean from time immemorial as a ghost protocol looking for an identify it deserves. According to this study, maritime security can gain identity it deserves by holistic integration with national security governance. This way human system will not have to disengage from the landclasp syndrome that has been the lifeline since people lost their umbilical cord when born over land and started clinging on to it for dear life.

The word "maritime" has many meanings. In one, it means pertaining to the sea; relating to sea-going or sea-trade; having a seacoast; situated near the sea; living on the shore; and having a navy and sea trade.[7] This is the nearest all-round connotation. According to maritime law, the word "maritime" relates exclusively to ships, seamen, harbours, and commerce on the sea.[8] The term "maritime" is widely related to merchant shipping for years. Though the terminology applies to all activities and aspects related to the sea, it has been known and used in commercial terms of the sea going trade. But the word "maritime" is much more than commercial shipping.

It is, therefore, important to define the word before maritime security is defined. Considering the usage of the word in national security discussions, the word "maritime" is also elevated in its scope and definition "as an amplifying word to those related to the oceans in all its dimensions." Within this perception, it can be said that maritime security deals "with all encompassing aspects of the ocean related to national security." This applies to all geopolitical entities irrespective of their proximity to the ocean.

Another example is in the use of the term "maritime strategy." It doesn't mean strategy related to commercial shipping. But the term still does not have universal appeal, and application of mental identity. The research on maritime security cannot be straitjacketed within the different meanings of the word, lest it should cause ambiguity in usage and application. The term does not find many definitions either; it is absent even in publications of maritime strategy. Maritime strategy often relates to maritime warfare and not to the holistic concept of maritime security. According to Julian Corbett, maritime strategy means the principles, which govern a war in which the sea is a substantial factor.[9] His work was originally published in 1911. According to author Raja Menon majority of the practicing professionals does not link their actions to any maritime school of thought when choices are being made. Menon also concludes maritime strategy as naval strategy.[10]

According to a US strategic assessment in 1999 the oceans would remain critical.[11] The assessment pointed out that the United States would need to maintain access to such traditional regions as Europe, North East Asia, and the Persian Gulf. Here the emphasis for the US is on access—the forward movement; whereas for some others it is the threat from—the inward movement. The perceptions vary, but the endgame is national security for every entity. The United States generally feel that on the whole, its maritime interests are far more secure than during the Cold War, though new regional problems are emerging.[12] They should be right in thinking that way against the backdrop of their constitution and national security policies. American author Jim Gaston quotes Paul Hammond in his article "*The Development of National Strategy in the Executive Branch: Overcoming Disincentives*" who questions whether too much has been spent on forward-deployed attack capability of maritime forces to the neglect of sealift and airlift.[13] The view expressed by him has undergone changes since then in American naval and maritime strategies by the turnaround of world order from the Cold War scenario to a direct mode of perceived unipolar system where political checks and balances are centralised. The unipolar scenario is changing gradually under the fundamental geopolitical gravity.

All these leads to the fact that the word "maritime" is used at convenience in a broader sense to depict anything that is related to the sea. In law it is related to carriage of goods and passengers by sea. In the event of law enforcement to curb transnational and national oceanic crimes including shipping crimes, it has to be looked in a broader sense encompassing all maritime activities. Maritime strategy, though widely used in its definitive form, explains naval warfare and manoeuvres. It did not cover the all-encompassing strategic aspects of national security identified in the process of this research. It is understandable because national security concept was widely believed to be military security.

Ultimately the arguments have to lead to the definition of maritime security if the term has to be applied sensibly. The author in his study found that it could best be defined relative to the already defined term national security which is a measureable and definite concept.

Within this appreciation, maritime security is defined as the *"the all encompassing complementary faction of national security of a maritime nation from an ocean specific terrain assessment applicable to that nation."*[14]

According to this definition, maritime security is a much larger concept than sea borne military security. The latter is a part of maritime security and inclusive of the military security element of national security. Accordingly, the term maritime strategy stands upgraded towards national security concept and not as military naval strategy alone.

Identifying the Factors of Maritime Security

Identifying the factors of maritime security is a challenging task. The factors are dynamic and varying with respect to the situation. These factors have to be identified from a terrain specific assessment for integrating with national security governance. In this case the terrain is the ocean. There are two options:[15]

- Option 1 is to compare the national security elements with ocean specificity.
- Option 2 is to generalise the recognisable oceanic factors complementary to national security and identify the factors.

The second approach is seemingly more definite and will restrict variations that can cause ambiguity within the definition. The option allows permissible variations to deal with the concept of ocean property explained earlier. It can be brought under the scope of research for examination. It is also an accepted fact that in today's scenario the international community does not view the oceans as vast unregulated voids. There is interest in protecting the seas, and defusing conflicts arising from competing demands for optimising ocean property.

Ocean property is the collective name attributed to the oceanic components of national security.[16] They are identified as ocean advantage, ocean resources, ocean environment and oceanic islands.

Table 4.1 explains maximising ocean property returns by maximising returns from its four constituent elements.

Table 4.1 Maximising Ocean Property Returns

Components	Objectives
Ocean advantage	Maximise advantage
Ocean resources	Maximise returns
Ocean environment	Maximise return, minimise damage
Oceanic islands	Maximise strategic advantage and returns

The ocean advantage is exclusive to the multidimensional terrain of the ocean: its complexity as well as candor included. The terrain provides facilities of transportation, mobility, surface and underwater military advantages, research and development, power projection, international relations, confidence building through goodwill exchanges between nations, etc. The ocean waters are vast pools of resources. Ocean environment relates to coastal zones, marine environment and climate dynamics that govern the sustainability of the ocean and the adjoining land territory. Oceanic islands are the geoproperty available to a maritime nation within an ocean. The islands can be close to mainland or distant from it in the ocean. Such islands are to be seen differently from island nations and archipelagic states. Island nations or archipelagic states may also have islands that could be brought under the concept of ocean property. Managing such islands that are identified as part of ocean property, therefore, is different. Effective implementation of UNCLOS means staggering opportunities for commercial companies providing enabling technologies within the classified marine sectors, seabed exploration, mining, maritime safety, law enforcement, environmental protection, scientific studies and resource conservation.

The objective, under all circumstances, is to maximise national security.

There were many turning points in the appreciation of ocean. The world recognised the importance of the oceans through the formulation of the UNCLOS regime that, in a nutshell, prevent ocean colonisation by the powerful. UNCLOS erased ocean illiteracy among people, at least among those who govern. This also explains why the ocean blindness existed among the public and governments in the early days as noticed by Mihir Roy. Perception of ocean differed largely among people until a global regime like UNCLOS came up under the combined efforts of the people and their governments. It bound the people on ocean providing a common platform even if the regime may not be all inclusive according to governments who have not ratified it. The governments became very much aware of the ocean and its importance in the 25 plus years it took to bring out the international regime on sharing the ocean. Later, the end of Cold War brought out a new awareness of the ocean. UNCLOS and the end of Cold War called for a fresh look at maritime strategic assessment. All these lead to a new look at maritime security and its governance. The specific factors identified in this study, that each geopolitical entity, will have to refer for itself for application in complementing the national security elements, are given below.

- Naval strategy and warfare
- Managing and governing ocean property
- Implementation of UNCLOS and other international legislations
- National legislations on ocean affairs
- Law enforcement
- Service at and from the sea
- Partnership and coordination of maritime forces
- Littoral operations
- Regional maritime cooperation and force coordination
- Management and security of limited waters
- Maritime border area management
- Limiting conflicts

- Control of critical choke points
- Sea launch
- Management of ocean habitats
- Humanitarian activities at sea
- Ocean survey and research
- Technological change and impact on ocean activities
- Consequences of sea level rise
- Others

These factors are identified as common to all the entities at one time or another. They are interrelated and inclusive. Often, they dissolve into each other. They are specific to a geopolitical entity. Even where they are common there will be variations in their degree of seriousness, sensitivity and priority. These factors will vary within each entity with respect to the period and time and also among the entities themselves.

Naval Strategy and Warfare

Establishing military security under the terrain specificity of the ocean is an important issue for the governments to examine under the changing scenario of ocean awareness in relation to military power. Under this context the term sea power in its connotation to naval power lap dissolves into the overall military power. A powerful navy alone cannot win a war. The Trojan War is a grand example of using the navy for reach to fight a war that may thereafter continue for many years. The Trojan War continued for ten years after the reach was established using naval power. Whether a legend or actual war, the idea still applies today in different forms of strategic application. While ground forces decide and end the war by holding ground, air and naval forces supplement their efforts through terrain specific approaches in the conventional and age old warfare system since the introduction of air power that still holds well. Additional terrains—outer space and cyber space—have already made entries into military strategy. [17] The best fought war is the one that takes advantage of all available terrains for maneuvering in the highest order of optimisation.[18] Here ocean has certain special characteristics of its own.[19] The two major aspects hidden in the ocean advantage element of ocean property are expansive reach and nearly indomitable stealth. Ocean is important in military parlance even for a landlocked nation because it can be attacked and annihilated from the sea if the adversary has the reach. Ocean provides the stealth element in all its dimensions—air, surface and underwater. It is only reach that matters. It is applicable even in a nuclear war when the ocean can be used more effectively, as on now and in the immediate future, as the most convenient terrain to launch an attack, especially in the second strike mode. Though nations have the choice to develop "anywhere, anytime" tools for second strike within minutes of being attacked, ocean provides a more convenient choice for preparation and launch. The strategy for naval warfare has to change considerably under the new approach from the old and orthodox belief systems that many navies follow even today. It requires a major change in the belief systems of governments and naval authorities. Such a change in naval belief systems will make integration with national security that much easier.

The scenario about warfare is changing fast. There is considered and hastened research in unmanned warfare. Future warfare is expected to be in a scenario of multiple functionality of unmanned technology. Human intelligence interface is expected to assume greater significance in war to coordinate multiple systems in consonance. Space, cyber space and asymmetric dimensions of warfare and advancement of various critical technologies, sensors, robotics, communication, advanced materials and electronics are expected to pave way for development of advanced and unmanned warfare systems. In future there is scope for developing unattended sensors, micro unmanned aerial vehicles (UAV) and unmanned underwater vehicles (U^2V), and autonomous underwater vehicles (AUV).[20] Unmanned combat vehicles (UCV) could be seen in all geophysical terrains. The next generation warfare is already at the doorstep.

Naval strategy applies to even landlocked sates. There are landlocked states with large and expansive lakes that demand maritime strategies in dealing with them. Among them are the nations with maritime forces including navies. Another interesting fact is about the NATO (North Atlantic Treaty Organisation) Navy. The NATO is an intergovernmental military alliance signed in 1949.[21] The NATO Navy is an extra-state navy with separate naval forces. The interesting fact is that there are landlocked sates in NATO. By being part of NATO virtually they too become part commanders of a naval military force.

Naval strategy and warfare policy thereby becomes a factor of any geopolitical entity whether landlocked or otherwise. Only the priority in governance may differ.

Managing and Governing Ocean Property

Managing and governing ocean property—ocean advantage, ocean resources, ocean environment and oceanic islands—for safeguarding the national security interests is a major activity for every geopolitical entity. This involves equitable and sustainable management of ocean resources, strategic appreciation of ocean advantage, the P^3C factors of marine environment,[22] climate watch, and island specific management in the national interest. An important aspect here is clarity of global commons within the ocean property regime.

Implementation of UNCLOS and other International Legislations

Establishing a globally acceptable legal framework for use of the oceans has been the central theme of the 25-year effort of the nations to achieve a comprehensive convention in the form of UNCLOS. The process began in 1958 with the first Law of the Sea Conference. This study postulates the dawn of ocean literacy from this date among the governments of the world. Without such literacy the participants would not have been able to negotiate the requirements and bring about a consensus in ocean governance without compromising individual interests. The debate went on for about 25 years. It was a serious matter and a first in the world about the ocean. The Convention was open to signature in 1982, and formally entered into force in 1994. UNCLOS is a comprehensive instrument in international law. 165 geopolitical entities have ratified the Convention. This includes 162 UN member countries, two territories—Cook Islands and Niue—and European Union as of October 2012.[23]

Though United States was actively involved in the Convention process, it has only signed the Convention, as it stands in 2013. It has signed the 1994 Agreement on Implementation. The consideration of the treaty was deferred for want of the required majority if it had come to vote in the Senate. Two Republican senators opposed ratification on 16 July 2012. According to them, "on balance the treaty was not in the interest of the United States."[24] The Convention, however, is supported by a wide swath of business interests, environmentalists and the US military. Some American commentators have warned that ratification of the Law of the Sea Treaty might lead to its taxing authority being extended to cover resources of outer space. The arguments in favour of ratification is that it would give the US more credibility with other treaty members when resolving maritime disputes and conducting naval operations. It was a view expressed by the Commandant of the US Coast Guard.[25] But the Senators who oppose ratification feel that it would yield US sovereignty to international law, impose environmental pollution fees and burden US companies with royalties for energy exploitation. They also note that some treaty members, such as China, do not abide by its rules. They often quote that the Law of the Sea has not helped in resolving the tensions and maritime disputes pointing to the South China Sea.

But the Law of the Sea has enabled countries with the legal framework needed to establish and maintain various management programmes, based on their environment and resources. Principle elements are categorised in four definitive areas: the Coastal Zone (CZ), the Exclusive Economic Zone (EEZ), the Continental Shelf (CS), and the Littoral Zone (LZ).

Nonratification will deny the countries even the "provisional status" to UNCLOS. It is a major issue for the international community. The status of nonratified countries with respect to UNCLOS can cause conflicting decisions and views.

According to international law and as per Article 1 of the Convention on the High Seas 1958, the high seas cover all parts of the sea that are not included in the territorial sea or in the internal waters of the state. According to this definition and by Article 2 of the Convention, "The high seas being open to all nations, no State may validly purport to subject any part of them to its sovereignty. Freedom of the high seas is exercised under the conditions laid down by these articles and by the other rules of international law. It comprises, inter alia, both for coastal and non-coastal States:

1. Freedom of navigation;

2. Freedom of fishing;
3. Freedom to lay submarine cables and pipelines;
4. Freedom to fly over the high seas."

This freedom, and others which are recognised by the general principles of international law, shall be exercised by all states with reasonable regard to the interests of other states in their exercise of the freedom of the high seas."[26]

Certain ambiguity arises here with respect to the definition of the high seas. This ambiguity can be seen in the UNCLOS Part VII that deals with high seas that says, "*The provisions of this Part apply to all parts of the sea that are not included in the exclusive economic zone, in the territorial sea or in the internal waters of a State, or in the archipelagic waters of an archipelagic State. This article does not entail any abridgement of the freedoms enjoyed by all States in the exclusive economic zone in accordance with Article 58.*"[27] Article 58 deals with the rights and duties of other States in the exclusive economic zone.

A third of the world's oceans, including entire seas, such as the Mediterranean, the Red Sea, and the Persian Gulf, is within the 200 nautical miles of the coast, and thus within 200 nautical miles of the permissible limits of the EEZs. The convention expressly preserves in the EEZs, the high seas freedom of navigation, over flight, laying and maintenance of submarine cables and pipelines, and related uses.

Since the UNCLOS, nations have been able to limit the international boundaries according to nine categories of considerations. Most of them were through treaties and third party processes. However, there are still many issues pending. Some of them may cause conflicts between countries that have not ratified and therefore remain outside the Convention. The nine categories mentioned are given below.

i. Political, strategic, and economic considerations
ii. Legal regime considerations
iii. Economic and environmental considerations
iv. Geographical considerations
v. Islands, rocks, reefs, and low tide level considerations
vi. Baseline considerations
vii. Geological and geomorphological considerations
viii. Method of delimitations considerations
ix. Technical considerations

The countries that have ratified UNCLOS are unanimous in the need to respect the provisions of it to resolve the issues at sea peacefully in relation to jurisdiction and rights. Nations that flexed their muscles on resolution of issues by force are slowly turning around to settle issues amicably. This is likely to be the future trend. Exploration and exploitation under a win-win situation is a permanent choice. This also means reaffirmed respect for the freedom of navigation in high seas according to UNCLOS between the countries under the Convention. It will also lead ways for assured bilateral relations and partnership for common benefit.

National Legislation on Ocean Affairs

To establish jurisdiction in the maritime zones in varying degrees and for suppressing unlawful activities at and from the sea by establishing the rule of law, nations will require strong enforcement capabilities and enforcement friendly legislation[28] related to ocean affairs. National legislation should be compatible with international law. The force level should be optimised for meeting the enforcement challenges. Codified maritime legislation appropriate to the security issues is absent in most of the littorals today. The international bodies are aware that extension of international law for use of the seas and maritime zones within it can reduce the potential for conflicts and contribute to stability in several turbulent regions. Under such situations there is a strong need for supporting national legislations in littoral states to ease out the law enforcement problems within the maritime zones for the security agencies involved. The national law should be capable of not only regulating illegal activities but also to punish the offenders. The law should be enforcement friendly.

The term "at and from the seas" is important when drafting a maritime legislation This is especially so on matters related to unlawful acts. The human concern is about the impact of the ocean over the land. The law has to deal with the unlawful activities that occur at sea as well as originates from the sea. Today the available law mentions about suppression of unlawful acts at Sea. An example is the Suppression of Unlawful Acts against the Safety of Maritime Navigation 1988. The term "from the sea" is absent. It can cause problems in appreciating the act in a court of law especially when it is about national legislation.

Law Enforcement

Transnational ocean crimes related to crime at sea on board vessels and platforms, shipping, poaching, smuggling, fraud, piracy, trafficking, illegal immigration, nefarious scientific research, maritime terrorism, etc., are those associated with unlawful dimension of maritime threat perception. There is also threat to marine environment. Managing maritime threats under prevention or preemption have to be examined independently, jointly and regionally with international support. The maritime forces of responsible countries should be able to meet the challenges of the future in relation to unlawful activities.

Service at and from the Sea

The coast guards of the world are primarily engaged in two activities at and from the sea—enforcing law and providing service. There are other agencies including navies that perform these two functions in various parts of the world. The capability of a geopolitical entity to provide service at and from the sea is a factor that will measure to its aspect of maritime security. Services will be required for search and rescue for saving life and property at sea by responding to maritime disasters and also to preserve and protect maritime environment and prevent and control marine pollution among others as part of national interest. Identified and capable nations are allotted national search and rescue regions by IMO that may even extend to miles beyond their exclusive economic zones. These nations have the international responsibility to coordinate maritime search and rescue operations within their designated region. Usually the national coast guards are chartered for such tasks.

Partnership and Coordination of Maritime Forces

Maritime forces operate more or less in isolation the world over. Considering the economic and multitasking aspects and expert jointness, this scenario is too insular for having an international regime on maritime security considering the characteristics of the ocean terrain. An idea that is yet to be thought out seriously is having an international regime offering a forum for the world coast guards to work together, where appropriate, for the common benefit. There are about 142 coast guards in the world (2008) according to a researched study by the author.[29] These forces, if come together under memoranda of understanding or agreement, could handle many issues that are matters of concern in relation to the ocean today. They could jointly assist in implementing the UNCLOS regime along with other international treaties and agreements. More treaties and agreements could be formed. An example is the Regional Cooperation Agreement for Combating Piracy and Armed Robbery against Ships in Asia (ReCAAP) concluded by 16 countries in Asia in November 2004.[30] It is the first regional government to government agreement of such a nature in the world under which the coast guards of member countries, where exists, are united. A worldwide coast guard regime under similar agreement or move is not foreseen in the near future. That would be a much desired approach, though. It will be revolutionary in maritime governance. But the international community is not going to take the wakeup call immediately. At least the world coast guards could perform together and exchange valuable communication in law enforcement and service where they have agreed to coordinate and cooperate instead of holding adversarial postures. This aspect has been tested under many situations by select coast guards yielding excellent results. It has been the forte of the Indian and the US coast guards. However the much desired synergy is lacking in getting at the decision making levels of various governments who hold coast guards. The advantage of the coast guards is that they are accepted by international diplomacy as service providers and law enforcers for the common cause and their presence are not seen as adversarial as in the military naval forces under most of the circumstances. Here the term coast guard includes all the forces that are otherwise nonmilitary maritime forces and engaged in law enforcement and services.

One of the important functions of the navy is in the geostrategic context. International maritime force partnerships are not at the coast guards' level alone. The more serious geostrategic involvement has to be established through the navy. The world navies can form coordinative postures in handling issues related to their charter, especially the geostrategic charter, at international level. The coast-benefit and other geostrategic factors have to be closely examined while dealing in such partnerships. The ability of a country in involving cooperatively with another through their maritime forces is a factor that is to be recognised while assessing the maritime security facet in the modern context.

Littoral Operations

Absence of predictable mid-ocean battles in the emerging world was instrumental for the much-needed downsizing of the navies today that takes away major chunk of national budgets for most of the fleets including that of the United States. Strategic focus shifted from war at sea to nearshore and restricted waters warfare. Shift to littoral warfare is a strategic reallocation of priorities for the global players. It is expected to hold in the future. Operating closer to shore, the navies will be dealing with more asymmetrical threats. Other maritime forces are expected to operate in the maritime zones and will continue in the enlarged scale according to the perceptions of threat to maritime security and in force assistance to the navies. More and more involvement of other maritime and dual forces (special operations forces, commandos, marines, coast guard, etc.) with the navy will be the focus of attention as a factor of maritime security.

However such littoral operations can be undertaken only by the navies that has the reach and operational endurance since littoral operations are not over own shores. This calls for not only readying the navy for such operations but also upgrading them for the desired reach and endurance.

Regional Maritime Cooperation and Force Coordination

Forces of the leading maritime countries were involved in wars outside their waters since the days of colonisation, trade and missionary activities. Today the nations with maritime enlargement in their vital national interest are still involved in global maritime operations. During the Cold War the US and Soviet maritime forces represented the archetypal symmetrical threat. Both the fleets prepared for decisive battles in mid-ocean. The scenario changed after the Cold War. In fact, in the US, there was budget cuts and even questioning of the relevance of the navy in the post Cold War world. The navy shifted its strategic focus from war at sea to littoral warfare. There are no navies in the world specially carrying out archaic fleet operations aimed at mid-sea battles with identified enemies. But the global interests prevail. These interests will lead to regional cooperation that will also include nonmilitary maritime forces like the coast guard and other marine security agencies.

Management and Security of Limited Waters

Limited waters or restricted waters including narrow seas around a maritime nation are critical for its security. The forces involved in protecting them have major tasks. Such waters are defined and included within the maritime zones of each country. The forces have the responsibility to safeguard the constituents of ocean property and related interests of the nation within the limited waters. Maritime strategy and operations in the limited waters are different from ocean strategy and amphibious mission statements. This subject deals with special emphasis on the limitations of terrain. It has to be studied. The view that a fleet can defeat an adversary in open waters can do the same in narrow waters is not true according to naval strategy.[31] It also applies to law enforcement. The issues are more critical in limited waters than in the open sea. The maritime forces should be competent in their respective tasks in the nation's limited waters. The constraints of narrow waters are different from that of the open ocean. It is the same as considering the terrain differences over the land wherein a low ground is different from a high ground. A hill is different from a valley in land warfare. In limited waters maritime operational intentions are achieving land-front objectives and safeguarding ocean property.

Maritime Border Area Management

Unlike the land border, maritime border is not a singular line or interface, but layered areas within different perimeters according to jurisdiction and allocation. These are coastal zones, territorial seas, archipelagic waters, contiguous zones, exclusive economic zones, continental shelf, legal continental shelf, mining blocks, search and rescue areas, historic waters and allocated areas external to them. There are also variable zones with protective boundaries. Strategic management of these areas will fall under the term maritime boundary management or maritime border area management. Managing these areas will be a specialised task tactically and strategically for the purpose of exercising selective jurisdiction and national defence. There are many nations between whom the sea boundaries are not earmarked. These are potential conflict zones. Delimitation of these zones through bilateral agreement for common and identified international boundary line (IBL) will reduce the risk of conflicts.

Limiting Conflicts

Limiting conflicts and conflict resolution between maritime neighbours is an objective that is continuous in the agenda of any coastal nation. This is achieved by preventive defence and deterrence and associated confidence building measures (CBM).

Control of Critical Choke Points

Choke points are the strategic chicken-necks of the oceans. Commercial trade will require transiting critical choke points: straits, canals, bays, gulfs, and other narrow ways of navigation. The areas prone to piracy, violence, and disturbance even in the open sea or close to shore, are also critical choke points for commercial trade. The choke points will also become important in conflicts whether the trading nation is involved or not. The nation state has to develop the capabilities to control and manage these choke points.

Sea Launch

Sea is a convenient terrain for launching weapons and space vehicles for those who have the expertise. Weapons of mass destructions in the hands of rogue states and militant activists can also find a place at sea in the future. Maritime security is also the capability to react and respond to the hostile actions of the rogue parties at and from the sea.

Management of Ocean Habitats

Ocean habitats are colonies that may be used in future demographic shift. There was a mention of a proposed design of a 1.2-km long "freedom ship" with a capacity to carry 100,000 people out of whom 40,000 will be permanent inhabitants. Such ideas are still in the conceptual stage.[32] Ocean habitats could also be developed for deep sea mining and other explorations. Condominiums at sea are not impossible dreams. Ocean realtors may be a familiar word to future generations looking for a place to live. Offshore platforms for oil exploration, extraction and production are already ocean habitats, though temporary, for the people engaged in it for long periods of time. Nations will have to manage and protect their ocean habitats.

Humanitarian Activities at Sea

Humanitarian activities are internationally important in the maritime scenario. It includes extending help across the oceans to the needy and assisting mariners in distress at sea. Maritime search and rescue is a widely recognised humanitarian obligation for nations. Each maritime nation has its own allocated region for coordination of maritime search and rescue missions. Reach is important in such activities. In addition, providing assistance in disaster situations by sealift, assisting United Nations in peace operations, evacuation, etc., are among the humanitarian activities expected out of capable and responsible maritime nations.

Ocean Survey and Research

Maritime survey and research is a high priority task in a maritime nation's ocean policy. It is also important to ensure that survey and research are not carried out surreptitiously in its maritime zones. Vital national interests can be damaged by covert marine survey operations for obtaining ocean floor and underwater profile signatures. These operations are bound to increase in the future.

Technological Change and Impact on Ocean Activities

Maritime strategy and security in modern times stand by technological change. Among the early examples of supremacy by technology was the use of nails by the Portuguese to construct superior ships when they plied the Indian Ocean. Revolution in military affairs (RMA) recycled to revolution in maritime affairs. Strength was the outcome. Warfare is heading towards network centricity in modern times. At the same time, the downside of technology is cost. Leaner, silent and lethal fleets will have to be more expensive due to technology input. Precise and decisive effects are expected in future conflicts. Human activities in the oceans are expected to be dominated by technology in the years to come. Such a scenario is not difficult to visualise. Technological edge matters a lot to maritime security.

Maritime technology is heading towards unmanned operations in ocean robotics that could break into military and unlawful activities also. Taking advantage of technological growth to deal with the issues related to the ocean is a factor of maritime security in the evolving world.

Consequences of Sea Level Rise

The sea level all around the world is bound to rise. The consequences will be unprecedented this time compared to the past. The world is highly populated today, especially near the coastlines.. The sea level rise will submerge low lying dry lands. Inland rivers will swell under floods of turbulent water flow—from the sea in one direction and of melting glaciers up in the mountain in the opposite. Some countries, especially island nations may submerge totally remaining that way for many years to come.[33] Kiribati and Maldives have already expressed their voices about the impending calamity.[34] Nations like Australia, India, New Zealand, Sri Lanka etc., would find external migrants from nearby island nations seeking refuge. The issues will be manifold. The prospective countries of refuge may have to seek responsible international and national regimes to protect their interests when flooded by climate change refugees. There is no such regime today that can handle the issues of a sinking world. Most of them rely on the conciliatory statements of experts who downplay the case of climate change refugees. According to them it will not be an alarming issue. But still, there could be serious issues demanding answers if things go wrong:

- How and under what condition will a host nation receive the refugees from an island nation that is about to go under?
- What will be the geoproperty rights and who will reclaim the land when the flood waters recede and the island nations come up dry, times ahead?
- Will the nations gone underwater hypothecate their submerged land to the host country (the country of refuge)?
- If so, how the rights under UNCLOS will be claimed?
- How will individual victims legally and physically reclaim their flooded properties when the waters recede?

There are many such issues, national as well as international, in an assured scenario of the sinking world that the governments have to ponder. All these relate to the ocean for which the decisions have to be over land.

Others

There are various other issues that may come up as factors of maritime security. Such factors are to be identified by the concerned geopolitical entity to incorporate in their national plans for governing national security by integrating maritime security. It is relative to the geopolitical entity's policy of governance besides being situational. It is for the policy makers to examine with respect to the situation.

Maritime Dimensions of Geopolitical Entities

Every geopolitical entity has its own maritime dimension according to its geostatus, heritage, historical perspectives, threat perception, ocean property, ocean based belief systems, ocean outlook, etc. The future perspectives of a nation related to its maritime security will be highly influenced by its maritime dimension. Maritime dimension of a country, thereby, becomes a matter of interest in political decisions and national governance. Some of the entities would have had strong relations with the ocean in the past. Some may have forgotten legacies. But with the introduction of the law of the sea every geopolitical entity has become politically and geostrategically connected to the ocean and thereby the ocean property when the eventful 20th century was about to be wound up.

There are many geopolitical entities that had never paid heed seriously to the ocean and its influence over their survival. There are others who are seriously apprehensive about their countries going down under the ocean when the sea level rises in the not so distant future. But most of them were callously indifferent on the oceanic issues in the past. Maritime security had not figured seriously in the national agenda of many countries. This argument also explains why many countries became victims to the colonisers who came by the sea. Their shores were landing grounds for maritime adventurers to plunder and colonise them in every respect, even intellectually. Maritime security still remains a curious term for all these countries.

The first to take to sea among the geopolitical entities would have been naturally the coastal people including the islanders. Under this argument it can be seen that usually none takes to sea in a landlocked country. That also explains why landlocked countries are not engaged in maritime affairs seriously even today whereas nothing prohibits them from venturing into it. For the coastal people across the world, the sea was their natural element for subsistence unless some of them preferred to keep away from the sea due to cultural and social taboos of misperception. Those who ventured out to sea involved in multi-economic activity, retaining their basic occupation—fishing and seafaring. They also engaged in more complex economic activities deriving from trade and commerce. Seasonal piracy also belonged to the realm of seafaring.

There was stagnation in indigenous maritime activities during the colonial period in many geopolitical entities of the world. The dictate of the colonisers subjugated and stifled the creative faculties of the locals. The colonial rulers jeopardised the maritime interests of the local traders. They coerced merchants and rulers into submission. They taxed the locals so that they remained under coercive colonialism. Local rulers who had the power over the land remained impervious to maritime matters where it did not affect them seriously. An example was the Mughals in India.[35] The nations obviously were not aware of the intricacies and importance of the sea. The awareness of the ocean dawned along with the world wars and thereafter got established with the preparations for the law of the sea convention in the late 1950s. All those who prepared for the convention and worked nearly quarter a century had to understand the oceans well to establish their points in their interest. That was a major turning point in understanding the oceans as explained earlier.

Still the notion of power and sovereignty continued to remain land-based as in the past which this study attributes to the landclasp syndrome acquired primordially by humans. The warrior ethics and prowess of a vast majority of people was not oriented towards the sea. People fought with their feet firm on the ground. Maritime jurisdiction did not figure in the evolving political agenda of the nations. This was considered to be ignorance of the sea or ocean illiteracy in the pre UNCLOS world. Today it still continues by practice though at least the governments of the world are fully aware of the importance of the ocean beyond military aspects. Ocean literacy is evident, among others, in the issues related to the maritime disputes all over the world in every ocean division. Without ocean literacy there won't be disputes on ocean property.

In the past, most of the geopolitical entities navigated in the ocean that lapped over their shores. Some went farther and established territories and spread their culture and religion. The Phoenicians, the Vikings, the Greeks, the Persians, the early Egyptians, the Dravidians, the Portuguese, the Dutch, the French, and the British, besides other coastal countries in the early days navigated in almost all ocean divisions. In the 19th century the British dominated the ocean.[36] For them the priority was to keep the sea lines of communication open to the British Empire to rule. They were particular about preventing European encroachments into their empire across the seas. Other aspects like checking the smuggling of slaves, and trade in the Persian Gulf and the East African coast were minimal. Russia was considered to be a threat to the British in seaward mobility and reach. There are recorded voyages of the Russian trader Afanasy Nikitin, 1466 through 1472, to India and other countries before the Portuguese discovered the sea route to India.[37]

Russia was a prospective ocean coloniser in the early world. But Britain succeeded in confining the Russian naval forces to the Black Sea. Britain had greater capability in harnessing the ocean advantage than Russia. British policy was centred on the assumption that "all the eastern sea lines led to the subcontinent that had become in two centuries the strategic centre of a commercial network that covered the whole Indian Ocean and the South China Sea."[38] The British therefore gave a great deal of emphasis both to the security of the Indian Ocean and in getting to know it well. The policy of the British in the Indian Ocean was "India centred" till India became independent in 1947. By 1967, British withdrew from the Indian Ocean. Political and security priorities of the Cold War brought the Soviet Union (resurgent Russia) and the United States into the region. New States, like Mauritius, Seychelles, and Australia emerged in the region with evolving nationalisms. Others like Sri Lanka and Maldives started looking towards the Indian Ocean for a new awareness. Naval doctrines changed since 1997 all over the world. The navies advocated regional presence. The United States had recast its operational framework after the Cold War. People's Republic of China has intentions to reach out to the northern Indian Ocean and seas surrounding. It is a matter of active consideration among the navies of the world. Other concerns are the problems of narcotics and arms traffic in the Asian region, and piracies and crimes on the high seas.

But, is there something special about the Indian Ocean in maritime legacy and geostrategic context irrespective of its relative backwardness in comparison with other ocean divisions? It seems to be so. This study does not examine this question. But it would be better for the countries of the Indian Ocean rim to take note though the prediction is that it will be a deep lake in 250 million years. That, for now, is a long way. It cannot be an excuse to neglect Indian Ocean or leave it the way it is today—rhetorically aggressive but complacently placid barring some exceptions.

Ocean routes of the world were the chords of maritime communication for traders, merchantmen, missionaries, immigrants, criminals and colonists. In the time of war these routes are blockaded to choke the supplies to the adversaries. These routes acquired the name sea lines of communication (SLOC) in course of time in maritime vocabulary. They became vital to those whose economic health depended upon sea trade in spite of being geographically disadvantaged. SLOC virtually connect the world, whether coastal or interior. Strategically, primary threats to SLOC come from ocean based unlawful activities and armed conflicts.

According to World Bank, the sea-borne trade is expected to reach 41,800 btm in 2014.[39] United Nations Conference on Trade and Development (UNCTAD) Report, "Review of Marine Transport 2000," indicates the world sea-borne trade is increasing. The trade routes are along the established lines of communication unless the ships engage in weather or conditional routing.[40] SLOC are maritime economic models for cost effective communication by trade and other means. In criminal or warfare parlance they may not be the same. Deviated SLOC may be necessary depending upon their intentions and objectives. For a nation state, its SLOC is a geostrategic ocean region, and most part of it will be outside its waters. It is a maritime dimension. A geostrategic region, this research defines, is a region outside the state that is not controlled by it, but within which it has interests related to its national security and it considers using political, economic, diplomatic and military instruments of power to safeguard it. Geostrategic region is time and situation related. The definition of geostrategic region therefore is of interest for every state in its maritime strategy as another maritime dimension. SLOC are to be seen from the type and density of traffic, threats and choke points.

The maritime dimensions of a geopolitical entity also indicate the maritime geostrategic asymmetry between them. It is very specific over that land because of the landclasp attitude of humans. It has to be studied specifically when it is about the ocean. When mutual advantage is a preferred choice, these asymmetries are often neglected. Whereas, the asymmetries play a serious role when the entities assume adversarial roles. All these depend on the factors of asymmetry in their maritime dimensions. Maritime dimensions may have similarities and dissimilarities between the nations. There is no standard formula to identify them. But the prerogative is to make sure the constituent parameters are identifiable and quantifiable to the extent their definitiveness can be established. They are examined in this study. The cosntituents that will go into a geopolitical entity's maritime dimension are enumerated and subsequently explained briefly below.

- Geostrategic maritime status
- Geolocation in relation to ocean division (landlocked, littoral, island)
- Status as a geopolitical entity (state, territory, disputed area)
- Membership in international maritime bodies
- Maritime zones
  - Coastline
  - Baseline
  - Coastal zone
  - Internal waters
  - Historic waters
  - Archipelagic waters
  - Territorial sea
  - Contiguous zone

- Exclusive economic zone
- Legal continental shelf
- Search and rescue area
- Extraneous zones (safety zones, variable zones, temporary zones, etc.) Art 60.
- SLOC
- SLOT
- Choke points
- Maritime border areas
- Maritime neighbours
- Maritime disputes
- Maritime forces
- Islands
- Territories
- Shipping
- Ports and harbours (major and minor)
- Ocean resource potential
- Weather and climate
- Marine environment
- Maritime resolve

The factors of maritime dimensions identified above are examined briefly below. There could be more in future.

Geostrategic Maritime Status

Geostrategic maritime status of a geopolitical entity is the traditional mindset and qualities it has acquired on matters related to the ocean collectively from its maritime endowments of the past including that of the very recent times. It is shaped out of its maritime heritage, historical aspects, direct and indirect maritime involvements, successes and blunders of the past, ocean influence and every other aspect that is capable of changing its maritime behaviour. Obviously the maritime status of an entity will keep changing as time passes especially those are littoral. The maritime status of an entity will be visible in its approach towards maritime issues. An example is Mongolia. The country has a strong maritime status. It is visible in its policies even though the country is landlocked today.

Geolocation in Relation to Ocean Divisions

There are five ocean divisions. Each geopolitical entity has a relative location with respect to them. Besides, the natural geographical character of the entity also matters. Among them the important aspects are whether it is a landlocked, coastland or island territory. Each one has its own natural characteristics in relation to the ocean. The issues an entity faces for its natural existence are different from another. Within this asymmetry, nations will have to be governed for their national security issues in relation to the ocean divisions where it has direct and indirect accesses. It has to be understood in any policy decisions interactive with the factors that complement national security.

Any country irrespective of its geolocation can be "reached" from the sea in the world today. United States launched two cruise missiles from Red Sea on 20 August 1998. One hit Afghanistan and the other the then Sudan.[41] The missiles caused heavy destruction under the code name Operation Infinite Reach. Mark the word—"infinite." The reach is from the sea. The results were devastating.[42] Afghanistan was landlocked and distant. Sudan was a coastland bordering the Red Sea in Indian Ocean. A landlocked country too faces challenges from the sea and relative to the sea. Hence the ocean cannot be discounted by any geopolitical entity. Ocean can provide infinite reach.

There were many interesting cases where in systems in a country ran extra governmental writs in the ocean contiguous to it and also elsewhere. While Somalis engaged in piracy deep in the ocean in the absence of a formal government, insurgents in Sri Lanka dominated their part of the ocean with an efficient sea going militia. Japanese whalers reached close to Antarctica in spite of resistances they faced from the nonstate seagoing environmental activists.

Status of a Geopolitical Entity

The status of a geopolitical entity whether a state, under a state as its territory, a disputed area claimed by more than one country, a part of a nation that is about be broken away, a global common, a state without a government, etc., matters while assessing its maritime dimension. Each such entity will have its relative prescription of the ocean. For a territory, it could be about its futuristic aspirations as a free country or as a part under protection of another country. All these aspects get intermixed with ocean perception and the maritime security imperatives that will change constantly.

Membership in International Maritime Bodies

The primary international maritime body is International Maritime Organisation (IMO) originally known as Inter-Governmental Maritime Consultative Organisation. It was conceived in Geneva in 1948 as a specialised agency of UN on maritime affairs related to shipping and the seas. It came into force in 1958 and was renamed International Maritime Organisation in 1982. Most of the geopolitical entities are members of the body irrespective of their geolocations and characteristics. The membership in these bodies makes a country to follow norms of international laws related to ocean and accordingly make changes in their policies. The country becomes member of a collective system in decision making on governance. There are 170 members including landlocked countries and three associate members in IMO (2013). The members are listed in appendix B.

Maritime Zones

Maritime zones are areas in the ocean and over the shore contiguous to the ocean where a nation has sovereign rights or limited authority in accordance with the national legislation compatible with the accepted international legislation. The coastline that also varies between tidal changes within an area falls under the purview of the maritime zones along with the baseline that is notified after demarcation. Into the ocean, these zones include territorial sea where a nation has full sovereignty and other areas under limited jurisdiction as allocated under international law and enforced under domestic laws. Such maritime zones are briefly explained below.

Coastline

It sounds simple. Coastline is where dry land meets the ocean maintaining each other's exclusive identity. But, according to this study, the coastline is the most complex and the least understood parameter in the study of maritime zones and the concept of maritime security in the larger perspective. Geopolitical entities seemingly have not understood the intricacies of coastline in the overall framework of maritime security. There are two important aspects that this study points out: 1) the coastline is a fractal, and 2) it changes every moment by sea level variations and coastal erosions and accretions besides periodically shifting longitudinally across an area determined by tidal variations. The coastline moves in a very complex manner changing the profile of the coast every moment. The only definite coastline is that of a landlocked country—zero, a finding of this study. Rest are under the so called coastline paradox[43].

For these reasons a coastline cannot be a precise line like the borderline over the land. It is a dynamic line that changes constantly. A coastline can be an open front or sheltered against an ocean.

The coastline is a fractal of nature. To avoid the complexity by overindulgent mathematical predilection, it is better stated that the length of the coastline will depend upon the measure according to the scale used to measure it. The smaller the scale the longer will be the coastline at any time it is measured. This is part of the coastline paradox mentioned before. An example is the measured assessment of the coastline of Great Britain. When measured using fractal units 100km long, then the length of the coastline was approximately 2,800km and when 50km, the length became approximately 3,400km.[44] The difference is large when compared to the total length.

The tidal variation takes place semi diurnally or diurnally according to the place in a day. The tide varies in height and time based on the forces that generate it. Every shore will have a mean lowest low tide line and the highest high tide line. The coastline moves across this area longitudinally in a complex and chaotic manner.

▶ Baseline

The breadths of the fixed maritime zones lying seaward are measured from the baseline determined under UNCLOS. Articles 5 and 7 define the normal baseline, except where otherwise provided for in the Convention, as the low-water line along the coast as marked on large scale charts officially recognised by the coastal state. The Convention provides further provisions for measuring and determining the baselines in various other cases. Baseline is critical for measuring the breadth of the maritime zones. The state has to establish it in compliance with UNCLOS. Article 7 defines the straight baselines that are demarcated where the localities are deeply varying because indentations, cuts, islands, deltas, etc. Here a part of the sea may come as part of the land domain while drawing the baseline. Article 47 provides for drawing the baselines of an archipelagic state.

▶ Coastal zone

The atmosphere, the sea, and the land meet and interact in the coastal zone. Human activity in the form of urbanisation, harbours, navigation, transportation, industry, domestic and industrial waste disposal, fishing, mariculture and recreation is maximum in the zone. It is vital for economic security. Coastal zones are also important for biodiversity with wetlands, mangroves and coral reef ecosystems. It is a spatial zone where interaction of the sea and land processes occurs

UNCLOS does not define coastal zone. But every entity that is not landlocked will have exclusive coastal zone. Coastal zones can be defined in many ways. Under the principles of coastal zone management a coastal zone is a corridor where the land and adjacent ocean space meet. Functionally coastal zone is the broad interface between land and water where production, consumption, recreation and exchange process occur in high rates of intensity. Ecologically the coastal zone is an area of dynamic biological, hydraulic, geological and chemical activities. It is a dynamic and vulnerable area that needs to be managed sustainably to avoid ecological disaster.

The term "coastal zones" may have general or regulatory connotations. The coastal zone may also include the inland tidal water bodies influenced by tidal action and the land area along such water bodies.

The profile of the coastal zone will be influenced by, among others, sea-land interface, mainland, creeks, estuaries, bays, islands, gulfs, border areas, coastal areas navigable waters within the baseline, rivers, inland waters and lakes and cliffs.

▸ Internal waters

Internal waters are sometime called inland waters. But strictly internal waters under UNCLOS are linked with the ocean for the purpose of navigation as an entry or exit point. They are actual part of the land territory of the entity over which it has full jurisdiction. The coastal nation has dominion and control over these waters. Internal waters also comprise of the sea areas lying within the baseline linked to the land domain. Such sea areas come under the regime of internal waters.

Article 8 of UNCLOS deals with internal waters as the waters on the landward side of the baseline except as provided in Part IV dealing with archipelagic states.

▸ Historic waters

UNCLOS does not define or refer to historic waters. Article 10 (6) mentions about the nonapplicability of the provisions of it to (so called) "historic" bays and article 298 (1) (a) (1) refers to dispute conciliation involving them. Article 46 (b) refers to archipelago which also means a group of islands regarded as such (an intrinsic geographical, economic and political entity) historically. Hence the concept and definition have to be envisaged elsewhere for clarity.

According to the Yearbook of International Law Commission, the concept of historic waters has its root in the historic fact that states through ages claimed and maintained sovereignty over maritime areas which they considered vital to them without paying much attention to divergent and changing opinions about what general international law might prescribe with respect to the delimitation of the territorial sea. According to another study, the doctrine of historic waters developed from that of the historic bays which had emerged in the 19th century for the protection of certain large bays closely linked to the surrounding land area and traditionally considered by claiming states as part of their national territory. The interesting aspect in this finding is that the visibility of the landclasp syndrome. Historic waters become an extension of sovereign land here. "Historic waters" is a concept that is closely related to the legal regime of "historic bays." But the terms, according to scholars, are not synonymous. "Historic waters" is wider in scope than "historic bays." Historic is a title that can be applied to various other maritime dimensions exclusive to a state.

The term "historic waters" was raised in the first UN Conference on the Law of the Sea (1958), also known as UNCLOS 1. But it was not discussed and defined appropriately for want of sufficient material and time. A resolution was adopted to request the UN to arrange for the study of a legal regime for historic waters including historic bays. The Conference, however, recognised the legitimacy of historic waters and historic bays. In 1962 the UN Secretariat published a study under the title "judicial Regime of historic Waters, Including Historic Bays" in Yearbook of International Law Commission.

No authoritative definition exists on historic waters. It is accepted that "historic waters" includes historic bays and other historic waters. The definitions are scholarly. One such definition (1964) reads: *waters over which the Coastal State, contrary to the generally applicable rules of international law, clearly, effectively, continuously, and over a substantial period of time, exercise sovereign rights with the acquiescence of the community of States.* According to another scholar *historical waters can be 1) bays claimed by States which are greater in extent or less in configuration, than standard bays; 2) areas of claimed waters linked to a coast by offshore features but which are not enclosed under the standard rules; and 3) areas of claimed seas which would, but for the claim, be high seas because they are not covered by any rules specially concerned with bays or delimitation of coastal waters (maria clausa*[45]). There are examples of historic waters belonging to all the three categories. But most of them are challenged and thereby lack universal acceptance.

This study could pose a definition to historic waters as: *Historic waters as considered from the maritime perspective are navigable and other waters at sea, in any dimension contiguous to the claimants' sovereign land territory, on which the state or states jointly have historically established jurisdiction that could be demarcated without variance for the claimant or among claimant if more than one under mutual consent and universal acceptance that has to be decided by a recognised international regime under the consensus ad idem of the parties to it.*

Under this definition many claims of historical waters may need a relook especially by the United Nations or any other body recognised by it.

However the world bodies are seemingly hesitant to examine the issue because discussions can only raise the complexities that may cause more problems and disputes in future.

Historic waters are influenced by heritage waters of a geopolitical entity.

- **Archipelagic waters**

Archipelagic waters are the waters around an archipelagic state in the sea within the baselines where the state can exercise sovereignty as over the land subject to the Convention and rules of international law. Archipelagic waters lie enclosed by the archipelagic baselines drawn in accordance with Article 47 of UNCLOS regardless their depth and distance from the coast. An archipelagic state may also have internal waters delimited by closing lines drawn within its archipelagic waters according to the Convention.

- **Territorial sea**

Under Article 2 (1) the sovereignty of a coastal state extends beyond its land territory, internal waters and archipelagic waters if an archipelagic state, to an adjacent belt of sea, described as the territorial sea. The sovereignty is similar to what the state enjoys over land. The territorial sea thereby becomes an extension of the state except that the sovereignty is to be exercised subject to the Convention and to other rules of international law. The maximum breadth a state is permitted to claim as territorial sea is 12 miles into the sea from the baseline. It is important to understand here that the often used term "territorial waters" is not the correct expression.

- **Contiguous zone**

  Contiguous zone is a maritime zone contiguous to the territorial sea where the coastal state can exercise control necessary to prevent infringement of customs, fiscal, immigration or sanitary laws and regulations within its territory or territorial sea and punish infringement of such laws and regulations committed within its territory or territorial sea. The breadth of the contiguous zone may not extend beyond 24 nautical miles from the baselines from which the breadth of territorial sea is measured.

  Contiguous zone is actually a buffer zone to suppress unlawful activities of the kind mentioned here occurring in the territory or territorial sea of the entity.

- **Exclusive economic zone**

  The exclusive economic zone (EEZ) is a specific and an important legal regime of UNCLOS. The zone extends from the baseline to 200 nautical miles into the sea to the maximum. Part V of UNCLOS deals with the EEZ which states it an area beyond and adjacent to the territorial sea, subject to the specific legal regime established part under which the rights and jurisdiction of the coastal state and the rights and freedoms of other states are governed by the relevant provisions of UNCLOS. The state has jurisdiction over the resources in the water column, seabed and below subject to the provisions of the Convention. The state, thereby, has sovereign rights,

  - for the purpose of exploring and exploiting, and conserving and managing the living and non-living natural resources of the water superjacent to the sea-bed, of the sea-bed and its subsoil and with regards to other activities for he economic exploitation and exploration of the zone such as the production of energy from water, currents and winds,

- for the establishment and use of artificial islands, installations and structures,
- maritime scientific research,
- protection and preservation of marine environment, and
- other rights and duties provided for in the Convention.

The Convention yields a wholesome package to the coastal state in the exclusive economic zone. The state will have to develop the expertise to exercise jurisdiction and avail the benefits. It is important that the coastal sate while exercising its rights and performing its duties under the Convention gives due regard to the rights and duties of other states and acts compatible with the provisions of the Convention. All states whether coastal or landlocked enjoy subject to the provisions of the Convention the freedoms referred to in Article 87 of navigation and over flight and for laying submarine cables and pipelines and other internationally lawful use of the sea related to these freedoms with due regard to the rights and duties of the coastal state in compliance with the its domestic laws and regulations and rules of international law on the subject.

Legal continental shelf

Legal continental shelf can extend beyond the exclusive economic zone where the surrounding continental area extends more than 200 nautical miles. Article 76 defines the Legal Continental Shelf (LCS) and outlines the methods to establish its outer limits in such cases. According to the article, the legal continental shelf of a coastal State shall comprise "*the natural prolongation of its land territory to the outer edge of the continental shelf, or to a distance of 200 nautical miles from the baselines of the territorial sea*", specifically excluding the deep ocean floor and its oceanic ridges. The important factors affecting the limits of a potential claim beyond the 200-nautical mile boundary are the 2,500-m isobath, the foot of the continental slope, the sediment thickness beyond the foot of the slope, and the relationship of the crust beneath the continental shelf to that onshore. The maximum limit of a claim cannot exceed 350 nautical miles from the baselines of the territorial sea or 100 nautical miles from the 2,500 m isobath. Within those limits the Legal Continental Shelf can be extended up to 60 nautical miles beyond the foot of the continental slope, called the Hedberg limit, or to where the sediment thickness is at least 1% of the shortest distance to the foot of the continental slope.[46] The Commission on the Limits of the Continental Shelf will examine those limits and engage states in the process called for by the Convention. The legal continental shelf is expected to extend the maritime zones of many countries further into the sea for which they will have to develop considerable expertise in exploitation, enforcement, and adjudication. In addition they will also meet with new neighbours across the legal continental shelf.

Search and rescue area

The ships at sea have an obligation to assist vessels in distress at sea traditionally as well as under international treaties. One such treaty is the International Convention for the Safety of Life at sea (SOLAS) 1974. The International Convention on Maritime Search and Rescue (SAR) of International Maritime Organisation created a search and rescue organisation that will coordinate a search and rescue plan at sea for the rescue of persons in distress at sea. The Convention was adopted on 27 April 1979 and came into force on 22 June 1985. Following the adoption, IMO's Maritime Safety Committee (MSC) divided the World Ocean into 13 search and rescue areas, in each of which countries responsible for search and rescue have delimited sear and rescue regions for which they are responsible. The countries have the obligation to provide search and rescue operations in accordance with the plan in these areas.

The Convention 1979 had certain limitations. It was revised in 19998 and entered into force in January 2000.

These areas form part of the maritime dimension of a country that has obligations within them for search and rescue operations. The coast guards are the agencies responsible for coordinating search and rescue operations in the ocean.

➤ Extraneous zones

There are various other maritime zones specific to country that it should consider in policy decisions on national governance. They are generally related to the ocean property regime. They are extraneous to the legally identified maritime zones to the extend they are purpose driven and varied and very much under a country's law compatible with international law. Such zones could be brought under various categories. They are examined below.

- There are research stations that are static and mobile. The country that owns them will be concerned about them and the area occupied by them will become fixed or variable maritime zones. Examples are research stations in Antarctica, whaling research stations and other platform based or robotic stations at sea.
- Deep seabed mining areas allotted to certain countries are outside their identified maritime zones. They need to be protected under national legislation under international legal consensus.
- Offshore platforms and other human made structures in the ocean for various operations of economic interest have to be protected by countries to establish rule of law as part of the national territory. They should have safety zones around them. They should also follow international regulations related to environment, etc. It will be the responsibility of the owner country. Under Article 60 (5) of UNCLOS the breadth of the safety zones will be determined by the coastal state taking into account applicable international standards. The maximum distance admissible from the platform is 500 m from the outer edge.
- There could be ocean habitat areas where human beings will reside in future. These too will settle in extraneous maritime zones for safety and protection.
- An interesting aspect is the zones where a nations ships including the warships ply. These ships should have a safe area around them in all the waters they are permitted to sail.

The country to which these ships belong will have to ensure their safety. It will be a variable maritime zone.

Sea Lines of Communication

Sea lines of communication (SLOC) followed by a nation for shipping is a critical passage route in terms of economics and safety for logistics movement. This becomes an important route for the nations shipping business and commerce for the carriage of goods by sea. It is the lifeline of a country and is applicable to all geopolitical entities whether they are landlocked, littoral or islands. SLOC, thereby becomes a maritime zone that is variable as well as joint for users.

SLOC are influenced by navigable waters. There will be SLOC only if the waters are navigable.

Sea Lanes of Traffic

Sea lanes of traffic (SLOT) is a term identified by the author in his research studies for routes that are normally followed by perpetrators of unlawful acts at and from the sea away and deviated from the normal passage routes followed by commercial shipping and other vessels on lawful passage and activities. They are variable and shifting lanes unlike the fixed SLOC. It is important for a country to understand the sea lanes of traffic around it and, if landlocked, the passages followed by the unlawful actors in the nearby seas in carrying out unlawful activities in their country. Obviously it will also include land and occasionally air routes through the neighbouring countries.

Choke Points

Though choke points are on the sea lines of communication, they are not part of them in the maritime strategic outlook of a country. They are special and need to be seen critically. The choke points can determine the approach of a country towards its maritime logistics chain. Blockade of choke points by the adversary can stifle a country's access to logistics. Adversaries, including unlawful activists, can block a choke point to deny resource to the target country. Resource denial is a strategic game plan. Choke points, therefore, figures seriously in the maritime security aspects of a country.

Chokepoints, as expressed here, are the heavily constrained parts of navigable waters. Only navigable waters will have choke points. To that extent, navigable water is that part of the ocean that is compatible for marine navigation. A major part of navigable water will be within the global commons. This is an important aspect of maritime transportation.

Maritime Border Areas

All the legislated maritime zones of a country across a recognised baseline and demarcated without conflict into the sea from the baseline define the maritime boundaries of a country. These maritime boundaries define various maritime boarder areas. The peculiarity of the ocean terrain is that the boundaries of jurisdiction are more with respect to the area than a particular boundary line unlike over the land habitats. Here the boundaries become important as a line enclosing an area when it is more with extraneous maritime zones including those that are variables. A vessel under way or making way in the high seas as well as in the territorial waters of another country where innocent passage is permitted has a virtual boundary moving along with it. It is important that such boundaries are formally respected under international law. This is an aspect that is important to ratify by countries so that no other vessel will have the right to curtail its movement unless the vessel is engaged in incriminating activities. Under this argument intentional and premeditated collision, restriction to manoeuvrability or boarding without reason could be brought under wrongful detention or curtailment to innocent passage.

The countries that are littoral or islands talk about coastal security. According to the finding of this study, coastal security is a misnomer. But the coastal area or zone including internal waters of a country can be included in one of the maritime border areas of a geopolitical entity.

Maritime Neighbours

Every nation with a shore towards the ocean will have a maritime neighbour with whom it will share a maritime boundary. The boundaries will be demarcated to establish long standing maritime relations. However, there are many maritime boundaries that are yet to be demarcated under *consensus ad idem* as there are conflicting view points. These maritime boundaries will remain notional or seriously disputed.

Maritime Disputes

Maritime disputes between nations can be about boundaries that separate them arcos the maritime zones or based on claims that are longstanding on land territories that could be inhabited or uninhabited. These disputes are unlikely to resolve in future as the international scenario is changing and use of force is not generally accepted, especially in territorial issues. Dispute resolution by means other than use of force is the only possible methods. Maritime disputes are challenging issues to the world. The resolutions may come, perhaps, when the disputed islands and ocean areas such as Senkaku or Diayou islands or Malvinas or Falkland Islands are brought under joint or multiple governance or similar procedures in future. This study does not agree the disputed areas in the ocean are potential flash points in the world. More so they are potential areas of opportunities for joint governance under mutual benefit that is yet to be examined by world entities.

Maritime Forces

A nation's maritime forces and their deployment are indicators of its maritime prowess and wisdom. The navy, coast guard, police, customs, and other forces engage in the tasks associated with them according to their design and purpose. The efficiency of these forces is another area of interest that determines the maritime dimension of the country to which it belongs.

Islands

Islands are part of ocean property. At the same time they are also considered extension of the mainland within its maritime dimension. Islands are therefore seen in this study as part of land as well as the ocean through its ocean property regime. The islands, therefore, hold dual values in maritime dimension.—one, as the extension of land and two, as part of the ocean property regime where the term "ocean property" is a maritime dimension of a geopolitical entity. Islands are ocean properties for a maritime nation under the geoproperty concept. The researcher finds that such a perception will advocate the principles of national security in a more effective way while considering island security. Islands can provide recluse for transnational crime syndicates besides being strategic chokers. The island property comprises island and rock territories.

Islands are two types: offshore and near shore. This is applicable to all entities that are not landlocked, according to this study.

Territories

The 73 territories established in this study are owned by nine of the other entities of the world. All these territories are coastlands or islands. Their maritime dimensions will also be included while assessing the maritime security factors of a country that holds it.

Maritime Transportation

The first advantage the humans identified with the ocean was mobility. It has not changed since then. People are depended on it for moving from one point to another and carrying goods in large volumes across the ocean. Today, the world is totally depended on ocean for carriage of goods. More than 90 per cent of world cargo moves through ocean. Oceans drive globalisation as a catalyst to various ancillary inventions like communication and information technology. Maritime transportation and the country's involvement in it is a major dimension that any entity has to examine while analysing about its maritime security aspects and the challenges the country faces.

Ports and Harbours

Ports and harbours are involved in transportation. However, this study looks at them separately as ports and harbours are not just the supporting elements of maritime transportation but also the integral part of the overall national security dimension. Ports and harbours facilitate various other aspects of national security related to the ocean and land. They are the entry and exit points involved in transportation. They link the ocean with the land habitat.

Ocean Resource Potential

The identified ocean resources are the living resources and nonliving resources. The living resources comprise general fisheries, planktons, nektons, benthos, pearl, and various other marine organisms and benthic animals. Most of them are renewable sources of protein rich food. About 90 to 95 per cent of the living resources of the ocean are found in the EEZ.

Nonliving resources are water, oil, gas, lime mud deposit, and minerals (magnesium, bromine, sand, gravel aggregates and placer deposits, phosphate, calcareous deposits, nodules containing manganese, copper, cobalt and nickel, and hydrothermal mineral deposits containing zinc, copper, iron, silver, and gold).

The potential of ocean resources should be included in the ocean property mapping.

Weather and Climate

Ocean controls weather through heat exchange. The heat exchange can get affected when the ocean is damaged. Ocean around the world could become an unknown reservoir of potent gases like nitrous oxide, hydrogen sulphide, etc., near the coastal areas from land wash and runoffs of fertilisers and other chemicals. Nitrous oxide is a potent climate change gas. Hydrogen sulphide can affect fisheries industry. According to some estimates nitrous oxide is 200-300 times more potent than carbon dioxide. The sea in and around the storage area of such gases becomes low in oxygen leading to the death of bottom living marine life. Increased input of nutrients from human activities has been said to be the cause. Such conditions can induce changes in climatic conditions like the monsoon.

Weather and climate, and induced changes become part of the maritime dimension of a country. Primarily the ocean controls them. Each country has its own attributes with the effect of weather and climate which are global phenomena in the totality of the maritime dimension.

Marine Environment

Keeping marine environment free from pollution is vital from the point of view of environmental security. Marine pollution in the ocean is a neglected area of study. There are periodic reports of metal and oil pollution near major cities along the ocean rim, more particularly in the coastal areas and along the oil tanker routes. There are reports of chlorinated hydrocarbons, various chemical metabolites and other toxic compounds in the ocean environment owing to large human inputs from many countries. Continuous monitoring of the marine environment for pollution is essential to evaluate the state of health of the ocean and to provide a basis for sound remedial measures against further pollution of the seawater and its organisms, particularly in coastal waters. The pollution level of an ocean contributes to the assessment of the maritime dimension of the associated country.

Maritime Resolve

Maritime resolve is the intent and the ability of a government to exploit the ocean for national objectives. The tangibility of the maritime dimensions so far discussed varies. Some of them even vary within themselves. Maritime resolve works on them and assimilates them towards national strength as a separate dimension. Without the desired maritime resolve an entity will not be able to turn the ocean towards its benefit. The resolve has to exist within the political system of the entity.

Maritime Signature

Analysing a geopolitical entity interactively in terms of its factors of maritime security and maritime dimensions are essential for understanding its overall maritime perspectives. A nation has to do it for itself and for others in terms of its policies on its geostrategic aspects in the international scenario.

The factors and dimensions provide for a maritime signature for each geopolitical entity. Most of them, or in fact all the identified geopolitical entity today lacks such signature as none of them have made an effort to examine their maritime factors and dimensions together to identify their maritime signatures. The importance here is not the signature, but the fact that each country will have a separate signature and that too will be varying as a function of time. The objective for every entity is to apply its maritime signature in the best possible way to maximise its national security. An entity will have to craft its maritime strategy after fully appreciating its maritime signature.

The sharpness of the maritime signature will depend upon the way the country is aware of its factors and dimensions and amalgamate them through policy decisions to maximise its ocean property returns.

The sharper the maritime signature, the stronger will be the desire and drive for integration. Maritime signature is an intangible concept that could only be appreciated in the overall factor and dimension of maritime security relative to the entity as the concept of maritime security is a ghost protocol.

Revisiting Maritime Security

Considering the human landclasp syndrome and the affinity of the humans to the land based governance of national security, it is not possible to perceive maritime security as an exclusive approach to maximise national security. The issues are much more complex than what could be envisaged. First the national security elements can be examined as separate and mutually inclusive. Maritime security does not have separate elements. It is required to identify the competent elements of national security for amalgamation with maritime security aspects taking into consideration the maritime signature of a geopolitical entity. Maritime signature varies between countries and within a country with respect to the policies of governance. Based on identification, it could be examined in relation to the elements of national security.

Maritime Security and National Security: Comparison of Elements

Maritime security has been defined as "*the all encompassing complementary faction of national security of a maritime nation from an ocean specific terrain assessment applicable to that nation.*" The concept is a component of national security, where the game is played relative to a terrain entirely different from land. Whereas the governance of national security is focused on land. Therefore, it is important to examine the relative aspects of national security elements with respect to maritime security before integrating maritime security with national security governance. The elements of national security have to be examined from the perspective of being complemented by corresponding elements of maritime security.

Maritime security being an all encompassing complementary faction of national security is not a standalone concept. For this reason, ideally, maritime security should comprise of only those elements that would complement all or part of the elements of national security. There should not be any element exclusive to maritime security. In that case the hypothesis of this study, possibility of integration of maritime security with national security becomes evasive and moves out in a different direction where it has to be chased for furthering the study. In any case, the complementary factions of maritime security are to be seen collectively with the overall elements of maritime security.

A comparative assessment of identified national security elements with respect to their equivalence in maritime security is given in Table. 4.2 Prior to that the elements are briefly examined.

1. **Military Security (m_s)**
   Military security is the overall military capability that is necessary to safeguard the interests of a nation in which the ocean plays an important and terrain specific part. Hence military security is very much an aspect of maritime security. It involves all the maritime forces that deal in military, preventive and preemptive defence and related strategy in relation to the ocean. It is considered a terrain specific independent element that is integral to overall military security. This establishes a complementary element of military security in maritime security.

2. **Economic Security (e_{s1})**
   Ocean property regime collectively with its elements is an economic bargain. Maximisation of ocean property regime maximises ocean based economic security. Integrating ocean with overall national economic security is necessary for it. Economic activities related to the ocean involves exploration of hydrocarbon, metals and minerals, commercial fishing and seafood production, shipping and transportation and various other economic activities including energy, tourism, etc. Future will identify many such ventures that will encourage economic security. This establishes a complementary element of economic security in maritime security.

3. **Resource Security (r_s)**
   "Ocean resources" is another element of ocean property. They are exclusive though interactive with economic security and other elements of national security. Ocean resource will

require exclusive governance. Under such consideration it complements the resource security element of national security.

4. **Border Security (b_s)**
   There are marked differences between land borders and maritime borders as seen while examining the maritime dimensions. Borders at sea have to be seen as zones or areas and not as straight-line borders. Coastline is not a border in relation to the ocean. The border zones are also seen from the angle of protection and obligation under varying rights and jurisdiction. Border security is much more complex at sea than over land. But the landclasp syndrome and perils of the sea keeps the activities over land extremely sensitive. Border security element of maritime security complements national security in this regard, though there is much to understand about it in security planning.

5. **Demographic Security (d_{s1})**
   The relevance of demographic security with maritime security is in its close relation with the coastal or near coastal zones of an entity. People move towards coastal zones in the process of internal as well as external migration. According to census reports, coastal population is ever increasing. Don Hinrichsen, United Nations consultant and author, observes that overwhelming bulk of human population is concentrated on just 10 per cent of land area of the earth's surface along or near the coasts.[47] As the coastal population increases demographics can sway the pattern of ocean governance. This in turn impinges on demographic security affairs. The element is, therefore, complementary to national security.

6. **Disaster Security (d_{s2})**
   Ocean based disasters are different from land based ones though the impact of any disaster is a dead ender for life and property, and damage to environment[48] that could be irreversible. Ocean disasters are managed through contingency plans and coordinated activities under national plans as in the case of disaster management over land. It is advisable to examine ocean based disasters along with national governance on disaster security as a complementary faction.

7. **Energy Security (e_{s2})**
Ocean is a powerhouse of energy and therefore a large contributor to the energy needs of the world. The ocean property element of energy is ocean resources. Ocean energy element requires exclusive governance. The element is complementary to the land-based energy governance. Offshore energy is a separate faculty for integration with the corresponding element of national security. It complements energy security.

8. **Geostrategic Security (g_{s1})**
Ocean has been playing a major role in the geostrategic context of nations since the early days. The equivalent part of maritime security element is ocean property in all its aspects including environment that will have universal implication. The ocean complements the element of geostrategic security.

9. **Informational Security (i_s)**
Information flow also involves intelligence gathering and information trafficking. Ocean is used for a variety of information gathering by evesdropping, clandestine research, illegal survey, etc. These activities as well as securing own information forms part of national security governance in a nation's governance activity. Hence ocean becomes complementary to informational security governance in a limited way

10. **Food Security (f_s)**
Ocean delves into food security seriously. That is also one of the reasons for the population explosion in the coastal areas. Food is one of the factors of human dependency on ocean. This is likely to increase in future. Maritime security, therefore, has a complementary element of food security.

11. **Health Security (h_s)**
Ocean can affect human health by the migration of microorganisms through water bodies as well as provide ingredients for developing new medicines supporting research in pharmacology in a credible manner. Ocean based health security element is complementary to the element of health security in the national security matrix.

12. **Ethnic Security (e_{s3})**
    Ethnicity is primarily affected by migration which was mostly land-based. But the influence of ocean is visible in the migratory tendencies from the density of the coastal population all over the world. It is increasing. Ethnicity also changes through illegal migration of people by sea. Hence ethnic security has its complementary faction in maritime security.

13. **Environmental Security (e_{s4})**
    Ocean has an exclusive environmental domain. Environment is a separate element of ocean property though it is directly linked with the entire planet. Marine environment has an effect on issues related to climate, sea level rise, etc., that will influence national security. These are for the long term studies. Maritime environmental aspects, thereby, complements the element of environmental security.

14. **Cyber Security (c_s)**

    Cyber security is in a terrain (cyber space) that is exclusive to itself under the terrain specificity approach to national security. But its impact is felt in the activities related to governance in the other terrains too. Hence, it is also natural to the ocean terrain. From the point of view of national security, the element becomes contributory in relation to maritime security. It cannot be cancelled totally or as null. It is, therefore, considered as a contributory element with respect to national security modeling.

15. **Genomic Security (g_{s2})**
    Genomic security is another exclusive element with respect to terrain specificity as it operates within the genomic terrain. But the maritime aspect may have either complementary or contributory role in the extended future in the yet to be seriously developed genomic security element of national security. In the meantime the element of genomic security will have null influence in relation to the national security matrix.

Table 4.2 gives the equivalency of maritime elements to national security elements and their symbols for modeling by assigning values appropriate to a geopolitical entity. The symbols identified in this study are similar to national security element with a subscript depicting maritime security as (mar) indicating the element is complementary or contributory. The null element is subscripted and preceded by n0. The symbolisation is basically to appreciate the national security elements for modeling studies and modeling. The symbols can be changed and used as required by planners and modelers.

Table 4.2 Equivalence of Maritime Elements with National Security Elements

	Elements of National Security	*Symbol*	*Maritime Equivalent*	*Symbol*
1	Military Security	m_s	Complementary	$m_{s(mar)}$
2	Economic Security	e_{s1}	Complementary	$e_{s1(mar)}$
3	Resource Security	r_s	Complementary	$r_{s(mar)}$
4	Border Security	b_s	Complementary	$b_{s(mar)}$
5	Demographic Security	d_{s1}	Complementary	$d_{s1(mar)}$
6	Disaster Security	d_{s2}	Complementary	$d_{s2(mar)}$
7	Energy security	e_{s2}	Complementary	$e_{s2(mar)}$
8	Geostrategic Security	g_{s1}	Complementary	$g_{s1(mar)}$
9	Informational Security	i_s	Complementary	$i_{s(mar)}$
10	Food Security	f_s	Complementary	$f_{s(mar)}$
11	Health security	h_s	Complementary	$h_{s(mar)}$
12	Ethnic security	e_{s3}	Complementary	$e_{s3(mar)}$
13	Environmental security	e_{s4}	Complementary	$e_{s4(mar)}$
14	Cyber Security	c_s	Contributory	$c_{s(mar)}$
15	Genomic Security	g_{s2}	Null	$n_0 g_{s2(mar)}$

The study identifies 13 complementary elements, one contributory element and one null element (depicted n_0). There are no elements exclusive to maritime security in the identified concept of national security. In that case the entire study related to national security so far would be negative especially in the assumption of terrain specificity.

However, the next examination is to see whether there is any likelihood of an exclusive and yet to be identified element of national security originating from the concept of maritime security in future.

It doesn't seem to be so in this study from the examination of the characteristics prescribed for qualification of an element. The possibility is very remote. It also confirms that maritime security is a complementary faction of national security and thereby possible to integrate in governance with it.

This study also identifies the concept of "ocean property,"[50] the "quantum" of which will be the prime parameter in decision making in maritime security matters. National security of a maritime nation can be enhanced effectively by managing its ocean property.

National Security and Maritime Security

National security concept, as envisaged, is based over land, the primary human habitat. But the interesting aspect is that the ocean is also over the land and thereby part of it. It is an established fact. A very special find of this study is that ocean, as it is today, is a geophysical terrain different from land terrain, which is nothing but a giant flood that prevails over land. It is also threatening to rise audaciously. The worst is that the flood waters are likely to rise and become more vigorous in future sinking the world deeper. In this process, the ocean will swallow more land. From that perspective, ocean becomes an exclusive geophysical terrain.

The objective here is to integrate maritime security with national security so that the ghost (in the) protocol of maritime security finds a body real for handling it right earnestly and practically in governance to maximise national security.

The ocean presently is an exclusive geophysical terrain under the terrain specificity principles of national security. It comprises the subsoil below seabed, seabed (ocean floor), water column in various layers[51], continental shelf, surface-air interface, sea-land interface, islands and inland extensions. All these entities will reflect in the maritime security statement of a maritime nation. The challenges will be terrain specific.

Each element of national security has to be assessed with respect to its equivalent, where specified, in maritime security for realistic assessment of ends, ways and means for achieving the goal. The elements thereafter have to be used for strategic mapping of maritime security.

This study could not find any strategy driven models of maritime security being used for integration with national security. Maritime strategy is not deeply and perfectly integral with the overall national security governance wherever it exists as on date. There are many generic and application models. One such model examined was that proposed by an Integrated Analysis Group of the National Defence College, New Delhi.[52] Most of them were meant to answer the "hows" and "whys" of national security from the point of military operations that would enable a government to coordinate, discuss, debate and decide the required course of action.[53] Almost all the models lack the idea envisaged in this study—integrating maritime security with national security. For that a government has to understand by competent analysis the parameters of maritime security specific to the entity that is being governed from the factors and dimensions preferably in a diagnostic manner. The model could evolve from this.

The parameters that can be inferred mostly on a varying scale from such diagnostics will include the following among various others that are entity specific:

- Strategic advantage acquired by geolocation of the entity.
- Potential to derive benefits from the ocean property available to it.
- Jurisdiction of ocean it can assimilate under various maritime zones.
- Nature and characteristics of its ocean policy statement.
- Nature and characteristics of its maritime forces.
- Human intellectual strength in relation to maritime security—policy makers, bureaucrats, force personnel, strategic thinkers, scholars and academicians, legal experts, ocean inclined public, institutional thinkers and scholars, writers and authors, etc.
- Scientific and technological knowhow.
- State of economy and funds appropriated for strategic application.
- Viability of maritime doctrine.

Understanding the diagnostic parameters of maritime security for an entity is very important to examine the hypothesis that a model can be built for maritime security of the entity and its feasibility for integration with national security. It is only through such diagnostic approach the ghost protocol of maritime security can be integrated with the national security effectively. Without integration, the subject will remain a terrain specific ghost protocol. The ghost protocol in any case will block the meta knowledge, the knowledge about the knowledge of integration, when handled individually, especially when assured uncertainties en route can scuttle the entire process of integration.

Under the concept of integration, the matrix of maritime security is relatively smaller than the matrix of national security since the former falls within it. National security has 15 elements that are symbolically assessed. The model builder or analyst is free to choose the elements with respect to the rows and columns according to situational priority and as perceived by the government. Whereas, in maritime security, elements are better compared with national security as 13 complementary elements, one contributory element and one null element. These are compared in the matrices below.

$$NS = \begin{pmatrix} m_s & e_{s1} & r_s & b_s & d_{s1} \\ d_{s2} & e_{s2} & g_{s1} & i_s & f_s \\ h_s & e_{s3} & e_{s4} & c_s & g_{s2} \end{pmatrix} > \begin{pmatrix} m_{s(mar)} & e_{s1(mar)} & r_{s(mar)} & b_{s(mar)} & d_{s1(mar)} \\ d_{s2(mar)} & e_{s2(mar)} & g_{s1(mar)} & i_{s(mar)} & f_{s(mar)} \\ h_{s(mar)} & e_{s3(mar)} & e_{s4(mar)} & c_{s(mar)} & n_0 g_{s2(mar)} \end{pmatrix}$$

(where $g_{s2(mar)}$ is a null element (n_0))

The matrices show that the overall national security elements are larger than the complementing maritime security elements being inclusive of them. Hence the choice for NS_{max} is only through integration. Any other forms of national security governance are not likely to provide maximum yield and thereby will cause national security deficit in spite of having strong supporting attributes.

Integration of maritime security with national security is feasible. It is necessary since strategic planning of maritime security in isolation is not a prudent idea of governance which in any case will be based on land perspective. Cohesive amalgamation of national security elements with maritime security complementary elements is possible only by such integration as a national policy.

Conclusions

Throughout the study, the concept of maritime security is deliberated as a ghost protocol that requires integration with national security for compatibility in proactive governance under terrain difference. National security governance is under land based approach for obvious reasons. Hence a concept under any other geophysical terrain will be a ghost protocol in relation to the approach of governance. This is the primary argument on which the hypothesis is based. It is not an assumption. The studies show that 1) maritime security as a concept exists in relation to the ocean terrain; 2) it exists as a ghost protocol as human system and its governance are land based; 3) it can be integrated, being clear and present, with the land based national security governance; 4) national governance (towards maxismising national security as perceived by governments) is land based; 5) maritime security will no more remain a ghost protocol if integrated with national security and 6) the nations will be able to acquire maximum yield from the concept according to the sharpness of the maritime signature they appreciate by integrating maritime security with national security. The yield from any other form of governance of maritime security including absence of such governance will always be minimal in relation to integrated governance.

This is the crux of the study.

Here, more than an assumption, the attempt was to prove maritime security a ghost protocol. That is why maritime security is a curious case. Once proven a ghost protocol, the concept is easy to assimilate for integration. It cannot be an assumption. An assumption has the disadvantage of abstractive assimilation. Such assimilation will make the concept with which it is integrated either cave in under cavity or buckle under pressure if the assumption turns otherwise. Hence it was necessary to examine maritime security to understand its relative reality with human governance. Maritime security exists because the ocean terrain is a high yield provider perhaps as much if not more than the land. It becomes a ghost protocol being in another geophysical terrain which is not the basic terrain on which decisions on national security maximisation are taken and executed. It would not have been a ghost protocol if human governance was not under the landclasp syndrome.

Everything about the sea is "at and from the sea" in a land based approach. It has been highlighted in this study as a finding that human governance is likely to remain land based.

Once appreciated, the ghost protocol needs to be strategically examined for integration with national security.

NOTES

1 IMO, www.imo.org/About/Pages/Default.aspx, accessed 10 April 2013.

2 The word trilateral is of great significance in maritime security as there are many trilateral connections in boundary issues in maritime matters.

3 Roy-Choudhury, Rahul, *India's Maritime Security,* New Delhi; Knowledge World, 2000, p. xviii.

4 Ibid., p. xiii.

5 Roy, Mihir K., *War in the Indian Ocean,* New Delhi; Lancer Publications, 1995, pp. 261-2.

6 UNCLOS is also known as Law of the Sea Convention and the Law of the Sea Treaty.

7 According to the *Wordsworth Concise English Dictionary,* Hertfordshire; Wordsworth Reference, 1988.

8 Saha, A.N, compiler, *Mitra's Commercial and Legal Dictionary*, Calcutta; Eastern Law House, 1990, p. 474.

9 Corbett, Julian S. *Some Principles of Maritime Strategy,* Annapolis; Naval Institute Press, 1988, p. 15.

10 Menon, Raja, *Maritime Strategy and Continental Wars,* London; Frank Cass, 1998, pp. xv-xvi.

11 Institute for National Strategic Studies, *Strategic Assessment 1999: Priorities of a Turbulent World,* Washington, D.C.; National Defence University, 1999, pp. 308-14.

12 Ibid., p. 312.

13 Gaston, James C., (ed.), *Grand Strategy and the Decision Making Process,* Washington, D.C.; National Defence University Press, 1992, p. 13.

14 Paleri, Prabhakaran, "The Concept of National Security and a Maritime Model for India," doctoral dissertation, Department of Defence and Strategic Studies, University of madras, Chennai, February 2002.

15 Ibid.

16 Ibid.

17 Paleri, Prabhakaran, *National Security: Imperatives and Challenges,* New Delhi; Tata McGraw-Hill Publishing Limited, 2008, pp. 104-16.

18 Winning a war without fighting is still the best option.

19 Every identified terrain has its own exclusive characteristics.

20 "Future Warfare Based on Unmanned Technology," *The New Indian Express*, Kozhikode, 9 Jul 2013, p. 9.

21 NATO has 28 members across North America and Europe, 22 participants in "partnership for Peace," with 15 others who involve in institutionalised dialogue process. The recorded naval force of the NATO Navy comprises research vessels. These vessels could be used for many purposes within its purview like a coalition mission for the collective security of its members. Stephen Saunders (Edit), *Jane's Fighting Ships 2007-2008, Cambridge, Cambridge University Press, 2007.*

22 Protection and Preservation of marine environment and Prevention and Control of marine pollution, Indian Coast Guard Sources, Directorate of Operations, Coast Guard Headquarters, New Delhi.

23 Law of the Sea, www.un.org, accessed 12 July 2013.

24 GOP Scuttles Law-of-Sea Treaty, blogs.wsj.com/washwire/2012/07/16/gop-opposition-scuttles-law-of-sea-treaty/, accessed 12 January 2013.

25 Rumsfeld Still Opposes the Law of the Sea Treaty, www.washingtontimes.com/news/2012/jun/14/rumsfeld-hits-law-of-sea-treaty/?page=all, accessed 12 January 2013.

26 1958 Convention on the High Seas, untreaty.un.org/ilc/texts/instruments/english/ conventions/8_1_1958_ high_ seas.pdf, accessed 15 July 2012.

27 Article 86, UNCLOS.

28 According to the author, a country needs enforcement friendly legislation. The term "enforcement friendly legislation" does not mean the legislation is with a bias or favourable to the enactors or enforcers of it. It means, as expressed here,

1. existence of legislation that clearly depicts the unlawful activities and punitive measures that serves the purpose of deterrence,
2. clarity of jurisdiction,
3. absence of limitations or constraints in enforcing it under intent (enforceability in the society),
4. expediency of judicial system and
5. resistant to abuse.

29 Paleri, Prabhakaran, *Coast Guards of the World and Emerging Maritime Threats,* Tokyo, Ocean Policy Research Foundation, 2009, p. 116.

30 en.wikipedia.org/wiki/ReCAAP, accessed 24 January 2013.

31 Vego, Milan N., Naval *Strategy and Operations in Narrow Seas,* London; Frank Cass, 1999, p. 11.

32 Menzel, Manfred , "Port Development Experience", Conference Compendium: India International Maritime Expo™ 2001,Mumbai, p. 43. Freedom Ship is a futuristic concept of a floating city at sea, 1.2 km long, 25 stories high, traveling around the globe every two years.

33 Paleri, Prabhakaran, Resource management in a Sinking World—Land and Geoproperty Rights, paper presented at the International Conference on Decisions in Management and Social Sciences for Sustainable Management, Indian Institute of Social Welfare and Business Management, Kolkata, 14 December 2009.

34 There was a unique case in a court in New Zealand where, for the first time in the world, an alleged climate refugee from Kiribati sought a decision for remaining in New Zealand on expiry of his visa on the grounds that his country was sinking under climate change. "Rising Seas may Give Rise to 1st Climate Refugee," *The Times of India,* Kozhikode, 18 Oct 2013, p.16. The court, however, rejected his appeal on the ground that he was not eligible as he was not a refugee under the UN Refugee Convention. The court also observed that he was not going to face persecution on return as his position was not different from any other Kiribati national. The argument was "unconvincing," the court observed. "New Zealand Court Rejects Man's Plea to be First Climate Refugee"' *The Times of India,* Kozhikode, 27 November 2013, p. 14.

35 Paleri, n.14.

36 Gupta, Ranjan, *The Indian Ocean: A Political Geography,* New Delhi; Marwah Publications, 1979, p. 1.

37 Check the Russian visitor to India. Russian Consulate Publication, Mumbai. *Afanasy Nikitin's Voyage beyond Three Seas--1466-1472.* Afanasi Nikitin died in 1472.

38 Gupta, n 32, p.2

39 Sakhuja, Vijay, Indian Ocean and the Safety of Sea Lines of Communication, *Strategic Analysis.* August, 2001: 689-702.

40 Conditional routing like hugging a cost out of fear of pirates.

41 The then Sudan has been divided into Republic of the Sudan (also called North Sudan) and South Sudan after the latter seceded from it on 9 July 2011 under consent.

42 Cruise Missile Strikes on Afghanistan and Sudan. en.wikipedia.org/wiki/Cruise_missile_strikes_on_Afghanistan_and Sudan_(August_1998). According to the United States, the attack was in retaliation of the terrorist attacks on the US embassies in Kenya and Tanzania.

43 Coastline paradox is a term used in this to explain the complexity of the coast and everything associated with it including the term "coastal security" that the concept of coastline is under indefinite variation making it a term that may not exist in an identified measure at any given moment hence not suitable to be used in border science or strategy related to land ocean interface. Instead the coastal paradox demands the coast to be termed as an area rather than a line as in the case of land border. This paradox extends further into the sea making all the marmite ozone measurements as areas

rather than perimeters that are under constant variation from the point of national security as a border area. Under the coastline paradox by being a vector and under constant alteration, coastline becomes just an abstract line that is not stable.

44 en.wikipedia.org/wiki/Coastline_paradox, accessed 16 January 2013.

45 A navigable body of water, such as a sea, that is under the jurisdiction of one nation and closed to all others.

46 Law of the Sea, www.linz.gov.nz, accessed 5 September, 2001.

47 Hinrichsen, Don., The Coastal Population Explosion, The Next 25 Years: Global Issues, Trends and Future Challenges for US National Ocean and Coastal Policy, p.27. www. oceanserivce. Noaa .gov/ websites/ retiredsites/ natdia_pdf/3.hinrichsen.pdf, accessed 17 January 2013.

48 Damage to environment is to be seen as collateral to the dead ender damage to life and property.

49 Paleri, Prabhakaran, *Maritime Security: The Unlawful Dimension,* New Delhi; Magnum Books Pvt. Ltd, 2010, p.31.

50 "Ocean Property" is the research-based modification of the term "ocean wealth" initially identified in the research problem, and comprising ocean resources, ocean advantage, ocean environment, and island properties of a maritime nation.

51 Rao, T.S.S. and Ray C. Griffiths, *Understanding the Indian Ocean,* Paris; UNESCO Publishing, 1998, p. 143. The water column is divided into Intermediate Layer (500-1500m), Deep Layer (below 1500m), and Surface Layer (0-500m) in oceanographic studies.

52 National Defence College, New Delhi, Report on Seminar on "Maritime Strategy for India, December 2, 1996, p.22.

53 Ibid.

Chapter 5

MARITIME SECURITY AND STRATEGIC PROCLAMATIONS

Till UNCLOS virtually drew lines on water across the ocean in the late 20th century, maritime strategy was naval strategy; thereafter maritime strategy has been hunting to settle[1] anew.

Maritime security is a concept that is often talked about in exclusive terms. This study asserts that the concept exists as a ghost protocol in isolation because humans are naturally huddled over land under the landclasp syndrome. Therefore, a strategic approach to govern maritime security will require integration of the concept with the overall national security governance for better results. Any attempt to examine or govern the concept of maritime security tends to become ghostly appreciation without serious outcome on the ground if handled in isolation or exclusivity. That is one of the reasons why humans have not been able to tame the ocean around them to maximise the gain from ocean property towards national security in spite of many strategic proclamations.

Ocean property in this explanation sums up all that the ocean can provide the world towards human wellbeing which in turn is what the national security governance is aimed at. Ocean was a mystery organ of the world in the ancient perception. Associated with the perils of the sea, the belief systems lead to a world of fantasy enamoured with weird tales of adventure, dodgy and demonic sea creatures, mysterious pirates, treasure chests and lockers, moving islands, flying ships, etc.

The ocean which is just a terrain of a different kind was even perceived as a god or had a god dominating it in certain belief systems. God is the ultimate in human belief system craving for security. No other terrain has a god safeguarding and ruling it among the believers. Many believed ocean had monsters living there. There were ships fitted out with weapons to attack not only enemy ships but also to lacerate imaginary sea monsters in the ancient days.

The focus gradually shifted to warfare, unlawful activities and exploratory and other voyages on specific purposes—trade, missionary activities, religious conversions, colonisation, adventure, fisheries exploitation, whale hunting, etc.. UNCLOS, the only evidence of overall ocean literacy and rational awareness in the world among governments is very recent. UNCLOS set in motion a kind of ocean renaissance in 1982 after 25 years of hard slog and debates—all reinforcing ocean literacy. But there were many strategic proclamations of maritime security starting with the ancient world. These varying viewpoints in time had also influenced strategic thinking on maritime affairs. An examination of these proclamations is one of the approach modes to understand integrated maritime security on which this study is focused.

Maritime Security and Strategic Aspects

Maritime security has increasingly been researched and spoke from the standpoint of the complexities of the ocean since ancient days. The concept changed over time. Today, and seemingly so in future, maritime security has to be seen as complementary to overall national security, and not as a standalone and inexplicable concept. Maritime strategic aspect should be in the overall geostrategic context. The strategic perception needs to be based against this background even while analysing the proclamations so far and beyond.

First, it is important to understand the meanings of strategy and its aspects. The difference between strategy and the related term, tactics is important in this examination. Though often used in every walk of life in modern times, the terms are not so simple, especially in their differentiation, to understand.

Both the terms originate from the study of military operations. Strategy is about the overall panning and conduct of military operations in its original sense. Strategy is a plan of action for achieving predetermined goals through objectives. It is a dynamic function. It is not a wish list, desire or belief system per se. Strategy needs to be visualised, focused, crafted, executed, evaluated, corrected, revised and then at the end, put back reactively into the system in a closed loop, abandoning any vain features identified subsequent to its implementation. Process of strategy changes only when the goal changes. It has to be recast completely thereafter.

In another way, strategy can be defined as the art and skill of using stratagems. In such case, a stratagem is the “smaller” version of strategy aimed at achieving an objective. But this definition does not hold much value in the macro sense of strategy. A stratagem is more a manoeuvre that could even be cunning, wily and deceptive at times. Such manoeuvres need not be an ingredient of national governance in its overall appreciation. Strategy does not have to be under imposture. It is a desired and recommended postulation of this study. It is not just under ethical studies alone. But strongly recommended for long term effect in interactive relations of human systems of all kinds, nations included.

A term that is closely associated with strategy is tactics. Tactics too come very close to stratagem though it is not exactly so. Knowledge seekers will always have difficulty in explaining the difference between strategy and tactics. Crafting and implementing them appropriately are relatively less difficult. But any strategist will have to appreciate them in clear perspective. Tactics though can best be explained as a manoeuvre to achieve an objective towards an identified and desired goal, strategy is the overall plan of action towards the goal. Tactics, used in singular, is contained in strategy. Strategy generates tactical manoeuvres. While the overall strategy continues as long as the goal is unchanged, the tactics used in achieving each objective towards the goal may change en route. Some may fail. Tactics thereby becomes an expedient for achieving a goal. The military definition of tactics is very clear. The military sets tactical objectives according to strategy. This study defines tactics as the art and science of the expedient processes for securing objectives set by strategy. And, what one has to understand here is that tactics lead to operations. Or rather operation is the next step in the line of tactics.

In its simple sense, the term strategy is larger than the term tactics as events transpire. While tactics is directed towards an objective for achieving a goal, more than one game of tactics will be required to achieve a strategic goal through the desired objectives. Strategy is the art and science of developing and using the necessary ingredients to maximise power to influence the objectives that are predetermined. Whereas, tactics is an instant of achieving an objective in the long chain of objectives towards strategic fulfilment. Strategy could be national, corporate, military or any other entity-based objective to achieve an authentic goal. In this study, it is used in the national and global sense of maritime affairs of taming the ocean for the best benefit of people towards their wellbeing which is the obligation of governments. Maximising the wellbeing of the people is the goal of governance. Wellbeing is national security. National security strategy should lead towards the goal of maximising the wellbeing of people.

Historical Perspectives—Maritime Strategy

It is left to cognitive hypothesis to appreciate and conclude when the world became aware of the ocean to develop maritime strategy for survival and wellbeing. Testing such hypothesis is possible in exclusivity. It can be otherwise generalised without deviating from the original proposition of the study.

It is argued by many that humans are unaware of the importance of the ocean. Certainly they would have been ignorant, in the very early days when they clung on to land for their dear lives. But they did appreciate the importance of the ocean slowly and rightfully as it came natural to them from the very ancient times. There are records of evidences to it. One of the reasons for noninvolvement with the ocean in the very ancient period could have been the absence of the need to venture out over the ocean for long periods and the apprehensions of moving into sea without secure platforms for support. The geographical entities of human systems of the past remained locally centred and almost in isolation without the need to get across the ocean. Ocean was a moat rather than a medium. The migratory tendencies were satisfied by passage over land. No one ever thought seriously about moving across the ocean in the early days of human settlement. Even those who dared to venture out into the sea would have gone ahead only up to where they could have been still in sight of land. Some of the geographical entities were continental land powers. They held on to land except for trading in a limited way. Military naval campaigns were not their forte in spite of the capabilities they had. Of course, the international system as it existed then was not interdependent and competitive as it is today. Most of the geopolitical entities that comprise the world today were fragmented and limited resource entities in those times.

The early humans never took the ocean seriously to augment their lives over land.

The concept of maritime security would have developed when the attention panned away from land security to seaward security in the strategic rationale, or something similar, if any such thing existed then. Slowly it developed into the question of (military) sea power and ocean rights. Examining the maritime history of the world to understand the human activities at sea will be very much generalised compared to regional and national approaches. Besides, the study of maritime history in relation to present day perspective will not be accurate with reference to various countries of the day since most of them have changed their national profiles. Many geopolitical entities that were relatively great sea powers have vanished from the map and new ones have been established through the historical transformations catalysed by time-induced demands over the pages of history. The study should be ideal if it is centred on human relations with the ocean rather than that of a specific geopolitical entity. It is the humans more than their systems that were responsible for changing the human-ocean interaction in the early times. There were no policy decisions of governance. It was more individualistic approaches until sovereigns or other kinds of their variety initiated themselves into war, trade, piracy and privateering, and selective explorations of commitment.

History, including maritime history, is a broad overarching subject. It is multidisciplinary in explorative study. The study should explore the maritime dimensions of economic, social, cultural and environmental history. Such recorded histories are available through various established researched publications and scholarly journals. In this exploration, there are separate paths to understand: carriage of goods by sea, military operations, explorations, colonisation, etc. Another approach is through human issues. It contains sociology, narrative studies, cultural geography, gender studies, social welfare, etc. Transportation through human interface gives rise to the next stage of unmanned or nearly unmanned mobility and warfare at and from the sea. It is in the futuristic perspective. But so far maritime security remained very much evolutionary more in a staccato fashion than linear and continuous. It is still relatively archaic. Mobility in other physical terrains—land, air and outer space—is relatively at a faster pace than in the ocean. The progress is relatively linear and continuous without interruptions or holidays.[2] Air and outer space mobility came much later than the ocean transportation.

While historians may record that seagoing was instrumental for the development of civilisations, this study would like to lean on the conclusion that civilisation, as explained in the early part, has been an ongoing unitary process. The developments are within the single civilisation. Human clashes originate within this unitary civilisation and not between civilisations. This has been emphatically stated. From this outlook it can be seen that human development where it took to sea has contributed in their advancement through ocean awareness and ocean interaction. These influences can be seen in many human systems. For example, the European powers that colonised the world in the later part of the second millennium have been influenced by sea. Second millennium is of utmost importance to modern human for it was the period that opened up the modern age. In the second millennium the human system became forceful and dynamic dotted by high middle ages, renaissance, colonialism, rise of nation states, industrialisation, science and technology, education and health care, space explorations, wars and no-war movements and indulgence in collective security. The world was entirely different from what it was during the first millennium. It is by the end of the second millennium the ocean became widely prominent in the human psyche forming an international regime in the form of UNCLOS specifying the rights and obligations of every nation with respect to the ocean.

Mobility at sea is limited by speed. Historically it has not changed much even with the advent of machines and engines for the simple reason that sea is a hard medium for vessels to move at high speed. It is not the restrictions or resistance offered by waves, water and wind alone but the danger of high speed impact on water and resultant damages to hull and structures. Besides, speed can also take away the stealth factor by noise. Stealth is very much a part of ocean advantage. Noise is also indicative of technical deficiency in design and construction of seagoing platforms. Hence speed was not a concern as speed gave way to carriage of goods under the economy of size. Underwater mobility is even much slower and limited in carrying capacity. While size and economy of carriage took precedence over sea, humans compensated for it over land and, especially, in the air to gain speed and expediency.

The first vessels that went to sea would have been dugout canoes of the Stone Age populations who might have used them for travel and fishing nearshore. They would have been made even before the ancient maritime history started. According to historical perspectives, the first seaworthy vessel would have been originated under the Australian hypothesis explaining habitation there around 45,000 years ago.[3] According to some records, the earliest representation of a ship under sail appears on a painted disc found in Kuwait dating to the late 5th millennium B.C. [4] Navigation as original science originated in Indus River around 5,000 years ago according to history. Ancient Egyptians had knowledge of construction of sails which contained the science of aerofoil theory that make the aeroplanes fly. In fact everyone everywhere was attempting innovation, some simultaneously showing leveled growth of intelligence in human evolution. Here the question of "who did it first" is not relevant.

Early records of fishing show that it was akin to hunting over land. It had reflections of the hunter gatherer mentality. People hunted what they did not tend or rear. Fish was major food source. Marine fishes belong to the commons even today. Humans, it is believed, began whaling in the prehistoric period. Whale was a big chunk of food. That could feed a community. Whalers drove the whales ashore using their tiny row boats to block the open sea. It was a kind of marine blockade. It was application of strategy towards food security. Such intellect coupled with physical efforts lead to maritime strategy.

Then entered the element of economic security along the experimental trade routes. Successful and safe trade routes became sea lines of communication. Earliest reference of establishing formal trade routes, according to some studies, leads to ancient India with the Mauryan Empire in 4th century B.C. The Indian subcontinent was the focal point of ancient trade route primarily due to its geolocation, a vital aspect of the maritime dimension of an entity.[5] The trade routes were through transshipments instead of straight long passages by sea. The subcontinent also witnessed volumes of coastal trade.

Trade by sea was recorded in the story of Indus Valley Civilisation.[6] It is said to be in third century B.C. There are also mentions about ancient India's interest in sea going activities in *Rig Veda* around 2000 B.C. It talks about 100 oared naval ships taking to sea to conquer other kingdoms. But they were quite isolated approaches in maritime affairs. Trade took precedence over war and colonisation in ancient India. There was a tidal dock at Lothal presumably constructed around 2400 B.C. Indian rulers had established trade relations with Rome, Greece, Arabian Peninsula, Persia and East Africa on the west and Southeast Asian Islands and China on the East. But under prolonged sovereign rules, the maritime affairs took a turn to the inward looking sovereign systems in India. This was accelerated after the European intervention. Actual decline commenced in the thirteenth century. Indian maritime strategy was almost non-existent during the period. European navies ruled the Indian Ocean for the next 400 years.

Maritime strategy evolved against the background of naval war and "empire" building which started very early in human system. There were many wars. War at sea is usually studied and examined under naval history. There were many wars in the pre-recorded history. Humans have been fighting wars at sea for more than 5,000 years, the pre-recorded history included. The earliest full scale war with a notable maritime element was perhaps the Trojan War according to this study. Trojan War was a mythological narration under legendary episodes in Greek literature which had an element of massive sealift by 1,000 ships that was crucial for the Mycenaeans (Greek) to fight against Troy (Western Anatolia) on the latter's ground for ten years. The war was said to have dated between 1260 and 1240 B.C. It was a wholesome war for the period and even today for analysts on the art of war involving coalition forces, land-sea warfare, sustenance, deception, resource accrual and inclusive objectives. The changes today are only marginal. But in relation to maritime strategy, the fleet manoeuvres were only for sealift of soldiers and logistics that was supplementary to the main war that unwounded over the land. The ground forces finally took control of war and established victory to the Mycenaeans at the end.[7]

There is no direct proof of Trojan War. It could have been a mythopoeian recording of sorts without direct traces of history. Mythopoeian hypothesis may need *a priori* appreciation. There seems to be an interesting find here from the first recorded war at sea. It was dated 1210 B.C. That was just around the time, rather a bit earlier than the assumed date of the Trojan War. It also involves the Hittites settlements and the geographical centrum. The Hittite emperor Suppiluliuma II defeated a fleet from Cyprus in the war around the area depicted in Trojan War. The emperor used Ugaritic ships similar in design to ships of Trojan War to defeat the fleet. Hittites were the powerful forces during the Bronze Age. They were linked to the Mycenaeans, the depicted victors of the Trojan War by proximity and period. The first recorded war also shows that wars similar to Trojan War would have been common in the area during the Bronze Age. It gives circumstantial evidence for Trojan War or similar wars. The Mycenaeans and Hittites existed during the Bronze Age and collapsed at the end of it. They dealt with sea extensively until the Sea Peoples, a confederacy of seafaring raiders, considered to have come from Southern Europe on the Aegean Sea, took over. All these meet the eye with respect to war at sea using ships for mobility, reach and logistics. The strategy of naval warfare was slowly unfolding.

More than its existence, Trojan War kindles the interest in maritime involvement of naval forces to gain reach in a quest for the rare resource of the period—tin, the prime ingredient in making bronze with copper. This must be true to some extent as the period was Bronze Age. This establishes the purpose for which ocean was used in the early days in history—resource mobilisation and security. Involvement of naval fleets in a serious manner, therefore, can be dated to the later part of the Bronze Age which was estimated to be between 3000 and 300 B.C. at various geolocations. An important aspect to understand here is about the ages of man as they were commonly depicted in human existence. The Stone Age, Bronze Age and Iron Age in prehistoric technological dating of various human systems were considered to have certain historical relevance. Human dependency on resources elsewhere enlarged during the Bronze Age. That required reach by ocean too.

There were many wars in the prehistoric period. They were not bursts of individual decisions but carefully thought out processes of the period. They were combined land-sea operations contributing to the evolution of human systems through experimentation and activity to live with the elements of nature. In the absence of formally recorded evidences, the studies had to depend upon *a priori* or intuitive knowledge, which could also be done by biomodeling the present. The sea was gradually becoming a tamable terrain to humans.

Most of the empires, brilliant in land warfare had to learn to get into the sea by understanding maritime strategies for survival even at the peak of their glory. It is another interesting find. Most of the human systems of the world got into the sea and learnt about it only when they acquired certain degree of profanity over land as empires. They did not achieve greatness exclusively by taming the sea. They tamed the sea when they attained certain degree of greatness remaining on land and then enlarged their hold. This also outsmarts the theory that one has to rule the sea to rule the world. Rome gained control of the Mediterranean after being transformed into a powerful nation. The mistake will be when an entity capable of fathoming the ocean remains hesitant about the ocean and ocean based integrated national security. It will be a costly blunder. Understanding the ocean and its value to national security require nations to achieve a certain level of credentials that comes only by advancement in governance. It is very much visible in the ocean based transformation of various countries, especially China in recent times, as evolving sea powers of the modern world. Many nations that can get into the sea and gain control over their ocean property regimes in the best manner suited to them are still reluctant to do so. Such an attitude, in spite of understanding the power of the ocean, could be a major strategic howler in the long term.

In the example of China above, it is important to understand that the entity was not in abhorrence with naval affairs as it was with the Mughals in India. The period of Warring States in China (481-221 B.C.) was often dotted with maritime efforts. Regional kings battled with each other before China was unified by Qin (pronounced closely "Chhin") Shih Huang Huang Ti of the Qin Dynasty (221-207 B.C.).[8] The emperor owed much to his unifying efforts to naval power. Chinese naval warfare in this period featured many indigenous destructive weapons including ramming strikers where ships were fitted with blades that will rip enemy vessels when rammed. The ancient naval warfare was extremely close quarter wars. What is interesting is the mystery of the sea was still not clear then. Chinese, like many others of the period, believed in sea monsters and one of the functions of the outwardly fitted blades was to chop them in case they were encountered on the way. These beliefs were common in spite of the fact that the Chinese were great inventors of weapons and machines. They modified their ships with stern mounted steering rudders that provided better control over ships. They also invented pontoon bridges and weapons and introduced newer design of fighting ships like the junk, a design that is multipurpose and still visible today in Chinese waters. Emperor Qin was credited as the inventor of the deadly crossbow. Ironically the founder of China, armed with his invincible cross bow, also went hunting for the mysterious monster that he believed to have been hiding in the lake. Was it schizophrenia that took him there?[9] We don't know. What we know is that since then China has been nudging slowly to establish its presence in the Indian Ocean for which it had to wait till it became an economic power in the early part of the 21st century.

From prehistoric times till the last seen war of the world on date, naval power remained critical in various ways—sealift, attack, preemptive strikes, eavesdropping, snooping, shadowing, launching platforms and the most important of all that is yet to be executed, the second nuclear strike from "somewhere in the ocean" in a scenario where an entity retaliates after being struck first by a nuclear weapon of the adversary. That is the ultimate in sea power unless something more serious comes up. Examining the wars based on ocean all along the past 5000 years or so will affirm this view point.

Wars became longer since 5th century B.C. Peloponnesian War between Athens and Sparta lasted 28 years. It was a land-sea war. It reinforced dependence over sea and the navy for winning over land. The disorder was amplified with the spread of killer plague soon after. Punic War between Rome and Carthage was another that followed. It lasted for more than a century ultimately bringing victory to the Romans.

Wars over long periods became a way of life. But not all the wars involved the maritime forces. Religion was one of the causes The Hundred years War between England and France that began in 1336 saw large scale naval manoeuvres. Both the countries contended with each other to take possession of the Channel and each other's territory. Generations of kingdoms challenged each other. In the meantime, travellers went around the world by sea. The world was slowly waking up from insularism. The old moat was gradually turning into a medium and a terrain of great significance. In some other parts of the world empires were being built and destroyed. Diseases too found better times to strike. In 1348, killer plague struck Europe as Black Death and the war was stopped. Interestingly it took an epidemic to interrupt a war though it could not stop it. The war resumed after six years as if humans cannot do without it. England made territorial gains in France. But ultimately the English were expelled from France. It was a period when powerful territories vied for domination through generations and the navy rose to prominence in war.

In the process, cruelty touched unseen limits. Religion ruled death. It is what this study mentions as clashes within a civilisation that is ongoing even in the 21st century. The war that later came to be known as the 30 years war went beyond religion. It started on 23 May 1618. It ended with various Treaties of Westphalia (Peace of Westphalia) dawning the era of sovereignty and nation states.

In spite of the treaty that triggered sovereign beginnings, wars continued as they were part of the essential human system. Matured transformation of geopolitical entities into sovereign states became a pretext for war to be fought in the name of sovereignty. Navy was ever present. The year 1700 witnessed the wars for Baltic. It was known as the Great Northern War. The wars started reaching out into the sea and thereby the world with the advent of colonisation. The wars became massive and scientifically structured for the day. Theoreticians and strategists like Clausewitz (1780-1831) and Jomini (1779-1869) established their theories on war. The First World War broke out with the assassination of Archduke Franz Ferdinand in Sarajevo, the 51-year-old heir to the Austrian throne on 28 June 1914. Within a year the war came to be known as the Great War that spread out into all the three geophysical dimensions—land, ocean and air. The war ended in 1918. There were 37 million casualties. Such things do not happen today. The same year Spanish influenza originated in China killed about 22 million in Asia, Europe and North America![10] Influenza scored over the First World War in killing average. In spite of such calamitous bolts human system persisted under supreme survival elements of the three geophysical terrains.

The inter period 1919-1945 witnessed more wars and culminated with the Second World War (1939-1945) with victory to the allies. The world witnessed the largest landing of troops on the shore in five sectors of Normandy on 6 June 1944 (D-Day) on a coordinated land-sea-air operation. That was the watershed event of the war. The operation was code named Neptune, the Greek God of the sea. 195,700 naval and merchant naval personnel, 160,000 soldiers, 6,939 vessels, 11,000 aircraft, 17,000 paratroopers, participated in the assault phase of the operation. Operation Neptune ended on 30 June 1944.[11]

Operation Neptune, primarily a British naval affair, was a masterpiece in naval planning, unprecedented so far. The operation also showed British supremacy in naval warfare. It was an operation that was never surpassed later in the real world. Among the vessels of eight different navies there were 1,213 warships, 4,126 landing vessels, 736 ancillary craft and 864 merchant vessels.[12] This was the largest and the most overwhelming fleet manoeuvre the world ever witnessed since the beginning of such manoeuvres and sea lift in the Trojan War period. The world may not need such manoeuvres in future to establish the point of ludicrous understanding of the activity called war. Navigation, during Neptune was guided by beacons supplied by midget submarines of Royal British Navy. The ocean advantage was getting firmly established in all its dimensions. The art of war was also getting enlarged tactically. In spite of the decisive ending of the war with Operation Neptune, the Allies caused a debilitating blow to Japan, one of the partners of the Axis, with the United States air forces attacking Hiroshima and Nagasaki on 6 and 9 August 1945 respectively with nuclear bombs for the first time in any war. There were many moral questions on the need for nuclear bombings and the just course of the war. Though such questions get dissolved in the fog and friction of war and the psychology of invention,[13] they simmer subsequently for ages in the post war world branding the countries involved in it on their absence of human values subsequently and hegemony of subjugation for ages. They are viewed suspiciously for everything they do for a very long time thereafter. Under the war-induced nuclear turnpike, the world needs to ride cautiously even when the intentions are gracious. The nuclear baggage at once percolated to the ocean too resulting in various activities that enveloped the world under paranoia.

The Second World War formally ended on 14 August 1945. An estimated 55 million people died and 10 million were displaced. That was the greatest ever casualty in war since the beginning of humankind. The war paved way for the United Nations on 24 October 1945 as a new symbol of hope for collective security.

Soon the world turned into a limbo of idiotic frenzy with a scenario where the winners of the war became mutually suspicious under differing ideologies. It was as if necessary for the human system to remain bipolar. The world was getting balanced fast into the bipolar regime. Soon the nations fell on either side—Western Block and Eastern Block, in cold engagement. It was aptly termed the Cold War. This study terms it the Third World War. A few countries for example Egypt, India and Yugoslavia dared to think differently and remained neutral and non-aligned holding over the quick sand of polarity more on socio-political will power than on national power. The Cold War that commenced in 1947 continued alarmingly keeping the world on the brink for the last nuclear war of mutual destruction until the Soviet Union collapsed under the containment policy of the United States on the Christmas eve of 1991. The world seemingly changed once again. But what is important for this study is the extensive use and development of maritime forces during the Cold War. It was unprecedented among those who were involved directly or indirectly. It also contributed to substantial development of naval technology. The contribution of Cold War rivalry for the development of naval technology deserves a serious study.

The post Cold War world witnessed many dislocations besides reviewed attempts to gain control of world resources, especially oil. Terrorism established through various fundamentalists all working for a cause according to the perception of the perpetrators. In the continuing situations and transformation of ideas on maritime security and maritime strategy there has been logistics and reach as support factors of warfighting, resource denial to rogue states and no state actors, preventing nuclear proliferation, containing and suppressing all types of unlawful activities at and from the sea,

All the time, naval warfare was aimed generally at logistics movement, sealift, and blockades and conflicts at sea. Central blockades and breaking the blockades over surface or underwater with the submarines became the chosen strategy. There was an expanded naval arms race prevailing the world over prior to the First World War. The United Kingdom was the dominant naval power of the 19th century. In the early 20th century the arms race was between Britain and Germany. While Britain was concerned about its status as an almost island country and its survival among other nations around,

Germany was keen on developing maritime power in proportion to their perceived economical, technological and military status to free them from dependence over the British goodwill for trade and commerce by sea. Both the countries had diverse forms of maritime strategy. The United States was another maritime power. But all these powers were greatly influenced by the findings of Captain Alfred Thayer Mahan (1840-1914)[14] of the United States Naval War College. That was a major turning point in the naval events related to military preparations and the beginning of arms race at sea.

Mahan put forward his view points through two publications—*The Influence of Sea Power upon History: 1660-1783* in 1887[15] and *The Influence of Sea Power upon the French Revolution* in 1892. According to him naval supremacy was the key for survival in the world of future. His theory was based on observations of great powers. He argued and categorically stated that such countries, from Rome to Great Britain, became powerful by their maritime prowess and prospered by ruling the waves. According to him, those lacked naval supremacy, quoting Hannibal's Carthage and Napoleons' France, failed from becoming great maritime powers. His observations were exploratory and revealed great facts that a country could not underestimate the ocean if it was aimed at becoming a great sea power. His hypothesis was absorbed by the United States as golden words that brought them out into the world over all the ocean divisions as a great sea power. They remained unchallenged at sea. Mahan also stressed the interdependence of military and commercial shipping for the control of the sea. The maritime domain is perhaps the only terrain where commercial activities supplement military operations as can be seen in Normandy landing and any modern naval warfare. Both the publications authored by Mahan greatly influenced the buildup of naval forces prior to World War I.

According to Mahan, the key to world domination was through the seas by controlling it absolutely. Today, according to this study, it is not so. Times have changed. No nation can control the sea absolutely in the post UNCLOS world. Every nation has the freedom to exploit its ocean property to the maximum. This is the turnaround.

The key to world supremacy is through economics and human wellbeing; it can be achieved through maximisation of national security that this study propagates. The most secure nation may not dominate the world, but the nation that enjoys maximum national security will be able to dominate the world as a super state[16] more than a super power. The world is changing. It is not possible to walk in and kill any more. Mahan's views were shaped by the 18th century naval wars between France and Britain. But these wars were for the domination of the English Channel in naval parlance and also were religious wars of a different kind. The British navy consistently prevented invasion and blockade by France. But externally for an observer, the British eventually defeated France by sheer naval superiority. This finding is only superficial. A similar practice in economics shows how comparative advantage can be used to create a win-win situation. France if changed the strategy instead of depending on naval warfare where it was weaker than the British would have brought out a sea change in the governance of English Channel. However a research project should not be looking into the theory of "would have been" because life is vectored unidirectional in a linear manner. The "would have been" theories will remain idle talk *ab initio*.

Mahan was popular propagandist for expansion. He advocated that the countries with the biggest navies would inherit the earth. He was a naval officer. His concern was the United States and its navy. He has to put it that way for gaining attention of those who governed his navy. In 1883, the US Navy transited from a wooden ship navy to an iron and steel ship navy. The rest of the world's navies were also engaged in the same activity following Mahan's advocacy. This led to the construction of more battle ships which in turn led to massive naval arms race. The naval race was exhibited in the Russo-Japanese war of 1904-05. The war and subsequent defeat eliminated Russia from the naval arms race for the time being. It provided lead to Germany. The result was a direct clash between Britain and Germany during WWI. Britain was already an established naval power. Was it a belief or a clever tactics by Mahan to turn around his hold on the job and make his country a power that can build ships with an eye on economic advancement than warfare? Mahan was a clever visionary of the middle and immediate; he was landclasped too, but understood the power of integration of ocean with land according to the period. He was in a rare class, indeed.

Prior to Mahan's pronouncement, naval strategies were commerce raiding and coastal defence. This ideology and outlook were changed by Mahan's proclamation. It was welcomed by investors, industrialists, nationalists, etc. Mahan's theories excited economics of the navy. They were absolutely appealing to the American government. That was what the money makers wanted. It changed the government's attitude towards the sea totally. The naval renaissance turned around, especially in the United States since 1890. Command of the sea became a serious slogan. Great navies, it was accepted, could bring greatness to the nation. But navies are very capital intensive outfits for a military. Hence only economically strong nations could ideally afford large navies and earn from them. But, "How powerful is the navy?" is a question that many finds difficult to answer. What are the yardsticks to assess the power of a navy that a nation possesses? Is it size, numbers, reach...? It is a study in strategy. But undoubtedly a great navy is the one that can establish geostrategic command over the sea from all approaches.

Mahan's ideas were shaped by various conflicts in the past and not premonitions of the future. He found the winner in the past always had an upper hand that came from ocean awareness. In the period of Mahan, control over seaborne commerce was radical and dominant. Mahan only looked at empires built by sea powers. He neglected or kept a blind eye on terrestrial empires and others who never felt modernisation and economic development sans maritime indulgence should also yield results. But those who argue on Mahan say his theories stood vindicated by the First World War. However, it is yet to be proved. He believed in sea based imperialism. It was in the "manifest destiny"[17] argument of the United States that demanded overseas bases. Mahan's ideology was purely American with the manifest destiny that argues North American settlers will expand all over the world and rule the world by sheer destiny. It was the belief system of the 19th century cherished by the migrant Americans. This is where Mahan's theories lean on the American belief system or rather a desire to make the American ideology of the manifest destiny real. The manifest destiny spoke on three basic themes of American people to rule the world: 1) the special virtues of the American people and their institutions, 2) America's dream to redeem and remake the world as a replica of America and 3) A divine destiny under God's direction to accomplish this "wonderful" task. Manifest destiny still prevails in the American psyche when the country talks about the new world order and also feels only America can lead the world in a unipolar environment. According to historian Fredrick Merk, manifest destiny on the outset was a sense of continentalism that was slight in support. The idea lacked national, sectional, or party following commensurate with its magnitude. The reasons were that it did not reflect the national sprit. The thesis that it embodied nationalism, found in much historical writings was not backed by supporting evidence.[18] But Mahan's theory was very much in close quarter with the manifest destiny. It was perfect then. Today the theory, according to this study, does not hold water. In other words, Mahan's strategic findings under his theory were for a limited period. It was not universal in time and place, especially so now. Does it mean the world forget them? No; not at all.

Mahan's findings created an era of naval explosion. All the eyes fell into the ocean around them. But very few could achieve such large scale constructions. Many of them turned inward as it demanded serious focus and strategic appreciation and a strong economy to reach out to the ocean. Many lacked it and lost the will. Mahan's idea was that countries with great naval power will have greater worldwide impact. It undoubtedly applied then; it still permeates in the US naval strategy as a ghost protocol to some extent.

Maritime strategy may take any shape depending upon the period; but it is the all time mastery of the seas that made nations victorious in war and prosperous in other-than-war situations.

Change Perspectives of Maritime Strategy

Maritime strategies existed from the very absence of it through the ages when use of force for plundering or warfighting became the prime objectives. Fishing and mobility at sea was in the hunter gatherer and nomadic mode. The wars that slowly enhanced in scale and casualty brought out naval attack and defence as the primary objectives of strategy. The wars however restricted the navy's role as the supporting force in the overall war where victory was decided by the ground held. Various strategies originated during these periods and still continue evolving. They are briefly examined in the following paragraphs.

According to Mahan, sea borne commerce produced national wealth and thereby contributed to the greatness of a country. His mentor was the then Swiss Chief of Staff Baron De Jomini. As already explained his prognosis on the sea power as ultimate to a nation's power was contemporary and situated to the period. His vision on overbearing sea power was a judicious combination of naval superiority combined with mercantile enterprise. The six ingredients of sea power, advocated by Mahan in his theory are summed up below.[19]

1. Geographic position—astride sea lanes and in the proximity of important trade routes as also adjacent to profitable fishing grounds. An advantageous geographical position, serviceable coastlines, abundant natural resources...
2. Physical confirmation—secured harbours.
3. Extent of territory—possession of adequate territory acting as strong economic bases
4. Number of population—people to handle the sea in hostile conditions.
5. Character of the people
6. Character of the government—ability to exploit the sea for national objectives.

In Mahan's finding, these elements were necessary along with a great navy for a nation to be a sea power. United States, as a great country had almost all these six elements as if on a platter when Mahan identified the elements. Did it influence his findings? To become a great maritime nation, all it needed was a great navy according to these findings. Through these findings Mahan could get the government listen and authorise expansion and modernisation of its navy. That the government did. Perhaps that would have been his idea.

According to Mahan's concept, a great navy is the one that is designed to engage an enemy at sea to win command over sea. That was the primary purpose of a naval fleet—attack to win. Commerce raiding and all the hoopla about *guerre de course* were secondary. The rest of maritime strategy for him was based on operations. Tactics were conditioned by changing types of naval armaments. Tactics were aspects of operations occurring after the beginning of combat and were conditioned by changing types of naval armaments.

Mahan's theories brought major change in naval appreciation of the United States and other countries in the late 19th century. Till then, the primary functions to which a navy was committed was commerce raiding and coastal defence. The US navy's renaissance started with Mahan. New battleships using Mahan's strategy of command of the sea also displayed the industrial development of the United States. But

Mahan was oblivious about the influence of technology in strategic development and planning. In reality, technology could impact upon the six elements and change the course of things. This was appreciated by some of the military leaders subsequently. In modern times it is also a question of the other aspects of strategy—policies of governments, national planning, etc., could make nations that are disadvantaged with respect to the six elements to gain maritime supremacy. It is also one of the objectives of this study. Maritime supremacy in this study means taking maximum advantage of the ocean property regime that is possible for any country in the modern world. Integrating maritime security with national security governance is one such method thereby advocated.

Mahan had also brought out strategic questions that are relevant today with minor modifications. One of them was about the function of the navy. It was to command the seas. But the posture of command at sea cannot be calibrated to measure accurately for validation. This makes it also difficult to understand the power of a nation's navy. How is it identified? Is it by size, number of ships, fire power or anything else? Such questions raise confusion in the cal-val[20] of the navy of a nation. For Mahan the objective of a navy is the command of the sea. But certainly navy's objectives should be much more than that. It has to be based on the national security policy of the nation under integrated maritime security. For Mahan, the navy should be concentrated in battle fleets. In today's parlance it should be according to the functions and the objectives of the navy. Mahan advocated basing the overseas coaling stations for ships at the geographic choke points. It may not be valid and practical today as a strategic decision. Instead endurance and reach based on coast-benefit analysis and resource mobilisation may gain precedence in decision making.

The secondary roles of the navy identified by Mahan were the operations that could not win a war or be decisive. This study disagrees with him vehemently in the appreciation that a secondary role that is less intense than the primary role will blunt the cutting edge of any military armed force by sheer human inertia, especially in the advancing age. A military that farms in the fields and hatcheries will not be able to fight the modern war. They will end up milking the cattle in the enemy camps if lucky to be alive.

Mahan has been a strong advocate of colonisation or acquisition of strategic positions geographically for basing ships. United States has been in the forefront of such activities that has paid rich dividends to it. But the cost of maintaining overseas bases is extremely high. There is also the political cost.

The United States was the foremost to be benefitted by Mahan's theory. In fact Mahan's book was one the select publications among those that were considered to have changed America's maritime perception forever. Mahan's theory was behind the United States annexation of Hawaii, control of Puerto Rico, Guam and the Philippines as coaling stations and perpetual lease of Guantanamo Bay in Cuba. Mahan was a no holds barred maritime strategist of his period.

Many other nations followed Mahan. France was one among them. Mahan was a household name in Germany. Most modern navies followed Mahan's principles that virtually caused the naval arms race in the world. In today's parlance Mahan went virtually viral at a time when the world was relatively in darkness with information! There wasn't anybody else that the world wanted to follow or was it that there was a kind of national hypnosis in the maritime psyche of the world because of Mahan's reach more than the naval reach? If that is so Mahan's theories were more a commercial and economic idea in naval production than in strategic application. It was more a business plan laced with politics that found favour with the governments and industrialists together.

French naval doctrine of 1914 was based on Mahan's theory. Accordingly the French prepared a navy for winning decisive battles and gaining mastery of the seas. But there was a change in the situation. The World War I brought a sea-change in naval applications unlike what was visualised in Mahan's times and earlier on which Mahan counted his theory. The place of the navy in war was found to be supplementary to the ground forces. In World War II the Allied forces found that Germans changed their tactics at sea. They refused to directly engage allied naval forces in decisive battles. The submarines found a larger application. The German U boats exploited the stealth factor (ocean advantage) and attacked at times where it hit badly, especially commercial destruction. For Mahan, commercial destruction was secondary, but the Germans engaged in sinking merchant vessels that was subsequently followed by Allies. This necessitated formation of convoys. That was a turnaround in naval warfare. All these are still followed today. There was never a battle that was only at sea; the convoy system is still found precedence to protect merchant ships in piracy ridden areas. The navy's role changed since the First World War and it is yet to achieve a new role which obviously should come by. These things prove the lines in which Mahan found his theory did no longer exist. This will call for a deviation from Mahan's strategy. But there are many scholars who advocate the applicability of Mahan's theory not only in the ocean but also outer space according to a paper that explains outer space as the ultimate high ground for warfare.[21] The scenario of supremacy can shift to outer space in the times to come by according to a study by the author.[22]

Mahan's observation, as mentioned earlier, was based on the past. It recounted the British success in becoming a maritime super power of the period. However, it is evident that the objective of an appropriate maritime strategy is to achieve the national interests integral to the grand strategy towards national security.

According to this study, Mahan's theory, though valid in maritime appreciation of national security, was not integrated maritime security. It was exclusively a sea power focused approach. The United States government cleverly incorporated the theory in integrated maritime security subsequently. Sea power is a term used to explain the strength of a nation's military naval forces. The idea of sea power should, according to this study, be termed as the power of a nation to maximise its ocean property returns. The ocean property is not equally distributed among nations of the world. But it is possible for a nation to maximise on the available ocean property more than another nation who has more at available level but fail to maximise it. This also means ability to counter the negative aspects of ocean property relative to that nation. A nation that can integrate maritime security regime with its overall national security regime can be said to be in the exclusive sea power club in today's parlance as this study recommends. Within that sphere how much a nation can do towards maximising the benefits of the ocean is what one has to examine in assessing the sea power quotient (SPQ). Here a new term, sea power quotient, is introduced. Sea power quotient is the ratio of the return from ocean property to the overall available ocean property. This can be assessed provided the elements can be measured in a universal module which is yet to be established. The next question is, "Can a landlocked or geographically disadvantaged nation possess more sea power quotient than a coastal one?" Ideally, it is possible provided the comparing coastal nation is not seriously concerned about its ocean property regime. In any respect, this study believes that integrated maritime security is the ultimate test on deciding upon sea power and it is not all about the naval forces. Mahan may not agree.

Mahan did not define maritime strategy. It came much later. It is credited to Sir Julian Stafford Corbett (1854-1922), considered to be Britain's greatest maritime strategist. He defined maritime strategy in 1911 as "*the principles which govern a war in which the sea is a substantial factor. Naval strategy is but that part of it which determines the movements of the fleet when maritime strategy has determined what part the fleet must play in relation to the action of land forces.*"[23] The statement is completed with the affirmation that *"for it scarcely needs saying that it is almost impossible that a war can be decided by naval action alone."*[24]

In this definition, maritime strategy is about the application of the ocean terrain in war—where sea is involved. Naval strategy falls within this maritime strategy. It is about the naval fleet manoeuvres in relation to the war fought by the land forces. Hence maritime strategy is not about the navy. It is all about the application of ocean in relation to war. The strategy applicable to the navy is naval strategy. Under integrated maritime security, the desirable situation is when maritime strategy is all about the role the ocean plays within the grand strategy of national security. The naval role within it remains as naval strategy. In fact both the maritime strategy and the naval strategy extend beyond war. Another comment by Corbett in his explanation about strategy is "*for it scarcely needs saying that that it is almost impossible that a war can be decided by naval action alone.*" This study disagrees with Corbett's statement on three grounds, though both the statements need to be tested seriously. The statement in this study is that there can be cases when a war can become decisive by naval action alone. The three grounds that form the lemmata for testing are 1) the sea based second strike paradigm where the navy fires (launches) the last weapon, 2) attack by an all terrain force (undifferentiated) that may come up in future and, the final lead to the hypothesis that may make it null, 3) integrated warfighting under joint (unified) force strategy where decisiveness cannot be attributed to a single force.[25]

Under the new theories and the modern way of thinking about maritime security, a geopolitical entity, especially a nation, will have to develop maritime interests taking advantage of the applicable maritime factors and established maritime dimensions to the optimum. The navy and the maritime forces should complement the land based approach as long as the landclasp syndrome prevails in the human mind and belief system. It will undoubtedly sail through eternity. The concept of the waterworld as the future ocean habitat without ever stepping over land is an absurd idea, at least for now. The benefit of doubt expressed here is intentional to avoid any debate on people moving out to sea on permanent settlement.

Mahan was not alone in articulating visionary ideas on maritime security. However, United States was the most prominent player in maritime activities since the days of Mahan. The change was in massive ships and overwhelming force at sea aimed primarily against adversaries in direct confrontations and everything about it.

Among the maritime players, the Indian heritage was especially in Southeast Asia. It showed India's extent of reach by sea in the early days. Many Indonesian terminologies originated from the ancient Indian heritage and the deep and ancient cultural linkages with Southeast Asia. The maritime tradition of India was strong but today India is oblivious to it for various reasons. One among them could be the validity of maritime security as a regular protocol in national governance. Maritime history is full of achievements of the so called western world. There is no word in the narratives about the eastern world where Indian and other countries did really engage in seafaring seriously. Perhaps it could also be that the involvement was not impressive.

Sardar Kavalam Madhava Panikkar (1895-1963), the Indian statesman and scholar, popularly known as K.M. Panikkar in his seminal treatise titled *India and the Indian Ocean* (1945) had depicted vivaciously the ancient Indian maritime tradition and the need for India to follow the sea for greatness as a nation. He was a lone Indian voice in those days. Panikkar argued that Indian Ocean witnessed the first oceanic activities in the world. This, he attributed to the geooceanic conditions pertaining to ocean navigation. There is a lot about the findings of Panikkar under the ocean property parlance depicted in this study as the ocean advantage and ocean environment, the two constituent elements. It was finding truth from facts in the true research methodological parlance. He contradicted the European finds about the Mediterranean waters, especially the Aegean, by the sheer fact that those waters were limited. He attempted to substantiate his statement that the Indian Ocean was brimming with activities much before any activity anywhere in the World Ocean. If that is so, Indian Ocean is a critical spot in the World Ocean that will have to be watched for. According to Panikkar, the most believed idea that Hindus had a natural resistance to going to sea was absolutely absurd. It is true as it can be seen in the ancient maritime traditions of India and the invention of the magnetic compass called *matsya yantra* for ocean navigation. Indian maritime tradition has been flowing from the ancient days through Mauryan Empire (5th century) to the day. India thereby has a great ocean property benefit that is yet to be seriously exploited.

As far as other studies in history go there are many statements that the Chinese voyagers discovered the globe before the Europeans. However, among the confusion of "who did what?" it is obvious that those who get exposed through maritime historians, selectively or otherwise, get the credit for discovering the world. And the credit goes to... is not a missing link that this study is exploring. Instead it is attempting to establish the fact that maritime security all the time remained as a land-based view for obvious reason and thereby remained a ghost protocol relative to the terrain to which it belongs—the ocean. It was not recondite. It is for the better to embody it with land-based governance in the modern world that needs to enhance national security governance at any cost to survive.

Returning to Panikkar, one can understand about this much less spoken about luminary even in India by reading his works of the period. He was considered to be the architect of India's then prevailing naval doctrine. He advised the independent Indians to take cognizance of the fact that the Indian Ocean was important to the country. He regretted the "unfortunate tendency" to overlook the sea in the discussion of India's defence problems. He was often quoted that India never lost independence till the country lost the command of the sea, better said in this study that only those who came by the sea colonised India. According to him a navy was not meant to defend the coast; he wrote in 1945. The coast has to be defended from the land. For Panikkar, the objective of the navy was,

- to secure control of an area of the sea,

- preventing enemy ships from approaching the coast or interfering with trade and commerce at sea,
- blockading the sea and
- Destroying enemy ships at sea.

According to him, a navy merely based on coast, degenerates into a subordinate service. He wanted Indian Navy, whether small or large, to understand it. Its role is to protect the seas and not the land and if it cannot protect the seas vital to India's defence it is better not to have a navy at all. But the policy makers in Government of India were not in a hurry to absorb Panikkar's views in independent India.

While China's maritime interests has been limited to the voyages in the past depicted by various historians, most of the scholars felt China intended to stay as a land power like the Mughals in India during their period. But in the 1990s China rose in its new avatar as a power determined to enter into the sea in a very serious way in its military outfits. But it had more economic sense than military intentions. It was more than what meets the eye. China certainly needs to safeguard its maritime routes in its quest for economic supremacy. China understood the need for integration of maritime affairs with national progress. The other view is that China was turning hegemonic in the Indian Ocean especially against India and attempting to find ways to choke it with a string of pearls. Whether a string of pearls or a hanging catenary lock of an Indian *dupatta*, China certainly would know better that dealing with India may have to be with other means of politics in geostrategy of modern times. China certainly understands. It is free to make decisions to gain access to Indian Ocean or any other ocean division like anybody else. There will be mutual suspicion between the two countries chorused by the bentline thinkers in both the countries and external to them. But China needs Indian Ocean and South China Sea guaranteed for passage for its economic stability and nation building activities in which it is engaged. There are other dominant powers in the Indian Ocean. China is aware of it. It is Mahan's theory in Chinese gown. Though the theory is old, it has still the power to induce arms race and associated cacophony. That is the worst or the ultimate that can happen. China's Indian Ocean vision is, seemingly, based on economics, energy and presence of other players who can cause a grumble over the waves. It is a prime agenda for China to please the countries on the Indian Ocean rim where it matters for confidence. It is not a question of any arc of influence as far as this study leads, but sheer economics of survival under ambitious plans to lead the world. China should know well that it is not hegemony that matters today but economics. But an interpretation of human minds is a different game. The nations should know.

China had issued a white paper in 2009 highlighting its intentions with modernisation. The country categorically denies that it would seek hegemony. According to the white paper, China's intention was "basically to accomplish mechanisation [of the military] and make major progress" in information technology by 2020 and "realising modernisation by mid 21st century."

The white paper was "updated, practical, consistent and systematic" according to Chinese defence ministry. On china's strategic guideline of active defence the paper said the guidance aimed at winning local wars in conditions of information technology. China aimed at developing a complete set of scientific modes of organisations, institutions and ways of operation. China's "NO first use" of nuclear weapon policy was explained. In peacetime the nuclear missiles of the Second Artillery Force were not aimed at anybody. The country will implement a self defence nuclear strategy. If China comes under a nuclear threat, the nuclear forces of the Second Artillery Force will go into a state of alert, and get ready for a nuclear counter attack to deter the enemy from using nuclear weapons against China. The second artillery force is China's core force of strategic deterrence. The Chinese military will take a more open approach with other militaries for world peace and stability. The maritime reference in the paper was primarily about the criticality of the situation in Taiwan Strait. The white paper said that China would never seek hegemony or engage in military expansion then or in the future no matter how developed it would become.[26]

For India, in relation to China, the probable approach in its maritime strategy would be to link it with geostrategic security and, thereby, with national security. This way the maritime relations in diplomacy get integrated with national security. Cooperating with China in building up an assured support under excellent confidence building procedures could take India a long way in its geostrategy. Every country needs to approach their maritime strategy in an economic friendly manner. Cooperation and jointness will also prove to be the best passage for dispute and conflict resolution. If that is so why not settle early to exploit the ocean jointly?

China had repeatedly mentioned that the overseas bases are for establishing energy security to ensure its growing economic activities do not starve. Having bases around need not restrict the movement of navies of other countries in the region. The ocean is a free terrain for manoeuvres for anybody as far as the jurisdiction and sovereignty of other countries are respected without exception. It is not power projection as envisaged in the old world. It is the need for power projection for one's own self more than others. Adding "coaling stations" is just another idea carried forward from Mahan's days. Today a country on the maritime loop could be more a banking station than an exclusive coaling station. It is the new strategy for integrating maritime security with geostrategic security element of national security and more if executed well.

China has become a naval power through hard work and planning. Therefore, it is natural that it will enter the waters where it has vital sea lines of communication. China has interests in the region for its own economic requirements as part of its national security concept. China is not becoming a sea power, but is integrating the maritime security with national security. China still believes in the old and tried out maritime strategies—access and allies around; increase naval power to respond under extended reach, etc. China has already established safety for its supply chain along the Indian Ocean lines of communication through the choke points from the Persian Gulf to its ports. It is not about encircling India or others. But in the process it can encircle India with some difficulty. The scholars should understand the way to China for India need not be through the Indian Ocean. It is too long.

India has taken for granted that Indian Ocean is India's Ocean. At least that was what China retorted earlier in one of the bumpy moments.[27] India could not project its power in the Indian Ocean; it remained in rhetoric. Maritime domain of the high seas today is a global commons barring the limited jurisdictional factor where it exists. The best India and China can do against this reality is to reduce mistrust and build confidence by regular and constructive engagement of militaries and economic forces. It has never been attempted seriously. The engagements have been mostly under diplomatic environment of dialogues. There are many other ways of engagement for improving relations.

It has been often reported in the media and elsewhere that India has been apprehensive of China's growing naval presence in the Indian Ocean. India had expressed apprehension in the past about the posture of the Americans and the British in the Indian Ocean. It did not substantially alter India's national governance preparations. India always had cooperative engagements with the countries of Indian Ocean region. India is expected to follow similar protocols with China too. There is no better option.

The sea areas around India are busy with large volumes of shipping. India's maritime diplomacy is also tested and practiced since long. There is no major change. India has a look east policy introduced in recent times. It cannot be linked with China's growing interest in the area. It was a policy that linked with various internal policies that were being introduced at that time for the country to turn around from the method inertia carried forward from the past. India's greatest diplomatic moves are its prolonged interest in the activities of the UN and the support it gives to peacekeeping activities around the world. The latter had earned it great mileage in establishing also at sea. India, US and China jointly supports Indian Ocean as a Zone of peace. China and the US have their priorities clear in the Indian Ocean. India too had it cleared very early.

In all respects, China will enhance its naval fleet on a fast track. It has no other option. India will be cautious on expansion but will certainly follow suit in its own pace. Most of the countries in the Indian Ocean Region (IOR)[28] will be geostrategically close to China and would not object to China in deploying forces in the Indian Ocean. China will not need their permission will be another matter. But the goodwill is always an asset in every geostrategic activity. It will only be the cost that will matter. India will have to balance the power if it takes the Indian Ocean seriously.

Russian military strength was tested to ground seriously in the First World War as part of the Allies. Russia existed as an empire prior to1922 and a federation post 1991. In the interim it was Soviet Union, a single party macronised country under the communist ideology. It had its roots in the Russian revolution of 1917 that overthrew the imperialists. It was a union of multiple subnational republics (Union of Soviet Socialist Republics (USSR)) in a centralised governing system though formally sounded federal. It fell on the eve of Christmas in 1991 and got micronised by fragmentation. What left behind became the Russian Federation. The Soviet Union was bound to fall considering the fallibility of its macronised structure though the fall was attributed to the US policy of containment to prevent the spread of communism abroad introduced as early as in 1946. It was an idea initiated by the US diplomat George Kennan in right earnest. It became one of the select polices of the US during the Cold War. The policy became a catalyst for the dissolution of the Soviet Union that was communist but did not succeed in expelling communism from the world. It shows the partial ineffectiveness of the policy and the weakness of the Soviet structure ab initio. The study of Russian maritime strategy is one of discontinuity. It has to be seen separately for Russia, Soviet Union and then for the Russian Federation.

Russian maritime advancement in the pre-1922 period was contained in the Baltic by European efforts. The Soviet Union regained its lost strength quickly once the communist rule was established. The Soviet Navy was replaced by the navy of Russian Federation formed in January 1992.

The changes in the naval forces of Russia was more or less on a continuous pattern as the country changed its existential profile that began with Peter the Great (1672-1725), also known as Peter I, who established the first Russian navy in October 1696 out of nothing. An interesting quote from Peter the Great after establishing a navy was "*a ruler that but has an army has one hand, but he who has a navy has both.*" For Russia of Peter I, the navy was certainly not part of the army but a force that was equal and additional to it. He needed it exclusively to win over the Baltic from the powerful Sweden at that time. This finding is important. But strategists in course of time allocated the supplementary role to navy to the ground forces in war though the navy is still counted as a probable game changer.

Peter I was the original architect of the Russian Navy. Ships were his passion. He made the Tsardom of Russia into the Russian Empire. He was modern in approach according to the period of his rule. He felt that the Ottomans who were his arch rivals could not be engaged without a powerful navy. He was proved right in his subsequent campaigns especially in the capture of Azov in 1696. The fleet created by him in part enabled Russia to win the Great Northern War (1700-1721) against Sweden. He initiated shipbuilding in Russia after gaining knowledge from his European well wishers and learning himself with their help. Russia is still a great player in the world of shipbuilding. He built a formidable navy for Russia in the British model. Russia rightfully considers him as the Father of the Russian Navy. Russia's entry into Europe and then into the modern world was exclusively through the navy according to author James Cracraft.[29] It also points out the geostrategic importance of the navy. It is not studied seriously. Geostrategic security is an identified element of national security.

Peter I correctly deduced the role of the navy as one that has to be incorporated into national governance. He created a naval academy to prepare Russians for the mercantile world. Peter learnt his lessons observing the British Navy and how it contributed to the British to become a maritime power that eliminated the Dutch supremacy in maritime trade.[30]

Russia's modern maritime strategist was Admiral Sergey Gorshkov (1910-1988) who oversaw the expansion of the Soviet Navy through the Cold War period. The Soviet navy became a formidable global force during his period. In late 1970 he was firm to announce: *The flag of the Soviet navy now proudly flies over the oceans of the world. Sooner or later, the U.S. will have to understand that it no longer has mastery of the seas.* [31]

However predictions of such nature do not hold much water in strategy especially when there are various factors whose interplay can change the course of history in a nation's life in many ways. Naval power is not dependent on itself. It can be affected by many other aspects of national security. Soviet Union collapsed leaving its powerful navy to split, drift and lay off in parts. There cannot be a better indicator to prove that maritime security depends on many other factors that are nonmaritime. This is another interesting find—while a navy can empower land, the power that energises it lies external to it over land. It serves as yet another argument to further the quest of integration of maritime security.

Post dissolution of Soviet Union, the Russian Federation regained economically in the beginning of the 21st century with new maritime policies and committed resolutions. The Russian navy has already entered the deep waters of the world as was visible in the Syrian imbroglio in August-September 2013. Russia is likely to keep the hold over the Cold War structure for the military forces including the navy under new strategic resolutions.

Naval strategy as seen so far is about warfighting at sea and from the sea. But maritime strategy is more than naval strategy. In the development of ocean based security appreciation, priority was to naval strategy and its application. It hasn't changed even in the beginning of the 21st century. But there are applications to the strategy among various nations. Warfighting is a small component of maritime strategy within the ocean advantage of the ocean property regime. While it was about colonisation and resource mobilization, the need for gaining control of the ocean applies primarily in modern times in clearing strategic passages at sea. The nations today have to ensure that strategic passages for movements of goods are clear for access by their carriers of goods. These passages can not only get blockaded by localised conflicts but also unlawful activities like ocean based piracy, etc. Piracy in Malacca and Singapore Straits and off the coast of Somalia became serious issues to passage security that has made governments to rethink ocean routing of ships in which even northern sea route to Europe from South China Sea had been examined. Every country has strategic interest in relation to ocean passages as they depend on them for resource accessibility. It is not exactly military interests.

Strategic Passages and the Ocean

Maritime strategists have not directly propagated the theory of clearing strategic passages without engaging in war of the nations. But modern world demands such approach. Nations are engaged in ensuring that through geostrategic interactions. The maritime forces of the military and nonmilitary nature have specific roles in it. China's intentions are visible in its expansion plans and establishing friendly bases in the Indian Ocean. The traffic should not stop at any given time for Chinese ships carrying goods to China and around the world. Indian Ocean is not alone in it. To understand the most prominent maritime strategy in today's world, it is necessary to appreciate the strategy related to ocean passage for carrying goods by sea. This is the bloodline of the modern world. It has to be protected.

Strategic passages are the thin lines of communication over the sea through which ships carry freight to their destinations from the supply points. With more than 90 per cent of cargo moving in this manner by sea, the strategic passages of the ocean become the bloodlines of global community. The space through which the global sea lines of communication pass is a limited space in the ocean for its economic viability. Sea lines of communication are thin and recorded for supervising safety of life and property against the perils of the seas. Besides, these are also with strategic choke points at various places based on the profiles of the continents. A geopolitical entity should have control over this space and choke points to ensure supply and delivery of freight. Detours and routing are common. They further add to the constraints of these passages. These choke points are narrow spaces in the open sea as suggested by the economy of goods movement. The maritime spaces avoid discontinuities and other constraints over land passage. It is unhindered except for the perils of the sea. It has to be established under the ocean property regime optimisation. Majority maritime circulation is along the coast whereas in countries like China there are also fluvial routes. The routes are located between major industrial regions in various continents. Various models of transportation like containerisation, etc. make the movements convenient. Maritime cargo transportation thus acquires a specific profile in maritime strategy appreciation and application for every country. The choke points can establish a long passage due to various reasons such as:

- geographic profiling of passage limitations,
- capacity constraints impairing navigation like canals and narrow straits,
- passage disruptions or closure due to local instability, unlawful activities, epidemics and pandemics, etc., and
- war zones in the normal routes of passage

The choke points, deviated lines of communication (DLOC), when ships are forced to deviate from their normal routes of passage, etc., impacts upon freight rates and other expenses.

Major transoceanic constrained routes for shipping on which the world is seriously depended are the canals, capes and straits. Some of them are also in relation to maritime disputes and probable conflict zones. All of them lie on sea lines of communication; hence are of strategic interest in maritime terms. A canal is generally an artificial navigational passage over land of the same country or different countries on either side; a cape is land that projects into the sea where a ship goes around it; a strait connects two water bodies by allowing passage between land masses. Not all of them are choke points in strategic parlance though parties may view them differently. Some of the critically constraint routes are given below.

- Panama Canal—Atlantic with Pacific
- Suez Canal—Atlantic with the Red Sea
- Strait of Malacca—Between Malaysia and Indonesia
- Strait of Hormuz—Persian Gulf and Gulf of Oman
- Strait of Bab el Mandab—Red Sea and Gulf of Aden
- Gibraltar—Atlantic Ocean and Mediterranean Sea
- Bosporus and Dardanelles— Aegean Sea and Black Sea
- Strait of Magellan—Atlantic and Pacific
- Cape of Good Hope—Around Africa where Indian Ocean meets Atlantic Ocean
- Bass Strait—mainland Australia and Tasmania
- Bering Strait—Alaska and Siberia
- Cook Strait—North and South islands of New Zealand
- Dover Strait—England and France
- Palk Strait—India and Sri Lanka
- Taiwan Strait—Taiwan and Peoples Republic of China

They are important for global freight circulation. Their continuous availability will determine the movement of traffic. All these waters have witnessed war and turmoil in the past. Some straits are also significant for wind and tidal power generation as part of ocean resource element of ocean property.

Among these constrained waters only a few are considered serious choke points. Choke points in maritime security are decided based on their strategic value. It is a relative expression and vital for a country in its strategic application of maritime security. The UNCLOS protects international access for all nations to sail through and fly over these choke points. Among them, the historically important choke points are the Gibraltar, Strait of Malacca, Bosporus and Dardanelles, Suez Canal, Strait of Hormuz, and Bab el Mandeb.

Other Forms of Maritime Strategy

The maritime strategy perspectives discussed so far has serious connotations to political appreciation. The bottom line is the political scenario and political power maximisation. Obviously governance is based on the political stasis. But this can be attained by following various unbeaten strategic tracks. There are other passages that are more open and at the same time discrete in the interest of the party examining it. They include the following:

- National interests
- Appreciated challenges and imperatives
- Forces and agencies perspective
- Ocean property mapping
- Maritime signature appreciation (dimensions and factors)

National Interests

The interest of a nation in the dynamics of national security governance is maximisation of national security—$NS_{max.}$ National interests on maritime strategy could focus on this single goal for appreciation. Each geopolitical entity will have and is free to decide on its own national interests related to maritime strategy. Identification of such interests is necessary prior to articulating them on its way to integration with national security.

The national interests in general may include the following among others:

- Deter conflicts at sea
- Win conflicts including war at sea
- Prepare for second-strike capabilities in case of a nuclear attack
- Enforce maritime laws at and from the sea
- Protect economic interests
- Ensure marine environmental security
- Assist mariners at sea in distress

- Support humanitarian activities
- Support disaster mitigation activities
- Carry out scientific and technological studies at sea
- Assure trade opportunities by sea
- Support global cooperation at sea
- Curtail and interdict transnational crimes at sea
- Support and influence regional cooperation and engagement
- Provide oceanic support by creating wealth for the people
- Protect sea-lines of communication
- Ensure bilateral confidence building measures
- Protect life and property at sea
- Protect the ocean global commons for the world.

Appreciating Challenges and Imperatives

Perhaps, appreciating challenges and then identifying the imperatives to craft the desired strategy is the best method for integrating a system with the process that is facing competition from every direction according to the author's studies on national security. Challenges can be identified by examining and analysing the threat matrix cube. A threat when accepted to confront becomes a challenge. This idea originates from various perspectives. In the modern world, any system comprises multitudinous elements. Any strategic process is a complex activity with infinite elements interacting with it at different times. For example, the survival of a company depends on the quality of product, service, value, availability, branding, and various other aspects including the moment in its organisational process and life cycle. The business environment matters all the time as a driver. Hence a company that harps only on the quality of a product but neglects other elements (customer service for example) may find eroding customer base in spite of a qualitatively acclaimed product. There are many such companies that can be quoted as examples. What they suffer from is integration deficit in strategic management.

Integration deficit is a major diagnostic finding in national security governance. Integration is a macro process. Every nation including the so called super powers could suffer from serious integration deficit in strategic governance. Appreciating the challenges and imperatives allows minimising this deficit provided it is handled effectively. The diagnoses matter.

Threats come in eight different dimensions, each with three components according to threat matrix cube. That is not all. The resultant threat can be a combination of all the multiple threats. The strategy to craft should be according to the identified combination of threats. Perhaps in no other field, threat analysis can be as complex as in national security governance. That is one of the reasons for the common integration deficit. But it can be overcome by diagnostic approach and adopting reactive strategy according to feedbacks that will be plenty once the process is set on role.

Threat perception is not a daunting tax, except for one major issue. The perception can be virtual or imaginary depending on the anxiety and apprehensions of the originator. Hence it is best left to the experts who have no stake in the matter. This will avoid threat perception under prejudice. Even then the originator will certainly be biased to a considerable extent. Hence the analyst will have a problem of convincing the originator who is the stakeholder. This happens in decision making from governments to the smallest of the organisations.

Governance of risk is different from threat perception and national security management. Risk is not threat. Threat in reverse is not risk. This has to be understood. In fact what governments do in the name of national security governance is managing the risks of governance. Most of the parts of legislative and administrative processes of contemporary societies are spent in managing risks or management by risks. It is one of the favoured ideas, though. Integrated governance could be absent in such procedures. Managing from eugenics to conflict resolutions and political dissent to terrorism has been a matter of risk management most of the governments in every country. It also applies to the units of smaller societies of human system. A risk is contingent on and shaped through the intersection of various social processes. It is analysed through risk perceptions. The success rate is marginal most of the time. It is a beaten track. Whereas threat perception is new and untried as depicted in this study. It is an unbeaten track for governments to examine.

The meaning of threat has to be understood to appreciate it. Threat is not risk or danger. It is a fly that may come and sit on the cake when not watched.[32] It is as real as the fly that no one has yet invited or witnessed on the scene. It will come when the object is threat attractive. Threat chases the target when the latter is threat attractive. A common term used for threat attractiveness is vulnerability. In the technical sense, vulnerability induces threat attractiveness. Vulnerability is more an abstract expression. It gives a feeling that the target can be made less vulnerable. In the real sense, threat attraction is more or less fixed with respect to time. It can be calculated to identify the threats that can fall within the attractiveness. It remains constant and real all the time. Every element in national security governance is threat attractive. In the example, the threat, the fly, chases the cake that is attractive to it. A threat will not home on to a target unless the target is threat attractive. The fly chasing a cake is a less complex situation. It is a simple direct-overt-external (DOE) threat under the TMC appreciation. It can be handled easily by prevention or preemption. A threat is handled through three parameter decision making—prevention, preemption or combination of both. It is the same model for the sugary cake and a complex geostrategic build up.

A risk is not interested in the target. It originates from process and process application. It is a two sum game—win or lose. Winning and losing can be to the extreme and thereby decision has to be based on the desired and acceptable extremity in both cases. It follows a two parameter decision making—acceptability and unacceptability of the outcome. It can vary with respect to the decision maker.

Risk and threat are associated. But in national security governance it is the threat to the element that matters for governance more than risk since the idea is to prevent or preempt threat and not dilute the sensitivity of the target as it will dilute the output desired in the process towards NS_{max}. Risk appears in the process en route. In standard expressions, especially associated with management, etc., a risk is considered to be a function of threats exploiting vulnerabilities to obtain damage or destroy assets and is expressed as,

$$R = A + T + V$$

Where, A = Asset (potential target)
T = Threat and
V = Vulnerability

Such studies also mention threats in three types—actual, conceptual or inherent. The threat may exist but if there are no vulnerabilities there is no risk according to such studies. Also it states that if there is no threat there is no risk but there can be vulnerability.[33]

This study does not recommend such an interpretation for absence of precision application in complex human systems like national security governance. Besides, the equation given above does not match with the subsequent statements mathematically.

Under this principle, maritime strategy evolves with the appreciation of maritime challenges the entity perceives and the associate imperatives to establish maritime security. Identifying the challenges and subsequent analysis and appreciation is imperative for crafting a strategy. Without such perception and appreciation, preparedness level can be costly and chancy with randomness. A challenge not identified and appreciated cannot be considered for policy decisions on strategic planning.

Proceedings of National Defence College, New Delhi, Seminar on "A Maritime Strategy for India" states that, "one significant way in which maritime threat differs from land based threat is that in the case of the former, it is not always possible to identify the adversary, since the adversary does not have to be an immediate neighbour. Maritime power must cater for a large number of contingencies and be aimed at protecting and furthering national interests." It means that adversaries to the maritime terrain could be from beyond the neighbours. The adversary can be visible or invisible. It could be human or nonhuman from the national security point of view. The threat matrix cube is a better approach where threats from invisible adversaries too can be appreciated and it is universal for any terrain.

The trend in maritime security is for overcoming regional nonresilience, which makes it imperative for security cooperation, according to Captain Lee G. Cordner of the Royal Australian Navy.[34] This statement came close to the end of the Cold War and reflects the immediate perceptions in any sea line of communication not just South East Asia as Cordner studied. Conflicts, and transnational crime syndicates involved in piracy and other serious crimes in the region were the threats that Cordner examined. The author advocated alliances for collective security through coalition warfare.

There will be problems for integrating maritime strategy with the overall national security strategy. But they have to be overcome. That is the role of the government. The seminar held at the National Defence College, New Delhi came up with following[35] conclusions:

a. Maritime strategy is vital for national security.
b. Power stems from economic, technological, scientific, and educational development, and military preparedness in a supportive role. This observation may be valid, but it could be said that a secure nation can exercise power.
c. Implied threat can be negated by regional partnerships.
d. India does not have a maritime strategy; it is traditionally land based.
e. India's threat is from economic competitors that will cause fractions in cooperative engagement. Such fractions may use military force against which credible deterrence is necessary. Military security is still high in the concept of national security. Therefore the navy is only for credible deterrence and its role needs to be defined and articulated.
f. Around the world there is consistency in governance with respect to national interests irrespective of the type of government in power.
g. Strategy is a definition of long-term goals. Policy, derived from strategy, is the method of achieving discernible results in real time.
h. The decision regarding the size of the navy whether for deterrence or all out war is to be taken after considering the economic, political, and military aspects. Therefore it needs to be seen what India is expected of its Navy by taking into account its role in national security. Deterrence is not achieved only by military means. It is used as means of policy when other methods are not conducive.
i. Influence stems out of power, and power is derived from economic, political, and military strength.
j. There are too many ministries involved in decision-making process with respect to the Indian Ocean.
k. Alliances are gudgeon pins of many victories.
l. India should start partnerships with the Indian Ocean Rim countries.

m. The perception that India is a regional bully needs to be corrected.
n. The first step in securing political involvement is articulation of strategy.
o. The aspects of strategy are economics, politics, and military.

The strategy for adoption, therefore, is a combination of all these, and changes in the evolving scenario that calls for on the spot analysis.

Forces and Agencies Perspective

The community element for attaining maritime objectives that a government has to consider in any nation will comprise forces and agencies that are capable of performing the roles identified for them. In maritime security governance the forces can be exclusive to the terrain as well as land as governance is under the landclasp syndrome. The maritime forces and agencies may constitute the following:

- Military maritime armed forces
- Non-military maritime armed forces
- Non-military maritime other agencies
- Offshore operators
- Shipping
- Shipping support agencies
- Ship breaking (recycling) agencies
- Hydrographic agencies
- Underwater operators and support agencies
- Marine environmental agencies
- Research organisations
- Ocean based space applications
- Cable and communication
- Intelligence agencies
- Maritime aviation agencies
- Underwater operations agencies
- Human element afloat, offshore and ashore
- Maritime law and treaty agencies

- Maritime non-governmental organisations
- Others...

Ocean Property Mapping

Ocean property mapping (OPM), in this study, breaks the conventional strategic thinking in maritime security by introducing a new singular concept called ocean property. The summation is that every geopolitical entity has been attributed with certain degree of ocean property in the post UNCLOS world. The ocean property can be assessed either as a singular wholesome concept or based on each of the four individual constituents. It is the prerogative of the entity based on its strategic approach. Such assessment is ocean property mapping. Once mapped, it will need revision periodically to incorporate changes and feedback inputs. Under such strategic assessment each entity should have its ocean property maps. The strategic objectives of OPM based on its constituents are given in table 4.1 (chapter 4).

Maritime power is not an absolute concept. Many nations in the world have the potential to become maritime powers. But serious integration of maritime security with national security is still an unexplored subject for most of them. Integration will be naturally involved in national planning if the ocean property can be mapped and included in national priorities.

Strategic Pronouncements and Geopolitical Entities

The geopolitical entities of the world in their process of integrating maritime security will have major tasks ahead if they are determined. This will follow through various steps in an entity specific manner that will include the following:

a. Constitution of a national security commission or a suitable agency that will work on behalf of the government on all matters related to the elements of national security towards NS_{max} and not just for the physical security of the nation as is being practiced today world over.
b. Mapping of nation's ocean property for integration with national security governance.
c. Integration of military armed forces under unified command.

d. Establishing accountability of non-military armed forces in their respective charter.
e. Avoiding duplication of efforts by government agencies.
f. Integration of intelligence services.
g. Training the government officials and peoples representatives in national security governance.
h. Establishing education in national security management and governance.
i. Restructuring the roles of all agencies accordingly
j. Continuous research, development and training on all elements of national security and their interactive governance for evolving strategies for NS_{max} governance preferably at educational institutions.
k. Establishing the national security index by appropriate means as a reference point for governance.
l. Reorganisation and restructuring of the apex decision-making bodies of the government to suit the requirement for integrated national security.
g. Reducing the gap between information related to policies and perception of the people by reviewing the information policy.

All these proclamations are from the macro level outlook.

Conclusions

The historical perspectives of maritime strategy lead the scholars to the ancient world that was bent upon warring for resources where navies had vital roles in support or independent action. All throughout the humans learned about the ocean. The awareness in the 18th century with Alfred Thayer Mahan breaking into the importance of the navy in leading the world with the ocean as the principal domain changed the outlook of sea power. His theory was based on the past glories of maritime nations. He gave a fairly intuitive vision of the immediate future that proved well in the First World War. Though the pattern of build up in the geopolitical scenario has changed especially in relations to naval arms race compared to the immediate period of Mahan's proclamations their validity still holds water. Mahan had many followers.

Elsewhere in China, Europe, India and Russia strategists were vocal on the importance of the ocean in national power. But the real take on the ocean game was with the introduction of UNCLOS by the world as a whole in the later part of the 20th century. The scenario of the post UNCLOS world has changed drastically. But many are yet to absorb the impact of the Convention and apply necessary reactive strategy in national planning. They may be slow, but it is not a serious matter considering the new dawn is just recent. There is no hurry. Maritime strategy even otherwise has been evolving at a very slow pace. Besides, the post UNCLOS scenario is going to stay for a very long time.

This study looks at maritime strategy from a different point of view compared to the foregone world. At the centre of it is maritime security, the complementary faction of national security. It is a terrain specific view. In this view the idea of sea power amalgamates with the national security maximisation. It is but not the sea power index that is going to matter but maximisation of national security with maritime security integrated with it. The modern proclamation of maritime strategy will be when it is made to cohabitate with national security in every aspect of national planning, not external to it.

NOTES

1 Hunting to settle is a nautical expression about the ships gyrocompass swinging to settle in the direction of true north after switching on.

2 In naval terms, a holiday means a break left behind, especially the space on a painted surface that is not covered.

3 en.wikipedia.org/wiki/Ancient_maritime_history, accessed 5 December 2012.

4 en.wikipedia.org/wiki/Maritime_history, accessed 5 Decemebr 2012.

5 wikipedia.org/wiki/Ancient_maritime_history, accessed 5 December 2012.

6 The study deviated here from its original concept of unitary civilisation for the purpose of explanation only. Indus Valley civilisation was part of the unitary civilisation at a different edge of the worm train according to the time and period.

7 There is no historical evidence of the war but many scholars believe there was historical core to the tale. The archeological site of Troy which is a world UNESCO heritage site today is located in Turkey. The historicity of Trojan War also points out that the war would have been part of the many Mycenaean sieges and expeditions looking for resources especially tin, the basic ingredient of bronze. The period was Bronze Age and the pricey metals of the period were copper and tin.

8 Encyclopaedia Britannica, Ultimate Reference Suite, 2004, CD-ROM. Also spelt Ch'in Shih Huang-ti (First Sovereign Emperor of Ch'in). Ch'in dynasty established the first great Chinese empire. The Ch'in, from which the name China is derived, established the approximate boundaries and basic administrative system that all subsequent Chinese dynasties were to follow for the next 2,000 years.

9 Emperor died by overdose of mercury, which he ironically took to become immortal.

10 Paleri, Prabhakaran, *National Security: Imperatives and Challenges,* New Delhi, Tata McGraw-Hill Publishing Limited, p.134. Also Ancient Aliens, History TV, 18 October 2013. According to some scientists the influenza came as if from nowhere and left the way it came. They attribute it to alien microbes from outer space carried by meteors and spread through meteorites.

11 World War II, en.wikipedia.org/wiki/D-Day, accessed 12 January 2013.

12 Ibid.

13 The psychology of invention is considered to be destruction according to

certain thought process as is evident in matters related to war directly or indirectly.

14 A commodore while serving; promoted to a rear admiral on retirement.

15 c250.columbia.edu/c250_celebrates/remarkable_columbians/alfred_thayer_mahan.html, accessed 12 January 2013 According to some scholars the publication year was 1890.

16 Paleri, n.10, p. 262. Super state occupies the top of the pyramid in the hierarchy of nations by maximising national security by governance according to author's study. The super state obviously will have the highest NSI over and above the prescribed limit for such consideration. It also means super power is not super state.

17 Manifest destiny is an interesting topic. It is about the destiny manifested in an individual or a group with respect to their potential. Manifest destiny to spread out to the world and influence it and thereby its destiny was not just an American behaviour system, it is nourished by various other societies and groups within the unitary civilisation of humankind. Appreciation of unitary civilisation throws light on manifest destiny as a not so obvious endgame. Many human systems believe in manifest destiny—as the future rulers of the world.

18 en.wikipedia.org/wiki/Manifest_Destiny, accessed 16 July 2013.

19 Mahan, Alfred, Thayer, Encarta Encyclopaedia, www.encarta.msn.com, accessed 14 November, 2001.

20 Calibration and validation.

21 www.airpower.maxwell.af.mil/airchronicles/cc/france1.html, accessed 21 January 2013.

22 Paleri, Prabhakaran, "The Dynamics of Power Projection in the Geostrategic Context, Long essay paper submitted to National Defence University, Washington D.C. as part of the curriculum requirement (unpublished), 22 March 1994.

23 Corbett, Julian, *Some Principles of Maritime Strategy,* Annapolis: Naval Institute Press, 1988, p. 15.

24 Ibid.

25 Not examined further.

26 "Will Never Seek Hegemony, Says China," *The Hindu*, Kochi: 22 January 2009, p. 13.

27 eyestreet.blogspot.in/2005/04/indian-ocean-is-not-indias-ocean.html, accessed 20 November 2012. A statement that Indian Ocean was not India's Ocean was attributed to a Chinese defence official in the past. India played down the remark. It is obvious that ocean divisions as a whole do not belong to any specific country

28 Also known as Indian Ocean rim.

29 Cracraft, James, *The Revolution of Peter the Great*, Harvard, Harvard University Press, 2003.

30 Ibid.

31 Russia: Power Play on the Oceans, www.time.com/ time/magazine/ article/ 0,9171,837933,00. Html #ixzz2a SOGKQEi, accessed 24 August 2013.

32 See Paleri, n.9

33 Threat, Vulnerability, Risk—Commonly Mixed up Terms, www.threatanalysis.com/blog/?p=43, accessed 13 June 2013.

34 Cordner, Lee Gee, Regional Resilience: the Imperative for Maritime Security Cooperation in South East Asia, Naval War College Review, New Port, Spring, 1994, pp. 41-56.

35 National Defence College. Proceedings of Seminar on "A Maritime Strategy for India," New Delhi, 1996, p. 13.

Chapter 6

GOVERNING MARITIME SECURITY: THE GHOST PROTOCOL

There is only one way to tame the ghost—reverse exorcise. That is integration.

> **Integrate** (inti-grāt) ***v. 1.*** *To make into a whole; unify.* ***2. To join with something else; unify. 3.*** *To open to people of all races or ethnic group without restriction; desegregate.*
>
> *Differentiate* (dif-uh-ren-shee-eyt) ***v. 1.*** *To constitute or perceive a distinction.* ***2.*** *To make or become different, distinct or speicalised.*

Governing maritime security is the crux of the matter. The finding so far indicates that maritime security evolved as an independent and exclusive concept of human system. The evolution was need-based and appreciation situated. It was punctuated in time but disjointed unlike the human system evolution over land that had a pattern of continuity. The continuity over land was natural as humans where firm on the ground under their survival instincts and not in the ocean. While the life and related aspects on land was continuous, ocean affinity was interrupted, often with a cameo projection. Ocean was a choice in life. It was brought in as and when needed. The requirement was often selective. The selective and otherwise detached approach towards the ocean still continues to the modern day. Many nations are yet to think about the impact of the sea on their national security seriously. People were mentally far from the sea and remained detached, though not insular, even while living along the coast. There were exceptions, though. Coupled with human apprehensions and natural perils of the dangerous terrain, humans exhibited a kind of numinous relation towards it. They remained curious about the ocean. The curiosity comes out of the mysterious appeal that the ocean had left in the human psyche over the period of time. It is interesting that people seems to be more familiar and cognitively privileged with the physical terrain of outer space than the geophysical terrain of ocean lapping on the shores at their backyards. That is why maritime security in this study has been treated as a curious case.

This attitude and mindset naturally reflected in human perception and percolated into the governance of human system from time immemorial as the way it existed then. Throughout the humans accepted that the sea was a diverse terrain and it could be exploited as it showed great potential for survival for them over land, the pedestal of their security. The ocean, unlike they think of it, is actually a part of the terra firma, though a different terrain for manoeuvres. It is a huge flood that is likely to rise and inundate more land in future declining to subside for a very long time. Probably the next ice age will begin with it.[1] Well, there is still time.

It is well-known that human system could be greatly benefited from the ocean irrespective of coastal or otherwise. The benefit can be maximised by integrating it with national security governance and not by governing in isolation or extraneously. It is integration that matters while dealing with a ghost protocol, not differentiation. Maritime security acts as a ghost protocol in a naturally land dominated governance. This will also give the evolution of maritime security the necessary fillip sans interludes. This is the basic argument.

The aspect of the ocean that first or foremost attracted the observant people or caught their attention was probably the mobility it offered. They found using platforms such as the dugout canoes, skin boats and other floating bodies they could move around the sea. It was not a knowledge find, but intellectual appreciation by observation. Principles of floating came much later in a scream—"Eureka!" Everyone knows it. The early people didn't have to know the science of vessel building or metacentric height as the platforms they created with whatever means they had served the purpose—floating and moving. This attitude rose to the limit when they made an "unsinkable" ship, the Titanic, as technology awareness grew. They believed and boasted the Titanic would not sink. Human fallibility with respect to sea was evident in the design of Titanic, which was a relatively modern seagoing luxury mammoth ever constructed by then. The construction was guided by the (limited) knowledge and certification facilities available at that time. After the Titanic disaster,[2] people knew there could not be an unsinkable ship. Every ship would sink when it loses buoyancy. And the buoyancy, it can lose unless jacked up over land. The idea, thereafter, became keeping them afloat as long as possible and in as bad a condition as could be expected. The attention turned towards safe ships and clean seas. Today, this statement has turned into a slogan by IMO—safe, secure and efficient shipping on clean oceans.

Warship designers too thought of unsinkable ships in the later years by manipulating buoyancy with reserve buoyancy, but did not succeed absolutely. There was competitive eagerness to make them also invincible. In this mad race, designers even lost their mind by absurd fixation on the problem by making them invisible. There was a time when the naval technologists thought that they could make the ships simply vanish from the prying eyes of the enemy lookouts using reverse magnetism by the degaussing techniques under the principles of the just thought out unified field theory. They tried it out, as reported later, in the disastrous Philadelphia Experiment. It was said to have been conducted by the US Navy in the Philadelphia naval yard under utmost secrecy on a naval destroyer escort USS Eldridge on 28 October 1943.[3] The US Navy, however, denied ever conducting such an experiment. The report stated that the US Navy felt making a ship invisible would offer it the perfect camouflage and help them win the Second World War that was continuing without signs of ending or victory to the allies. Absurdity gets generated at critical situations even in the most intelligent mind by situational expediency.[4] In dealing with the ocean, it is also associated with the mystical nature of it. The report on the Philadelphia Experiment surfaced in later years, notably against the background of the hocus-pocus "now-you-see them, now-you-don't" Bermuda Triangle, an area of the Atlantic where there were reports about ships and aircraft vanishing mysteriously. The Philadelphia Experiment was also reported along with it stating an experiment was conducted to make a naval ship invisible that ended up in surprises to all involved not only on invisibility but also teleporting! The less said about it is better since there is no scientific or recorded evidence.

For anything, such reports show the way the ocean settles down in the minds of people within the inherent abstractionism of human thinking even in a period that was reasonably advanced. There is no story about any such endeavour over land-warfare or in military aviation. Of course, there were stories about unidentified flying objects (UFO), again in the United States. They were straight and simple—unidentified, period. Leave it there. That had nothing to do with the mystery of the airspace as a terrain.

All these also indicate that curiosity of the unknown never leaves the ocean. Ocean is simply seen as an alien terrain and behaves that way—mysterious. Keep off it; but don't leave it!

Today, in a better and advanced knowledge environment, ship design and construction are much more accommodating than in the days of the Titanic or Eldridge. Warship designers too are aware that it is not possible to design an unsinkable or invisible platform. But they can continuously thrive for better stealth, buoyancy, firepower and sustainability under extreme harms-way (EHW)[5].

The ship is the camel of the sea. It dominates the sea. Without a ship the humans cannot involve and deal with the sea seriously. The ship holds the sea for the humans to be there. In these statements the ship means any vessel[6] as legally defined according to international law.

The study of shipbuilding slowly developed against this understanding and branched out into an art and science combo with many variations. Shipbuilding became a technology oriented subject. It is interesting to note that shipbuilding did not become the monopoly of those who were good in it in the ancient days. Ideally it should have been. It also explains the interruptions in maritime security thinking mentioned earlier. Shipbuilding prowess changed hands. Countries with focused governance and marine orientation relative to national governance became masters of composite shipbuilding not only with respect to technology but also with the human element. Today anyone with such integrated governance can get into the field. The countries that were traditionally excelled in shipbuilding where pushed behind not only by the aggressiveness of the new entrants in the field but also due to the absence of focus in their governance and over and above failed governance in relation to the subject. Some countries, India for example, attribute the distressing decline of its ancient position as an exemplary shipbuilder to British colonial subjugation. Blame-throwing has no meaning in the dynamics of governance. It sounds a matter of rationalisation under incompetent national governance. India had sufficient time post independence to develop and refresh its ancient shipbuilding prowess by modernising the approach and integrating it with national governance seriously. But it did not have the acuity of governance from this perspective. This incompetence is seen in its dependency in shipbuilding in spite of huge and expensive projects undertaken by its many shipyards. But the pace is too slow and the competence too low to drive the future. A number of countries like India had lost their ancient prowess in shipbuilding giving way to modern entrants. There are many newcomers who have established by careful planning and governance. Why many traditionally sound countries failed in nurturing their skills or many who never possessed any such skills are developing and transferring shipbuilding knowledge today will make an interesting study leading to integrating maritime security with national security efforts. Shipping is not the only example; it was probably the earliest example of appreciating the interaction of humans with the ocean. There are various aspects including shipbuilding dealing with maritime security that need to be examined to understand how their integration promotes national security governance.

The Case for Integrated Maritime Security

The case for integrated maritime security vacillates on various aspects related to the ocean starting with shipbuilding in a chronological hierarchy. This study identifies the following in the line of appreciation:

- Shipbuilding
- Shipping
- Warfighting and naval military forces
- Law enforcement
- Service
- Resource exploitation

- Research
- Establishing rights
- Others in future

Shipbuilding

The world builds ships today with steel plates welded together or other advanced materials. The ancient shipbuilders of repute were China, Egypt, Greece, India, Phoenicia, Rome, Scandinavia, Mediaeval Europe, Iraq, Melanesia, Polynesia, etc. The oldest dock identified was at Lothal, modern day India, estimated to have been built around 2500 B.C. Today, shipbuilding is a multifaceted area of technology. It encompasses shipyards, ship repair yards, ship recycling and demolishing yards, marine equipment manufacturers, offshore platform and habitat builders and many related service and knowledge providers. It is a strategic industry that has particular reference to skilled workers, industries providing components, infrastructure for movement of materials and the nation's need to manufacture, maintain and repair its own warfighting vessels for military security. Shipbuilding in modern parlance is a wholesome domain of national security and, thereby, more than a part of maritime security. The countries that hold command over the world in shipbuilding in the early 21st century are China, South Korea, Japan, and European Union, in that order, the last one in a very limited way, at just about one per cent. Among them only China can be credited with an ancient shipbuilding heritage. Remainders are new entrants. China did neither loose the hold over it nor disregarded it. The reason for being the world's number one shipbuilder (2010) arises from the fact of China's attempts to integrate its terrain specific aspects of national security governance.

Considering the various elements and interactive processes involved in shipbuilding, a country can acquire the leading role only if the national security system is integrated. For example, shipbuilding is associated with shipping and commercial transportation, and maritime operatives for other than commercial operations that include military operations, law enforcement, service providing, research, exploration, exploitation, etc. Shipping is a facet that is economically needed for any country. Without movements of goods, countries and other geographical entities even if landlocked or geographically disadvantaged cannot survive. The rest of the activities are very much essential for every country and other geopolitical entity in varying degrees to maximise the returns from its ocean property.

Shipping

Like shipbuilding, shipping too is not just an ocean based activity. It is an important aspect of commercial shipping. The entire activity except transportation occurs over the land in various geopolitical entities. There is no business like shipping where every element of the business profile comes from or engaged with different parts of the world. These include the nationality of the owner and the crew, port of registry, cargo source and destination, managers, agencies, etc.

Commercial shipping was very much there in the ancient world. Earliest reference to commercial shipping is believed to be in India during the Mauryan period (323-185B.C.). There was a fusion of Indo-Greek elements during that period as recorded mostly in Greek history.[7] In fact almost all the countries that have been credited in ancient shipbuilding were also good in commercial shipping. Primarily they built ships for the purpose of the period as per demand. But none of them including China or India can boast a good maritime track record in modern times. The countries that were great sailing entities once upon a time do not have a place in the glorious growth of commercial shipping as holders of commercial tonnage. But China is slowly emerging from the fog as the recent reports indicate. It was ninth in the world in terms of ship registration in 2010.[8]

The reasons for decline in ship registration among traditional countries were many. Among them was the rise of "flags of convenience" (FOC). Since World War II, shipping tonnage grew rapidly in open registry system which was under the flags of convenience. The modern practice of registering ships in foreign countries to gain economic advantage came into practice in United States in the era of World War I. The term flag of convenience came into usage in 1950. From five per cent of the world tonnage in 1950, the tonnage held by flags of convenience grew to 68 per cent in 2011.[9] Flags of convenience provided ease in regulatory and manning costs. The national owner could register ships in another country that offered concessions in regulation, registry costs and operating costs. Flags of convenience provided less stringent regulations, low rates of registry which moved around 30 to 50 per cent at times and 12 to 27 per cent reduction in operating costs. The savings in operating costs are from lower personnel costs. Of course, the wages and other benefits offered to the crew are normally at reduced rate. Because of this reason, the large ship-owning countries today are flags of convenience. The top 10 countries of the world in terms of tonnage registration are Panama, Liberia, Marshall Islands, Hong Kong, Greece, Singapore, the Bahamas, Malta, China and Cyprus, in that order in 2010, according to the Office of the Maritime Administration, US Department of Transportation.[10] Among them the Bahamas, Cyprus, Liberia, Malta, Marshall Islands, and Panama are flags of convenience. China, Greece, Hong Kong and Singapore are not open registry. They are more serious about ship registration and their hold in world tonnage is seemingly increasing. Here, again, China's advancement in maritime security matters is convincingly conspicuous.

All types of ships are registered in these countries—dry bulk, container, tanker and others. Regulations are lax in flags of convenience. Ship registry is a source of additional income for any country. Flags of convenience take a major chunk of this money. It is economics for them. Addressing problems associated with flags of convenience vessels can be daunting but for the countries it adds to the economy and for the owners it is all about convenience and money saved. There are also heavy criticisms of the flag of convenience system alleging that they flout safety, treat crew badly, engage in maritime fraud and are uncared about marine environment. There are occasional complaints that some of the flags of convenience vessels deal in unlawful activities at sea.[11] In modern times doubts are expressed about the possibility of terrorists using ships with preferred choice to flags of convenience. Another criticism against them is that the flags of convenience states avoid ratification or failing to enforce important international treaties related to safety of vessels that come from International Maritime Organization (IMO) and International Labour Organisation (ILO).

An important and encouraging aspect is the involvement of landlocked countries like Mongolia in ship registry services. Under the international law, a merchant ship has to be registered in a country. It becomes the flag state with a civil ensign that the ship flies. The flag state has the responsibility to establish the ship seaworthy under the law. Open registry permits avoidance of tax and other mandatory laws in terms of labour, etc., of a country by adopting the flags of convenience mode of registry. The question is, "Can such laxity impact on maritime safety?"

According to International Transport Workers Federation (ITF) there are 32 flag of convenience registries.[12] There are also ports of convenience according to a report of ITF in 2006. The ports of convenience operate like the flags of convenience according to them where concern for dockworkers wellbeing is limited.

It can be seen that the choice to become a flag of convenience or, for countries like China, to view seriously about shipping is about integration of commercial shipping with national planning as integrated maritime security. The countries do not visualise maritime security in isolation. It is a considered approach and decision aimed at the element of economic security among others.

The world of ships is the major part of the ocean property regime under the ocean advantage. Nations take it selectively or rather partially without being absolutely concerned that the entire ocean property regime needs ships of all kinds to manage. The first principle of managing any terrain under terrain specificity is the appropriate platform. The ground is the ultimate platform for the humans. But they have to enter other terrains also for governing national security. Here they encounter serious limitations. The most appropriate platform needs to be identified for manoeuvring in national security governance by playing the game over the terrain, incompatible most of the time. For the ocean, it is the ship. It has to meet the purpose. A ship is the ultimate engine of commerce, naval warfare, law enforcement at and from the sea, ocean research, marine environmental protection, oceanic island protection, ocean residence, climate change management and various other activities associated with the ocean. The ship has to be seen from the ocean property regime point of view as required by the nation instead of selectively from the purpose point of view. Otherwise there is a chance of over or under playing the requirement. Both are damaging to national security requirements. Planning ship requirement includes the number and types of ships required for national security governance based from the point of view of national security maximisation. Ships are necessary to harvest the ocean property. It is not necessary that a country has to be littoral to benefit from it; it is available for landlocked and geographically disadvantaged states too. Mongolia is an example as already mentioned. Mongolia, an ancient maritime country, said to have had the world's largest navy in the 13th century, is landlocked today. It has shown interest in shipping activities as part of economic development. There are other landlocked countries too who, once in a while, dabble in maritime activities. Laos had shown the maritime will to take a stride into the ocean using the Mekong River through Cambodia and Vietnam. But it is yet to venture deep. It can, by focusing on integrated maritime security. Many landlocked countries are members of IMO and signatories to various international maritime agreements.

The study of ships and shipping requirement is in two parts—building and operation. The nation can take decision on buy, make, hire, lease and even outsource operations. But there are many limitations. The decision could be well decided based on purpose. For example, any equipment related to war will be best made in the country itself. It is historically proven that war is won with own weapons and not bought, borrowed or leased ones. Yes, there are borrowed and leased weapons and means of warfare inventory including ships that had been demolished or sunk in war. A leased one may provide experience in managing it. Ships may be bought or hired from elsewhere or made in one's own country with an objective of export in a globalised world. These decisions can be taken only after mapping the overall ocean property and targeting on the requirement of maximising the benefits from it. Further, it is a question of integrating appropriately with national security governance.

Integration of maritime security is more a rational activity. It begins the moment when the government looks at maritime security as part of national security and not in the exclusivity of detached governance. It will be interesting to introspect and explore into the style and priorities of chosen governments including one's own to understand integration of maritime security in their national security governance.

In the integration of maritime security, ship design, building and operation become a national obsession. It has to be a centralised activity at the highest level from where the activities converge to the specialised sector. The policies should originate from the central focus on shipping activities. The apex body of national planning should be aware of ocean property signature of the country and the ways to maximise the returns from it.

Today most of the nations, barring those who are serious and aware, look at commercial shipping, naval warfare, rule of law, service providing, ocean research, etc., separately as if they are mutually exclusive. It could turn out to be a mistake in planning and policy according to this study. Vessel operations should be highly integrated. They cannot be separate. It will be clear from the fact the largest and decisive marine landing in World War II was with the maximum support of the merchant marine fleet. The naval ships need to escort merchant ships on their passage through piracy infested waters even in modern times. There is a symbiotic strategic relationship between national shipping and national maritime forces that should reflect even in national commercial tonnage. No country looks at ship building in this manner, as an overall policy of the nation in relation to design and construction of ships for various purposes under a single window decision making. The decision should show the end for ocean vessels of all types a nation needs, whether to make, buy or charter them, etc., and how they would be operated. In this decision, it is imperative that warship design, production and research should be exclusively a national activity if the purpose is warfighting, which it has to be. Decisions on merchant ship building can be based on advantage. Warship building should also be export targeted as in any weapon or associated system from the economics and geostrategic point of view. Otherwise, the aspect cannot be integrated in the overall national security governance. Here the term warship is used for a ship belonging to the armed forces of a state as defined in Article 29 of UNCLOS. Any sample examination, barring some exceptions about shipbuilding programmes will show disconnected linkages in the system. That is indicative that the system is not even integrated within. In such cases integrating the overall maritime security aspects of shipbuilding and ship operation including combat requirements with national security will not be exact. A nation that has integrated maritime security in this fashion has to be watched for speed and alacrity in gaining maritime supremacy in the modern world and not just focusing on the maritime strategies examined so far. They are outdated for the modern world.

Warfighting and Naval Military Forces

Naval war is engagement in combat in, on, over and from the sea. The sea remains the combat zone. The primary platform is the ship, the ultimate habitat of the ocean—surface or underwater. A ship's journey through war and beyond commences from the design stage followed by keel laying and construction or production as legally appreciated.[13] The "only" purpose of a naval ship is warfighting. If not, it is not ideally a warship; it may be legally, though. A warship has to be war compatible. Every other purpose for which a naval combat ship is put or naval personnel deployed will not only be secondary but also pose the danger of blunting its cutting edge in many ways. A surgical knife has just one purpose. Once used for something else it can't be on the surgical table again.

Warfighting is not just engagement between adversaries at or from the sea. It has a lot to do with geostrategic security for which the navy is the only suitable force among the military forces. Geostrategic security is not about posing in an adversarial manner with naval fleets stationed close to the target nation's backyard waters. It was a tactical manoeuver in the olden days with an apt name "power projection." Flexing muscles is not modern day power message unless diplomatic snag is acceptable in the overall national security governance. Power projections today has to be achieved through sublime suggestions of what a country can do when the need arrives. The navy can be used aptly for such purpose as in the earlier version of power projection. This aspect can be seen from all the activities ongoing with respect to the show of presence at sea, geostrategic interactions through goodwill visits, joint exercises and operations, acquisition of overseas bases, cooperative engagement in resource sharing, support in disaster situations, etc. The country should be clear about this ultimate purpose of having a navy. It is very important for the country to understand that using its navy for law enforcement or providing service in the routine manner is an extremely reckless and shortsighted policy approach driven by traditional baggage and reluctance of the naval personnel to be combat minded. It is very imprudent. It is not sufficient for naval warfighting to have ships with punch but also people who are combat oriented and compatible. The latter is quite important. A navy that indulges in law enforcement or providing service in the usual manner will end up in a different area of expertise. Besides, normally a military force is not used for law enforcement unless the situation demands under the modern constitutional outlook. There are other agencies for law enforcement suitably empowered. The navy being a military armed force will not only fail to appreciate warfighting but also will lose their combat orientation by extraneous soft core indulgence. Losing the combat orientation is more dangerous as it is highly irreversible, especially when the navy is equipped for war and is aiming towards establishing sea power. Ideally, a naval ship, however powerful it is as fitted out, will not be combat ready unless "everything and everyone" in it is "engaged" in real or virtual terms in combat and geostrategic operations constantly, in modern times. It is for the government to examine and audit. It should not be "chartered out with crew" for other purposes such as law enforcement and services unless they are to be executed with military precision or of similar nature. Among the 107 navies, identified by the author in a study in 2008,[14] there are hardly a few that may fall somewhat within this paradigm. Among those who tend to follow the principle of "exclusive regimen of military and geostrategic integration with national security" can be counted. They too have a lesson here to stop and interlude in serious introspection. Simply put, under the principle of integrated maritime security, every navy in this world that calls itself a navy need to brush up to be of value to the state. Most of them may even change their title into other maritime force. Hybridism means disaster for a military force that has to have affinity with EHW, similar to the legendary salamander's affinity with fire. It is more so when they are handled by humans. Humans are the weakest link in the operation of a highly advanced technological process. This statement is a warning to check human efficiency degeneration in any such process.

One of the roles in which the military forces are deployed is disaster relief operations. The conduct of such operations should be on war footing if carried out by the military so that it becomes a training ground for military operations. One of the ways to assess such operations is from the finesse sans accidents and other casualties. A military that meets with accidents in its missions or standard operations in other-than-war situations including disaster operations or exercises have a reason to sit back and seriously introspect. The "more you sweat in peace, the less you bleed in war" is a forlorn jingle. First of all peace is an abstract term, especially in relation to a government. Secondly sweat is common; it is blood that a force has to think about. "The force that bleeds in other-than-war situation is the one that is likely to be drained off it in war" could be more appropriate. Everything what a force, especially a military force, does should be an evolution, the one that has to be executed fastest in a way that is more than perfect and precise, where the drills and procedures are to be better than the best. Accidents are always warning signs to a force. There is much to learn from accidents and mishaps, even the minor and neglected ones, in relation to combat capabilities of a military armed force. A military force has to be accident free. Accidents can expose the chink in the armour to the keen observer, internal as well as external.

The navies were more combat-ready and oriented towards war in the early periods of the 3000 years or so when they were at sea in combat with the elements, if not with the enemy, almost every day. Among the 107 navies of the world (2008), as mentioned earlier, only a few have combat experience or compatibility. Naval strategy has been considered as the maritime strategy in the earlier periods. It ended there. There was also nothing else in maritime strategy. It has changed for both maritime strategy as well as naval strategy. Naval strategy has dissolved within the overall maritime strategy on one hand focusing exclusively on the military aspects; on the other, it has come out and spilled over to the national security strategy expanding into various other elements, especially geostrategic security, economic security, disaster security, etc. This can also be said about the coast guards and other select maritime forces and agencies. Many of the tools of maritime strategy have external linkages towards national security elements. These requirements highlight the importance of the need for integration of maritime security with national security without which a nation cannot acquire maximum benefit. One such integration is with the new and changing concept of geostrategy. Geostrategy is not a military function. It is a diplomatic function dealing with foreign policy and affairs. War is when it fails and no other means are available. War is just one of the instruments of foreign policy even today. It is more in the dark sense in modern times. That is the difference. Navy and, to some extent, other maritime armed forces like the coast guards have serious roles in the geostrategic context. Naval strategy in its original framework was maritime strategy. Even then it was about the planning and conduct of war at and from the sea according to one definition. But it needs to be elaborated further to include not only military security but also the other elements of national security in the integrated approach. As mentioned earlier, the navy is an excellent tool for geostrategic interaction and security. Navies can be engaged in cooperative strategy in handling situations at sea. The cooperative strategy is not only external but also among the nation's own maritime forces and agencies. However, it depends entirely on the compatibility genesis of the maritime forces of the country. This includes the navy too.

The United States set an example of the cooperative strategy by internalising it with the Marine Corps and the coast guard in 2007. This model may not work for other countries as the genesis of the compatibility of their maritime forces can be different. They may have to consider other models suitable to them when crafting cooperative strategy among their maritime forces. The danger is about domination of the navy over smaller or considered smaller maritime forces. It is a very serious matter and undermines the overall national security strategy in many ways including duplication, cost and isomorphism of human and organisational element into less intensive operations. Domination of other armed forces by the navy, which is a military armed force designed for higher intensity operations, causes more harm to itself than other forces that it attempts to dominate and control. It is self destructive in the long run. Most of the nations face this problem. Such human element will never be able to perform in EHW situations subsequently. The navy, in general, feels historically that it should be the only force at sea especially where governance is inept in integrating or unifying the armed forces. In countries where decision-making lacks prudence, the navy may even oppose creation of another force besides them in the maritime field. The thinking, if at all it is there, is based on the absurdity principles that have been carried forward in maritime aspects from the historical periods when navy alone rode the waves. That was sufficient then as their role was not so intense and missions so diverse within the two functions—warfighting and geostrategy. But the mindset holds. The navy is conditioned to resist the creation of another maritime force or dominate it if the government goes ahead with the induction conception as in many countries today. Under domination, the essence of cooperative strategy gets dissolved totally. Not only the purpose gets diluted but also the individual forces lose their glitter in their respective duties and functions. The accountability gets concentrated on the dominant agency totally absolving the rest in the collective framework which will not be a cooperative format anyway. It will also impact upon integration of maritime security with national security. One of the ways to understand the possibility or existence of integrated maritime security in a nation is to examine the interactive matrix and the assigned roles of the maritime forces of that country. The individual authorities of the maritime forces should be assured of their freedom in decision making according to their charter and reminded of their accountability at all times to the government under such charter in a cooperative strategy. Among the dangers of the naval domination of other maritime forces is blunting the cutting edge of the navy and eroding the accountability of other maritime forces towards the government. Complacency sets in fast in an organisation, like gangrene in human body, when accountability is eroded. There are many more problems. The alliance will be mutually destructive. It has to be facilitated by their design, charter and integration. This is especially so as ideally a navy should be designed for global operations including external littoral operations and not localised brown water management of the country more in a defensive posture. The navy should have the "headway" from own shores. It should not lose it. The US perhaps is the only country that has been definite in this mandate as seen from the powers of the US Congress "to provide and maintain a navy" in the Constitution and the operational doctrines of the navy, marine corps, and the coast guard, which is also a military armed force in the United States. It is not so in many parts of the world. The navy is not strictly meant for defence unless defence is part of the offensive strategy. The US Navy is there for a definite purpose that obviously implies to external matters.[15]

The role of the navy is changing. More and more, the role is supplementing national security efforts which are beyond maritime security aspects. Maritime security is also expanding into various other fields. It means the navy will have to slowly switch beyond the exclusivity of the ocean. The navy may crawl onto the shore like many life forms that originated at sea. This is not a mythical statement. It is real. What do the marines do? They crawl "into the mud" in their own slogan. The future of the navy will also be land based. This will make maritime security too to take cover over land under the principles and concepts of national security.

The role of the navy in warfighting and geostrategic security context has to be highlighted seriously. In the initial days, the navy was deployed for sealift of land troops and supplies, combat at sea, combat from the sea, antipiracy operations and ocean based exploration. Importance of the navy varied for nations. For example, the role of the ancient Egyptian navy that has a history as old as the country itself was different from those of the Greeks or the Romans. It depended on the perception of governance. Still the ancient Egyptian navy transported additional troops and logistics for the campaigning Egyptian army. The Egyptian kings of the New Kingdom reorganised the navy with a new role—maintaining Egyptian power and influence abroad. It was geostrategic security at the prime. A very ancient role, indeed. Navy was moving beyond maritime security even then. The combat at sea in those days was based on archery, boarding for armed combat as well as ramming till the cannons evolved. The largest war the ancient Egyptian navy involved was, according to some scholars, against the Sea Peoples in the 10th century B.C. Rameses III during his reign (1182-1151 B.C.) prepared a navy that created a formidable wall at the mouth of the Nile against the invading Sea Peoples who had already created havoc and destroyed the mighty Hittites in the Levantine region.

The role of the navy is ultimately winning the war by supporting other military forces in a terrain of its own. Thus the nation makes an integrated team for warfighting and combat scenario during war and other-than-war situations. The latter is the normal period when nations are not engaged in a declared war. This study does not recognise the term "peace" when it is about national security. The term is fine in fictitious conceptions and idealistic interludes. It is best to leave the term peace in peace forever.

Navy is the most useful tool a government has for diplomacy. No government is aware of it. It is not surprising. It can be attributed to the landclasp syndrome of governance. But matured governments are able to understand it and the navy is becoming prominent as floating ambassadors of national power projection through diplomatic engagements. So far it is good. It can be made better. Diplomacy is not between governments in a bureaucratic fashion but between people to people who in turn regulates governmental thinking.

The identified functions of the navy in the early days are summarised below.

- Transportation of troops and supplies to where required (sealift and reach).
- Serving as a platform for archers of the land force to fire arrows upon the enemy at sea or from the sea (attack and defence).

- Destruction of enemy ships and sailors by boarding or ramming (attack and defence).
- Power projection at sea on neighbours and distant coastal entities (adversarial geostrategic security).
- Passive cautioning of adversaries by presence and posture at sea close to them (geostrategy).

Naval strategies adopted by the countries historically and in modern times included,

- logistics movements and sea lift,
- battle at sea,
- blockade (sea denial),
- commerce raiding,
- fleet-in-being,
- costal defence,
- power projection,
- nuclear deterrence,
- air traffic support and
- forward missile defence.

The priorities of the purpose varied among the entities and were as decided by the situation and decisions of governance in whatever forms they were.

Today, the role of the navy remains much the same, but in a different apparel. The navies may not know it, but they are the best suited for these roles according to this study. The identified roles of the navy are,

- warfighting and combat engagements in support of other terrain forces in every respect,
- transportation of troops and supplies to the scene where needed independently or through convoys and
- geostrategic affirmation under the principles of the element of geostrategic security in support of the nation's diplomatic policies.

All the three functions are highly intense and complementary to national security. They are the primary roles of a navy. Ideally there should not be any secondary functions. But, of course, the navies cannot get away from them. In most of the cases, a good number of navies will be performing only the secondary roles.

These roles are important for a navy to be what it should be. But all navies are not capable of doing it. Or their national policies may not converge on to them. The ultimate navy in its role as seen from the overall naval strategy of the United States can be different from what the other 106 navies are. But that is what any navy has to aspire for. A general summation is given below.

- Provide the necessary reach in war and other-than-war situation in every respect to the country effectively utilising the ocean advantage.
- Prevent and preempt the threat to national security at and from the sea along with other maritime forces with due respect to their charter of duty and without diluting their accountability.
- Support the national security efforts of the ocean terrain.
- Prepare for strategic posture in the nuclear war scenario under the adopted nuclear doctrine of the country.
- Support national security efforts in confidence building measures (CBM).
- Spread out to the world in geostrategic missions in a cooperative posture.
- Support other national security efforts of the country without duplication of efforts.

The Cold War style power projection is no more the factored mode in the modern world. The Cold War nations have refrained from it since 1992. Some of them even drastically downsized their navies. Geostrategic influence has to be gained through friendly gestures and approaches with established presence of the navy. It is the Chinese practice today even though there are coercive reflections, especially where there is dissonance in maritime claims. China seemingly is on the forefront of the modern naval theory that is yet to unfold in a definite form. This is more a hypothetical statement. Friendly power projections inducing fear as the key in a sublime manner is what the navy can achieve provided it can get out of the mental shackles that keep it on the native shores when it can afford to get out into the sea.

For a nation, sea power should be in support of its national objectives. Ideally, for every nation, the national objective should be maximisation of national security. It is not likely to be for a very long time, as the principles of national security, this study advocates, are not universally accepted as a converging format for inception by governance. Hence it will remain as an idealist philosophy or finding at the moment that is engaged selectively by the governments. The time is yet to come. It will. This is in spite of the fact that the principles of national security can be implemented without serious mishap. The governmental systems, however, will need a major overhaul to adapt to the new national security principles envisaged in this study.

But what are the functions of a navy in support to the national objectives? It cannot be stated unless the government articulates the national objectives. Often navies fix their roles and functions without understanding the national objectives. There are also situations when the nation has not articulated its objectives in the absence of a formal national security plan. But the problem with the human element of an armed force is the haziness in understanding its role and functions. It doesn't matter at the lower echelons. But ignorance can be a bane in the hands of people in authority. A government may wreak havoc under ignorant governance. Often this happens with maritime security. It takes time to get to know the damages which often will be categorised under whimsical terms after passage of time. Understanding the functions and roles of the navy in achieving the national objectives is a must in any policy decisions by and for the navy of any country.

The mission of a navy originates from this. The only country that has been seen in this study with an articulated mission for its navy is the United States. The mission of the navy is categorically stated in Title 10 of the US Code. It states that the navy must be prepared to conduct prompt and sustained combat operations in support of the national objectives.[16] It clearly indicates the role of the navy on national interest. Such role can be performed by the navy only if maritime security is integrated with national security. It also means that the navy must assure continued maritime superiority for the United States. The US Navy must be able to totally defeat any threats to the continued free use of the high seas by the United States.

One of the aspects that have not changed so far since the world wars is the situations in which the forces fight and the theories associated with war. It will be too mild if the situation is mentioned as "harms-way." A combat is extreme harms-way (EHW). It is not just a situation of danger. It is beyond that. That is why war machines including the personnel today will have to be seen as fighters even when under debilitating hits. It is more so with the machines. People can succumb to EHW disaster faster than machines. People need the confidence from the "machine" in an EHW situation like war. A naval ship meant for combat (they should be only for that) should be able to fight under extreme harms-way. A ship should be functional even after it is hit. The ability to carry on combat even in EHW is what the designers have to see. This is not a new concept. It has been seen on many occasions in the past where ships could withstand hits.

The naval doctrine of some countries may have a clause stating that the navy assures maritime superiority of the country in the ocean by destroying hostile aircraft, surface ships and submarines that threaten seaborne forces of the country and its allies. It is far from truth about the role of the modern navy. Navy is not on a Kill Bill mission today[17]. The navy will have to exercise caution in maritime engagements unless there is a declared war. Today it can be done through cooperative engagement which is a serious aspect of geostrategic security. Prudent nations will engage cooperatively. No other forces can be as effectively deployed as the navy in such engagements since these forces can be made mobile worldwide overwhelmingly, if planned well.

Any efforts or mission of the navy has to be within the framework of the national policy. It will require coordination, cooperation, integration and jointness at every stage. It also will have a lot to do with national security strategy. Unless integrated, the national strategy will be with gaps. National security strategy is a broad course of action designed to achieve national objectives in support of national interests. Military forces are required to maintain sovereignty of a country by achieving physical security and political independence that is identified as the military security, the oldest element of national security. For this process, the forces will be capable of deterring aggression in overt and covert forms and to prevent or preempt coercion. The armed forces of a nation also help in geostrategic security and partially other elements by influencing other nations to shape the future events conducive to the country in a value based manner. It is important that negating another country's interest could be counterproductive. A country will be successful only if the rest of the world is successful. Most of the difficulties encountered by a nation that is otherwise successful come from those that are unsuccessful. National objectives are specific activities leading to the desired goal identified. The objectives lead to the goal. They can change en route without a change in the goal. They can also change when the goal modifies. The armed forces, therefore, will require the desired flexibility and reflex. Often this is absent in a military system. The government will have to be attentive to this paradigm. If not, the forces will be on a different approach path from what the nation desires at a particular moment. This inertia is very serious and often leads to military dissatisfaction which may not have immediate outlets. Most of the unexpected political scenarios in the world occur by this inertia. The government and the forces, therefore, will have to be in synch at all times. Such synchronisation is easier when the military command is integrated with the national security format of the country. Under such integration communication downwards will not be a casualty. Though may not announce in public or express outwardly, governments are always apprehensive of losing power to the military. Constitutions may not provide absolute immunity to the government from military takeovers directly or indirectly. Governments may resort to various means under such apprehension. One of them is to leave the armed forces totally independent and exclusive from each other. It can affect integration in the absence of effective leadership at command level. The balancing act of the government may not work all the time. National interests in socio-political paradigm are generalised conditions frequently of a continuing nature, the pursuit or protection of which is perceived to be advantageous to the nation. National interests can often get mixed up with political interests causing conflict though such conflicts are also necessary to balance governance. An approach to maximise national security, as defined in this study, has the advantage of understanding the deviation by all concerned. Under such appreciation the role of an armed force, the navy here, will be clear and defined well in relation to the particular country that has a naval force. Navy, like any other military outfit, is a costly proposition. A country will have to identify its optimum navy to balance the cost. It is a long drawn out process. No government applies its mind seriously to it. Often, it is thought the larger the better. There are exceptions of governments engaged in enlarging and downsizing the navies. China is an example on the outset for enlarging the navy towards optimum as it envisages in the beginning of the 21st century. Whereas, the US downsized to the optimum after the Cold War. There are no other examples that this study can quote. The navy that a country holds today could be either above or below the optimum size required. Both ways it impacts on national security. The utility of such navy in value is mostly under integrated maritime security. Understanding the optimum size and character of a navy or any other maritime force and agency is possible only when maritime security is integrated with national security. It should not be planned under wish lists that too prepared without serious thinking.

Sustained combat operation at sea is the primary function of the navy. It is about military security. But a navy will be capable of performing non-military operations too. It is important for naval commanders to see that such operations where they get engaged in the nonmilitary frame should not in any way blunt the cutting edge of the navies. This is a serious matter as long as navy is manned by the human element, which it will be for a very long time. The human element the military has a tendency to drift into the mediocre, where mediocre means anything that the humans can do or are designed to do. For this purpose even the highest and the most competitive activity a human performs as a record or genius is mediocre, because the very performance of it shows it can be performed by a human; hence mediocre relative to war. War is the only activity that this study considers outside the perimeter of the mediocre by its nature and demand. It is an exceptional task for which human beings are not designed, especially when it is about winning. Humans will have to perform beyond the designed human capabilities (physical and mental) in war. This is the underlying principle of art of war. The danger of a navy becoming mediocre means it may stop behaving like the navy—a force that has to perform the beyond mediocre task in the EHW environment. Hence it is important that navy is above the normality in a psycho-physiological posture for fighting wars. There is a lot to do in preparing a navy for EHW missions. It is also important for every other military armed force. The navy becomes a navy only when it is detached from the mainland. It should not be an inward looking landclasp force. The adaptation of integrated maritime security by a country can be easily visualised the way it uses its navy.

There are other parameters too. It also amounts to assessing its sea power quotient which is a factor that contributes to the overall sea power status of the nation. It also means, according to the study, the sea power status of nation in modern times comes from various inputs in which the navy is a major contributor. Navy is not just ships. It will include every platform and weapon designed for operation at sea and from the sea along with the people behind them.

Warfighting is also about suppressing enemy naval commerce and logistics movements. In war, the sea should belong to the navy. The navy should be able to control and blockade the ocean terrain of its interest in war. It is not just about sinking merchant ships. It is also about establishing naval supremacy in the area of interest. The vital sea areas should be under naval control.

Naval warfighting is aimed at providing support to the ground forces that will ultimately hold the ground at the decisive moment when the war will end. The hold gives the bargaining power at the time of end-of-war resolutions. This is applicable to the declared war. There can be many undeclared war situations in which also the navy may participate. It may not be as much as the ground forces engagement. It is a difficult situation. The combatant will be nonmilitary or military. The situation will be other-than-war. It is extremely important when the world is turning towards external decisions for engaging in war such as that of the United Nations and also has to face many nonmilitary combatants in the form of terrorists, pirates, insurgents, etc. Such wars are more difficult to tackle in the modern world because of various restrictions. Alleged violations in an undeclared war are viewed more seriously. It is also difficult to establish war syndromes to argue for in undeclared combat situations as often the enemy is within.

The complexity of naval functions has to be examined frequently to establish a doctrine. The doctrine should not be mistaken for the function of the navy. A country will not require a navy unless the two functions mentioned above are important for it. There are other maritime forces to take care of rule of law, services and management of ocean property. The pressures on the navies will be obsolescence (from ship design to weapon technology), balancing operating cost, idling of people and machinery, depreciation of warfighting tonnage, balancing the hi-low mix aspects, meeting the new requirements (scientific warfare, unmanned combat, netcentric warfare, nuclear strategic changes, communication, etc.) The hi-low aspect is the concept of balancing the procurement and acquisition of low cost-high cost platforms and combat equipment. Improvement in weapon system is another hi-low mix concept. The two functions of the navy are both technology oriented.

Geostrategy is not just sailing around in flag showing visits. But also about commanding the oceans and influencing the countries around, including the landlocked. A geostrategically dominant nation should be able to make the best use of its global commons in the ocean as its ocean property and also establish claims to see that there is no effort by other countries in resource denial. An example was the Russian underwater manoeuvre to the Arctic in its territorial claim in 2007 when the scientists dived down 4261 m below the surface and planted rust proof titanium metal Russian flag on the seabed on the Lomonosov Ridge.[18]

There are many other terminologies used in naval terms about the missions of the navy. Strategic deterrence is one of them. It is a geostrategic function. Strategic deterrence is not necessarily an adversarial stand. The world has to move away from primitive postures of aggression and intimidation to the more friendly projections of cooperative engagement enabling diplomacy to yield more positive and long lasting results. The ultimate truth of globalisation is sovereign symbiosis. A country that has to survive in a situation of wellbeing needs a neighbour who is successful. This was never understood. It is dawning today, very slowly. Deception and aggressive postures have lost their pick in the modern world. Both are counterproductive in modern diplomacy of the changing world and thereby the geostrategic approach a nation can adopt.[19] Strategic deterrence is an expensive offer. It has to be made into strategic appeal by improved diplomacy. Deterrence of any kind is tagged heavy. Nations may find the new method the cost effective way of approaching geostrategy. Strategic deterrence of the old mould is aimed at preventing or discouraging attack by others. Strategic deterrence of this nature has not worked seriously so far since the enemy can use methods that suit them. Terrorism is born out of this cast. Another objective of strategic deterrence is to inflict dead end damages to the attacker in the event of an attack. This objective comes out of the feeling that the first objective may not be feasible all the time. Then why should a nation go for such an objective? Building objectives over objectives assuming the previous one may not work (with a fancy title called Plan B and so on) will add cost to the exchequer in national security governance impacting on the element of economic security. Another objective is to make the nation and its allies stable and secure to withstand and respond to any attempt of blackmail or attack on them. It is more a military strategy than exclusive maritime concept. The navy is a suitable platform for it unless space based systems are developed and accepted for assured second strike capability in a nuclear scenario. But the element of stealth is not very attractive in space. There are other dangers too. Second strike attack is the old fashioned term still in vogue for the capability to take on the enemy in the case of an all out nuclear attack in which the nation gets annihilated. It is simply the retaliation of the dead and almost dead in assured mutual destruction—attack by the zombies. It is more a placid undertaking of the dead end human thinking. Such thinking will prevail any way for a very long time. The navy is the most appropriate retaliatory platform according to the accepted wisdom of the world wars. It incurs heavy coast and every nation cannot achieve this capability. But those who achieve such capability will be paying a very heavy price for it, literally and figuratively. No naval vessel, surface or underwater, has ever been used in the world so far for a second strike even in fantasy movies. It is also not proven that the absence of a nuclear attack on a nuclear power is attributed to its second strike capability. The maximum achievement in second strike will only be the "on the beach syndrome."

"This is the way the world ends

Not with a bang, but a whimper." [20]

The world perhaps will not end that way even in a nuclear war. It is a Nevil Shutian hypothesis. This study does not engage in it further being out of context.

But, the above observation of Nevil Shute, author of the novel *"On the Beach,"* reflects the thought process prevailed among nations and political strategists of the period immediately after the Second World War. Surviving in one of the last US nuclear submarine near the shores of Australia after the perceived Armageddon of the fictitious World War III,[21] was a bunch of downhearted crew awaiting certain death. It is a great setting for a novel, and a novel alone. But is it so for a strategic doctrine? May be; perhaps may not. But in modern times the second strike mode underwater is for deterrence. Though of limited use value, such a posture provides high esteem and exchange values for the nation as a sea power, provided the navy sticks to its functions and the nation integrates maritime security with national security. But still the cost value of such outfits is extreme.

The question is, "What next if such a scenario is envisaged?" It is a very serious matter for countries burdened on poverty to think of nuclear war unless it is only for the rhetoric and cacophony. Submarine is the backbone of such a doctrine. The second strike mode is expected to limit the haste in a panic nuclear attack. It may not, when the adversary is not averse of self destruction. A nuclear war in future, if ever happens, could be in the least expected mode, like it was when it first came,[22] within the fog and friction of combat declared or undeclared. The second strike is aimed at a state as a matter of punishment. But, what if the attackers have no state?

Another objective of strategic deterrence is sea control. Sea is a global commons except for a relatively small part close to the shore. UNCLOS has demarcated the use of the sea elaborating the rights of nations on it. Controlling the ocean global commons, therefore, is not a rightful approach. Sea control thereby becomes a wishful thinking. Any effort on that can involve wasteful expenditure. Even if it is exercised it will be in limited waters that are already under the control of the concerned entity.

Sea control is generally attempted by various tactics in the traditional mode of the navy. Among them are sortie control, chokepoint control, open sea operations and local engagement. These methods are outdated under the geostrategic contest of the present day in other-than-war situations. They are followed when the previous one becomes ineffective. The decision making here drifts into skepticism unless backed by confidence. There could be alternate plans. But believing that the tactics may not work and, therefore, it needs to be supplemented by another is not a professional approach. In littoral warfare the navy should be able to reach the target country's nearshore areas. The reach and ability to deal in littoral waters are the decisive points and capabilities that the navy has to examine through friendly visits, joint exercises, joint engagements in maritime aspects, tactical air and submarine projection, etc. All these are old methods that still hold value. Only the approaches are modified. An example is tactical air projection. Tactical air operation was the typical Cold War projection of power ashore that had ended up in fiascos many times. Today deep penetration or presence of an alien aircraft without the approval of the concerned country even in a civil flight can receive condemnation and attract worldwide displeasure. It will be long lasting. The party involved in such an act may be viewed suspiciously.

The navy should be capable of acceptable responsive operations in the geostrategic context. Presence of the navy near another shore is an adversarial posture. But it will not be if it is in the confidence building or reassuring mode. There are nations whose goodwill had been dented by unwanted and unfavourable power projection attempts.

A navy should develop offensive capabilities more than defensive capabilities. The power of the navy comes from its offensive demeanour. The defensive capability of the navy should be inbuilt by default. The navies generally divide its platforms as offensive and defensive. The warfighting tonnage of the navy grows if the defensive role is integrated with the offensive role by tactical design. War fighting tonnage is what counts.

Every country that is serious about its navy has its own priorities about naval strategy. But none of them seriously examines the cost of keeping a navy and the accrual of benefits. Even if it is done, the mix may not balance. Some countries believe in defensive posture, some in offensive and yet others in dual postures. Use of overwhelming force is still one of the mottos of the day. But the difference is that unlike the forces of yore it need not be in the combat zone but in the naval power of combat and geostrategy acquired by competent governance of national security. No navy should take a challenge lightly. This is an aspect that is still prevailing. There is always the future price one has to pay in military expenditure and posture. Often the ultimate victims of defeat are the next generation of the population and probably also those who come after that in a relayed system unless someone corrects in between. Damage control is what goes on rather than most of the new innovations. Aren't the victim nations of the Second World War still struggling with the scars of war that hinder their future? Aren't the new generations mostly involved in every part of the world attempting to mend the damages caused by their predecessors? Isn't climate change and global warming the undoing of the present generation by the past generation? Isn't the mistake being repeated by the present generation? The problem is not the continuing damage control and firefighting, especially in military aspects, but the opportunity cost of it in national progress. Integration of all these aspects with national security may be an answer as it becomes worse when it is handled in isolation. A country should not build a navy because it doesn't have it or its navy doesn't match the past glory. It should have it if it needs one. At least this is clear and implied in the US Constitution; sorry, nowhere else.

Whether such a scenario is factual or not, it is important that the navy restricts itself within the twin functions in this study—warfighting and geostrategy, without separating them as primary and secondary. Both are equally important and there are no other functions for the navy though the government can delegate additional authorities without diluting the two functions.

From these analyses it can be concluded that the role of the nay in modern times will be,

- providing war support to the nation and its military armed forces under EHW situations,
- integrating itself with geostrategic functions of the national security regime and
- providing support, as needed, to the other maritime forces and agencies of the country in governing its ocean property without diluting its twin functions.

The third is a supporting role that the navy may be tasked by the government that it will have to perform without blunting its cutting edge. The two identified functions (combat and geostrategy) and the associated roles are not likely to change in the near future.

Assessing naval power or rather analysing the power of a nation's navy is a major task. Presently these assessments are done as appreciated by analysts whose parameters and benchmarks can vary. This study suggests a different approach which, of course, may also suffer from similar syndrome. The recommended parameters are based on the proposal of this study for integrated maritime security where the navy is a vital component and, hence, it is imperative not only to know the navy of another country and its intentions but also be aware of the strengths and weaknesses of own navy for integration. The capability of the navy in carrying out its functions and roles and the strength and vitality it can acquire by doing so decide the power of the navy and the overall naval power of the country. Some times what matters is more from what the navy is doing or put to than what it is not. For example, an underemployed and under engaged navy without a constructive profile may not be powerful in actual operations though its characteristics may show otherwise. Assessing naval power of a country originates from assessing the power of a navy. It is an expert task that demands serious input and analytical ability. It becomes more complex since it is a function of time. It needs continuous analysis to understand a navy and the way it is steering into future.

Determining the power of a navy has never been simple. It becomes more intricate with the complexity of times. There could be many contradictions in the assessment of the power of a navy. Often such contradictions can be attributed to the compatibility of the navy with the changing times. The power of a navy can decline and rise with respect to changing times.

The power is expressed in various ways: number of ships and aircraft, number of personnel, the growth rate in numbers, budget allocated, presence, etc. They are some of the usual standards to measure the power of a navy. But do they hold?

For example, does the number matter? Or is there something called the optimum number for a particular time and period? The United States Navy had 245 ships in 1916. In 1917 it was 342. By the end of World War II the number rose to 6,768. In 1987, at the height of Cold War the number was 594. Post Cold War, subsequent to downsizing, the number of ships became 278.[23] It was the variation of the seasons. The main opponents too had matching figures at different times. In the beginning of the 21st century the US feels it does not have a peer competitor. The US enjoys unquestioned naval superiority by not sheer numbers, but capabilities. Numbers still figure though, in the form of aircraft carriers, nuclear submarines, etc. What others lack in comparison is what the assessment parameters could be. That is not just numbers. Three major parameters stand out—warfighting tonnage, capability and reach.

Various nuances can be encountered while assessing the power of a country's navy. This nuances demand additional corrective factors with respect to each country. The nuances may come from ideological, political and other differences of governance. For example, a country may be lavish in spending, whereas the other may have to restrict and still gain control. Gauging a navy has to be with the application of the country factor. It is a variable. For example, China of the day is different from the China of Cold War era. It can also be seen in the changing pattern of the number of US naval ships. The war fighting mode also changes. 1916 was different from 2014. Besides, every country will have its identified potential enemies. The policy may change according to the potential enemies and their capabilities besides what they are up to. The threats too have to be examined. Some of them may not be relevant to deciding naval power.

There will be many arguments on quality and quantity. Can quantity be the ideal substitute for quality? Certainly, not. This is one of the aspects to observe while optimising the navy. It is also necessary to optimise response. A navy in the modern world should be capable of multifaceted response especially from the surface, air, space and underwater using effective intelligence.

Naval power is not just naval combat power. It is the power it contributes to the nation through its functions. This is the change in the paradigm today. The power has to have international acceptance and recognition which should not be from the adversarial stand point. There should not be anything factoid about naval power assessment.

When does a navy becomes the world's greatest? Is the greatest navy the ultimate navy? When should a country feel apprehensive about the potential adversaries' naval plans? When will a country's navy raise hackles in another? What should be the next move in such case for both? These questions are quite difficult to answer. Some analysts may say that the world's greatest navy is the one that has no peer competitor. But even then that navy need not be the ultimate. The ultimate navy in another approach is the navy that is very well optimised for the country's needs and spread out in every aspect to meet them.

The navy is required to have surface power, underwater stealth, air power, missile power, and ground power. It also has to have power to counter enemy's strategy and manoeuvres.

Numbers do not matter in assessing the navy's power. It amounts to counting hulls. It is like counting skulls and deciding victory in war. Navy needs intelligence. Intelligence may come from satellites and other electronics (don't forget humint[24]). It also means the navy needs the terrains other than the ocean to survive. It has to be integrated with them.

The parameters of naval power according to this study in realist analysis include the following under the assumption that the navy is compatible for national security integration:

- Design parameters
- Degree of indigenisation
- Combat tonnage
- Ratio of combat tonnage with noncombat tonnage
- Level of optimisation
- Role definition
- Usage role
- Level of Integration of maritime security with national security
- National concept of the navy
- Degree of nuclear doctrine Compatibility
- Reach
- Alien littoral capability
- Sealift capability
- Speed and mobility
- Assessment of present activities
- Capability for multifaceted response
- Vitality of Human element
- Random tests
- Actual Vs. potential gap
- Interactive matrix with other maritime armed forces
- Readiness: strategic and tactical
- Positive maritime heritage

The factors of naval power are briefly examined below.

- **Design Parameters**

  The design parameters with respect to obsolescence and redundancy of naval platforms, weapons, sensors, EHW capabilities, ergonomics, etc. are important factors. This has to be examined not with respect to the period of design but the period of time when they are likely to be used. The quality of design with respect to the likely period of use matters.

- **Degree of Indigenisation**

  Ideally any equipment of war has to be designed and manufactured locally within the classification. Outsourcing abroad where the adversary also can access it is a great mockery of the art and science of combat. However, many nations cannot afford the luxury of indigenisation unless they develop research, design, development and manufacturing capabilities. In such cases only the relative merits can be assessed. It is as ridiculous as outsourcing people to fight a war. Perhaps, worse.

  The counter point is that indigenisation may not have that much teeth. Here is where the secret lies. A country that does not have control of the production of its platforms, weapons and sensors cannot be competent in war, unless the opponent is worse, as it lacks the background. Even in the Stone Age the stone sharpened by the hunter was the one he used more effectively.[25] If a country's arms and equipment outfit are procured or acquired from elsewhere, it will face many limitations and constraints in using them. One will have to be weary of a nation that has an indigenised navy or other armed forces. War means "knowledge and knowhow" of the combatant. It is reflected in the combat outfit of the adversary. A combat outfit should be home grown and developed for the desired punch in a continuous process.

  Indigenised navy and weapons matter in assessing the value and strength of the navy of a country. Indigenisation can be in building, retrofitting, reverse engineering, etc. It could also be done depending upon the factors of production. A country can make its outfit even abroad under its own supervision and expertise, even if shared, in modern times. Blind buys through shop windows and corrupt routes have critical limits.

- **Combat Tonnage**
  The combat tonnage includes platforms, weapons, sensors, equipment, people compatibility, etc. The combat tonnage of a navy comprises everything that is designed for direct combat. A navy can have large inventory tonnage with only a limited faction capable of placing in combat. Such navies are not a force to worry about. Besides, an inflated navy with noncombat tonnage will be a burden for itself. Flab is not a good thing for armed forces too.

- **Ratio of Combat Assets with Noncombat Assets**
  The ratio of combat assets with noncombat assets will be one of the parameters in assessment. While the right ratio for a country cannot be ascertained without serious study, navies that have a ratio that is less than one have reasons to wind up immediately and allocate the budget for more fruitful national efforts. At a higher level, the tonnage factor also includes other assets of the navy converted into combat or noncombat tonnage. Such a study is yet to take shape seriously.

- **Level of Optimisation**
  Optimisation means nothing more-nothing less. A military output today has to be optimised. It has to be need-based for the country. Often national navies may be over emphasised or under emphasised. This has to be compared with the need to arrive at the optimisation factor. Optimisation has to be in relation to strength, size, dominance, lethality, projection, etc

- **Role Definition**
  The role definition of a navy is an important factor in assessing its value and power. The aim is to keep the navy lean and lethal.[26] The role definition will depend upon the charter assigned to it by the constitution, political governance as well as various doctrines. For example, the US Navy is often called an "offshore balancer." But the problem here is the term offshore balancer itself. It is a strategic term that describes the strategy of a great

power in checking the rise of potential hostile countries using favoured regional powers. It is an age old strategy. It also arguably favours the great power in reducing cost of deployment of own forces as well as limiting own casualties around the world. The US used this strategy in 1930 and as late as 1980-1988 Iran-Iraq war, all in the name of democracy. In modern role definition advocated in this study, a navy can be seen a geostrategic balancer by using non-adversarial posture, at the same time projecting the capability to be adversarial if situation demands. Such a role definition—combat and geostrategic readiness without adversarial or hegemonic intentions is what the nations have to project to be in the "sea power club."[27] The navy's contribution is more than other military armed forces in maintaining geostrategic balance though it is not an exclusive agency for it. The closeness of role definition towards this objective is what makes it powerful.

Increase in role will decrease lethality. This can be proved. Hence the best option for a navy is to limit its roles to maintain the EHW compatibility.

- **Usage Role**

  While the navy may have a role definition in its doctrine, the actual use to which it is put including idling can be very well observed across boundaries of nations. Here the gaps in the navy's role will be clearly visible to keen observers and analysts. It is a sign for assessing the suitability of the navy for combat at a later date. The usage of the navy will also be indicative of the energy policy in relation to armed forces, personnel capabilities, internal issues, etc. It will be visible from the actual role the navy is performing in relation to its sorties, missions, constructive occupation and even from accidents, mishaps, discipline and maintenance procedures.

- **Level of Integration of Maritime Security with National Security**

  The government's approach towards national security as a wholesome concept, as envisaged in this study, and view point about maritime security and its integration with national security for governance with an objective of NS_{max} will give a fairly good indication of how the navy will be. This theory is also applicable to the state of the other maritime forces or any other indicator that a country is looking at with respect to another. A determined approach by a government should indicate a determined navy.

Each country appreciates its maritime security according to the government's policy on national security. Accordingly its navy also will undergo policy connect with national governance. It is an indicator of how the navy will perform when situation demands. In a system of governance where maritime security is integrated with national security, the navy will be with a definite charter in relation to military operations and geostrategy even if the force is at low tonnage and capability. It can be an effective navy for its power and capacity.

- **National Concept of the Navy**
  Every navy is expected to have a naval doctrine. But it is the doctrine that is practiced for a period of time that matters and not what is written down in white paper. This can be observed in a continuous analysis of the respective naval force with respect to its deployment particulars and national level consideration. The navy's operational policy with respect to its functions matters. The navy could be integrated with other military armed forces under a joint command or independently operating on its own. It could be coastal, littoral, multi-ocean, blue water, multi domain, multifaceted, outward looking, inward looking, dominating, dormant, constabulary faddist, etc. All these provide indications of the national concept, if not obsession, with the navy with respect to the target country for a keen observer in analysing it especially about its capabilities.

- **Degree of Nuclear Doctrine Compatibility**
  For a nuclear capable country, the navy slips into the centre of gravity of the policy in the maritime terrain under integrated maritime security when the nuclear show-down is certain and whether the policy is first strike or assured second strike. The compatibility of the navy with respect to this doctrine is a vital clue about the navy's capability.

- **Reach**
  The reach of a navy is important in war and geostrategic context. The analyst can examine the capability of the navy to reach out and establish ocean presence to understand even the country's policy and interest in international affairs. This is valid even if the navy doesn't physically go around. Navy's access to global commons and capability for resource denial to the adversary is a vital clue.

- **Alien Littoral Capability**
  Another indicator of enhanced competence of a navy is its capability to operate in alien waters close to their territorial waters. This could be on friendly engagements including cooperative engagements as in joint exploratory operations or exercises.

- **Sealift Capability**
  Sea lift is a serious function of the navy since ancient days. Navies of the world were used for transporting troops and cargo since the very beginning. It is a continuing process under various patterns. The sealift capability is a clue for extended value and reach also.

- **Speed and Mobility**
  The ancient Greek Triremes created panic among the adversarial forces by its advanced mobility during the period. Mobility is still of value for the navy. The mobility aspect is a considered indicator for a navy's strength.

- **Assessment of Present Activities**
  The operational and other activities of the navy that is being analysed could be examined through its activity profile for an identified period. There will be signs of growth, for example in earning geostrategic goodwill, new commissioning activities, etc., as well as decline at times through mishaps, personnel controversies, etc. All these information are vital for incorporating in the naval power assessment of a country.

- **Capability for Multifaceted Response**

  The navy's capability for multifaceted response is an indicator of its power. The navy in such cases will be able to withstand the threats from various dimensions. The ocean is a multidimensional terrain. The naval ships have to be compatible for responding to the multidimensional issues.

- **Vitality of Human Element**

  Most of the time, the human element is seemingly the most misunderstood constituent of any armed force, military or nonmilitary, and perhaps the weakest link on it. The navy is no exception. Personal quality standards should be of highest order. But the exclusive aspect of human element is that it can be molded and invested effectively under human investment management.[28] However the basic effectiveness of human element is essential to develop them. It starts with the selection, recruitment, training and post training development. Serious gaps can exist in all these procedures. The gaps will be visible in performance. Personnel quality standards of a navy can be accessed through various means including training process, operational performance, disciplinary issues, career engagement, turnaround of personnel, satisfaction level, indulgence in corrupt practices, politicisation, etc.

- **Random Tests**

  Analysts examining the quality of the target navy undoubtedly have to be engaged continuously on it examining various parameters. However they will not be able to maintain this continuity for close observation. Here is where random tests at times will help. These tests have to be devised by themselves appropriate to a country's requirement. Random tests are actually observations at varied times. Examples are piracy engagements in joint operation or independent operations, disaster scenarios, comparison of naval forces deployed by two nations with politically opposing views, internationally accepted patrols, exercises and post exercise behaviour, etc.

- **Actual Vs. Potential Gap**
  The actual power is calculated with respect to a particular time in the present. This situation can be visualised by calculation for a particular time in future. The difference will show whether the navy is progressing or declining. From this examination, the navy's future potential can be determined for a required or identified time.

- **Interactive Matrix with other Armed Forces**
  Navy alone cannot win a war. But there are various scenarios when navy can be deployed independent of other military armed forces. Even then, the interactive matrix and cohesion with other forces and agencies holds the key to the power of the navy. A navy that prefers to operate in the independent mode or is particular about dominating other maritime forces may not yield much result however powerful it may be on white paper.

- **Readiness: Strategic and Tactical**
  Readiness depends upon the big question: for what should it be ready? A navy will become complacent unless it is kept at the highest level of preparedness. That is the problem all over barring some exceptions. There can be strategy deficit. Tactics will be as it comes. Tactical requirement is based on situational demand. Strategy is a long term requirement to reach where it should be according to the national policy. The navy therefore should get inputs from national security agency or associated agencies regularly. If not, the navy will lose its heading and bearing. It will amount to drifting with power on (underway). In an integrated defence system of jointness the gap will not be felt seriously. In such case the naval strategy will be much more synchronised with the national requirement.

Readiness can also be assessed based on the threats and challenges the country faces. A country always on the edge will be at a higher degree of readiness than if it is not. Its potential and perceived adversaries can be identified while assessing the threat perception. It is not the state of readiness of the armed forces here. It is how well prepared the navy is in terms of strategic readiness and tactical applications as and when required. This state too can be identified independently or assessed comparatively with another. The preparedness of a navy can be estimated under a colour code, level bars or any other suitable means for comparison. Here the purpose is comparison and understanding the naval power of a country at a particular time.

- **Positive Maritime Heritage**
  Every nation has a carried forward maritime heritage. It still reflects in their behaviour even if it had lost touch with the ocean years back. It is an amazing reality. The bulging membership of landlocked countries in IMO is not just because of their international strategic interests including trade and globalisation. There is a sublime suggestion of the ocean link from their maritime heritage factor. A piece of the Mongolian story and mindset reflects in the context. This is the positive maritime heritage that is explained in this study. Many countries boast their maritime heritage from the nationalist stand point. That is not a factor to assess their naval power.

All these factors need to be analysed scientifically and continuously making naval analysis a constructive process. This is not further studied, analysed, or examined here. Besides, the analysis will also vary with respect to the government's policies and policy changes. But this is a study that is more valid for nations to self examine if interested in their navies.

Value Assessment

This study does not examine the methods of assessment of values of these parameters. It is a different topic. Such study has two purposes: 1) comparative analysis between navies of the world 2) optimising own navy in comparison with what is needed. An optimised navy is a need based navy. Here assessment of need of the navy on the same parameters becomes another task for the analyst. Another aspect of assessment is that the methods adopted need not be universal. It has to be as preferred by the analysts according to the national policy. Different analysts may follow different methods. The methods may be exclusive and classified for a country. The assessment process has to be accuracy driven.

Law Enforcement

Law enforcement in relation to the ocean is about dealing with the unlawful acts at and from the sea. Within the boundaries of law, the term "unlawful" implies that the associated activity would have been forbidden by law. It also means there is the requirement of legislation to suppress the unlawful. That is a conditional requirement. In the absence of law prohibiting an act, the act doesn't become unlawful in the strict judicial sense. This is especially so in the domain of the ocean as there is no permanent human habitat there.

War is governed by the laws of war. It applies to naval warfare too. Nations engaged in war fight lawful combatants. But in the case of proxy wars and terror strikes there will be a dilemma in dealing with enforcement of law. In a high intensity encounter, nations will be fighting against unlawful combatants to establish rule of law at sea. There are questions. Is it correct to kill a pirate who waylays a ship on an innocent mission of cargo carriage? The pirate can turn out to be an unlawful combatant. What are the laws that will contain ocean based terrorism? Can a maritime force attack and take on identified terrorists in the high seas? Can there be privateers in modern times even if they are called private sea guards or security privateers at sea? There are many such questions.

The ocean terrain provides certain difficulties in enforcement of law in terms of clarity of jurisdiction. But that shouldn't make the ocean a perfect place of crime. There is clarity jurisdiction. It is a question of enforcement which also includes legal proceedings. One of the assumptions of this study is that every unlawful act at and from the sea can be prevented or preempted. Of course, the issues at sea could cause a blur for the uninitiated if not examined under national and international laws in the appropriate manner to the satisfaction of the concerned authorities. The state sovereignty is limited to the territorial sea or similar seas that vary within the extent prescribed under the law of the sea (LoS) as per UNCLOS. In the ocean, beyond this limit, international law comes to the fore along with national laws applicable to specific jurisdiction of a country under UNCLOS.

International customary law considers state sovereignty as a negative concept. It is the jurisdiction that matters as its positive complement.[29] Sovereignty means omnipotence in the unitary state's concept. Each state is expected to accept it in reciprocity. Otherwise it will lead to conflict. This complicates the issues outside the territorial limits. Jurisdiction, in whatever form, will have to depend on international law. International law functions under the principles of civility and ethicality and calls for fair trials of accused. It was not so in the past when each sovereign state had unlimited jurisdiction in its own territory except where limited under international customary law and treaties. International law prohibits appropriation of high seas. The distinction between limited and unlimited jurisdiction is to exercise legality among the subjects of international law under the plurality of states. The objective is to minimise conflicts between states.

There are many unlawful activities based on the vantage points at sea. A pirate will be positioned near the SLOC through which ships transit. A smuggler or a human trafficker may take route via the SLOT in the hope of avoiding detection. Both SLOC and SLOT becomes alive and active when an unlawful activity is about to take place. This demands overall surveillance of the ocean by the law enforcement agencies of the government within their operational domain.

The various unlawful activities that can take place at sea or from the sea are,

- maritime fraud,
- illegal sales and dealings,
- illegal transfers,
- piracy and armed robbery,
- crime at sea on board vessels and platforms,
- smuggling,
- trafficking,
- poaching and illegal, unorganised and unregulated (IUU) fishing,
- marine environmental crimes,
- terrorism and insurgency support ,
- eavesdropping and espionage,
- illegal survey,
- carriage of illegal goods,
- infiltration,

- hostage taking,
- barratry,
- insurgency and militant support,
- terrorism,
- agitation and clashes,
- attacks and murder, etc., etc.

A variety of unlawful activities can be traced to the ocean from historical times. Many new crimes can develop surreptitiously under the silence of the sea in the future. High seas could be used to commit activities that are prohibited under law over land or jurisdictional waters. Unlawful activities at and from the sea can affect not only the economy of a country but almost every other element of national security. Future may witness new challenges. Hence it is imperative to integrate maritime security with national security for establishment of rule of law at sea.

There are notified areas outside the sovereign waters of nations demarcated for purposes like deep seabed mining or as special areas, particularly sensitive areas, search and rescue areas, etc. Often enforcement of law in such areas by the particular nation may be a difficult and daunting task. It will be almost impractical to carry out monitoring and surveillance in such areas.

The crimes at sea and from the sea could be individually committed or organised. The crime could be localised or transnational. Most of the crimes mentioned could be seen in both modes and matrices. Some of them, like human smuggling or trafficking are exclusively transnational by their nature. Organised syndicates play great role in such crimes where the stakeholders will be many. Organised transnational crimes are also matters of serious concern among United Nations and other international organisations.

Rule of the law at sea is to be established by national forces and agencies. There are various maritime forces and agencies to carry out the functions at sea under national governance. These forces include the,

- navy,
- coast guard,

- customs,
- police,
- shipping,
- fisheries,
- environment,
- wildlife,
- mining,
- intelligence,
- investigation, etc

The navy is a military force. It is not meant for law enforcement. Its functions have been already explained. It could support the agencies in law enforcement under special situations and conditions without diluting its original functions. Hence the involvement of the navy n law enforcement, ideally, is on a case-to-case basis. In many countries the navy is the sole law enforcer at sea. Such navies, as mentioned earlier, will not be combat ready or combat capable because they perform the coast guard or police missions. All these agencies vary in their designations and attributes with reference to countries. Some of them may perform multiple roles. As in the case of the navy, the effectiveness of these forces and agencies in performing their roles are not a matter that is seriously thought about by the governments. Often the duties and functions are duplicated though the charter or the act relevant to them specifically mentions about avoidance of duplication of efforts for obvious reasons. Most of the agencies may seriously complain about their roles being diluted by other agencies but the governments are not aware of the fact that along with such dilution their accountability to the government also gets contravened making them naturally slip on their track of efforts. Diluting accountability generates blame throwing behaviour. These agencies and forces will be useful to the country only if the government is serious about integrating maritime security with national security under appropriate accountability. Each agency and force is specifically important for maritime security governance and establishing rule of law as well as providing service at sea in their own niche and charter. Authority, responsibility and accountability of these forces and agencies should be adequately balanced.

Among them, the coast guard is a new idea that fits in very well in the post UNCLOS world. There are 142 coast guards in the world (2008).[30] It is a not a new concept. Coast guard as a force has been introduced by the Swedish Government as early as 1638. It is, to that extent, the oldest coast guard in the world.

In spite of this antiquity and also the modern touch, the governments have not been able to make effective use of the coast guards in the post UNCLOS maritime appreciation. Coast guard is an excellent force and can be effectively used under integrated maritime security.

In every respect the navy and the coast guard provide the essential duality to maritime security force projection. Balancing them, according to the requirement, is for the governments to do.

Service

Service at sea and from the sea came up much later. There was no provision for organised search and rescue in the early times. That was evident in the case of Titanic. Life saving was left to the person in distress and the nearest life boat. The situation has changed. The P^3C aspects of marine environment show the concern of the international community towards keeping the oceans clean. IMO has established excellent regimes in marine safety and environment. Service to people in distress has everything to do with the perils of the sea. People in distress at sea under such circumstances needed help. More than the criminal activities, it was the disaster scenario and marine casualties that made the national governments to collectively examine the issues of search and rescue, disaster mitigation, environmental protection, damage control, etc. Safe and clean seas became the motto for the international seafaring communities. Today most of the nations have contingency plans and designated forces and agencies charted for maritime service.

Resource Exploitation

Ocean resources are collectively seen as one of the elements of the ocean property. They fall in the category of,

- national resources appropriated to the state under international law and
- global commons

Maximising their exploitation in a sustainable manner where applicable is what a country has to see under resource security, an element of national security. Presently, except for fisheries, minerals and gas, the nations are not seriously engaged in the exploitation of ocean resources.

Research

Obviously ocean research is an area that may go much beyond the land based research. It is evident that ocean research to a great extent is limited by the arrogance of the ocean itself or, rather, the cap installed by the mysteries of ocean that is deeper to the modern world than that of the space and the universe itself.

Establishing Rights

A country's prowess to establish its rights in the ocean is the more obvious factor than the rights it has over the ocean. The rights are basically sovereign rights and in addition to resources including global commons, shipping passages, innocent passages, establish rule of law, etc. There are efforts by various countries to establish rights over the natural resources deep under the Arctic. It is an example. Countries are busy mapping the ocean to delimit the boundaries. The way to establish rights is through the international law. Nations have to establish their rights in the ocean legally. Some of the countries are yet to ratify the law of the sea. The UNCLOS generally is sufficient for any nation to establish its rights over the sea. The nations, under UNCLOS, will have to prove their underwater geographical boundaries also.

The law that supports underwater profiling for resources comes as follows:

- Rights in the continental shelf extending past 200 nautical miles of the exclusive economic zone, up to 350 nautical miles from the shore or to the extent of continental shelf whichever is less.

- If a country can prove its territory is connected to an underwater ridge, sovereign rights to resources could be extended even further out along the ridge. This will be useful to claim and establish rights in the Arctic for neighbouring countries.

But many claims of countries can be in opposition to those of others and may remain so for decades and beyond.

Others

In addition, there will be various other aspects related to the ocean that a country will have to examine while streamlining national governance for integrated maritime security. They will be country specific. These aspects may change from country to country depending on their characteristics, political requirements and, more so, their geographical nature as land locked, coastland or island states.

Integrating Maritime Security Elements

Integrating maritime security elements with national security elements is a functional aspect of time and the period and approach of governance. The process has to examine the integration of an element of maritime security with the appropriate national security element. The national security model examined in this study comprises 15 elements. The identified maritime security elements can be complementary, contributory or null with respect to the national security elements. This is not for universal application. It is for the entity to decide and incorporate in its planning. The concerned geopolitical entity should conclude the affiliation and import of the corresponding maritime security element in its national security governance. The opinion may vary among the planners as well as political representatives in this regard. The more prudent in decision making will reap more benefits. For example, a tsunami, a cyclone or a major oil spill can be complementary to the disaster security, environmental security and other national security elements for Japan or India. These countries may incorporate and integrate the effects of it in their national disaster contingency plans and preventive or preemptive measures.[31] It can be contributory for Nepal or Bhutan or null for Afghanistan or Chad. It depends the way the national planners visualise them. The situation can also vary in such a way that the impact of disasters at or from the sea can be either complementary or contributory for all countries in the world since there could be collateral damages in one way or the other. One can visualise accidental or intentional detonation of a nuclear weapon at sea. The impact can be worldwide in differing degrees. It is all a matter of time and approach to governance.

The scenario and situation can change. While the identified national security elements can peter out and new one can appear in course of time, terrain specific security element will always remain complementary, contributory or null, according to this study, in relation to national security. The entire study is based on this fact that the elements of maritime security will not have any exclusivity with respect to national security; hence incapable of inclusive generation. If that was not so, integration of maritime security with national security will not be ideally possible. This is a factor that supports the theory of integration in the first instance.

In the complementary relationship, the terrain specific element will be forming or serving as a complement that strengthens the overall impact by integration. In such relationship the integration will support the supply of mutual needs or offset mutual lacks as in the case of any symbiotic relationship.

In the contributory relationship it will be an add-on as a support to bring about a result. The contributory element will be different from and exclusive to the main element but useful to it as an added value if integrated.

The null element is where the supplementary faction does not have a suitable element to complement or contribute but can otherwise integrate as it is.

The relationship of maritime security with national security elements—complementary, contributory or null, can vary among the geopolitical entities.

In chapter 4 this aspect has been examined and found that maritime security can complement 13 elements of national security. Two other elements are considered null for the time being. However there is a caveat that the method of integration and deciding the compatibility of the elements are prerogatives of the respective geopolitical entities concerned as the situation and the parameters of national governance can vary significantly between each entity. The decision has to be based on the case and situation as desired by the respective geopolitical entities.

The elements are reexamined below for their general compatibility for integration. The examination is in the chronological hierarchical order explained earlier.

#1 Military Security (m_s)

Military security basically originates from maintaining the territorial integrity by defending it from aggression that originates external to it. Safeguarding territorial integrity is a difficult task. The common perception of defence is not a singular activity of lining up against the enemy and preventing the forces from entering into the territory. To defend, a nation may also have to take the offensive route. Under this concept the very theory of art of war can change. Offence could be preemptive defence in the case of a nation who appreciates a possible threat and determines to eliminate it. This is an aspect that the organisation of nations has to understand and appreciate in clear perspective while deciding about war against another in a strictly defensive argument. The game of war always occupies a domain where it is played on a specific terrain. Ocean is a terrain that has multiple domains under the macro concept of warfare—surface, underwater and air. Even the seabed and benthic layers can be different domains where a submarine can lurk, mines can be laid or robots can snoop. For convenience, they are considered underwater. It is too early to treat them as different domains for military purposes. But the day will come when the benthic surface becomes a war zone. Sea bed may still take a longer time to become a war zone. Can the world ever imagine a military domain on the seabed? It sounds more atrocious than science fiction. But there are many such atrocious sounding decibels that are realities today anchored under reality perception of human survival.

Military security is indomitably linked with the navy especially for a coastland and island country and hence with the ocean. It is an element of national security that is linked with all the identified terrains. Defending territorial integrity of a nation from external aggression means unification of maritime security relative to it with national security. Integrating the warfighting forces under a unified command concept is one of the means of such integration. However it is not the only choice as long as the government can integrate them with other means.

#2 Economic Security (e_{s1})

The famous statement of a former president of the United States, *"It is economy, stupid"*[32] speaks about it all. Governance deals with economics. Priority in governance is seemingly given to economics. Or is that so? Is economics the most important aspect of governance? According to the theory propagated in this study (every element is of equal importance and their relative importance will shift with the situation and time) it is of equal importance with other elements, though in the chorological hierarchy, the oldest element past military security. Its relative importance is for the individual human as well as the government to decide accordingly. But a nation's affluence is normally measured, at least for now, by its economic prosperity and strength.

The political catch phrase "*it is (the) economy stupid*" has additional relevance too. The importance of this phrase in real caricature of life reflects and resonates clearly and strongly when nations experience the choking feeling of recession. But economic security creates a more resounding impression over the people. The world has lately realised that the decline of an economy can impact others too. It is a kind of economic pandemic with a difference. Pandemic strikes as a disease. Health doesn't spread around the healthy person. Only disease spreads around in certain cases. But in economics, economic health or wellbeing as well as disaster spreads around. Hence economic security is not strictly a nation's internal issue. The element, like various other elements of national security, if not all yet, has an exogenous influence in national security governance. A country can manage its economic security element better if the global economy is booming. This is also an important aspect to see in future studies as one of the prerequisites for identifying an element of national security from various conditions and factors.

The ocean has many domain values leading to economic security within its ocean property regime. It all starts with the ocean advantage of mobility that allows shipping commerce, the blood line of global trade which is only enhancing as time passes making the global community more and more interdependent. All the economic aspects of economics of ocean property thereby should get integrated with national security planning as a complementary element.

#3 Resource Security (r_s)

Ocean resources are part of ocean property, hence complementary to national security element of resource security. In the earlier times there was a tendency to explain about ocean resources as ocean wealth. Today it is clear, though coast effective exploration and exploitation of such resources are limited to technology. It is expected that the ocean will provide strategic resources that are not available over land terrain. For a country it may not be urgent to exploit all the ocean resources, but it is important to sustain and protect them till being exploited.

The earliest familiarity of humans with ocean resources is fisheries. It is a major resource for food security. In all respects ocean complements resource security.

#4 Border Security (b_s)

Border security aspects based on the ocean is much more complex than over land. While a border over land is just a line that separates two territories, border in the ocean is a multifaceted geophysical phenomenon related to the geographical position and nature of the domain. Border security in maritime security relates to of various maritime zones that also act as border areas. The maritime security element, therefore, is complementary to national security.

#5 Demographic Security (d_{s1})

Demography is integral to ocean as the major portion of world population is concentrated over the coastal zone. The coastline of the world is a fractal continuum in the strict sense. The ocean area of the territorial sea and the coastal zones are complementary to demographic security in governing national security. Demographic security cannot be assured without relevance to the coastal zones and the oceanic influence.

#6 Disaster Security (d_{s1})

Ocean is known and accepted for the perils associated with it. It is accepted even in legal regimes as natural association. Disaster situations related to the sea is based on activities that could cause disasters ashore. Primary agent in this case is a tsunami that could be caused by underwater earthquakes or volcanic eruptions, benthic landslides, etc. Disaster is an effect on people's lives and properties. The disaster is when people lose their lives and properties. This could happen under the ocean property regime related to the ocean environment and climatology besides other causes. Hence disaster security element of national security has a complementary faction in maritime security.

#7 Energy Security (e_{s1})

Ocean is associated with energy as part of the ocean property that could also be seen along with the ocean resources. Already oil and gas are readily accepted as ocean given. In all its creditability offshore energy exploration is considered as an ocean given benefit to humanity for its survival along with transportation and fishing. Energy security through its inclusiveness with other elements copes well with national security planning with ocean background and the ocean property regime.

#8 Geostrategic Security (g_{s1})

Ocean links the world even for a landlocked country in geostrategy along with other terrains. One can reach across the world over air and ocean. Outer space is also a terrain but that is not likely to be a medium for transportation across the world. Ocean transportation is slow, but it has the advantage of the economy of volume and cost. It is the right medium and will remain so for a very long time for carriage of goods. Air space is preferred by commuters. The nature of the two terrains is very different, especially in the sense of a country's borders. Geostrategy starts from where the border ends. Ocean has a peculiar character in the geostrategic context that made the scholars and strategists in the past to observe that "he who owns the ocean will command the world." Though it may not be strictly an ideal statement especially in the military context where the outer space becomes prominent, ocean's importance cannot be underestimated here. Hence geostrategically ocean is an important terrain which also points out the importance of military and nonmilitary maritime armed forces in geostrategic applications.

#9 Informational Security (i_s)

While reliable ocean information is a matter of interest for navy and other maritime forces and agencies besides the users, the ocean as a terrain can be used for gathering and managing information required for maintaining informational security, a vital element of national security. Ocean is an expansive terrain that could be used for gathering and disseminating information in many ways. In the olden days ocean remained secretive. Gradually the people started getting ocean related information. Even maritime transportation is a means of communication for information; hence the routes the ships follow is called the sea lines of communication.

Any innovative method could be adopted for using the ocean for informational security. One of them is crowd sourcing. Information gathered through mariners and other seafarers of all kinds—merchant personnel, fishers, sail boat crew, stationary platform personnel, cruise vessels, etc.—could be vital for informational security in relation to not only the ocean and activities there including marine safety, but also for maritime border security and other elements of national security. It will be interesting to note that any information available to a mariner or seafarer at any given time will be insufficient as it will not be in place in real time. Latest data will make the information close to real-time and that much more useful and actionable. In view of this condition maritime security aspects have exclusive understanding of informational security. Most basic information for any mariner is incomplete and out-timed in many areas unlike over land. The navigational charts, notices to mariners will not be precise about the ocean information in real time.

Ocean at any time comprises people with purpose—travelling, carrying cargo, exploring, producing, fishing, etc. National governments have to reach out to them under informational security as the people over land.

In the integrated maritime security governance, collection of ocean data by scientists, meteorologists, seafarers and mariners as well as space and air agencies could be an imperative part of their assignment. Governments should encourage it and share information deeply under a national ocean policy for integrated maritime security.

#10 Food Security (f_s)

Maritime security is hardened contributor to food security since the time people went about hunting fish in the ocean space. Today, it is not only a terrain for food hunting and gathering but also what the scientists believe the natural silo that can store food to meet the entire nutritional requirement of the future world. Ocean farming of fish and seaweeds may come up in future. A nation with sufficient ocean property with a fertile continental shelf can seriously engage in ocean farming and change the present nature of primitive hunting gathering techniques into a productive arena with large scale employment opportunities for people. It is also one way to develop the continental shelf from destruction. The land could be free for other economic processes that a nation requires in its journey towards NS_{max}. Ocean can be used for farming seriously. Mariculture and various other forms of farming are already being attempted.

#11 Health Security (h_s)

Ocean can provide access to and transport various diseases. It can also provide health support through medicines. Pandemics like the black plague were carried by rodents on ships along with infected crew and passengers. Ocean can carry diseases to the people over the coastal belt and hinterland. Toxic algal blooms may hazard the health of the coastal population. Ballast water transportation by ships from one point to another can cart various ocean species that can turn predators and host organisms for disease carrying microbes where they are discharged. Cholera stains originally seen in Chittagong can now be seen spreading in European waters carried in ballast water of ships. Ocean stasis has to be monitored regularly to reduce public health risks.

Public health and ocean is a very speicalised subject. Most of the people even among coastal population are unaware that the ocean can harbour risks to public health. The health of the ocean is tied to human health too. A healthy ocean produces the major portion of oxygen the humans breath. Ocean can assist humans to derive life-savings drugs. At the same time contaminated seafood, ballast water organisms, polluted beaches, etc., can affect global public health.

#12 Ethnic Security (e_{s3})

Ethnicity as explained in the study of national security is a vast subject much beyond the racial perceptions that separates one from another. Major aspects of ethnicity in skin colour, religious and other human combinations originated through migrations and other means. These movements from one point to another and amalgamation by reproduction created a world full of humans different from each other physically and psychologically. Migrations and human movements either as slave trade or though smuggling and trafficking have shaped the world into a big ethnic cauldron of mixed living human gumbo. People moved over land in the early days. Very few went across the sea. Subsequently there was a flow of ocean based movements. However, the base system of socio-cultural differences originated over land in the varied ethnic formats.

Coastal area is highly populated. It could also brew ethnic issues. Already there are simmering discontents in various parts of the world about coastal population getting involved with ethnic differentiation of specific kinds. The governments may do well being alert on such issues.

#13 Environmental Security (e_{s4})

Marine environmental security is a four pronged activity profile—protection and preservation of marine environment, and prevention and control of marine pollution. It is also known as the P^3C aspects of marine environment appropriate to any mission statement of the agencies like the coast guards who are legally chartered with it. [33] This is an aspect that easily gets integrated with the environmental security element of national security. Damage to environment is also not domain specific and cannot be contained at the border of nations. The damage that occurs in one place will have an impact on another. For the same reason the P^3C aspects of all the physical terrains, including outer space has to be seen together.

#14 Cyber Security (c_s)

The performance domain of cyber security is in the cyber terrain. It is an exclusive terrain. There is no similar element so far in the realm of maritime security that complements national security. But cyber security is vital in the ocean terrain in modern times. A serious example is naval warfare and netcentric military operations. Besides, there are various other aspects, especially those related to informational security, cyber snooping, law enforcement, ocean research, etc., that are in the realm of cyber security. Hence in the integration process of maritime security with national security, cyber security becomes a contributory from the ocean perspective .

#15 Genomic Security (g_{s4})

Genomic security too is activated in another terrain—the genomic terrain. The element has various constraints for takeoff. It is delayed, not annulled. It shows big prospects in future once it breaks the mold. In that case maritime security will certainly be involved in integration as life in its original form began from the ocean. It is expected that the ocean may provide variety of revelations and contributions on matters related to genomic security. It is only a matter of time.

About Integration

Integration in national security governance is a macro system approach. The idea here is different from business or systems integration. For example, in business there could be vertical, horizontal and conglomerate integration and custom models of enterprise integration. There is also integration of subsystems like maritime force or naval systems integration. But the integration of a subsystem like maritime security with the core national security is an entirely different process activity dealing in national or global governance. Human system governance is different from organisational management. In governance, integration is an all encompassing manifestation of human authority under participation, legitimacy and accountability for the common good.

"Integrated maritime security" is maritime security assimilated within the wholesome concept of national security for the objective of maximising national security by governance. Maritime security even if integrated within itself is not integrated maritime security for this purpose unless assimilated with the concept of national security. The process of integrating maritime security with national security is a complex task, especially since national governance is yet to take this aspect seriously for various reasons. Any government that is seriously desirous of looking at national security in its wholesome concept may face many hurdles in governance in the first place. It will be a rough ride for a very long time. Many traditional methods and belief systems carried forward from the past will have to be demolished abruptly under great opposition and resistance to change at all places. The days of overnight revolutionary changes are things of the past. Besides, national security governance is not a subject for abrupt changes. The shift has to be gradual at its natural frequency. It will happen or, perhaps, is already on. This study could be part of it. The present process of governance had taken deep root in the psyche of those who govern because it is not only a familiar and a well-beaten track that is easy to follow but also beneficial to them. The alteration to the new system—governance by NS_{max}—has to come from the human quest for survival in the long run. It will take time under the law of invariance according to which transformation in a society takes place at an extremely slow pace that is difficult to appreciate at the time of change. It is like the wave of a tsunami that is heading to the coast at the speed of a locomotive but not noticeable in the open sea under a ship as the wave form will be too low and long.

Ideally, integration should be possible only when the national security concept is accepted as the wellbeing of the people, as explained in this study. Presently governance is about the welfare of the public, as perceived and practised by governments, or just about the military and other forms of physical security of the nation. Even then, such governance can absorb maritime security by integration though the results may not be as encouraging as by governance towards NS_{max}. Integration of maritime security is easier if the governments accept and consider the idea of ocean property as a single window regime to design and develop maritime strategy applicable to them according to the situation. This will call for ocean property mapping and corresponding changes in maximising the returns from it according to situational demands in the process of maxismising national security. It is the ideal form of integration. It means that governance at national level turns towards national security maximisation (NS_{max}) and nations compare themselves under the national security index (NSI) internationally worldwide. It is not possible as long as the governments of the world follow their own agenda familiar to them besides the overwhelming method inertia[34] of governance that is not easy to stride out.

Integration, in this study, technically means joining the probable system with the core system in the desired process through a select alternative. The systems (core and probable) will be ideally common to every geopolitical entity in their nature but not in endowment because of various factors, dimensions, parameters, situations, demands and time in governance. The systems will be common when definitions and their appreciation are universal. Everything else varies from entity to entity. Primarily it is the select alternative process of integration that may be different because the choice of approach may vary. In this study, the process is national governance. The minimum condition for the probable system for integration with the core is that it should be compatible and, thereby, qualify as a "probable,"[35] and also with other probable systems if it is a multisystem integration with the core. The core system will be unitary. For the core system, the compatibility comes from its ability to absorb the probable systems and manifested superiority according to demand as a process driver. National security is an all terrain concept the governments deal with under the landclasp syndrome for the desired result maximisation in perceived governance. The perception of the concept may not change if the definition (whichever it may be) is accepted by the governments universally.

Integration is also mentioned for the process of joining or combining parts of a system so that they work together or form a whole. Here the integration is between subsystems of a system. Maritime security is said to be integrated under this assumption when its subsystems are conjoined effectively or when the maritime security as a concept is integrated with national security, the core concept of governance. This study is about integrating maritime security with national security. Hence integrating maritime security with all its subsystems has to be taken up prior to that. It is done by envisaging the concept of ocean property. In all these processes integration is a process opposite to differentiation.

National security is an all terrain concept. It is the core system concept in national governance as advocated in this study. Each terrain security concept—in this case maritime security—is naturally integral to it.[36] They just have to be integrated with it. Integrated maritime security is when the concept of maritime security relative to a nation gets integrated with national security in totality. Here the entities may differ in the process of integration and so will be the results. Any process of integration will contain various styles within it while it is ongoing. The process of integration will not be uniform in its style all the time. Adopting different styles balances the overall process of integration. Some of the styles are mentioned below and briefly examined thereafter.

- Phased integration
- Direct integration
- Adaptive integration
- Reactive integration
- Cut back integration
- Fixed integration
- Flexible integration
- Isomorphic integration

All these styles are applicable to unitary system integration or multisystem integration. In unitary system integration, a single probable is integrated with the core. In multi system integration, the core will still remain unitary but the probables will be more than one. There are multiple methods of integration in such case. In one, the probables are integrated with each other before integrating with the core. In another method, a single probable is integrated with the core and the next one is integrated with the resultant. If the probables are too many, some of the probables could be integrated together and then with the core or the resultant. The choice is with the planners. The resultant system will have all the similarities of the core system but the character and effect will be different and much more enhanced. If the resultant is worse or valued less than the original value of the core then the integration was a failure. The purpose of integration is to competitively maximise the value of the resultant many times more than the core system. Each probable system gets value added to it in the process of integration and thus gains in identity and impact.

- **Phased Integration**

  In phased integration, the process of integration is phased in a planned manner without causing a break. The continuity is maintained. The governments may find it difficult to ensure continuity especially when there are changes in governments.

The results of integration will take time to be felt and appreciated by the public.

- **Direct Integration**

Direct integration is normally getting the probable system assimilate with the core system at the planning stage without any change subsequently. But, in normal case, the probable system that is to be integrated is considered similar to the core system. The core system thereby is given additional "boost" to cover the probable system also. An example is budgeting for the probable system but utilising it for the core system in the name of the probable system. The probable system can get totally neglected if such thing happens. Most of the process of integration in governance, even system integration through subsystems, is done in this manner. Direct integration is when phased integration is not possible or when the time required for phased integration is not acceptable.

- **Adaptive Integration**

Adaptive integration is just a terminology. In fact a system unless adaptive cannot be integrated with the core system or another subsystem. Adaptiveness is a compatibility requirement. Every integration, therefore, has to be adaptive.

- **Reactive Integration**

The process of integration becomes reactive when the activities of the process respond to various stimuli. There are many situations when the corresponding stimuli within the process may induce responses that will have to be keenly watched and steered to avoid conflicts.

- **Cut Back Integration**

Many original processes that initially had been found good for introduction may subsequently turn out to be rejects. They should be abandoned immediately if integration has to be successful. Often there is a tendency to keep the rejects in process in government due to public opinion, legal obligations, etc. Reluctance to cut back can cause damage to the process.

- **Fixed Integration**

  In fixed integration there is no alternative. The process continues as planned in spite of the need for changes due to various pressures. Part of the integration process may become fixed.

- **Flexible Integration**

  In flexible integration there will be provisions for introducing changes at the appropriate time and as and when required in any number of times. This will be different from fixed integration.

- **Isomorphic Integration**

  Isomorphism in mathematics is about bijective homomorphism. It is seen and verified in organisational process and governance dynamics as institutional and process isomorphism. According to one of the definitions, the notion of isomorphism implies a constraining process that leads to an increased resemblance of one unit to other units that face the same set of environmental conditions.[37] A newly created institution can ultimately take the shape of another existing one. A new department expected to be different from others in a university can soon take the shape of another existing one in governance and administration thereby defeating the original purpose. A new process of governance dynamics can gravitate towards an already existing process. It is isomorphism. There can be normative isomorphism, the standard and usual one, mimetic isomorphism where the tendency is to mimic another or coercive isomorphism where the institution or governance dynamics come under pressure to follow another. Isomorphism can affect integration and also help it to speed up. It is left to the planners and executors to manage and steer through it.

A process of genuine integration in governance is bound to follow all the above styles and more if new ones come up in its correct perspective and proportion. It is for the planners and executors to decide. The process of integration in governance is not a new subject. Most of the governments are used to various integration processes and are familiar with it.

But the issues will be different from the usual, when maritime security has to be integrated with national security and incorporated in national governance. What makes the process different are articulated below for examination by governments because the process of integration is exclusively the domain of the governments of the concerned geopolitical entity.

- The concept of national security differs from entity to entity with certain similarities in relation to military security and rule of law. The former is an element of national security and not national security by itself. The latter is a condition of national security, more so a constitutional function of the government.
- Almost all the entities integrate maritime security in their national governance according to their perception. Mostly it is selective and limited.
- This study envisages national security different from what any of the entities, except a few partially, perceive. The study looks at it as a wholesome concept including and beyond military security as a measurable concept towards wellbeing of people of a country.
- Maritime security according to this study is not just naval power but a wholesome concept from which the landlocked and geographically disadvantaged countries too can benefit more or less equal to the littorals if they can appreciate their ocean property.
- Accordingly the recommendation of this study is to integrate maritime security with national security for the purpose of national governance and give it an identity in conformity. The governance dynamics is the prerogative of the concerned nation.
- The findings of this study are relatively new and therefore bound to take time for further research and application. They touch different aspects of governance according to various identified elements of national security. The entire concept

proclaimed and identified in this study has local, national and international reach and validity for governance.

- The recognition of interfaces between national security elements and their corresponding maritime security complementary elements are important for integration.

It is not possible to make a model that is universally acceptable for integration. It is a matter that the entity has to envisage. Not only the models will be different for entities depending upon their maritime signature but also within themselves depending upon the situation, time and demand. Such integration however is imperative for integrating maritime security and thereby providing the concept the desired recognition as a vital element of human existence.

Conclusions

The case for integrated maritime security is strong and clear. Maritime security is a terrain specific statement that needs to be integrated with national security for positive results and neither to be left isolated or seen separately. Maritime security gets integrated only when it is amalgamated or assimilated within the national security governance as part of it. Though the concepts of national security and of the ghost protocol, maritime security, are widely different for the nations and other geopolitical entities, integration in whatever form they are perceived should start early. The integration could preferably be in a phased manner as the concept of national security itself is evolving under the pressures the nations and other geopolitical entities face. Integrated maritime security is relevant to every geopolitical entity. But there are differences. Each of the process of integration will be country specific until they all converge one day. Even then there will be no standard pattern of governance. It is a continuous process.

The governments could do well if the concept of ocean property is brought on board as early as possible. It is easy to see the ocean from the ocean property perspectives as a unified organic entity than a kaleidoscopic enigma of fragmented sorts, however the pieces may look. Ocean is not a blind man's elephant; it is a unified terrain of life saving chattels that the world collectively owns. However, it will be a long wait for the principles of national security as envisaged in this study to be accepted by all under the inertia, primarily of the natural law of invariance. But things are bound to be different.

NOTES

1 Paleri, Prabhakaran, *National Security: Imperatives and Challenges,* New Delhi: Tata McGraw-Hill Publishing Company Limited, 2008, pp. 238,346, 445.

2 Blame it on Wrought Iron Rivets from Uncertified Suppliers? materialstoday. com/view/1618/what-really-sank-the-titanic/, accessed 24 August 2013. The ship would have remained for a longer period afloat after collision with the iceberg if the rivets were of better material quality, according to some findings.

3 Saunders, Alex, The Philadelphia Experiment: "The invisible Ship Experiment," keelynet. com/ energy/ philad1. htm, accessed 10 February 2013. In another frivolous situation the government of India is "officially" digging for an invisible treasure of 1,000 tons of gold worth US$ 40bn under an ancient temple in the village of Daundia Khera based on a dreamy revelation of an old and "holy" man in the village. While the obsession for war could become the nemesis for economic security for the United States, India could end up in the dump by the people's craze for the yellow metal. India imports 2.3 tons of gold on a daily average. The entire gold goes into offerings, jewelry or hoards. The digging and the justification by the government officials and politicians in India or attempts to make a naval ship invisible and the official denials are not laughing matters if the psychological compulsions behind such incidents are examined. If it was war induced anxiety illusion in the United States, it was "psychonomics" at play in Daundia Khera when the government was down in the trash economically and by allegations of corruption from the opposition at a time when the election was round the corner. See Bhan, Chander, Alexander Smith, NBC News, worldnews. nbcnews.com/_news/ 2013/10/ 18/ 210245 81-india-digs-for-40-billion-gold-bonanza-based-on-holy-mans-dreams?lite, accessed 19 October 2013. Of course this is just a small price the governments will have to pay for taking the easy route in governance.

4 It happens to any human system, as group behaviour, even to advanced governments when they come momentarily under intellectual confinement and decision impotence.

5 Military machines, equipment and people are not meant just to face "harms-way" as it is a natural situation for which humans had the capability all the time. That is why human beings are the only non-endangered species. "Extreme harms-way" (EHW) is a notion of this study that means a war machine including the people should be capable of facing danger at all times beyond their natural human capabilities. A war machine including people should be EHW compatible. If not they will be annihilated in no time.

6 According to Section 3 (a) of International Regulations for Preventing Collisions at Sea 1972 (COLREGS), published by International Maritime Organisation (IMO) the word "vessel" includes every description of water craft, including non-displacement craft, wing-in-ground-effect (WIG) vehicle, and seaplanes, used or capable of being used as a means of transportation on water. A wing in ground effect vehicle is one that attains level flight near the surface of the earth making use of the aerodynamic interaction between the wings and the surface known as the ground effect. Also called sea skimmer and by other names. Not widely used.

7 indianchild.com/mauryan_empire.htm, accessed 10 February 2013.

8 people.hofstra.edu/geotrans/eng/ch3en/conc3en/registships.html, accessed 10 February 2010.

9 Ibid.

10 Ibid.

11 Neff, Robert, "Flags that Hide Dirty Truth," *Asia Times*, 19 April 2007.

12 As assessed by ITF based on the ability and willingness of the flag state to enforce international minimum social standards on its vessels, the degree of ratification and enforcement of ILO Conventions and recommendations and safety and environmental record. en.wikipedia.org/wiki/Convenience_flag. According to Neff, ibid., there were 40 FOC registries.

13 Is a ship an industrial product, or a constructed or built habitat or platform? Though all arguments are valid, considering a ship as a platform where people leave at sea, it could be taken as a built item rather than a manufactured product. It is also a matter of usage for convenience in taxation where a product may attract a different assessment of taxation compared to the one that is built or constructed. In regular usage a ship is normally built or constructed.

14 Paleri, Prabhakaran, *Coast Guards of the World and Emerging Maritime Threats*, Tokyo, Ocean Policy Research Foundation, 2009, p. 116.

15 Section 8, the United States Constitution, www.usconstitution.net/const.html, accessed 10 February 2010.

16 Title 10 deals with the armed forces.

17 A term borrowed from a successful Tarantino movie.

18 Denmark and Canada are also claiming part of the ridge. en.wikipedia.org/wiki/Lomonosov_ridge#site_note-interfax-9, accessed 23 August 2013.

19 Paleri, n. 1, p. 259.

20 "On the Beach," a novel by the British-Australian author Nevil Shute published in 1957 ended with those lines. Shute, Nevil, *On the Beach*, New York, NY: William Morrow and Company, 1957.

21 Ibid. This study refers to Cold War as World War III. Hence it was not fictitious

as far as the study is concerned but the specific the incident was. In fact the movie "On the Beach" was an evidence of the Third World War in its cold avatar.

22 The bomb dropped in Nagasaki was meant for another Japanese town named Kokura. Weather changed the destiny of many.

23 Shoefield, Matthew, Assessing Navy's Strength Requires More than Math, www.military.com/daily- news /2012 /10/24/tallying-navys-strength-requires-more-than-math.html

24 Human intelligence.

25 Here the word "he" is not gender biased. The hunter in a Stone Age family was always the man. The women helped in household activities, not in combat.

26 A force has to be lean, lethal and focused on the special doctrinal objective. For example a navy according to the author should be lean, lethal and silent; a coast guard or a service force should be lean, lethal and visible. It is for the policy makers to decide.

27 This is a nomenclature used in this study. Unlike the other "geopolitical" clubs such as the nuclear club, etc, the sea power club membership may have to be decided by the country itself by self evaluation. It is not based by any other hard and fast rules like acceptance by others etc.

28 A subject that has been practiced and being explored by the author. First mentioned in Paleri, Prabhakaran, *The Role of the Coast Guard in the Maritime Security of India,* Second Edition, New Delhi, Knowledge World, 2007, pp. 27, 29.

29 Schwarzenberger, G., *International Law,* Delhi: Universal Law Publishing Co. Pvt. Ltd., 2000, p. 90.

30 Paleri, n.14, p. 116.

31 A fine example of effective integration of maritime security, though very much situational, can be seen in the handling of the powerful cyclone Phalin that lashed the east coast of India on 12 October 2013. The government machinery carried out a never before disaster prevention plan that was strictly land based. The predictions of the Indian Meteorological Department (IMD) were very accurate. The railways showed excellent sense of governance under the threat that came from the sea—direct, overt, and external. Of course, the DOE threat is the least complex in most of the cases. news.rediff.com/commentary/2013/oct/12/liveupdates.htm, and www. orissadiary. com/ CurrentNews.asp?id=45106, accessed 25 October 2013.

32 Bill Clinton, during his second election campaign for the office of the president of the United States. Also title of Chapter 18 of the Book *The Next World War* authored by James Adams (London: Arrow, 1999), p. 307. It's the economy, stupid" is a slight variation of the phrase "The economy, stupid"

which James Carville had coined as a campaign strategist of Bill Clinton's successful 1992 presidential campaign against the then president George H. W. Bush.

33 From the mission statement of the Indian Coast Guard on marine environmental security.

34 Explain if not done earlier.

35 Taken as a noun similar to subsidiary.

36 National security study has identified six terrains—land, ocean, air space (geophysical), outer space (physical), cyber space and genomic space. Human mind could follow, but not so far though can be influenced through psychological intervention. Informational security that covers the human mind is considered an element of national security in this study.

37 (DiMaggio & Powell, 1991, 66), Lodge, Martin and Wegsrich, Kai, Control over Government: Institutional Isomorphism and Governance Dynamics in German Public Administration, www.questia.com/library/1G1-133188224/control-over-government-institutional-isomorphism, accessed 26 November 2012.

Chapter 7

FUTURE PERSPECTIVES AND THE GORDIAN KNOT

If maritime security is a ghost protocol, then national security is a Gordian Knot.

The future will turn out the way the world will perceive national security. Or rather, that is how the nations and the generations will wake up to the future. But what if the national security is a Gordian Knot? It is, but that should not be a serious problem. There will be enough Alexanders to cut and loosen it threadbare, when the situation arises.[1] That is the future; it is more than crystal gazing.

It has been difficult for the humans since the time social systems thrived for survival under group governance. Wellbeing of people remained at stake under misperceived governance all the time. Every government had its own prerogatives. Priorities changed. Governance became selective. No government thought about governance with the sole objective of the wellbeing of the people. They focused on welfare taking it for wellbeing. It was easier than governing for wellbeing. The returns were immediate. The span of governance for each government was short for focused long term governance. Each government was in a hurry. Governing for wellbeing is a long drawn out process that cannot be done in staccato fashion by short term planning of five or so years unless continuity is maintained. The long term damages to the system by governing for welfare were naturally not a concern for governments as they rolled out welfare freebies that pleased the public, at least a section of them, who returned their gratitude by appreciating governance. This is a traditional way of governance as even the Greeks practiced it centuries before. Many nations collapsed under such governance within the century itself. Many nations became couched dependencies of the strong and powerful. Most of the nations became simply welfare states at different levels adding to the vows of the successive governments and non-beneficiaries. There are many examples of disappeared nations or union of nations, which this study leaves to the reader to examine. They were not exactly failed states, but examples of failed governance. A state fails under bad governance. Welfare is not wellbeing as long as it is doling out benefits to a select few. Some call it vote bank politics. This study does not think so for reasons that are much more serious.

Maximising and managing the wellbeing of a people in a social system is undoubtedly a difficult task. No one has proven it so far except in mythopoeian diaries or idealist proclamations. Many believe maximising wellbeing is simply impossible. Whereas, they believe, providing welfare is easy, practical and pragmatic. Nothing can be far from truth if the reason for governments deviating from wellbeing to welfare is examined seriously. The governments simply do not know about such governance. A simple biomodel that will explain it can be seen in the compensation regime where governments quickly puts the lid on a serious mishap by declaring monetary compensation to the unfortunate victims that their successors claim months or even years later. The dole of compensation closes the chapter and shuts the mouths immediately in a welfare state and opens the door for a repeat. Governance aimed at NS_{max} is different from doling.

It has been going on in governance of every human system from time immemorial because everyone makes the common mistake of attempting governance from within as it is comparatively effortless. Governing national security in its wholesome concept is meant for the tough professionals in governance. It is similar to kicking a ball in the desired direction to achieve an end goal through objectives. One should not endeavour to kick the ball remaining inside it. The governments have to break the inertia of being trapped within and get out engaging the intractable problems of national security governance externally. They got to cut the Gordian Knot and create fresh ends to unwind it. They need to view national security as advocated in this study, from outside. For that they have to be tough, professional, persistent, pragmatic, competent and determined. It may take a very long time in future for nations and their governments to reach that level, looking at the past. But human ingenuity at the time of crisis can do wonders. It can surpass any mishap. The world turns out better when things go seriously wrong.

Under this assumption, the initial attempt to appreciate the future is to examine the prevailing situation. It leads to interesting findings.

No government in the world governs national security from outside, positioning external to it, from the perimeter inwards. It includes the world's successful governments, normally proclaimed quoting various indices. It is visible with the fixation of national security far from national wellbeing with war and conflicts that threaten the governments and those who govern, not the state, if visualised seriously. More than highlighting the peaceful efforts of the Organisation for the Prohibition of Chemical Weapons (OPCW), the Nobel peace prize for 2013 awarded to them highlights that even in 21st century the craze for genocide prevails unhindered among those in power. Otherwise why should the fragile but determined OPCW be there as the global chemical weapons watch dog? More than the elimination of chemical weapons, the OPCW actually prevented America entering the war in Syria in 2013, by taking over the responsibility to tame the chemical Syria on themselves. Syria behaved intelligently. An American war in Syria would have been genocide of a different kind—an Afghan and Iraqi repeat. Does a government go to war unless its own existence or that of its members is at stake? Does a government suppress insurgency or militancy because it is impacting on people's wellbeing or is it because it challenges the government and the authorities?

Everything about national governance is on a case to case basis in a fire fighting mode in which those in authority situate the appreciation. There is no integration in governance even in the land based approach. "Internal security or rule of law" is governed as elements of national security whereas they are only conditional to it. Looking internally to an issue provides an inside gut view while it needs an external perimeter view for governance. All round perimeter view is a must for national security governance.

While the governments are busy with national security governance the way they perceive it under the landclasp syndrome, maritime security wanders outside as a ghost protocol. It is a Catch 22 situation.[2]

A ghost protocol such as maritime security that can influence national security waits outside to get exorcised in reverse by integration. Whereas the body to which it has to be integrated is hidden within itself! Here it is important to understand that a large number of ghost protocols exist all around the main body of national security for decision making in relation to integration. Maritime security is just one among them upon which this study stumbles. Governments should know. Others are not highlighted in this study.

Hence the first question is, "Will the governments manage national security as a wholesome concept standing external to it in future?" The answer is, "No." The finding is from the history of governance. But from the visible projection of modern day advancement in thinking and renascent governance that is visible in some parts of the world since the fall of Soviet Union, the answer could be, "Can't say." The visibility is in traces and flashes. And there is hope. Nations will have no escape from the forces of decline if they follow the same old selective governance. The situation will demand them to do better, to perform for survival. Those who heed to this call may attempt new methods from the tried out easy and complacent ways of internalised governance. Survival is the biggest challenge to humans. And when the very issue of survival is at stake humans will rise to the occasion. But, not all. There will be tremendous disparity among people the world over. The disparity will also be visible within each entity. The gap will widen in course of time. There will always be gaps in wellbeing within the human system but the good news is that the thinking process in governance may change for the better among the wise and prudent with foresight and vision. Others may resort to violence or pray for it. This is the first insight of this study.

The future of nations and national security, the concept leading to the wellbeing of people, has to be seen from this perspective. It will be difficult to get into the real national security. The problem is that the national security benefits the governments can provide to its people are much less than the perceived security they strive for. Beyond that the governments are helpless. Apparent security is not "what people want." They want perceived security. But still they can be contended with apparent security the governments can provide. There are many other outlets people can find with or without government support to chase perceived security. The governments can maximise apparent security by effective governance. But mostly, even in the most powerful nation, the point of national security maximisation will be distant. History shows that every golden age in governance whimpered out after a short while for this reason. It is the subsequent societies that recognised them as golden eras. It is visible in modern age too. The great political slogan "India shining," bargain hunting with "Asian Tigers," the Greek saga of "Olympic hype and prosperity," the much touted "Mexican Bonanza," etc., were such golden age candy flosses of recent times. The governments did not succeed improving everything that would kindle the wellbeing of the people because what the people want is (unlimited) perceived security. Perceived security is like the ocean horizon observed from the bridge of a ship. It moves farther as much as the ship moves forward. Perceived security is a chimera. Apparent security is "what people need." But the governments will not be able to maximise it under present day governance.

Another problem is what mentioned earlier—governing national security from within. Every kind of governmental system including democracy governs national security without coming out of it. That is why they are unable to break the Gordian Knot. Within this scenario or rather helplessness of governments, maritime security will be out of grasp even for the powerful, being in a terrain the political system is not used to. The example was of the powerful Mughals in India. In the study of the future, the main question is, "Will the national governments be able to cut this Gordian Knot at any time in future?" Simply put, the world is yet to witness governance that provides the best possible feeling of wellbeing to people. A change for the better may be possible if the wholesome concept of national security with its elements is acceptable and governed towards maximisation. At least that will do well with apparent security. This study is strictly about integrated maritime security. Here the underlying issue is how to maritime security will figure in future.

Factors of the Future

The governments will govern their nations the way they would like to go about it. It will be worthwhile examining, therefore, the factors associated with the general parameters of maritime security examined in this study and their importance in the future world. The factors examined are,

- Maritime trade
- Maritime transportation
- Maritime forces and ocean order
- War at and from the sea
- Ocean property exploitation and governance
- Law enforcement at sea
- Other possible exploitations of the sea

Governing them in the future perspective is a task the governments have to arrive at according to their identified priorities and policies.

Maritime Trade

Maritime trade or trade by ocean dominates the world to a considerable degree. It is also called the shipping trade. The dependence of the world on maritime trade will naturally increase. The world unlike during the period of the Dunkel Draft[3] or earlier, has become more conscious about the concept of trade and welfare. It has been a slow progress, but progress in which the world understood the importance of trade between nations for common wellbeing. The maxim of foreign trade, "trading between countries is good for parties involved" is gaining ground in the mindset of people and those in governance. It is not just a matter of comparative advantage alone. Protectionism, though still persists under various games the countries play, may have its ups and downs as the global community will not be able to keep a blind eye towards the feel good necessities of life that will be available only through trade. Maritime security related to the economics of trade will gain more significance under this paradigm. Ships and ship transportation will increase in a balanced manner and so will be the safety aspects and insurance market. Foreign trade is important to maintain stability and the global order. Ocean trade has to flow smooth under the coast guard slogan "traffic should flow." Disputes, conflicts and unlawful acts in the maritime scenario could challenge the determination of the world to advance forcing the countries to look for new routes and modified SLOC. Cost of carriage of goods by sea will increase. Ships can become more vulnerable in routes that have not been tried so far. The common impact will be on consumers of various countries. But with the growth of global economy, the people should be able to bear the load in the name of advancement.

Nations, including landlocked countries, could benefit from the increase in maritime trade by integrating maritime security with national security. It is time the nations broke the jinx that only coastal nations will involve in maritime trade. Under integrated maritime security, a country hidden among mountains far from the ocean could become a great shipping power economically by involving in shipping, maritime business and education, and absorbing the employment benefits for seafarers. The future doesn't see it happening.

The new drivers of ocean trade that surfaced as challenges are many. Among the challenges there are unlawful activities of all kinds including piracy and fraud, climate change regulations like carbon footprints, rising consumer demand for speed of delivery, cost of freight, currency domination of shipping markets, marine environmental security, rogue state involvement, etc. The opportunities are increased support from international organisations, export promotion policies of governments, influence of World Trade Organisation (WTO), globalisation of markets, etc. All these challenges and opportunities are going to linger on in future with more opportunities and encouragements forthcoming through international cooperation and understanding. Maritime trade will flourish. Unlawful activities, at and from the sea will be suppressed by world governments with all force including diplomatic moves. Hopefully the Somali piracy will be the last of it with such intensity since it all began even before the advent of maritime transportation when pirates used the sea to raid over land causing mayhem. Finally maritime trade will outlive at least the Somali type of high intensity piracy. But piracy at sea, however, is difficult to eradicate because of its inherent strength of the historical past as a livelihood of maritime hooligans for whom it is more an adventure or a blood sport loaded with money and power than a crime.[4] There is excitement in it. More dangerous in maritime commercial world will be other unlawful activities, especially maritime fraud. National governments and international organisations will find ways of containing them under increased awareness.

The consumer demand for early delivery of goods and services will increase in an impatiently moving world. Consumers may reconsider their decision to purchase goods and services if they have to wait. Unfortunately shipping services cannot provide expediency. Traders may have to anticipate demand and arrange for transportation much earlier. The risk in maritime trade, thereby, will increase whereas the risk of the perils of the sea will not be that serious by advanced designs and personnel quality standards in shipping and aggressiveness of insurance factors. Cost of freight will shoot up by energy expenses as well as currency fluctuations world over. The US dollar plays dominant role in ocean trade. Shipping rates, bunker cost and other expenses normally will have to be met in US dollar. Even the ransom demanded by the pirates is in US currency. Value of other national currencies against the US dollar including hard currencies will fluctuate drastically. This will be a challenge for maritime traders. This may create currency consortiums that will hold the balance of currency against the unitary currency stronghold. Such thinking from the maritime point of view also complements the element of economic security.

Nations will rely on foreign trade for improving the quality of life. Since the absolute majority of foreign trade is by sea, the ocean, especially the SLOC will become crowded by trade traffic. It has its advantages in establishing marine safety by buddy support. The trade tonnage in all the ocean divisions will increase substantially. The choke points will find heavy density of traffic causing delay and increase in energy cost. Concentration around choke points will be a matter of concern from the safety point of view.

Markets are expanding due to globalisation, movement of factors of production especially labour and capital, and the ambitious strategies of multinational enterprises. The multinationals have created supranational markets around the world that creates the demand for increased maritime trade. Increasing interdependence in the world will increase demand for foreign trade that will mostly flow by the ocean. International division of labour is changing because of capital flow. All these will add to maritime trade in future. The expected areas of increase in maritime transportation are container traffic, liquid and dry bulk cargo and cruise tourism.

Maritime Transportation

The future of maritime transportation is likely to shape in accordance with the present day trends and the way the industry has been behaving in the past. It will be a kind of straight line progress. Maritime transportation also includes ports, harbours and other relevant infrastructure development. Examination of the elements of the past and present day trends points out the changes will be incremental as well as innovative but not in a fast pace. Structural changes in international trade will have a direct impact on maritime transportation including port development.

The shipping industry will continue to carry more than 90 per cent of the world's trade by volume. At the same time, the world tonnage would have multiplied. With increase in maritime trade, the transportation scenario is naturally expected to expand. Maritime transportation is not just merchant marine cargo transfer. It includes all kinds of vessels. There is considerable demand for various types of vessels for commercial transportation. The main constraint will be energy.

The changing transportation needs will require tighter integration of production chains. The demand will be for versatile and flexible vessels. The focus in anyway will be on energy efficiency which may turn builders to liquid natural gas (LNG) for driving ships as the marine fuel alternative. Other energy sources are yet to be developed for commercial use. Switching over to LNG may be comparatively easy. Change factor management will be crucial for development of designs for energy efficient and weather compatible ships of all kinds—cargo liners, passenger ships including cruise liners, pilgrim ships, regular transport ships, etc. The biggest challenge will be energy constraints. LNG is the immediate choice for study by those who are in a hurry to find energy solutions in maritime transportation. But there are others who argue for hybrid power and fuel cells. But that will cut on the economics demanding storage space for hydrogen. Experiments will even continue with coal and biomass.

Ship design will also undergo major change. One may see no ballast or limited ballast ships as ballast water can become a strict no-no near shore. Ballast water when pumped out in a different location near a port can pollute the local sea with alien organisms shipped in from the previous port. The alien organisms normally turn predators in their new environment. Mid sea transfer of ballast will not be a safe idea.

There are chances of the climate change impacting future maritime transportation. Climate change can induce extreme weather events. Surges and storms could be more intense according to future predictions.[5] Increased maritime trade and transportation will raise the demand for ports, harbours and loading points. Marine infrastructural development will become an important area in national planning. The density of ports will increase to accommodate increase in traffic. Increase in maritime trade, research and development in marine transportation and marine infrastructural development will generate integrated maritime policies on maritime transportation and trade in the seafaring world. Different maritime modes will be integrated. These policies will be an opportunity to integrate maritime security with the national security regime, if the nations so decide.

With the environmental fears turning out to be realistic, the world will look forward to green maritime transportation. That perhaps will be the ultimate challenge for the seafaring community. The maritime transport sector will look for advanced maritime business perspectives to overcome the change induced barriers. The overall objective will be sustainable economic growth and the development of maritime business related to strategies, planning, competition, routing, innovation and financing. The maritime business models will undergo drastic change. Companies will engage in cruise tourism, offshore industry, research charter, passenger transportation including pilgrim ships, marine renewable and services, etc. These are opportunities to strengthen maritime transportation business all over the world.

Production has been intermittent in the past according to the fluctuations in trade with ships getting laid off when the seasons thinned out. This trend will continue in future as production will depend upon trade fluctuations. Major boost is expected to cruise tourism with increase in investment. Superships like mega container vessels and luxury liners will serve the industry. The container terminals should be able to service and turn around such vessels at fast pace with port to port logistical service for meeting client demand.

The role of the government will be in macro economic reforms related to ocean trade and transportation. It will work better in an integrated environment under the changing nature of maritime transportation. According to some observers, the changes will be more than just incremental.[6]

Maritime Forces and Ocean Order

In the ever intricate ocean scenario dotted with conflicts, the maritime forces may find their role of keeping the order enhanced but without firm commands and directions on terms of engagement and reference. This is going to be natural under the perils of the sea and the fog and friction of scenario build up. Mistaken identities, confused manoeuvres, panic attacks, unforeseen disasters, private security blunders, etc. will rule the roost at sea. The forces of the future will have to decide on their way and engagements through such challenges. In the overall outlook, the world maritime forces could behave as if they got into a limbo of development inertia. There will be exceptions. Maritime forces have seemingly slowed down in their design, policy transformation and usage. The post Cold War "depression" has caught on seriously in the absence of stern competition in technology advancement related to arms and weapons. There was highly demanding competition in destructive designs since the commencement of the world wars that gave birth to the ultimate weapon—the nuclear bomb. Chances are that the future of the war designs may turn towards the objective of zero combatant and civil casualty instruments of war. Zero casualty principle applies to own forces in combat including elimination of friendly fire casualties. The focus may shift to smart weapons and unmanned instruments of destruction. But the pace will be slow. The change may be felt in the ocean also. The use value of a navy or a coast guard is ever increasing but the forces are not on track with demand. They have seemingly deviated from their desired roles and slowed down in design, development and indigenisation efforts compared to the past. This could be costly for nations who need to integrate maritime security with national security urgently to meet the future. In the absence of a serious bipolar chill the world may lack direction and balance related to war and conflict engagements to rev up technology. This is a relative expression.

In naval warfare, there could be moves for more unmanned activities and stealth platforms compatible with EHW engagements. Ocean robotics may pick up momentum for warfare, intelligence gathering and research. The problem in finding the direction is that the threat is not easily perceptible today. But the navies can look into the common requirement under universal threat in warfare and conflict scenario. For example, irrespective of the scenario, they could still examine,

- Advancements in ship and platform design
- Reduction of personnel

- Advancement in weapon and sensor design
- Communication
- Intelligence generation

All these activities will involve cost, but have collateral advantages if executed strategically under integrated policies and plans. Nations could also get into strategic and tactical research in relation to the roles and missions of the navy under improved geostrategic context. While the navies are involved in advancing various capabilities like stealth, early warning, mine countermeasures and underwater attacks, and modernising the existing systems to the next generation portfolio, what they have to visualise with respect to the future is the compatibility of the naval outfit with the extreme harm's way (EHW) scenario in future. EHW could itself be a wholesome package for military naval development. It has to be combined with geostrategic requirement. It is a full time activity for any navy if supported by the policies of government in geostrategic security. The navy is the best ambassador a country could have, especially in the modern world, is a finding of this study. It is reiterated here.

The navies, like other military armed forces, will hold exclusive signatures. The signature of a navy will be different from another for obvious reasons. But irrespective of the signature, the navies may have to face signature strikes from ratpack nonstate actors with or without proxy support of regular state actors. This could happen to any navy large or small depending on which country is targeted by the nonstate actors or unlawful activists. The strikes will carry more or less common signatures all over the world. For example the terrorist attack in Mumbai, India on 26 November 2008 provides stunning similarity at the core of the Kenyan mall attack on 21 September 2013, to the extent it could leave an analyst to believe the Mumbai attack was a trial run for the Kenyan one; a template of sorts. Some analysts believe the terrorists use India as a staging ground to try out new methods of attack though carried out by different agencies who may share information. As it is, they believe the terror groups consider India as a trial ground for trying out a new style in the changing terror scenario to practice elsewhere. Such statements lack scientific investigation. Besides, terror strikes and criminal attacks of a period will look similar elsewhere.

Cooperative engagements between navies may increase to study each other's operational culture for preparing for jointness when required. Scientifically, in all bijective probability, the forces with varied signatures when called to operate together as a team in a joint force ambience should transform isomorphically into similar naval signatures in course of time. It means joint operations between two navies on a common ground should make them behave and develop into identical forces. That is the belief. But that is not likely to happen. The signature of a navy will depend upon the maritime signature and the style of governance of the country it belongs to. Sheer joint operations may help in understanding each other but not in mutual transformation. The option here for the navies is cooperative engagement, not transformative engagement, with other navies as well as other armed forces for handling signature strikes that will be at higher EHW than it can handle. It could be practised within own country among various forces. There will be great opportunities for the navies to cooperate not only with other navies but also with other military and nonmilitary armed forces to balance their respective signatures in meeting higher threats. Since this is also true for other military armed forces, navy will not be an exception in warfighting or combat preparedness in cooperative engagement. It also means integration of military and other EHW capable armed forces will hold a lot for the future. It leads to a question. "Will the world witness an all terrain armed force in the near future?" Perhaps, not. Because near future is close and one can see it better. It can't be said for the long term. But the necessity exists. Here, all terrain includes every terrain under the terrain specificity principle of national security—land, ocean, air space, outer space, cyber space, genomic space... But forces could be multi-terrain specific.

A navy will have to predict the future if it has to stay ahead and remain integrated. How far into the future? The answer is relatively easy—to the limit of obsolescence or redundancy. It is time to change when the adversary has the advantage. Every military equipment has a period design. Military technology becomes vintage specimen very fast, mostly unused. Strategically speaking a war is best fought and won when the force has superior system than the enemy. It means the system is valid only for one operation or is mission specific. However a military cannot function that way. Therefore the idea here is to have comparatively better platforms, systems, weapons and personnel at any given time. It is possible by forward design—designing and inducting the system competitively for the time or period it is likely to be in use.

The future of naval warfare will be continued supplementation of other forces including strategic nuclear operations. People will need better training to improve their quality standards. The navy will be costlier than before. Energy efficient naval systems will be an advantage. While nuclear power will be a choice to manage energy it will not be within the reach of most of the navies. Those who have the expertise and wherewithal may think of change over in a convincingly safe manner. There will be constraints caused by public, powerful nations and law and treaties in design and use of militaryware.

The ocean order will be complex with various disputes lingering without getting resolved. Mostly, the disputes will be governed by UNCLOS. The UNCLOS allocated regime will govern national thinking. Landlocked states and geographically disadvantaged states will not be forthcoming or will be slow in placing their claims under UNCLOS because the flow of the regime and redressal of grievances originating from disputes may take considerable time. The nations may be short of technological capabilities to put forward their claims with deserving evidences.

The ocean order can be visualised under two different perspectives—national policies and the ocean-stasis. The policies as well as ocean-stasis change with respect to time. The more serious situation is when the national policy does not match with the ocean-stasis at a particular time. This dissonance often makes a nation follow an ocean policy which may not have definite objectives. It will end up as awesome waste in finances. Here, integration helps considerably to synchronise the ocean policy of the government with the ocean-stasis and bring in the necessary convergence without any kind of resonance in ocean order. The resonance in ocean order occurs when a nation's policy is asynchronous with the ocean-stasis relative to that nation at a particular time. It happens with almost every nation. It can be seen when their ocean policy is analysed with the ocean-stasis relative to it. It could also be seen when nations change their ocean policies in relation to changes in governments or when devoid of any kind of ocean policy. The future maritime scenario with respect to national ocean order is likely to follow suit with respect to the present and followed situation.

Ocean order of the future, therefore, need not reflect in the national ocean policies of the governments. However ocean policies will give some hints about their expectations of the future ocean order. The ocean order has not changed since UNCLOS (1992). It is expected to continue for a long period into the future. The only change expected is increased concern sans serious activities about resource and environmental protection. More serious nations who have the capacity may initiate policy level dialogues and discussions on protecting and restoring ocean resources and environment with implied admission that they are in danger. The admission validates the ocean-stasis of the day. The ocean needs concern. This concern will reflect in future too as things can go further wrong. This is an indication that UNCLOS, though a fine regime, hasn't been able to establish a new universal ocean order except establishing rights for all so that the powerful nations do not dominate the ocean. The Convention has shown respect to the ocean based global commons to a considerable extent.

Nations are likely to voice concern on all matters related to resources, environment, coastal zones, and adjacent navigable waters internal to nations. Some nations will establish comprehensive ocean policies with respect to their appreciation of the ocean-stasis. But none of the nations is likely to view integrating maritime security with national security seriously. Because most of them believe it is being done as their national plans advance. Maximum that can be expected is integration of ocean agencies and stakeholders for governing the ocean independently. This may include costal and marine spatial planning, scientific activities, and preservation of environment including critical biosystems, etc. Still, there will be conflicting and overlapping mandates among various agencies in many countries which will be an indication for the absence of integrated maritime security. The ocean order, added with unresolved maritime disputes will remain chaotic. This will be complicated with the issues of sea level rise under the climate dynamics. It can create ocean refugees. These refugees may have to find place elsewhere when their belongings including land go underwater. And those who accommodate them will have to establish their geoproperty rights collateral to it for claims when the flood waters recede or not. There will also be internal refugees in the sinking world. They will have rights over their sunken property to pass on to generations ahead. Perhaps this will be the biggest challenge to the future ocean order. There are already distress signals emanating from the yet-to-be-marooned island nations. They are seriously concerned about their nations sinking in the not too distant future.[7] According to Environmental Justice Foundation, climate change will create around 150 million people looking for relocation in the world by 2050.[8] This statement has been challenged too.[9] There are questions too. Is climate change going to be treated as a natural disaster? Or is it a human induced one? It could also be hybrid. There are no studies that will examine the underlying econo-legal issues of climate refugees. Perhaps they may not be another class or variety when called as refugees. But their wellbeing should be the concern of their nations and the prospective countries of refuge. It requires a national security regime that will look into these matters as wellbeing and not welfare or disaster relief.

Another issue of the future is the faster rate of acidification of the ocean which will cause mass extinction of many ocean living resources. Ocean acidification takes place when the p^H value decreases in the ocean.[10] It is caused by the uptake of anthropogenic carbon dioxide which will be human induced. Human inducement comes from human activities that will also be the cause for climate change.

The ocean order, therefore, can turn serious and difficult to manage if necessary caution is not exercised by governments. In addition to ensuring marine environmental security in all respects under efficient P^3C regime, the national and international governmental systems should also device legal regimes for taking care of ocean refugees of climate change and establishing rights on their geoproperties that have been lost in a sinking world.[11]

War at and from the Sea

While the centuries old scholarly treatises on war and art of war still holds good in tactics and strategies of warfare, the pattern of the cues for the occurrence of war, especially limited war have changed considerably since the last part of the 20th century. War needs the approval of the international community. However the same cannot be said about the next global war as it could even escalate out of an "approved" limited war. Prediction is possible, but it could not be dared to, except for exercises and war games. How many global wars the world has been involved so far? This study takes it as three. This includes the Cold War (1945-1993) between two sides and their respective allies, though serious shots were not fired. There were death and casualties all over the world in the shadow of the Cold War including regime changes. It was a shift from the hot war but generated all the heat with special attention to nuclear tests starting with the first underwater nuclear test at Bikini Atoll in 1946.[12] The Cold War reflected all the characteristics of a global war. The world came close to escalation and nuclear showdown on few occasions. In comparison, it is not so today even though the world (another find of the study) is balanced between the inevitable bipolarity. The world can never remain unipolar because of the inertness. It will have to be bipolar or in a stage of hunting for bipolarity as long as it has to power human life.[13] It need not be under the conditions of cold wars, but in a more matured fashion. Uniploarity is a freak assumption or illusion in a human system, especially of nation states.

Strategists continue to toy with the idea of global war. The argument is that multipolarity can induce wars. It could happen even when world is unipolar even momentarily. War does not seem to have any connection with polarity. The next global war according to this study is World War IV.[14]. But the appreciation by various schools of thought is World War III. There are many predictions and games on it. In one such premonitory assessment, the next global war breaks out between two sides headed by the US and China respectively. The rest of the nations align on either side based on their choice of polarity. The war breaks out on 1 September 2029 and ends on 11 November 2036 with victory to the former. Obviously the scenario was envisaged by the hopeful. It was a scenario that may not happen as the world advances. But war could happen. The scenario could be more serious than what has been envisaged.

The appreciation of the war in the scenario mentioned was based on the Syrian and Iranian appendages (though different) as they remained in 2013. In reality, the situation unwound under international public pressure more than national leadership opinion. The pressure from the public ultimately generated new directions. There was diplomatic deadlock on Syrian issue that the United Nations could break to make the powers on other side agree on a draft UN

Security Council resolution aimed at Syria abandoning its chemical arsenal. Why this did not succeed in the case of Saddam Hussein's Iraq could be a pop up at this juncture. Of course, pop ups can be blocked. The answer simply is that it was in the past and the world had moved that much on the road to rationality by 2013. It is a healthy sign. Besides, the polarity was getting sharpened. Russia legally obligated with underlying responsibility to make Syria to give up what the other party reluctantly desired. The "understanding" was hammered out according to Russian foreign minister Sergei Lavrov.[15] So much for now in a world that is poised to improve.[16]

Iran too expressed a change of mind. They had declared that they do not want to "walk in the dark" by international isolation by chasing the bomb, on 15 October 2013.[17] All these points out a future world that is "war choked"[18] and not "war ravaged." The changes can be very different from what is witnessed so far. Immediate predictions may lack accuracy. Thinking about the unthinkable may lead us to fancy but wary predictions.

War is visible only in the human system; it is a behavioural pattern for survival. War is unpredictable. These are the two fundamental laws of war between nations. Much deeper it may also have the primordial code that the animals at the apex of the pyramid of evolution will have to destroy themselves to balance the life systems. This is a hypothesis. War is not the only means by which the humans can successfully accomplish the feat.

According to the observations of this study, the chances of a global war diminish every day the world moves forward. The world is getting war saturated because of the growth in human intellect and fear of death.

It is under this hypothesis and the corresponding assumptions the war at sea in future has to be examined.

War at sea will be to supplement the war efforts on land when needed. It will, therefore, aim at reach rather than clashes at sea. The military use of the navy will be restricted for this purpose in active war scenario in future. This will not diminish the navy's growth. Geostrategic functions and high intensity conflict resolutions will keep the naval forces growing with special momentum where reach coupled with stealth is a necessity. Accordingly, the platforms, weapons, sensors and systems will undergo serious modification in high end navies that will be the privilege of a few. There will be new ideas in human capital strategy as well as human investment in naval affairs. The most important requirement here is to cut the personnel strength. This applies to every maritime force.

There are many talks about netcentric warfare as a concept of the future. It is not a new system that will emerge in future but only a modification of the action information organisation and force integration system that was bound to happen in the process of system evolution. The naval warfare scene, especially in the multi-terrain mode, will be enlightened by modern systems as part of the evolution. The navies should not be missing out the process under complacency or political hold back. Otherwise they will be living with the old.

The navies of the future will have to be fast, agile and geostrategically centred. They have to be ready for creating situational awareness that has never seen so far. The objective of reach demands such alertness. This demands identification and induction of future technology. As mentioned before, nations with access to own developments in future technology will have better command over the use of their navies at sea. Integration of maritime affairs with national security governance will make it easy for indigenisation. Many nations will experiment with these ideas as their status of governance improves. But the success rate will be varied.

Ocean Property Exploitation and Governance

The benefit, a country, including landlocked and geographically disadvantaged, can accrue from the ocean is from its ocean property, not from the ocean as it is. The benefits have to be generated from the ocean property. It is possible only by effective ocean property governance towards this objective. However, the nations have been involved in ocean governance in various ways and not in ocean property governance. Ocean governance and ocean property governance are two different approaches though some of the characteristics may overlap. For example, fisheries exploitation, law enforcement or military preparation can be included in both the approaches. Still there will be differences. The scenario can change for a nation by strategically focusing on the constituents of ocean property directly available and can also be accessed jointly with other nations by cooperative engagement or legal agreements. This is not likely to happen in future, because the nations are yet to accept and examine the concept of ocean property. The awareness of ocean property rights and obligations is yet to breed in many nations, especially the landlocked ones. The primary requirement is to understand and appreciate the concept of ocean property. Thereafter the nations will have to map their respective ocean property.

Ocean property mapping is the initial step towards ocean property governance aimed at maximising the returns from it. Nations are a long way from it. It is the primary requirement for effective integration of maritime security with national security. However integration could still be attempted otherwise. But it will lack the effectiveness required. Presently each nation adopts its own method of ocean governance. Starting with landlocked states that are not aware of their ocean property and ending at the small island entities that are virtually "at sea" with the ocean around, there are different regimes for ocean governance. Though each nation has its signature system of governance including the absence of it, none has looked at the ocean from the point of ocean property governance so far. This is irrespective of the fact they voice equally and competitively for benefit in international organisations like IMO for their rights and concerns about the ocean. The status is expected to remain unchanged for a very long time in the future.

Ocean advantage also involves ocean disadvantage though not a preferred term for mathematical analysis. Ocean disadvantage means diminishing ocean advantage. For example sea level rise or ocean induced cyclonic or tsunami damages can decrease the ocean advantage. Countries will have to be on the watch for them in future too. Ocean resource exploitation will be primarily in fisheries, oil and gas. No major change is expected in future as deep seabed mining and other exploitation will be limited not only by technology but also by demand.

Oceanic islands are one of the constituents of ocean property. The profiles of the islands constantly change like any shoreline for various reasons. Tectonic shifts due to earthquakes, underwater landslides, dry land coastal erosion, sea level rise, etc. can alter the shoreline and inland profiles. Islands can go underwater or new islands can be born. Generally all of them are forces of nature. There were underwater nuclear tests based on remote islands in the past that were very damaging to the islands and the ecosystems. The tests were banned in 1963 by the Partial Nuclear Test Ban Treaty. The Comprehensive Nuclear Test Ban Treaty (CTBT) 1996 further prohibits underwater nuclear tests.

Many islets come up due to the forces of nature and other reasons. Many vanish without caution. There were reports that the islet Bermeja vanished without traces in Gulf of Mexico. The island reported since the early 16th century on the Yucatan coast was not found in a survey in 1999. Explanations for its apparent disappearance include erroneous reporting of early cartographers, shifts in the geography of ocean floor and rising sea levels besides conspiracy theories that the United States did it to expand their exclusive economic zone.[19] There are cases of islets popping up and vanishing under natural forces in other parts of the world also. This calls for a vertical ocean regime to include underwater benthic heights in ocean property rights. Perhaps the future world may think of it as technology for ocean research and exploitation advances, climate change swallows more land masses and ocean reality, more than awareness, dawns among governments through integrated maritime security.

The future maritime scenario can get complicated when islets or even large islands come up or vanish. To avoid geostrategic issues, any new island other than those come up within the sovereign waters of a state may be concluded as global commons for jurisdiction and exploitation unless a country can claim it undisputedly and irrevocably under the international law without a counter claim. The regime should also specify about islands that have gone underwater or are already underwater and claimed by various countries. All these are going to be mammoth tasks, though very much practical. The future world will get into ratifying many regimes related to such issues. It may take considerable time. All these are maritime issues and show the wares that are very much in store to be studied under maritime security in future. Whereas, new issues over land, air space and outer space are likely to be less complex, compared to the ocean. This is a find of this study in the futuristic perspective—the relative importance of ocean with respect to the other two geophysical terrains—land and airspace, and the physical terrain—outer space, will be more complex in future as there are many scenarios that are yet to unfold.

Still the governance of national security will be land-based. Hence it is all the more important that maritime security is integrated before it turns complex and wildly unmanageable by all nations in the world in an equivocal manner. This cannot be predicted. Some among the responsible nations may venture into such governance. The reasons for such a situation originate from the complexity of the existing scenario in the ocean property regime. It lacks recognition. Ocean property focuses on its four constituents—ocean advantage, ocean resources, ocean environment and oceanic islands. Hence the behaviour of ocean property regime will be in accordance with the scenario with respect to the four constituents.

Ocean advantage is very specific to naval transportation, maritime trade, maritime warfare maritime research, etc. Interestingly, even landlocked countries can benefit from ocean advantage. But it is not likely the governments will get engaged in serious studies of ocean advantage and how to maximise it for the benefit of the state. It is wrong to believe a country that is landlocked will get seriously involved in having own ship bottoms in maritime trade or citizens competent for marine employment on board ships. It is not likely they would pursue maritime research seriously though nothing can prevent them if determined. A landlocked country may not venture out to establish a wind farm in a leased part of the ocean of another country or global commons to generate electricity and distribute it to other countries willing to purchase power. All these are practical and pragmatic ideas except that the mindset is not likely to turn towards them.

This goes to ocean resources including global commons also. The landlocked and geographically disadvantaged countries have their rights over ocean resources and global commons. But how much they will exploit is yet to be understood. Hence the scenario in the immediate future is not likely to be changed unless the countries turn around in their system of governance and think seriously of integrated maritime security. Ocean resources however will have much greater say in national planning in terms of food and energy in future.

Ocean advantage is more or less fixed for a country. It is also a global common. It is for the country to exploit. The changes can be minimal in future.

Ocean environment is a major issue that will find many changes in future. The largest change, perhaps, could come in preserving and maintaining the coastal zone where the impacts are directly felt by wave, wind and tidal actions under changing climatic conditions. While for some countries it is coastal erosion more or else at sea level, for some it will be cliff erosion and sand dune disappearance. Along the coast, the sea behaves as if the shore belongs to it. The sea persistently makes attempts to snatch the shore. It comes back again and again, sometimes more ferociously riding over the wind and the waves. One day it takes away the shore only to return and reestablish its rights in a discontented manner. This problem that is happening continuously can get further aggravated with the rising sea level in future. The issues can be resolved in a better way if the coastline is managed as a global continuum that has no beginning or end.[20] The levelled up coast, sand dunes and cliffs breakdown and disappear changing the profile of the coast continuously. Any effort to prevent or preempt it will cause unexpected and serious trouble elsewhere along this continuum. Cliff erosion will be a serious matter for many countries hanging on it against the sea. In certain countries, owners of coastal properties form associations to safeguard their coastal zone interests unaware of the damages their efforts can cause at another shore in another country. Sea can break any veritable wall. Adding to the environmental woes will be marine pollution of various kinds—oil, chemical, land based, bio, algal bloom, radioactive, medical waste, etc. The pollution will increase closely followed by new legal instruments to prevent them.

Governing islands will be different kind of organised human activity. There are different types of islands. The ocean property regime actually looks at islands that belong to a nation and not an island nation by itself. Nations whether land locked, coastlands or islands could have islands besides the mainland, either as part of mainland or as territories or autonomous regions. There is no landlocked nation owning oceanic islands today. The islands complement national power and are drivers of change in national progress and strength. However, nations do not appreciate these powers seriously. Instead, the islands are treated as a kind of reserve territory that could be exploited as and when the times come in many cases. This trend may not change. The island states too will govern their national security under the landclasp syndrome though may possess characteristics and behaviour pattern of states surrounded by ocean, especially by small island nations. This can be seen in the governance of many small island developing states

(SIDS). But the greatest danger for an island, even if mountainous, is sea level rise. It will be more visible in future.

Maritime security strategists often talk on ocean habitats or hydropolis—surface and underwater. It is a technologically possible and viable idea for people to live in the ocean surface and under it. While there are evidences of erstwhile human habitats that had gone underwater, there is no chance of people staying in the ocean permanently. The concept of water world is mere fantasy. It is not likely to happen, according to this study, at least in the near future because humans cannot let go their landclasp syndrome. Notwithstanding, there could be people investing in ocean real estate, just like buying a piece of Mars or Moon. Though, both are fantasies under extreme superciliousness with self, the number of those who bets on the planets will be more and more rationally vulnerable than the ocean migrants. Leave it to the landclasp syndrome.

Law Enforcement at Sea

Law enforcement at sea will depend upon the changes in the pattern of unlawful activities at and from the sea in future. Comparing with the past, the present has not witnessed any serious change except in the frequency and location of such acts. An example was Somali piracy. Maritime piracy was known since the beginning of ocean transportation or even earlier to it when pirates came by the sea and raided and plundered coastal villages unleashing mayhem. Soon piracy confined to sea and maritime forces engaged them. Piracy has been an organised crime even before. It retains its character today. The situation is similar in other unlawful activities also. The future may not witness any major change except fluctuations in frequency and location. The only difference is that unlawful activities like piracy may not keep its lustre as before when the world progresses economically and politically towards better environments. Somali piracy as seen in its culminated form in 2011 could be the last of the blockbuster piracies.

Whether there is change or not, the maritime terrain will have to be swept and sanitised constantly by the enforcement forces and agencies of responsible governments. Systematic monitoring, control and surveillance are necessary for response. It calls for a regime, preferably international, that comprises ocean monitoring, control, surveillance and response (MCSR). Without an MCSR regime backed by effective intelligence, suppression of unlawful activities at sea will be difficult. Even then, it is a matter of cooperative engagement. Besides, identifying law and having jurisdiction over the unlawful activists is another matter. The world is hindered by them. This state of affairs is likely to continue. The unlawful activists will take advantage of the situation. Coastal nations should have legal prowess in establishing rule of the law at sea. There should not be any asymmetry between the unlawful act and the law that needs to contain it at and from the sea. But the situation will remain unchanged in future. There was no indication that showed situational change when nations were struggling to contain the menace of Malacca Strait piracy or Somali piracy. Piracy will end when pirates decide. Pirates will decide when they do not have to do it anymore. That goes with all unlawful acts. Hence, suppression of unlawful activities in future is going to be a serious issue.

One of the reasons for the confusion is seemingly the wrong approach. The solution for suppression of unlawful activities lies seriously over the land according to some political analysts and scholars. The best way to resolve a piracy or other enforcement issues at sea is politico-legal. It is land based process. It was clear in the case of Malacca Strait piracy related to the political unrest in Aceh in Indonesia and marine fisheries issues in many parts of the world.

UNCLOS is so far the best thought out and articulated international legal regime for the sea. But it has limitations in law enforcement. While piracy is the most noticeable, there are various other unlawful activities that need the attention of national governments and international organisations. This includes crime at sea on board vessels and platforms, poaching, smuggling, insurgency and terror support, environmental crimes, etc. While there is not likely to be any spurt in unlawful activities in all likelihood they will prevail and test the effectiveness of maritime law enforcement agencies. Maritime nations will need to examine cooperative engagements and agreements for handling such acts. All of them are expected to continue similar to crimes over the land. Unlawful acts never get eliminated. They have to be suppressed. Continuous surveillance and effective rule of law will be the only solution. Nations will have to prepare for it. It can be more facilitated by the integration of maritime security with national security than governing in isolation externally. This will call for maritime law enforcement forces like the coast guards to be equipped with measures to interdict unlawful activists and bring them to trial under enforcement friendly laws.

The chances of further developments in unlawful activities at and from the sea cannot be ruled out, though remote as the world wakes up to the realities. However, when the world ocean order turns to unexpected directions, situations can go out of control. For this reason the law enforcement aspects should be kept on the edge.

There is always the surprise element in unlawful activities. Situations may arise when an unlawful act may be committed when least expected. Under such situations the law enforcement agencies will be found wanting especially in matters of judicial action. Some such activities could be collateral to other issues.

Ocean can witness many "never before" incidents in future. There was such an incident in Indian waters in 2012. Two Indian fishers were allegedly killed at sea while engaged in fishing on the west coast of India by shots fired from an Italian merchant oil tanker *Enrica Lexi* on 15 February 2012. Within hours, the vessel was located and directed by Indian Coast Guard to Kochi, the port nearest to the location of the incident. Two Italian soldiers, understandably from the ship's Vessel Protection Detachment (VPD), who fired at them were arrested and charged under sections 302 (murder), 307 (attempt to murder), 427 (mischief) along with section 34 (common intent) of the Indian Penal Code (IPC) 1860 in addition to booking them under the Suppression of Unlawful Acts Against Safety of Maritime Navigation and Fixed Platforms on Continental Shelf Act 2002.[21] The charges may hold or likely get modified later after detailed investigation. The marines were in active service. The case was said to be of mistaken identity. The marines allegedly mistook the fishers for Somali pirates. The ship was close hugging the coast of India instead of venturing into deeper waters, according to authorities, to avoid Somali pirates who had extended reach miles away from Somali shore. Handling such issues will be a serious problem not only from the point of view of the alleged crime, but other issues of law enforcement. There are many issues besides the case of murder and other charges against the two Italian marines. Some of them examined in this study are given below.

- What is the authority for serving military personnel carrying weapons to be on board a merchant ship allegedly to provide security to the ships against piratical attacks?
- How such vessels are to be considered while making way through a nation's jurisdictional waters or otherwise?
- Do such vessels have to be considered as armed merchant vessels? If so, what are the rules related to them for innocent passage?
- How do the maritime agencies of nations along the passage of such a vessel will board it if required under suspicion?
- Do such vessels have to inform or take permission from the port state while on passage close to the coast?
- What is the relationship between the master of such vessel and military personnel on active duty on board the vessel?
- Do the military personnel on board have to take permission from the master of the ship before engaging the suspects?
- What are the powers of such military personnel with respect to the crew of the ship?
- What actions are to be taken against such merchant vessels by the port state when they transit deviated from recognised SLOC, close to the coast increasing the risk of intentional and unintentional pollution to marine environment, collision with other unsuspected vessels, hindering fishing activities in the area, etc.?
- How such incidents can be eliminated in future?

India, Italy and IMO have joint responsibilities in deciding over these issues and more, besides meting out justice to the families of the victims of the incidents and the Italian marines involved in the case. Meanwhile, the case is sub judice (2013).

Another freak case is that of a ship boarded by the Indian Coast Guard in Indian waters on the east coast on suspicion, and subsequently detained by the state police at the port of Tuticorin (*Thuthukudi*) on 12 October 2013. The international crew comprised 35 people. All of them were arrested for charges of illegal entry, fuel transfer at sea and carrying arms.[22] The ship allegedly on private security duties at sea got into the area in its efforts to steer clear of the category 4 cyclone Phalin that hit India on the east coast in Odisha a week before. The ship needed fuel and logistics. The personnel on board were charged under Indian Passport Act, Indian Arms Act and essential Commodities Act. The vessel registered in Sierra Leone was owned by a US company. The ship was not involved in arms trafficking and all the arms and ammunitions held on board had proper registration according to the company. There are reasons to believe that the vessel was employed to provide assistance to ships against piracy at sea. It is a new trend in which the private security agencies are entering into the sea based on demand. But the sea, being perilous and with too many uncertainties and limitations that were not bound by any country, is a dangerous place for the crew and the ship when apprehended by the forces of a state on suspicion. This is especially so for a ship that is a new entrant in a new business in modern times that does not recognise privateers or ocean vigilantes. In fact, traditional pirates will find more at ease at sea in carrying out their job than a legal security ship, being a new entrant, in an assignment for which there are no precedence or formal guidelines.

The company that operates the ship claimed it had been providing comprehensive maritime security solutions to the commercial shipping industry.

Such involvement, if the statements of the owner and the company are proven after investigation, draws out more questions:

- Under what law private security agencies are to be permitted?
- Under which law such ships have to be treated?
- How the ships operate? Is there a mother ship in the area decided for operation for logistics support?
- What are the collateral damages including illegal activities the ship can engage in with the arms on board?
- How secure are these arms for preventing unauthorized use?

The question that comes to the fore under such situations is the limitations of the emerging maritime security industry and its future. Piracy at sea had given rise to the state approved privateers in the early periods. Today it has given rise to private maritime security providers and industry. Merchant ships feel seemingly comfortable in employing them. There is a steady increase in the use of privately contracted armed security personnel (PCASP). The two cases mentioned above are descriptive on the complexities that can arise from public and private security personnel employed at sea. More could follow. The PCASP is seen as an effective piracy mitigation strategy and reduction in naval dependence that is very cumbersome for the merchant marine community from the individual ship perspective.

Maritime security companies are on the increase with the new ISO/PAS 28007: 2012 voluntary quality management system that will focus on training, development and validation (TDV) of PCASP.[23] But it will not solve the suppression of unlawful acts other than piracy at and from the sea.

IMO should take note of the issue of private security provisions in the high seas firmly and create an international regime so that the courts and ships are clear about the charter and the way it has to be executed. It may not get the consent of all. The discussed case unless otherwise established after the investigation, is about mishandling of situation and procedural lapses all around.

There are more serious issues that may come up in future. The non-state unlawful actors may challenge the sovereign nature of the state in the name of crime. There are also lawful non-state actors of the global variety—the media, multinational corporations, non-governmental organisations, environmental organisations, social activists, etc. They will have a greater say in the national and international security affairs, but they will lack the ocean perception being over the land. This can lead to contradictions unless the ocean is integrated with land. Transnational as well as national organised crime syndicates working with support from high places will avail every opportunity the ocean can provide. Trafficking in all commodities from humans to weapon materials will be the order of the day unless maritime forces with the backing of actionable intelligence and the will of governments are prepared to take on them. Worst is when such syndicates leech into organised business at sea with unlawful activities running parallel.

Other Possible Exploitations of the Sea

Looking at the present trend there are no other ways the ocean will be exploited in future. Any exploitation of the ocean will be related to trade, transport, law enforcement, ocean property and associated regimes, climate change and geostrategic context including military missions. No other possible exploitations are in evidence. Even if gritty syndicates exploit the ocean to commit acts that are not possible over land under law such as cloning, assistance to euthanasia, illegal research, information trafficking, etc. they can be tagged under any of the topics already mentioned. But lately there are concerns expressed by human rights activists that governments can use ships, especially naval ships for illegal detention and inhuman interrogation of high end suspects.[24] The concern is that lawful governments who are reeling under pressure may use the wilderness of the ocean in their safest and most secretive platforms, the naval ships or hired merchant ships for nefarious activities and playing dirty tricks including human rights violations far from the prying eyes of the media and humanitarian activists. Ocean can provide expansive and trouble free space for the powerful to carry out dangerous activities that otherwise would be in serious violation of law if committed in a nation's territory including the ocean. Who else but strong governments can have access to it? They are not supposed to engage in such activities; but they might, when their backs are against the wall.

Integrated Maritime Security—the Future

Integrated maritime security is maritime security integrated with national security in land based governance, where national security is a wholesome measurable concept of governance towards the overall wellbeing of the people that is not limited to the physical security of a nation alone. By doing so, maritime security gets assimilated with the overall national security governance.

This study does not foresee a change from the present form of governance of geopolitical entities in the near future except certain modifications as demanded by situation. National security concept is likely to remain the physical security of the nation especially from the point of view of the military and high end internal conflicts like insurgency, terrorism, etc., that may challenge human lives. It is more so because the governments would like to protect themselves and their political establishments. In fact, the governmental machineries will be used for this purpose and not for the overall governance of the public. Governance will be very selective.

Until such situations and demands continue, the governments may not have the will to change towards the overall wellbeing of the people in national governance. Hence rationalised governance is a long way ahead. Till then, it will be selective in the politico-legal outfit often panic driven where primary need of survival is not for the nation or people but for the government.

But even under such governance, maritime security can be integrated with national security governance in any prevailing form. It will be a kind of phased integration for a very long time. This is provided the governments appreciate that maritime security should not be treated in isolation. It has to be governed as part of national security. Then only it becomes integrated maritime security. There are a few nations who have been serious about it and practising it. An example of attempted integration of maritime security with national security is in the perceived concept of China. China's attempt may lead to new maritime strategy, hence worthy of watching.

Most of the entities of the world, especially the coastlands and islands, are gradually going through the stages of sensitisation with regards to the potentials of integrated maritime security. This awareness may come to Africa collectively in the near future.[25] Africa has 54 fully recognised sovereign states (2013) among them 38 have coastal fronts.[26] The implications of not integrating maritime security are considered perilous by the African strategists lately. They call for a collective approach to contain and curtail the cross border implications of the unlawful acts at and from the sea. What they have not taken seriously is the integration of maritime security with national security and getting the overall benefit of integrated maritime security by also keeping the 16 landlocked countries also on board with respect to maritime security. They too have rights over the ocean and the global commons.

Africa recommends and ponders on collective strategy for enhanced maritime security for the continent. The recommended approach is grand strategic from political perspective, military strategic from interagency perspective and operational level strategies.[27] Most of the nations in the world may think of collective approach in integrated maritime security in future. Already there are successful models. Fresh approaches can face serious imitations under international politics and geostrategic interests of the entities. Even if the attempts succeed, the maritime security concept will still wander as a ghost protocol without integration with the overall national security. Collective approach is not external to governance of a nation. It has to originate from within each nation integral to national governance. Often this does not happen in reality. Collectivism should be molded as part of the geostrategic element of national security of each participant. It has to be applied in geostrategy by fusion. Otherwise the plans will remain on paper as a desire. This is likely to happen. Even then such thought processes will be encouraging as the world moves towards discovering better systems in political approach.

Integrated maritime security will be accepted by the world collectively emphasising international obligations to safeguard the international maritime community at least in principle barring a few exceptions who may have their own interpretations.

With all the future proclamations, finally it will be the results on the ground that will determine the wellbeing of the people of the global entities. Predicting the exact advancement in wellbeing is not possible as it depends on the nature of governance of each entity internally. It is left to the governments whether they are effectively functional, functional, dysfunctional or shut down.

Conclusions

The envisaged concepts of national security and integrated maritime security are the themes of the future. Both have to be clearly understood and seriously studied for national governance in right earnest and perspective. The future is examined under this caveat. The outcome of national governance will depend upon the perception of the governments about national security and integrated maritime security. It is not likely to move out of the mould practised by the governments for a very long time. But there could be modifications depending on demands from the public and survival quests of the nation.

According to this study, the world will be embroiled in all the problems of the past in future also. Relief will come from various international regimes and general awareness that are renascent. International trade will grow as the demand for goods and services increases with the population. Most of the trade, as usual, will be through the ocean for obvious reasons. Demand for ships will increase when ocean trade increases and should ideally balance each other. Suppression of unlawful acts at and from the sea will continue to be a concern for governments and their maritime forces and agencies chartered into it. The war at sea will be modern and different from the past wars. The forces will have to be prepared for it catering for redundancy. Obsolescence will set in fast like gangrene in a human body unlike in the earlier days when decades old ships could be inducted into war after minor modifications. It means the forces of the future should be designed and equipped today for EHW engagement in advance. Today's asset production should be based on tomorrows design and exploitation. It will be the greatest challenge to naval planners, designers and operators.

There will not be any requirement for specific integration of ocean elements as mostly thought out by the term integration, if the ocean property regime is established. Ocean property orientates and unifies the ocean concept and prepares maritime security for direct integration by assimilation with national security. But it may take considerable time for nations to get or fall into this groove. Still, integration of maritime security with national security in whatever form envisaged by the governments will yield better results in governance for every geopolitical entity. This could be established in future. Otherwise maritime security will be under isolated governance wandering as a ghost protocol.

Ocean can spring up uncertainties anytime that may impact national governance. The effect of the impact could be dampened and turned to positive action by following the principles of integrated maritime security.

NOTES

1 The Gordian Knot is a metaphor for an intractable problem—disentangling an impossible knot. According to legend associated with Phrygian Gordium, Alexander the Great untied the Knot after slashing into two with his sword. A Gordian Knot will call for "out of the box" thinking. This study considers issues of governance that are intractable, get caught under method inertia and become Gordian Knot of sorts. They can be still be untied and separated for governance.

2 Catch 22 is a situation introduced by author Joseph Heller (1961). The word in the English language means "a problematic situation for which the only solution is denied by a circumstance inherent in the problem or by a rule." It has become a common idiomatic usage meaning "a no-win situation" or "a double bind" of any type.

3 Arthur Dunkel (1932-2005) was director general of General Agreement on Tariffs and Trade (GATT) now replaced by World Trade Organisation (WTO), between 1980 and 1993. He drove the negotiations in the Uruguay round of the GATT affirming the importance of trade for global benefit. When faced with stiff opposition based on inward looking appreciations of nations he came up with a draft called Dunkel Draft in 1991 that provided an arbitrated solution to issues on which negotiators failed to agree. It was accepted and became the foundation of WTO that presently leads affairs of the world trade along with other international organisations.

4 Paleri, Prabhakaran, "Piracy Victims—The Indian Experience" in Griffiths, David, N. (ed.), *The Human Face of Marine Piracy,* Islamabad, Fazaldad: Human Rights Institute, 2012, pp.141-54.

5 epa.gov/climate change/impacts-adaptation/transportation.html, accessed 15 September 2013.

6 Gallegos, Carlos, Trends in Maritime Transport and Port Development in the Context of World Trade, www.studymode.com/essays/Trends-In-Maritime-Transport-And-Port-1194947.html, accessed 15 September 2013.

7 Paleri, Prabhakaran, "Resource Management in a Sinking World—Land and Geoproperty Rights," paper presented at the International Conference on Decisions in Management and Social Sciences for Sustainable Management, Indian Institute of Social Welfare and Business Management, Kolkatta, 14 December 2009.

8 Kiribati Man Seeks to become World's First Climate Change Refugee , *The Times of India,* Kozhikode, 19 October 2013, p. 19.

9 Verma, Suchit, Why Create another Class of Refugees? Ibid. The author states the refugee issues will not be serious as feared.

10 p^H value is a measure of acidity or alkalinity of a solution. It is numerically taken as 7 for neutral solutions; the value increases with increasing alkalinity and decreases with increasing acidity.

11 Not all cases of sinking could be attributed to climate change and sea level rise. There could be many causes. Satellites Show Venice is Sinking @1mm every Year. *The Times of India,* Kochi, 1 October 2013, p.11.

12 The first nuclear test was in 1945 at Alamogordo, New Mexico in the United States. Over 2,000 nuclear tests were carried out externally since then before wrapping up by the Comprehensive Test Ban Treaty of 1996. The world was seemingly in a hurry averaging about 40 tests per year. More than 50 per cent of these tests were conducted by the United States of America, the ultimate winner of the Cold War. All the tests caused heavy damage to environment and people leading to deaths. India and Pakistan conducted their last tests in 1998 with North Korea reporting tests in 2006, 2009 and 2013. The tests post 1996 broke the de facto moratorium established by the CTBT.

13 There are monopolar or unipolar systems but normally that is short-lived. Human systems have never steadied on unipolarity. Instead human systems survived in multipolar mode before settling down as bipolar.

14 The Cold War (World War III for this study) was the longest with the world divided in two parts with a belligerent attitude. The war was fought without seriously firing shots but with far too many covert and overt operations with intentions to destroy the other. The next global war, if it occurs, is considered to be World War IV for this study.

15 US, Russia agree on Syria UN Chemical Arms Measure, news.in.msn.com/international/us-russia-agree-on-syria-un-chemical-arms-measure, accessed 26 September 2013.

16 A serious issue which causes reluctance on one hand and the opposite on the other among decision makers in the United Nations is the conflict or rather gap between Chapter 6 and 7 of the UN Charter. For a balanced approach of a more civilised dictum, it is time the charter of the world body has a chapter in between so that the wiser among them do not have to negotiate through an imaginary Chapter 6 1/2 (six and half). Under Chapter 7, the council could impose punitive measures if Syria had refused or failed to comply.

17 Shields, Brian, "Iran Offers New Nuclear Proposal," news.kron4.com/news/iran-offers-new-nuclear-proposal/, accessed 23 October 2013.

18 Human system desires war (ironically) for survival. The affinity for war promotes inventions. The affinity will still remain but will be blocked by the inability to execute it at will. This will stifle those who believe in war for

survival. They will be "war choked' a feeling that may become progressively visible in future.

19 "*Dweep Kananilla; Mexicoyil Vivadam" Mathrubhumi*, (Malayalam), Kozhikode, 13 September 2009, p. 13.

20 Paleri, Prabhakaran, Marine Environment: Management and People's Participation, New Delhi: KW Publishers Pvt. Ltd., 2009, note.2, p. 79.

21 en.wikipedia.org/wiki/Enrica_Lexie, accessed 17 September 2013.

22 www.dnaindia.com/india/1905301/report-usiship-detention-arrest-of-35-members-legitimate-says-bharat-verma, accessed, 21 October 2013.

23 ISO/PAS 28007:2012 provides guidelines containing additional sector-specific recommendations, which companies (organisations) who comply with ISO 28000 can implement to demonstrate that they provide Privately Contracted Armed Security Personnel (PCASP) on board ships. To claim compliance with these guidelines, all recommendations should be complied with. Compliance with ISO/PAS 28007:2012 can be by first, second and third party (certification). Where certification is used, it is recommended the certificate contains the words: "This certification has been prepared using the full guidelines of ISO PAS 28007 as a Private Maritime Security Company (PMSC) providing Privately Contracted Armed Security Personnel".

24 Lendman, Stephan, US Globalised Torture Black Sites, www.globalresearch.ca/us-globalized-torture-black-sites/5353706, accessed 12 October 2013.

25 "Creating an Integrated Maritime Security Strategy for Africa," Key note address by the chief of the naval staff, Nigerian Navy at the Maritime and Coastal Security Africa Conference, October 2011. www.affmd.org/news-updates/item/151-creating-an-integrated-maritime-security.html, accessed 15 July 2013.

26 Ibid. There are other territories and de facto independent states also (2013).

27 Ibid.

Chapter 8

FINDINGS AND CONCLUSIONS: GAINING HEADWAY

Integrating maritime security with national security is the only way to maximise the yield from the ocean in national governance; if not, it is bound to remain as it is–enigmatically indifferent.

The rationale for this chapter is to consolidate the key points mentioned in the study to ponder further over the lines of reasoning to invoke research interest among scholars and practitioners on the subject of national security, and also to point out identified strategic actions for integration of maritime security for gaining governance.[1] The central theme of the chapters so far was national governance by integrating maritime security with it through the ocean property regime that holds the key to maritime security in the concept projected here. Maritime security, a much spoken about concept in strategic circles and centres of governance is considered a ghost protocol for very special reasons. One of the reasons is the diverse ways the concept is expressed and practised in governance around the world, all aimed at the central point of national security which is also appreciated differently. But being central to governance, national security is the core protocol and hence, not a ghost protocol even if practised differently. A ghost protocol is a requirement for execution by the designated executors sans sufficient clarity, backup and support, but without any dilution in accountability. The rule of engagement (RoE) will not be clear while handling ghost protocols. Back up and support will be available to the real protocol and the RoE will be specific, being the core. Individuals and groups, including governments, will come across far too many ghost protocols under various situations. Execution of a ghost protocol is not only stressful but also unyielding if handled as a normal task however serious it may be. The first principle under such situation is to give the ghost protocol a "body" by integration with the prime factor that drives through the core.[2] For this, the body (the core protocol) to be integrated with has to be compatible with the ghost protocol. Once integrated, it is the body that is driven not the ghost protocol. For example, governing maritime security has to be through national security governance. For that first it has to be integrated with national security. Maritime security integrated with national security, as practised, is integrated maritime security (IMS).

The study shows maritime security is compatible with national security for integration. The compatibility is established from the findings that include,

- land-centric national governance,
- terrain specificity of maritime security within the concept of national security,
- the importance of ocean for every geopolitical entity irrespective of proximity to the ocean,
- ocean being part of the global commons and
- the inclusivity of the elements of maritime security in complementary, contributory and null relationship (absence of exclusivity) with national security elements, hence supportive of model building.

The identified concept of national security has been considered an approach path in the process of maximising human wellbeing by governance. Various findings of the author and other researchers have been referred to in the explanation. The most important among them is the reference to national security as a much larger concept than being talked about and practised based on fixation with war and military. The reference also brings out diverse corollaries on which the idea of national security and maritime security, the key points of this study, are conceptualised.

National security is the duty of the government in whatever forms it is practised. A step ahead, the duty is to maximise it. The government has the authority. In modern times, every citizen is more or less a partner in governance besides being a stakeholder. This statement applies to every kind of governmental system including "absence of governance" where a formal government may be absent. People are participants in national governance in one way or the other even in a system where they are subjugated. The subjugation will have an impact on governance. That shows the people connection in governance of any human system. This is an important reminder of sorts. Opposing governance critically,aimed at achieving progressive wellbeing of people, is a constructive attitude. Constructive opposition is not only a part of governance but also the requisite to keep it exciting. It is a natural phenomenon in the human system. It should not to be misconstrued as resistance. It is only by opposition and decisive observations, national governance can be steered towards better results. It happens that way in spite of various internal and external interferences. It is visible in many countries. In the case of Somalia, people took over the control of the country when there was no "government;"they governed their country as they felt. Modern constitutions give the right to the people to govern their countries"the way they want." Here, the difference is in how people govern their country, not whether there is a government or not.

India is a resounding example for changing times in national governance where the constitution is well connected with the people including the media. The opposition in government has been persuasive in keeping checks. To that extent, opposition in governance does not mean blind resistance for gaining power at the expense of the other. Opposition, in the constitutional sense, is not conflict but constructive governance through critical findings. But the opposition as opponents may meddle in power play in the process as accustomed. In spite of evidences of constructive and stable governance, India, like any other country, is far from appreciating the changing concept of national security and integrating maritime security with it. The past traditions, belief systems and associated method inertia in governance refuse to leave. Introducing the wholesome national security regime and integrating maritime security with it is still a far cry in every country though the levels may differ.

It is important that interested nations examine the approach in governance to yield more from what they got. It applies to the governments and the people, where they are partners in governance. Without the consent and participation of the people, the governments will not be able to take care of their wellbeing. It is for the people to understand it clearly. On the reverse, it is for the governments to make them understand their role in governance and carry them along.

A change in governance does not mean a change in the constitution or political belief systems. Every political system can offer wellbeing to the people. Only the approach to governance needs to be altered. For that it is important to understand the concept of national security and terrain specific integrations in clear perspective. The most complex terrain to integrate is the ocean. This study is a pointer.

The bottom line of national security is that it is not the type of government but governance and the nature of it that makes the difference in people's wellbeing.

About the Findings

As projected elsewhere, the findings in this study are based on exploratory studies of two different periods. The findings of the first period comprise those that have been already established based on previous studies. The rest are those that are correlated with them on integrated maritime security.

The study begins with the idea of national security as a concept of human governance, applicable to any human system, but specifically focused on national governance. National security is a term that has been widely used in national governance. The term creates a forceful sensation by semantic noise in communication that national security is all about the security of a nation. The breakaway starts from here under the forces that make governance for the people a complex task. Rest of governance, the charter of the government or the duty of the king, breaks away from the wholesome concept, leaving behind the military aspects of national security as national security. Looking for an easy approach path the governments nudge the rest of the elements into a conundrum of gimmickry to promote political ideologies and individual interests. What is left behind as national security is the singular element of military security which is about the overall security of the nation from all aspects. Hence national security remains as everything about the security of a nation, internally and externally, not the wholesome wellbeing of the people. Actually the perceived national security is only an element of it—mentioned in this study as military security where the term "military"has the connotation of use of lawful force for providing protection to the target population. The term has to be seen beyond war under the context of modern governance.

The separation of military security from the rest of the elements of national security, regrettably, is not easily appreciable. All the breakaway elements of national security conjoined and assimilated into political governance. Here, political governance means governing by political objectives that often become objectives of the concerned political party. Still, political governance will have to ensure physical security of the nation and the people even from its political standpoint. This function is carried out as perceived by the government, which it calls national security. There is a huge conceptual deficit here. The gap is between the actual concept of national security and what the governments provide as national security. It is this gap that is being filled academically by the definition of national security and by the study in general inviting pragmatic approach in governance.[3]

One of the tribulations the governments may not be aware of in considering military security alone as national security is that their control over the military can erode slowly. The military may get separated from the rest of governance and can become a power centre in its own authority. The loss of control of the government over military will get projected in various ways. On one side it will be visible as resistance and difference of opinion between the military command and government. Slightly at higher level there will be direct sacking of senior officers including the chief of the force when government takes an aggressive posture out of a kind of helplessness. In some other cases there will be mass sacking of senior officers of the military under sheer helplessness that the government may feel under certain situations. The sacking will be on certain grounds that may look as firm action by the government. The worst is when the military takes over governance and send the government home either in a coup or under coercive extraction of power. Opposite of this under the same situation is when the military leaders trying to woo the people in authority in government for fringe benefits. Military sycophancy with politicians and to some extent the bureaucrats is an interesting phenomenon. Every country faces the associated issues of "military" shift and exclusiveness of national security in one way or the other. However, no example is given as these comments are not with reference to any geopolitical entity. Such military-politico situations can be overcome when governments take over the wholesome national security as the prime path of governance considering military security as one of the 15 elements of national security that are highly interactive and yielding if governed professionally. The military forces will get an entirely progressive outlook in governance in such case. But till then, it is disjointed governance by separation of elements of national security.

The term, national security, originated in English language was more or else in existence with the formation of sovereign states. The initial focus was on protecting the sovereign rights from aggressive aliens. As a result, the military approach to protecting sovereign rights became a separate issue with the rest of the governance becoming totally political. Governance as a whole parted and drifted away from the concept. The governments and their approaches towards governance changed after they engage in a war most of the time. It was more obvious with the beaten. It is the critical evidence that war was not part of governance but an entirely different behavioural approach in the concerned human systems. According to military theory, war is an instrument of national policy. It can be questioned. Ideally, according to the theory, war should lead to establishing a national policy. A government could engage in war anytime, not necessarily when all the other means are failed as the "art of war" says. But a prudent government refrains from war because of collateral damages, some of them long lasting and even irreversible. Even when engaged, war is not meant to change the governments but the policies and procedures of their governance. The idea is to achieve the desired policy. But mostly wars change governments still keeping the policies on the back burner where they continue burning. But achieving the desired policy is possible if wars are fought or unlawful acts are suppressed under the wholesome concept of national security. Under the national security governance, wars, conflicts and law enforcement can be handled by limiting them. Winning a war without actual combat or establishing rule of law without fiendish enforcement (also means the same) is possible under national security governance. This is a realistic find.

All wars, therefore, cannot be called instruments of national policy. The war itself can be a policy. A country needs a strong military even to win a war without fighting. In fact there are many "wars" the countries win without fighting. Such situations may miss the notice of the public. A war is not a war unless it is visible; hence a war not seen will not be counted and appreciated as a war by the people. It is a tragedy. From a different perspective, it can be seen that many wars were fought on individual policies that subsequently may have been converted into national or international decisions.[4] This is a major deviation from the projected theory of war and its practical execution. But there is also an interesting question under any syllogism like this study itself: "Is a war that is not fought a war?"[56] The question will invite serious debates on the theory and laws of war from ancient times. Under the predilection of the "fighting war," a war that will not involve in change of governments or other vitriolic interpretations of policies (eat grass to make the bomb, etc.) can be considered as an instrument of national policy. Simply put, the war should end where it ends after the objective is fulfilled. A war that is won without fighting could be the national policy itself, not an instrument of it. This too will need a strong military. The basic dictum is that the objective of war should not linger on further after the war.

As mentioned, on one hand, the early concept of national security was separated from the form of governance desired for national wellbeing as war and associated conflicts of force disposition. On the other, there were attempts to identify its constituent elements other than those related to military security in various forms of governance. It started more or less along with the establishment of the concepts of sovereignty in the human system. Actually, the concept of economics, geostrategic context, etc., that were subsequently thought out were the existing but unrevealed elements of the original concept that had broken away from it similar to the continents that broke away from the super continent and became nation states and other geopolitical entities. The broken away pieces of continents are still wandering probably with the hope of rejoining one day as predicted by researchers. Similarly convergence of the driving forces is a natural process of social dynamics and so it is possible the elements of national security get recognised in one form or another as parts of the original and governed accordingly. The identified elements have always been the constituent parts of the national security concept in relation to the human system. They have been actually rediscovered as quoted in this study. To that extent the elements are not new and additional to what have been already existing but not conjoined in governance. A few elements came up subsequently as a process of evolution. This can be seen from the chronological hierarchy of the elements. The governmental systems could not recognise them collectively as the wandering national security elements. The attempt in this study is to bring them back as the lost pieces of the jigsaw puzzle and create the whole picture and modify the concept of governing a human system, especially a state. The time is now.

The reason for such separation need not be that the concept itself was a misnomer. It is probably hidden in the difficulty of getting the public"what they need" as governments show serious disposition bias[7] in political power and survival instincts. That is why wellbeing was never taken as a governance objective. Its place has been taken over by the more populist and easy to execute welfare governance by social doling. Every state and political system is expected to isomorph ultimately into a welfare state and welfare politics respectively unless the trend reverses to wellbeing. This also leads to a lemma— welfare can mask wellbeing in a social system. Government and people may take welfare for wellbeing.

As mentioned, the elements of national security, therefore, are rediscovered and conjoined without changing the term. They are not new. They existed all the time in the concept of wellbeing. The expressions came much later when scholars started negotiating national security as it should be. Specific characteristics had been assigned to a national security element and only those that follow the characteristics were qualified as elements.[8] Through the findings, the concept goes through five different terrains since governance is strategic terrain application of constituent elements. Such applications need to be manoeuvred for which the terrain understating is essential. The terrain understanding is brought in under the terminology of terrain specificity. The identified terrains of national security elements are land,ocean, airspace, outer space, cyber space and genomic space (genome). The first three belong to geophysical terrains. Outer space is a physical terrain. Cyber space and genomic space are exclusive terrains in which they resolve as unitary elements for the time. They are relatively new. There are also possibilities for new elements developing in these terrains. New terrains may develop in future though there is no evidence as on now except for the efforts to control human mind that was ongoing since the time of Cold War and even before. Still the world has not been able to control human mind except for a small part of influencing it. The efforts to deliberately control human mind through psychological means fall under the element informational security. Human mind is still inaccessible to agencies and forces external to it for absolute control. The chances are it is likely to remain that way.[9] The reason, perhaps, is that human mind can be controlled only from within. Hence human mind can never become an exclusive terrain though the efforts to control it are ongoing since the end of the Second World War.[10] The world is weary; it can drain out reason.

The study has invoked a very specific find that could cause serious differences in appreciation. It is about the "law of invariance." The decisions on any form of governance have to understand the presence of the law of invariance so that it neither underestimates nor overestimates the rules of change. Most of the decisions in governance and human appreciation of the social system have gone overboard in appreciating the future. The law of invariance simply states that the changes in a human system is largely incomprehensible when it is going on and also that the changes induced by agents of change are visible only after substantial time is elapsed and by which time the humans and probably other life systems (not tested) would have been adapted to them as if it has been there all along the past. The law of invariance is more appreciable at the macro level. It has to be made visible through reductionist mechanisms at the micro level. Even then it will need very close and careful observation to understand the change. For example, to understand the results of an election accurately, one will have to wait till they are announced, but the change elements would have been already at play once the last elections were over and the government was formed. Even for a psephologist, it will be hard work through various surveys and analysis to predict the results with some accuracy. The word psephology itself exhibits the law of invariance. The origin of the word psephology is attributed to pebbles that have been used by the ancient Greeks to cast their votes. Not only the word but also the methodology of election has not changed since then. To that extent the law of invariance is highly perceptible in the words used for verbal communication in any language between people. There is no change, or change is not appreciable. That denotes the state of invariance. There are other examples too that are closer to life system dynamics. One of them is the process of communication. Communication by electrical impulses has never changed since it has been invented, but the instruments used for such communication has undergone alterations under induced and market driven innovations. A society that talks about innovations as a major change driver is not aware that under the law of invariance innovation does not change the core idea. War is war in every innovative way it is fought. Maritime security remains as a ghost protocol even if integrated within itself. Hence it has to be integrated with governance even in its integrated status. Integrating within itself is by the idea of ocean property and advocacy of ocean property mapping according to this study.

The relationship of law of invariance and national security governance can be explained in simple terms. One is that the human system will not change in the near future to the extent of eliminating war and conflicts permanently, but the ways and instruments of war will change drastically. This condition will not change and remain intrepidly within the law of invariance. Hence national security governance is not change management but enabling itself for human wellbeing within the law of invariance. Any form of governance or management will have to look at change management from the perspective of the law of invariance to avoid underplaying as well as overplaying change.

Human appreciation of wellbeing will be the perceived state and not the apparent state. Perceived security is endless and virtually impossible to achieve, whereas apparent security is what is needed to survive. The efforts towards perceived security kindle hope and expectations which provide a sense of achievement. That in turn triggers the sense of perceived security. Human beings indulge in various activities towards triggering sense of perceived security.[11] But they become distressed when there is a deficit in apparent security. This is what the governments have to see.

The landclasp syndrome that directs the people to feel secure and comfortable only when they are over land highlights the law of invariance hidden in the primordial behaviour of human beings. Hence everything about human governance will have to be land-based for effectiveness. Looking at the ocean as a flood over the land is acceptable, though not vital to appreciate integration with land-based national security governance. The landclasp syndrome reflects in every human activity on the planet but is much more amplified in national governance.

Human system is governed by conditioned behaviour and belief systems mostly interactive with primordial instincts of survival. The resulting behaviour at times becomes extremely intricate. That is why human system governance is a complex task. It can be seen in the pace at which human belief system changes. The change in belief system is much slower than the changes noticeable in human ingenuity. This causes a lag in human adaption to ingenuity. The change in belief system is not visible on the go but the change brought out by ingenuity is instant. For this reason "change" for humans means innovation using the skills which is only temporary transformation, not a change in human perception of life and security. Hence the study of human security remains affirmed in the law of invariance—nothing changes when change cannot be noticed. It is not a Catch 22 situation. Under the law of invariance, however vital the ocean may be for human security, governing the mindset will still remain primordial and land-based. The concept of integrated maritime security originates from this observation.

The concept of unitary civilisation is another find, brought out from the earlier period, used to explain the security concern of people in this study. The idea of unitary civilisation declines to consider human beings by differentiation of advancement as it is more in external outlooks than internal personality developments. Their security concerns remain primordial irrespective of whom and what they are. There is no (serious) difference between human beings in relation to their primordial security concerns. The laws of personality (behaviour) apply to all. The human beings are the most advanced form of life that is constantly developing much faster than any other life forms in their intellectual usage. For these reasons and more, they are together within the unitary civilisation. There they form a long train of compartments with people at different stages of intellectual advancement in their external forms and personalities but remain basically primordial and similar to each other in existentialistic behaviour. Therefore wars, conflicts and clashes between human systems are considered internal to this unitary civilisation, not between civilisations or the illusory compartments of the unitary civilisation. The approach of unitary civilisation supports the theory of human wellbeing based on national governance that is measureable and comparable. It takes away the long pursued human differentiation that has been stifling progress seriously. Unitary civilisation does not consider any type of sectoral differentiation such as east and west, occidental and oriental, capitalist and communist, civilised and uncivilised, rich and poor, etc. The concepts of governance and national security could be null, if not negative, if a nation or the world itself comprises people belonging to different civilisations. Hence the classification of human beings under different civilisations is admissible only for historical studies based on limited geographical space and period factor. It cannot be applied to studies on national security and governance, especially in modern times, under sovereign statehoods.

An individual human nurtures physiological and psychological needs similar to any other human but possesses exclusive individual biometric signature. It is a kind of situation where there is symmetry in needs and asymmetry in physio-psychological structure. The governments of the period will have to meet the needs of its people that will be identical. But the behaviour and response of each individual will be different. The purpose of national security governance is to provide maximum wellbeing to each and every one of them. It is possible by governance under this finding—give them what they need and allow them to find what they want within the limitations of governance. A government that supports art and culture, religious needs, information flow, freedom of media, creativity, entertainment, sports, games, etc., just achieves that to a considerable extent.

The study identifies the ocean as a terrain that is more expansive than land and an indispensable life supporting system of the planet. Any damage to the ocean can damage the earth. However the advocators of ocean control did not clarify the methods of controlling the ocean except for naval dominance for a select few who had the capabilities. But in the modern world, especially post UNCLOS, the governments and people including those of the landlocked countries have become aware of the ocean and its importance to them.[12] Under the changed ocean-stasis, the governments have to look at the ocean beyond naval power and also channelise naval power towards geostrategy and strategic applications of war, especially in a nuclear scenario including forward missile defence, etc. Role of the navy in geostrategic security is an aspect advocated in this study. The postulations of naval strategists including the early strategist, Alfred Thayer Mahan, have to be seen against the period background that does not exist today. Maritime strategy has to be under the future perspective. Though most of the earlier theories talked about the future, the postulations on intuitive analysis were actually based on the historical past including tried out methods. The element of future was absent in their studies. The tunnel of the past need not essentially lead to the future. The world will have to rely on strategic governance to get to the future. For example, with the beginning of the law of the sea convention in 1958, the world would have looked ahead to predict that soon there will be a situation when no nation will be able to control the ocean absolutely. The evidence lies in the fact that still there are nations who have not ratified the Convention.

The study has brought in another term—the "sea power quotient (SPQ)." Sea power quotient is the ratio of the return from ocean property to the overall available ocean property. This can be assessed provided the elements can be measured in a universal module which is yet to be established. Both the factors of maritime security and the maritime dimension of the concerned entity will dissolve in its ocean property regime. The term ocean property is developed from the earlier term ocean wealth that denoted only limited resources. But ocean can be taken as unitary terrain specific provider of national security in every aspect. Such a unitary approach will also support modeling and appreciation for integration. The analysis of sea power quotient is an example under both the arguments. A nation should persevere vehemently to enhance its sea power quotient as applicable to it from the strategic point of view. The sea power quotient will help the nation in analysing its overall ocean yield. It can also carry out analysis of the ocean quotient of others based on information. It will be interesting to ask a question, "Can a landlocked or geographically disadvantaged nation possess more sea power quotient than a coastal one?" Ideally, it should be possible. In any respect this study believes that integrated maritime security is the ultimate test on deciding upon sea power in modern times. It includes naval power.

Considering ocean quotient derived from ocean property can have extreme variations in calculations as there will be many factors that will defy precision measurement, it is best acceded to by under valuing one's own SPQ and overvaluing those of the others in relative assessments. Such under-over assessment of a power factor in comparative assessment is a strategic game plan for better performance in governance. In strategy, blowing one's own trumpet could help to make deceptive moves but one can also get trapped by self deception and geostrategic discomfiture when known. It is not a fair thing to happen.

A nation is limited by its land boundaries in isolation, but through the vast expanse of the ocean it can reach out in a big way to the world. This is one of the findings based on which the integration of maritime security is recommended. The expansiveness of the ocean that belongs to every nation provides opportunity to each one of them to look outwardly at the world. It should ideally dissolve insularism. It is also the evidence for the essentiality of globalisation. The hidden influence of ocean in human life establishes the fact that globalisation is an essential part of human existence and is not a concept that has to be invented. Shutting the doors to globalisation will be self destructive. Ocean provides the window for living with the world.

Globalisation will also balance the polarity of the world. While the world will remain under multiple polarities which will always be hunting to settle to the equally distributed bipolarity, the nations that govern better will be able to gather bargaining positions in the global system. The idea of a permanent unipolar world does not seem to be practical unless it amounts to superpower status of a country in the hierarchy of nations. Power gets negated in a situation it cannot be used. A country that goes in for maximum national security (NS_{max}) is bound to become a much preferred super state, not a super power, a status that no nation has achieved so far.[13] Of course it is too early considering that human advancement has been extremely slow. It is only recently, past the midpoint of the 19th century, even compassion developed roots in the otherwise cruel and sadistic human system that comprised rich and poor and kings and paupers. Every one of them lacked compassion to the fellow human. There was no conscience. Perversion in every which way ruled the world in human behaviour as we look back. It continues today with a small difference. It can be seen in the evaluation of the criminal history of human kind.[14] Everything in a human system takes time to turn around for the better.

Gaining Headway—Integrated Maritime Security

Gaining headway is the concluding part of the study on integrated maritime security presented so far. The intended headway is in national governance. The study and comments thereon are futuristic. Concluding a topic that is in a futuristic mode can turn out to be an anomaly in experimentation. This is especially so when the topic is in the ultimate public domain—national governance. The difficulty increases when it is about a topic that is yet to be practised as projected. There is no way to appreciate the outcome of the change in governance. Hence, the study is concluded with prospective strategic actions that any geopolitical entity could examine for governance as deemed fit under the political system and constitution.

Besides the introduced concepts of national security and maritime security, both largely deviated from the existing visualisation and practices, the term governance too needs explanation to support the recommended approach to NS_{max}. The literary meaning of governance is administration of public policies and affairs. But the concept of governance has gone much ahead of mere administration of the public.

The authors contention of governance is from the activity pyramid of human engagement in which a person, or otherwise said, an individual, gets involved in various tasks to satisfy the physiological and psychological needs which is at the root of the perceived security. Within this pyramid, one performs daily tasks either guided by self or guiding others in the formal or informal group system according to the authority, responsibility and accountability balance.[15] What one performs through others becomes managing or governing in the modern sense. Management is achieving organisational objectives through delegation and decentralisation for the overall benefit of the organisation according to its vision and mission statements by optimising resources. Whereas, governance is managing the organisation keeping the overall wellbeing of the target population, not the organisation. Here the target population is more vital in governance than the organisation itself.[16] Governance that way is much larger than corporate or organisational management. A nation, the ultimate organised human settlement, is governed by managing for the benefit of the population based on their apparent needs. And the benefit is maximised by the provision of wellbeing, not welfare. A government governs through its forces, agencies and other organisations. To that extent a government employee is expected to serve the public through the respective organisation by and under governance. Whereas, in a private organisation, the employee performs by and under management for the benefit or wellbeing of the organisation to meet its apparent needs. In modern times, the organisation also has the task of caring for the public primarily as a legal requirement in the garb of corporate governance which in turn also talks about the whimsical (according to this study) corporate social responsibility (CSR).[17] Corporate governance as an obligation could also fall under business ethics where companies may govern their organisations with a virtuous eye on the public including stakeholders in the external business environment. In all respects, governance is a step higher than management in the human activity pyramid. This study does not intend to elaborate it further.

Every entity is expected to have an exclusive maritime policy that it could follow in augmenting its maritime interests in relation to its national governance. The policy where it exists will be aimed at the short or long term requirements primarily related to security or ocean development in the vague terms of a wish list. Integration of maritime security with national security governance is not likely to be a seriously implemented affair. Besides, the policy will be highly situational and focused to the cause or appeal that on the first hand forced the government to generate it. For example, if it is based on a terror strike, the policy will be in the antiterrorism mode. Most of the entities are not likely to have a firm and consolidated overall maritime security policy (MSP) leading to strategic actions and integrated governance in national security as projected in this study.

Every maritime security policy has to be consistent with the respective national laws, customary international law and treaties and agreements to which the entity is a party. The policy may also contain the intention of the entity to become a party to various select international treaties and agreements in future as it may find needed while drafting the policy. The policy, among other things will be specific on the maritime interests and the identified domain for extending it. This is the first strategic action an entity has to take in integrating maritime security with national security.

The maritime security policy will have to be suitable to the entity. It should be classified appropriate to the entity's requirement. The policy of government in relation to its national security governance is another part. The maritime security policy is the leading document that would assist in integration. Here, as seen so far, the concept of national security will be different for the governments of every entity. No one will be following the wholesome concept of national security as projected in this study. However it is not a serious matter as far as integration is concerned. The governments could at least integrate maritime security in governance instead of treating it as a separate element of national security, in the wholesome manner as projected by analysing its overall ocean property. Ocean property mapping and serious strategic appreciation will be necessary. Integration of maritime security does not have to wait for a major shift in national security governance as identified in this study. It could very well be done with the existing practice of governance. But integration of maritime security with national governance, in whatever form it may be, is important.

Integrated maritime security, once implemented, will require continuous analyses and study along with the application of the findings strategically in the national security governance. The integrated maritime security is what the national planners have to incorporate in planned governance with continuous feedback and reactive corrections. Once integrated, it will be a continuous process. Nations will develop the necessary expertise in integrated maritime security by practice. It will require serious infrastructure that could be prepared by rearranging the existing infrastructure available in most of the countries. Even the ministries and other governmental organisations will require structural changes. There will be countries that will require fresh start. This study does not intend to bring out any specific examples of geopolitical entities but would like to have a look at the existing and continuously rewound or altered policies of governments. It may be appropriate for governments to think about the compatibility of the plans they have adopted or not yet adopted but thinking of implementing in the near future with respect to integrated maritime security. A few examples of the 21st century meddles with governance are given below. It will be interesting to see how much integration such changes would have brought in gaining headway in governance though they are not analysed in this study.

- **Terror Strikes in the United States—11 September 2001**

  United States was never been jolted since the Pearl Harbour strikes on 7 December 1941 until terror struck on 11 September 2001 on its waterfront under the coast guard in Manhattan and elsewhere over land. One of the results of 9/11 was the homeland security model that attempted to integrate maritime security as appreciated. Why the powerful country, the best in the world, could not preempt or prevent the attack is a mystery to the analyst. Wasn't there any actionable intelligence? There was a conspiracy theory that the Pearl Harbour attack was known beforehand, but the governments, who were aware of it, especially the British, wanted to let it happen to get America into war. And America got into it the next day. It was true that without America World War II would not have been decisive the way it was. Similarly, were the 9/11 attacks known? Did the government want it to happen? Did it give the right to hit where it wanted the very next day? If so, the Homeland security model is just an eye wash, nothing worth talking about even in America as a modern strategic model. If the attack was a surprise, then the model has some meaning. That too gets dissolved in time since it has been designed and generated subsequent to the incident. It will only serve the purpose of preparing to face a similar attack in the future. The attackers also learn from such models. Normally attacks are not repeated in the same fashion but for the rhetoric. Yes, it would have been something special if America had prevented or preempted 9/11.

- **Terror Strikes in India—26 November 2008**

  Indian maritime security makeup came under fire from the public and media subsequent to the terrorist attacks in Mumbai on 26 November 2008. The public has lost hope in them. The government and the security agencies hurriedly whipped up some plans with the navy controlling coastal operations. Simply put, the government reversed the navy to the shore. Hurriedly the government provided compensation packages to the coast guard in the form of new acquisitions and personnel. A marine police that was already on the cards was urgently brought up for the states and the union territories. An analysis of the so called 26/11 will prove much more behind the scene activities. As in the case of 9/11 that too came across the border. Did the Indian government know such a strike would take place? It could be wrong to say the government had intelligence at least two years before that prospective terrorists were being trained for a seaborne operation in Karachi. Why would the government have to allow it to happen? The response of the government of India to the attack did not lead to any such conclusions. Certainly the government of India would have received broken information much earlier but within the kind of helplessness it would not have been able to prevent it. The trauma of the incident refuses to die. A book in 2013 informs that there was a mole, a Pakistan double agent, who helped the attackers to home on.[18] But the fact remains that India could not prevent it a la the United States. Whatever may have happened subsequently were only mitigation of impact, not preventive or preemptive governance. The government seemingly has not been able to integrate maritime security with national security. The forces and agencies seem to be highly unaccountable stamping on each other's toes while groping in the dark. What should the country do next?

▸ The Twilight Saga of an Indian Submarine

The Indian Navy lost a Kilo class diesel electric submarine *in situ,*alongside in harbour by an explosion allegedly by torpedo malfunction.[19] The incident that occurred in the early hours of 14 August 2013 showed the chink in India's maritime armour and the flaws in its attack profile. This study considers accidents asthe telltale signs of decline in the EHW prowess of armed forces. The probe report will not be known to the public and may not come out with the truth. But the incident will remain a national stigma. Such occurrences speak a lot about the urgency of naval indigenisation as part of integrated maritime security, not the kind of touch and go ocean governance the nations practise. Three months later, in November 2013, the only development was the cautionary warning by the defence minister that the navy should not fritter away such valuable assets of the country.[20] The defence minister said, "It must be ensured that safety mechanisms are accorded topmost priority and standard operating procedures adhered to strictly and without any exception."[21] What is the safety mechanism here? Can the navy conclude? But is it ignorance of safety, non adherence to standard operating procedures (SOP), dependence on external sources or sheer incompetence in rank and files that causes such accidents? The defence minister, on the other hand, expressed satisfaction that the Indian Navy had maintained a fairly high operational tempo on maritime and coastal security in collaboration with other organisations and agencies, though he expressed his displeasure in certain incidents of moral turpitude.[22] The reference to navy's tempo on coastal security contradicts the navy's role as EHW machinery in maritime strategy. In addition, where does that everything-is-not-fine- feeling of moral turpitude take the navy? India, as a responsible country, with a confirmed and accepted second strike doctrine, perhaps needs to rethink about the functional applications of its navy and home on to them. The earlier it is, the better it will be. The integration of maritime security will pave way for it. This is applicable to any nation.

▸ Death in the Chilling Netherworld—Russian SSN Kursk

The Russian nuclear submarine Kursk allegedly exploded underwater and sank in the Barents Sea on 12 August 2000 for reasons not clear on the public domain. Here it is the case of an instrument of war that was completely designed and built by the user. All on board (118) were killed. As usual in similar cases, the incident opened up to various theories. There were statements that torpedo malfunction was the original cause. Russian Federation faced a series of military accidents since its formation in 1991. The casualties were largely attributed to cutback in spending, lack of maintenance of hardware and fall in personnel quality standards which encouraged the deadly criminal gangs and syndicates of Russia to steal parts.[23] The navy virtually was rusting and every effort to regain the reach of the Soviet era was plagued by disasters. As is the practice, post such incidents, Russia too took to immediate shake up. Many naval officers were sacked. The government removed the naval chief, though much later, without giving any reason. All these show the pathetic state of the Russian Navy who reels under the sense of urgency to showcase its old glory in the wee hours of the the new century. In the bargain, it meets with disaster.

Will Maldives and Kiribati Sink?

For some, especially the Maldives and Kiribati watchers, the question is not, "Will they sink?" It is "When?" It may be the world's first underwater cabinet meeting; It happened in Maldives. The government of the Maldives held an underwater cabinet meeting in October 2009 to attract international attention to the dangers of global warming.[24] President Mohammed Nasheed and his team were underwater across a horseshoe table conducting the meeting in diving gear for 30 minutes. In 2007, the UN Intergovernmental Panel on Climate Change (UNIPCC) warned that a rise in sea levels of seven to 24 inches by 2100 would be enough to make the country virtually uninhabitable. But the problems will start much earlier.

Kiribati too is worried. If the solutions are not found early, Kiribati and many other islands will become uninhabitable creating a wave of refugees. When life becomes unsustainable, people will have to move out. But there are many who won't agree with the anxiety expressed by the islanders. Obviously they are not living in these islands. They are clasped to the land elsewhere. Is there a threat? If so how to handle it? Is it by prevention, preemption or limiting threat attraction? The threat, if it exists, is direct-overt-external, the easiest to handle. But there is no international action so far. To that extent it is new because it is yet to happen. And unlike what has been mentioned so far, more challenging.

- **The Tohoku Earthquake and Tsunami—the Japanese Syndrome**

  On 11 March 2011, Japan was hit by the most powerful earthquake ever recorded. The underwater earthquake occurred at Tohoku created a tsunami with waves 40.5 metre high that destroyed everything on the shore where it advanced creating havoc on the way. The tsunami waves overtopped the seawalls around the nuclear facilities. The Fukushima Daiichi nuclear power plant was worst hit. It was by all versions an apocalyptic nuclear disaster. Three years later the Fukushima meltdown is still uncontrolled. Simply speaking, seawalls are not an answer to prevent a tsunami. Indian politicians were talking about sea walls to stop the tsunami impact when the country faced the Javan tsunami in 2004. More than the sea wall what is needed is integrated maritime security against disasters at and from the sea. Japan, the great island nation should know.

All these cases are to contemplate and debate over the ocean. They are not conclusive. There are many such cases the strategy analysts can ponder. There will be different views. The actions were taken by the national governments as part of their ongoing governance. After initial analysis it may be seen whether the actions, as and where taken, will resolve the issues in future or complicate them further. All the above comments are on situation based maritime security planning. Is it the right approach to change plans depending upon situations or to have an integrated plan beforehand? Does change in governance towards NS_{max} require a situational prompt? Actions under situational prompt indicate the government was unprepared. Every entity suffers from it.

The method inertia of governance will be the main constraint in incorporating changes in governance in modern times. Most of the governmental processes will have to undergo major alterations to incorporate integrated maritime security to their present system of governance. Every government experiences far too many constraints under political system changes and selective commitments.

The very purpose of this study lies in the desired action in governance in relation to maritime security by every geopolitical entity of the world. The study is aware of the constraints in coupling integrated maritime security with the existing systems while in motion. The study also believes it could be done against all the constraints and in many cases, the nations will be forced to do it by their own exigencies. The research throws light on a few issues so that the governments can attempt such changes under clarity of perception. One of the suggestions is that change, especially in national or any large human system governance is better incorporated prior to a situation than after it. It has many advantages in governance. Any system introduced subsequent to a situation that demands such change will be purposeful only for that situation that may not repeat in the same form and seriousness. Besides, it will be short lived and governance will get back to the original complacency again waiting for the next. The next situation for a change is assured; it may take a long time, though. Sometimes as long as the time taken between the attacks on Pearl Harbour and Manhattan, at a distance as far away.

Strategic Actions

Acceptance of national security universally could be difficult as the world moves under the design of the worm train in the unitary civilisation. Still the concept of national security with its 15 elements, and integrating maritime security with it for governance aimed at NS_{max} could be suggested as the preferred way of providing maximum apparent security to people. That will amount to wellbeing maximisation within the limits of competitive governance. Competitive governance can be interpreted as the methods of governance between governments of a nation or between governance of different entities. Governing national security or, otherwise known as governing by national security, should be a practitioner's delight, not a grind.

It is not possible to prescribe any specific method and identify procedures for advising governments on how to govern a country. It is for the governments to design, experiment and follow. Integrating maritime security with any form and practice of governance is what this study advocates. It has been reiterated for reinforcement. The strategic actions for integrated maritime security that any government or procedure of governance can follow, are mentioned below. These actions may change with respect to impending situations at times.

- Carefully draft out a national maritime security policy that will have strategic value, even if a landlocked country.
- Introduce wholesome national security concept and prepare for national security indexing on appropriate scale based on

the principles of the new concept and where it does exist, by comparative analysis by factoring the existing system. This has to be done, preferably, under a global regime. However any individual nation can also practice it as an introduction that may prompt others to follow once the results are seen on the ground and benefits are appreciated.

- Immediately appreciate the folly of considering military security as the concept of national security. Mistaking an element for the concept often by superimposition is extremely grave.
- Analyse the threat perception under the threat matrix cube and model the interactive matrix and probable outcomes of the national security elements to understand their situational underplay. This involves understanding the threats from every quarter and classifying them under the threat matrix cube for decision on preemption or prevention.
- Have threat response plans ready for handling issues by preemption or prevention on the aspect of every element and their interactive matrix.
- Incorporate the threat response plans in the national plan.
- Understand the importance of the ocean and analyse maritime security by ocean property mapping, not by estimating or appreciation.
- Crate means for continuous evaluation and incorporation of ocean property changes.
- Establish strategic objectives in relation to the constituents of ocean property and integrate them with national security objectives at the planning level.
- Integrate maritime security for governance under the national plan as per national convenience.
- Integrate all the military armed forces under a unified command or as combined defence services under unitary command and control. This is one of the essentials of integrated maritime security. Integrated maritime security otherwise will be an impossible idea to execute seriously. The situation will

become worse and more somber when the complexity of the navy increases.[25]

- Bring the warfighting tonnage of the navy to the optimum limit.[26]
- Limit noncombat naval tonnage to minimum.
- Define and limit the role of the navy to maximise benefits from warfighting and geostrategy. Use the navy for extended diplomacy in geostrategic context.
- If nuclear, keep a flawless and all inclusive zero error command and control (C2) over the nuclear warfare doctrine of the country without any time holiday. This could ideally be followed even by a landlocked country.[27]
- Streamline the nonmilitary maritime forces and agencies according to their charter under absolute accountability for law enforcement and service. Accountability is the key factor. Under no circumstances it should be diluted.
- Initiate action for international regimes and protocols for:
  - refugee asylum seekers and geoproperty rights of asylum providers when the flood gates open by sea level rise,
  - ocean monitoring, control, surveillance and response (MCSR),
  - force cooperation,
  - protection and preservation of global commons,
  - global piracy control and counseling of piracy victims,[28]
  - prevention of human rights violations and other nefarious activities by governments or others in the high seas,
  - abolishing of armed securities in merchant ships, and private security agencies at sea and
  - any other matters that will be of global concern at sea.
- Initiate action for serious penalties to governments in case their nationals involve in maritime piracy activities or blockade of traffic, as a special case for eliminating piracy under the UN regime.
- Identify nations to form part of a coalition under IMO and operate independently for select periods on anti-piracy duties

under specified rules of engagements in identified areas where there is no government or the existing government is too weak to control or contain piracy. At any one time there should be only one navy deployed at sea that will provide cover for all against piracy in the notified piracy block.

- Create effective intelligence agencies for maritime intelligence at national and international level.
- Create recovery plans for disasters and distress incidents in maritime security.
- Have maritime outreach plans to integrate all domestic maritime operators for cooperating with national governance as stakeholders.
- Link with the national plan for suppressing unlawful activities at and from the sea including use and transportation of weapons of mass destruction (WMD).[29]
- Totally abolish the term "coastal security"with respect to maritime security and replace it with the term "maritime border security (MBS)."The term coastal security can be used for land based coastal operations such as patrol or policing as part of MBS. It will also have the much needed psychological impact on people involved at all levels.
- Augment international cooperation in the geostrategic context—bilateral, regional, and global based on the national maritime security doctrine. This has to be done on an as required basis after careful examination. It is often possible that the country or countries with whom a country wants to work together may not be forthcoming under various socio-political holdbacks. This can be resolved better through diplomatic and political relations under integrated maritime security.
- International cooperation in integrated maritime security is possible between coastal and landlocked countries. The transboundary Mekong River had helped Laos to get to the South China Sea with Thailand, Cambodia and Vietnam as providers. Nothing prevents these countries in having cooperation on maritime security at a much higher level. India can provide assistance to Nepal to extract its ocean property

better than any other ocean neighbour. Ideally it is possible even for landlocked countries to come into maritime agreements based on their national objectives under integrated maritime security.

- Emphasise terrain specificity and awareness (sometimes known as domain awareness; originally an American concept)[30] among all concerned about integration of maritime security.
- Keep the awareness as a regular and ongoing system requirement periodically modified with respect to changes and alterations in the maritime scenario.
- Integrate and codify all forces, agencies, organisations, establishments including research organisations related to ocean property governance within an entity.

There could be more strategic actions specific to each entity. A case is that of maritime dispute resolution. Geopolitical entities could examine such specific actions according to their respective national policy statements.

The accomplishments of strategic action are more important than the action itself. It depends on governance. In relation to maritime security as projected, it will not be readily possible by the localised actions alone to accomplish success. Success is the ultimate, not action. Success in maritime affairs will require international cooperation and global connectivity in today's world. There should be an international front promoted by like minded nations or international organisations. In most of the cases it will be bilateral or regional. Global approach is for nations with global outlook in maritime security. This issue makes maritime security integration all the more important for national governments. Direct attention of national governments at the highest level is imperative. It will not be forthcoming if maritime security is taken in isolation for governance. A global level approach is much welcome if there is identity of mind (*consensus ad idem*) among global nations. In fact that is what is preferred in most of the cases. That is geostrategy, the core application of maritime force and power in the modern world in the open.

A strategic mission has to be operative under zero failure. Zero failure is technically not possible as the very law of chance will be negated. There is an interesting find in the law of chance—in a system where an item is totally focused for perfection there can be unexpected failure or short coming elsewhere that the operator will come to know only when it happens.[31] It is there, everywhere. Zero failure systems or governance is an impossible dream.[32]

Enablers of Strategic Actions

Mere strategic action pronouncements are not going to take the national security governance anywhere near to success unless the enablers of strategic action are activated. This will be visible in the widening gap between the vision statements and actual achievements.

The strategic actions should be executed successfully. One of the methods successful strategic executors follow is activating the enablers of success at the time of launching action and subsequently following them till the result is achieved or, in rare cases, the action is abandoned. These enablers have to be identified by the executors. Some of the enablers of integrated maritime security are given below.

- Maintain interest among all, especially at the higher levels of activity and among the stakeholders in the governance environment.

  This includes governments, public, media and the executors throughout the period of action. This also shows that for a particular form of governance to be successful, the interest in the end goal and transitional objectives should remain kindled the entire time. The awareness related to the strategic action should be retained. Otherwise it is virtually impossible to achieve the strategic objective. This is a difficult task especially considering there will be various levels of governance and far too many executors and stakeholders. But national governance, being a macro level engagement, can reachout since it has the authority and the required machinery. That is also the reason that such activities should not be diluted by non- integration or isolation.

- Be aware of threats and the best possible way of handling them at all times.

  A threat is created by the target. The intensity of the threat will be according to the threat attractiveness of the target. The moment born, the threat starts moving towards a target like a fly,by the force of threat attraction. The target should be protected from the threat hitting and damaging it. Sometimes the damage can be total. Because once the threat hits target there is only mitigation of damage as the subsequent action. For example, a measure to control inflation could be preemptive, preventive or mitigative. It depends on the time and the nature the measure is taken. Ideally the target could be protected from threat by prevention, preemption or eliminating the threat attraction of the target. Normally in any human situation even under superstitious belief systems (the evil eye syndrome), the easy approach is to downplay the attractiveness to keep the threat away. Sometimes even the target is destroyed (female foeticide or infanticide when seen relative to demographic or ethnic security). It is not a strategic solution whatsoever. Because reducing the attraction of the target will amount to decline in its value and thereby decline in the results of its management. Hence the choice should be to prevent or preempt the threat from striking the target. If not succeeded, there should be mitigating measures that are best suited.

- Keep the finger of governance on the pulse of the geostrategic context.

Kiribati and Maldives have taken efforts to raise the sound across the oceans on their problems of sea level rising. But it was not so with Somali piracy. Piracy is a heinous crime against humanity. What heard around the world was only a whimper when hundreds of seafarers were humiliated and traumatised for life by a bunch of dollar peddling hooligans and their henchmen on a very selective basis. Either the nations should have the will and capability to destroy the evil doers or the ability to gather international cooperation. Whatever happened around the waters of Somalia with the so called coalition forces or independent operators was nothing but the show of helplessness in the absence of a maritime policy and capability to manage maritime security in an integrated manner. The pulse of the international scenario is an enabler of integrated maritime security. Because a world that does not cooperate is destined to sink together. The primary terrain for international cooperation is the ocean. Ocean provides great challenges to the world. It is the common space for international cooperation for proactive existence and wellbeing. It is yet to dawn in the minds of most of the governments.

- International cooperation also means exchange of information and intelligence about the ocean terrain.[33]

Intelligence is intention that is actionable. Information may further lead to actionable intelligence by analysis. Intelligence is a private affair even among agencies within a state. Nations may share them in a limited manner for mutual cooperation. Maritime intelligence mentioned here is from the point of view of the ocean as global commons. A global intelligence system to understand the goings on in the ocean that is dissipated to every entity in every respect as decided by them under a global protocol will be one of the essentials of the world tomorrow. However, it may be a distant possibility under many activities nations may perform at sea under secrecy.

- Ensure guaranteed free flow of shipping around the SLOC at all times without fear and disregard.

This will require comprehensive plans for assured maritime supply chain under constantly improving international regulatory framework.

- Establish worldwide MCSR regime without waiting for situations to develop.

Often a change occurs anywhere in the world in governance as an effect of a calamitous situation. It is the wrong practice because the response to the change just happened may not be able to handle a new situation. The correct procedure is to foresee the calamity and take action prior to that to prevent or preempt it. In case it develops, still the procedure is to find the future development and take action. Any new action taken subsequent to a crisis or disaster will not resolve the issues permanently. Preemption and prevention of such situations will be possible to a great extent under enhanced MCSR that covers the entire ocean terrain.

- Minimise the gap between governance and governed (people).

This is not only an enabler but also one of the objectives of national governance. Large deficit exists all over the world within nations between the outcome of governance and the wellbeing of people. This makes the people psycho-sociologically drift away from their governments and their governance. It is visible in every governmental system today even in the most developed countries. Under this situation people will take their lives in their own hands along with law losing confidence in governance. The much touted human indices like those of happiness, development, influence, etc., becomes highly irrelevant and archaic. It is the NSI index that matters in modern governance. No nation is practising it today.

Concluding Enabler of IMS—Transform IMO

Integrated maritime security calls for cohesive national efforts for governance under serious deviation from the present practices all over the world. The ocean, unlike the land terrain, which is highly insular (within the great mental walls of line boundaries of the landclasp syndrome), is actually an open roadstead that permits outreach. This awareness had sunk in gradually among the nations today. Ocean has transformed from a moat to an outreach territory. One of the deviations in governance that the nations have to appreciate is that "domestic governance" has become a true part of international governance and it can be highly benefitted with an effective international regime in place in regard to ocean because of its special characteristics as an outreach terrain and a global commons. For this, the world needs an international organisation that will facilitate the governance of ocean property as a whole and not just the maritime commercial transportation, which will substantially assist nations in their domestic governance integrating maritime security. The most suitable agency for such a regime change is the highly successful and responsible IMO, the UN agency. But it has to be transformed for it. It is a better choice than creating a new one for obvious reasons.

IMO—the International Maritime Organisation—is the United Nations specialised agency with responsibility, as on now, for the safety and security of shipping and the prevention of marine pollution by ships.[34] That is all about it, a hard core shipping regime. There is no international organisation for focused and exclusive governance of the rest of the ocean property.

Since its inception in 1948 as International Maritime Consultative Organisation (IMCO),[35] subsequent to a convention adopted by an international conference in Geneva, IMO had performed commendably and consistently to bring order in shipping commerce and transportation. Its importance can be seen from the membership of large number of landlocked countries and participation by various non-governmental agencies who are concerned about the ocean. Limiting its charter to shipping alone could have been examined for a possible enhancement immediately after the UNCLOS regime. IMO would have extended to everything about the ocean leading to ocean property governance and imparting education through its excellent knowledge centre at the World Maritime University (WMU). But IMO, according to this study, preferred to remain, grounded by specialisation in regulating maritime transportation. This satisfaction, the feeling of absolute contentment was heard, in Tokyo when the then secretary general, Mitropoulos,[36] expressed his blissful satisfaction with the achievement of IMO stating that if there was anything that IMO had not looked into, it must have been inthe standardisation of the champagne bottle used for the ceremonious launching of a new ship. This he said in an address on 22 October 2008 to celebrate the 60th anniversary of IMO at the Nippon Foundation. He was right; one could agree with him. But in a subsequent dialogue, he expressed his concern and apprehensions with an emotion of helplessness in tackling the Somali piracy at its peak then. There was nothing, he felt that was within the mandate of IMO to handle such issues. He was right again.

Helplessness of an international organisation reflects the world over. Most of the nations may not come to know about it. Every nation in the world may have to work together under stiff resistance to transform IMO into the guardian of ocean property for the benefit of the entire global community without wait. This is much preferred to creating new fragmented international regimes for ocean governance in select fields.

Even otherwise, IMO can engage with the human element more seriously than being done under its mandate. IMO should interact with seafarers directly through its officials and member nations for keeping them aware and involved. This could be a task of the IMO knowledge centre at the WMU. The engagement should be to bring a value and courage based human element in the ocean environment which should not be left insulated. They should be able to brave the trauma and tribulations of the ocean life like the way they ride the waves. One of the suggestions made by the author in a human rights institute meeting in Karachi in 2012 to reduce the post piracy trauma of seafarers was to pre-counsel them by trained counselors to prepare them for facing human tragedy that may strike anytime.[37] Post incident counseling has its limitations. Those who brave the oceans should be capable of braving life's sufferings too. They can, with alittle help from the people who know; the WMU can do that.

To that extent IMO should even look into the six billion dollar treasures held over the world by the ocean.[38] Why not?

NOTES

1. Gaining governance is a term borrowed from a nautical term "gaining bearing," which means moving up relative to the other vessel normally on a parallel course. Here gaining headway in governance means moving ahead in governance towards NS_{max} relative to another country. That should be the strategic objective of a nation.
2. The word "body" is used for easy understanding of the theme. Similar words are used elsewhere for ease of explanation.
3. There could also be deficit in achievable wellbeing and achieved wellbeing irrespective of the approach in governance. The recommended approach—governance under the wholesome concept of national security—helps to minimise the deficits. But there is no "surplus" in national security.
4. Under this principle, behind every coalition in a war there are individual wars won without fighting between the partners in which the more forceful wins and makes the other to join in. This principle of coalition forces can be seen from the time of Trojan War. That war was perhaps the earliest rendition of the coalition warfare theory. See about coalition in Paleri, Prabhakaran, *National Security: Imperatives and Challenges*, New Delhi: Tata McGraw-Hill Publishing Company Limited, New Delhi, 2008, p. 128. How Agamemnon gets the partners in war to go with him will show how he won over them without fighting.
5. In this study the syllogism—the major premise, minor premise and conclusion often appears together for clarity while reading on the go by reiteration and not separated like in scriptures, canons or academic theses. More so, this study did not originate from any question or for seeking clarification. Hence syllogism is mixed with the premises that self conclude.
6. This question can be examined seriously by syllogism, fist under the major premise, followed by the minor premise and then concluding with the finding as the answer to the question.
7. Disposition bias makes people to keep what brings them loss in the hope they will yield better in future. In the general sense, people retain things that are old and have crossed their use value for reasons that may not be clear to them. In the macro level, the process of governance today will be retained by governments in spite of the disaster they cause in governance, under the disposition bias. It is necessary to understand here that the disposition bias is not resistance to change.
8. See Paleri, Prabhakaran, *National Security: Imperatives and Challenges,* New Delhi: Tata McGraw-hill Publishing Limited, 2008 and "The Concept of National Security and a Maritime Model for India," doctoral dissertation,

Department of Defence and Strategic Studies, University of Madras, Chennai, February 2002 for a detailed understanding of the identified concept and its elements.

9 Ibid.

10 The statement here refers to various studies carried out by nations and their militaries for controlling mind and communicating with forces through paranormal media like telepathy, telekinesis, closed vision, etc., at the heightened period of Cold War. Still, it is understood, there are studies underway on these subjects using ultrasounds, biochemicals and other scientific means for individual and crowd control.

11 See Paleri, n.8, *National Security,* pp. 18-19.

12 The spirit of UNCLOS had declared the sea as a common property of humankind.

13 Paleri, n.8, pp. 258-78

14 Wilson, Colin, *A Criminal History of Mankind,* London: Granada Publishing Limited, 1984, p. 101. According to the author, the public conscience began to wake up in the middle of the 19th century largely as the result of the work of humanitarian novelists such as Charles Dickens and Victor Hugo. The novels that depicted human sufferings touched the minds of people for the first time. Attention turned to abolition of public executions and other cruel ways of handling people. Still the world remains as criminalised as in the past. Human concerns attempt to swim parallel to it. But the modern governments should understand that governance aimed at wellbeing,not welfare, can bring the desired change. However the findings of Colin Wilson may not be applicable to the world as a whole as there were geopolitical entities like India whose culture irrespective of variants was built on the firm foundations of human concern and the right and wrong value systems as early as the Vedic period.

15 According to the human activity (task) pyramid devised by the author as part of study in business environment as well as human investment management (HIM), the humans at any given time may engage in five different levels of activities depending upon their activity profile. Level one is when the individual is engaged in an activity for self without any monetary consideration. The next three are for monetary and other considerations (Maslow). In level two the individual performs the task directly for another, in level three the individual performs the task through others for the benefit of the organisation (managerial function) and in level four performs similar to level three but for the wellbeing of the people (governance function). The peak is at level five where the individual performs without any consideration at the self actualised level (Maslow). An individual can go through all these five levels on any given day. But mostly they remain at the levels based on their way of life and career. An important aspect of the human activity pyramid is exclusively for the evaluation of one's own activity profile and

not that of the other.

16 Paleri, Prabhakaran, Management is Passé; Governance is Trendy: Applying the Principles of Management in the Twenty First Century, in Mishra, R.K., Shital Jhunjhunwala, and Mridula Sahay (eds.), Corporate Governance: beyond Boundaries, Delhi: Macmillan Publishers India Limited, 2010, pp. 1-8.

17 The author finds certain anomalies in the very concept of CSR; hence the mention of it as whimsical. These are not highlighted here except the argument that according to the management theory of authority, responsibility and accountability, responsibility cannot be given or delegated. It is a sense of feeling on the part of the entity or individual to be responsible under the delegated authority. This feeling (the feeling of responsibility) can vary among individuals and entities under identical authority and accountability. Hence it cannot be called corporate social responsibility under any legal documentation. While ethical business practice can permit it, CSR under the obligation of law becomes the corporate social obligation, not responsibility. This aspect is overlooked while naming it (reference to company law). Responsibility is a state whereas obligation is binding oneself under social, moral or legal tie. It will be better to call the concept as CSO (corporate social obligation) instead of CSR (corporate social responsibility), especially when enforceable under law.

18 "Pakistani Mole in Indian Agencies Helped 26/11 Attackers, Book Claims,"/ news.in.msn.com/national/pakistani-mole-in-indian-agencies-helped-26-11-attackers-book-claims, accessed 9 November 20123.

19 The torpedo of the Russian Kilo class submarine, supposed to be CET 65E (pronounced SE.AT in Russian. The E in 65E stands for export variety), according to experts, cannot malfunction that easily considering the safety levels applied to it. The main levels of safety cordon that demands water pressure, electric supply and influence by proximity or impact is not easy to breach even under human negligence. The torpedo cannot explode over dry land or even when roasted under fire, experts opine. But there could be problems of short circuits and software malfunctions in advanced weapons and equipment that need to be tested frequently. The Indian Navy, perhaps, will never know the exact reasons for the explosion and the sinking of the submarine for the simple reason that the equipment that caused the accident was not an indigenised one, not withstanding that the submarine, a 1995 vintage, had played some credible roles under able commands in its life span. In spite of such credibility the user should know that there will be many unknowns in an instrument of war that has been borrowed or purchased off the shelf or on line (pun intended).

20 "Antony Pulls up Navy on INS Sindhurakshak Sinking," ibnlive.in.com/ news/antony-pulls-up-navy-on-ins-sindhurakshak-sinking/435370-3.html, accessed 22 November 2013.

21 Ibid.

22 Ibid.

23 en.wikipedia.org/wiki/List_of_Russian_military_accidents, accessed 12 August 2013.

24 Waleed, Fakhroo, Maldives Government Meets Underwater to Show Effects of Global Warming, www.lite-news. com/maldives-government-meets-underwater-to-show-effects-of-global-warming/,19 October 2009, and Andre, Vitchek, Will Tiny Nation of Kiribati Sink? www.zcommunications. org / will-tiny-nation-of-kiribati-sink-by-andre-vltchek.html, 18 October 2012, both accessed 9 February 2013.

25 This is applicable to other military armed forces also.

26 Optimum limit is preferred to maximum limit with respect to cost. Even otherwise managing maximum limit will require more efforts that may be counterproductive.

27 Theoretical expression; not amplified further. This statement is neither aimed at encouraging nuclearisation for military purposes nor does it support the idea of nuclear engagements. The study believes in absolute elimination of nuclear weapons from the world except to meet the common interests of the planet and its life forms under an international regime. For example: to destroy a speeding meteoroid on a collision course with Earth. The high seas of the ocean will be vital for such terrestrial missions.

28 Counseling means precounseling also. Precounseling means dealing with the trauma prior hand either directive or, sometimes nondirective. The seafarers can be counseled before they take to sea on the difficulties and the experience they can expect and prepare them for that. See Paleri, Prabhakaran, Piracy Victims—the Indian Experience, in Griffiths, David, N. (ed.), *The Human Face of Piracy: Consequences and Policy Options,* Islamabad, Fazaldad Human Rights Institution, 2012,pp. 141-154.

29 As defined by the concerned entity or under international regulations. In the US the WMD is defined in section 921 of the 18 U.S. Code § 2332a(c).

30 Domain awareness is within the terrain awareness. Terrain awareness is preferred in this study as it is about macro level appreciation.

31 Rastrigin, L, *This Chancy, Chancy, Chancy World,* Moscow: Mir Publishers, 1973, pp. 18-22

32 This makes the proposition for nuclear weapon system or nuclear strategic command system a dangerous idea. See note 27 also. Such systems will not be fail proof under the impossibility of zero error systems under the law of chance.

33 Information is not intelligence. Intelligence is intention. Intentions can be refined by analysis from information.

34 www.imo.org/About/Pages/Default.aspx, accessed 15 September 2013.

35 The name was changed to IMO in 1982, the year of UNCLOS.

36 Efthimios E. Mitropoulos was the seventh secretary general of IMO (18 June 2003- 31 December 2011). He was a rear admiral and the direct general of the Greek Coast Guard with exemplary accomplishments in maritime affairs.

37 Paleri, n. 28, p. 153.

38 According to an end of the scene display in the Hollywood movie "*Into the Blue*" (2005). This is nothing. According to Popular Mechanics it could even be around 60 billion US dollars, ten times larger than the *Into the Blue* statement. As seen in www.popularmechanics.com/technology/engineering/gonzo/whats-the-total-value-of-the-worlds-sunken-treasure, accessed 3 September 2012.

ABBREVIATIONS

AGP	Assam Gana Parishad
AUV	Autonomous Underwater vehicle
BBC	British Broadcasting Corporation
BC	Before Christ
BM	Biologically Modified
btm	billion tones metric
CBM	Confidence Building Measures
CIA	Central Intelligence Agency
CLCS	Commission on the Limits of Continental Shelf
COLREGS	Convention on the International Regulations for Preventing Collisions at Sea 1972
CS	Continental Shelf
CSR	Corporate Social Responsibility
CS3	Centre for Strategic Studies and Simulation
CSO	Corporate Social Obligation
CTBT	Comprehensive nuclear Test Ban Treaty
CZ	Costal Zone
DBO	Daulat Beg Oldie
DCE	Direct-Covert-External (threat)
DCI	Direct-Covert-Internal (threat)
DDT	Dichlorodiphenyltrichloroethane

DLOC	Deviated Lines of Communication
DNA	Deoxyribonucleic acid
DOE	Direct-Overt-External (threat)
DOI	Direct-Overt-Internal (threat)
DOM	Department d'outre-mer
EC	European Commission
EDS	Economic Defence Spending
EEZ	Exclusive Economic Zone
EHW	Extreme Harms Way
ER&TRP Act	mergency Regulations & Protection of Terrorism Act
EU	European Union
FADA	Federally Administered Tribal Areas
FAO	Food and Agricultural Organisation
FOC	Flags of Convenience
FOIA	Freedom of Information Act
GATT	General Agreement on Tariffs and Trade
GDP	Gross Domestic Product
GNH	Gross National Happiness
GoM	Group of Ministers
GOP	Grand Old Party (The Republican Party of the United ates of America)
GP	Ghost Protocol.
HIM	Human Investment Management
IBL	International Boundary Line
ICE	Indirect-Covert-External (threat)
ICI	Indirect-Covert-Internal (threat)
IHO	International Hydrographic Association
ILO	International Labour Organisation
IMCO	International Maritime Consultative Organisation
IMD	Indian Meteorological Department

IMO	International Maritime Organisation
IMS	Integrated Maritime Security
INCSEA	incident at Sea
IOE	Indirect-Overt-External (threat)
IOI	Indirect-Overt-Internal (threat)
IOR	Indian Ocean Region (also Indian Ocean Rim)
IPC	Indian Penal Code
ISA	International Seabed Authority
ITF	International Transport Workers Federation
LAC	Line of Actual Control
LCS	Legal Continental Shelf
LNG	Liquid Natural Gas
LoS	Law of the Sea
LZ	Littoral Zone
Ma	Megaannum
MAD	Mutually Assured Destruction
MAR	Mid Atlantic Ridge
MBS	Maritime Border Security
MCSR	Monitoring, Control, Surveillance and Response
MSC	Maritime Safety Committee
MSP	Maritime Security Policy
NASA	National Aeronautics and Space Administration
NATO	North Atlantic Treaty Organisation
NIO	National Institute of Oceanography
NSC	National Security Council
NSI	National Security Index
NS_{max}	National Security $_{maxima}$
OPCW	Organisation for the Prohibition of Chemical Weapons
OPM	Ocean Property Mapping

P^3C	Protection and Preservation (of marine environment) and Prevention and Control (of marine pollution)
PCASP	Privately Contracted Armed Security Personnel
PLO	Palestine Liberation organisation
PMR	Pridnestovian Moldavian Republic
PMSC	Private Maritime Security Company
PRC	Peoples Republic of China
PTI	Press trust of India
ReCAAP	Regional Cooperation Agreement for Combating Piracy and Armed Robbery against Ships in Asia
RMA	Revolution in military affairs
ROC	Republic of China
RoE	Rules of Engagement
RoI	Return on Investment
SAR	Search and Rescue
SIDS	Small Island Developing States
SLOC	Sea Lines of Communication
SLOT	Sea Lanes of Traffic
SOLAS	Safety of Life at Sea
SPQ	Sea Power Quotient
SSN	Submarine (Submersible) Ship Nuclear
TAAF	*Terres Australes et Antarctiques Françaises*
TDV	Training, Development and Validation
TMC	Threat Matrix Cube
U^2V	Unmanned Underwater Vehicle
UCV	Unmanned Combat Vehicle
UAV	Unmanned Aerial Vehicle
UFO	Unidentified Flying Object
UN	United Nations
UNCLOS	United Nations Convention on the Law of the Sea

UNDP	United Nations Development Programme
UNEP	United Nations Environment Programme
UNESCO	United Nations Educational Scientific and Cultural organisation
UNCTAD	United Nations Conference on Trade and Development
UNIPCC	United Nations Intergovernmental Panel on Climate Change
US	United States
USA	United States of America
USI	United Service Institution of India
USSR	Union of Soviet Socialist Republics
VPD	Vessel Protection Detachment
WHO	World Health Organisation
WIG	Wing-in-Ground
WIGEV	Wing in Ground Effect Vehicle
WMD	Weapons of Mass Destruction
WMU	World Maritime University
WTO	World Trade Organisation

APPENDICES

Appendix A

(Refers to Chapter 2)

Geopolitical Entities of the World (2013)

	Entity	*Nature*	*Land Border (km)*	*Coastline (km)*	*Ocean link*
UN Members					
1	Afghanistan (1946)	Landlocked	5,529	--	--
2	Albania (1955)	Coastland	717	362	Atlantic Ocean
3	Algeria (1962)	Coastland	6,343	998	Atlantic Ocean
4	Andorra (1993)	Landlocked	120	--	--
5	Angola (1976)	Coastland	5,198	1,600	Atlantic Ocean
6	Antigua and Barbuda (1981)	Island	--	153	Atlantic Ocean
7	Argentina (1945)	Coastland	9,861	4,989	Atlantic Ocean
8	Armenia (1992)	Landlocked	1,254	--	--
9	Australia (1945)	Island	--	25,760	Indian Ocean Pacific Ocean

	Entity	***Nature***	***Land Border (km)***	***Coastline (km)***	***Ocean link***
10	Austria (1955)	Landlocked	2,562	--	--
11	Azerbaijan (1992)	Landlocked	2.013	--	--
12	Bahamas (1973)	Island	--	3,542	Atlantic Ocean
13	Bahrain (1971)	Island	--	161	Indian Ocean
14	Bangladesh (1974)	Coastland	4,246	580	Indian Ocean
15	Barbados (1966)	Island	--	97	Atlantic Ocean
16	Belarus (1945)	Landlocked	3,098	--	--
17	Belgium (1945)	Coastland	1,385	67	Atlantic Ocean
18	Belize (1981)	Coastland	516	386	Atlantic Ocean
19	Benin (1960)	Coastland	1,989	121	Atlantic Ocean
20	Bhutan (1971)	Landlocked	1,075	--	--
21	Bolivia (Plurinational State of (1945)	Landlocked	6,940	--	--
22	Bosnia and Herzegovina (1992)	Coastland	1,538	20	Atlantic Ocean
23	Botswana (1966)	Landlocked	4,013	--	--
24	Brazil (1945)	Coastland	1,6885	7,491	Atlantic Ocean
25	Brunei Darussalam (1984)	Coastland	381	161	Atlantic Ocean
26	Bulgaria ((1955)	Coastland	1,808	354	Atlantic Ocean
27	Burkina Faso (1960)	Landlocked	3,193	--	--
28	Burundi (1962)	Landlocked	974	--	--
29	Cambodia (1955)	Coastland	2,572	443	Pacific Ocean
30	Cameroon (1960)	Coastland	4,591	402	Atlantic Ocean
31	Canada (1945)	Coastland	8,893	202,080	Arctic Ocean Atlantic Ocean Pacific Ocean

	Entity	*Nature*	*Land Border (km)*	*Coastline (km)*	*Ocean link*
32	Cape Verde (1975)	Island	--	965	Atlantic Ocean
33	Central African Republic (1960)	Landlocked	5,203	--	--
34	Chad (1960)	Landlocked	5,968	--	--
35	Chile (1945)	Coastland	6,339	6,435	Pacific Ocean
36	China (1945)	Coastland	22,117	14,500	Pacific Ocean
37	Colombia (1945)	Coastland	6,309	3,208	Pacific Ocean
38	Comoros (1975)	Island	--	340	Indian Ocean
39	Congo (1960)	Coastland	5,504	169	Atlantic Ocean
40	Costa Rica (1945)	Coastland	639	1,290	Atlantic Ocean Pacific Ocean
41	Côte d'Ivoire (1960)	Coastland	3,110	515	Atlantic Ocean
42	Croatia (1992)	Coastland	2,197	5,835	Atlantic Ocean
43	Cuba (1945)	Coastland	29	3,735	Atlantic Ocean
44	Cyprus (1960)	Coastland	150	648	Atlantic Ocean
45	Czech Republic (1993)	Landlocked	2,290	--	--
46	Democratic People's Republic of Korea (1991)	Coastland	1,673	2,495	Pacific Ocean
47	Democratic Republic of the Congo (1960)	Coastland	10,730	37	Atlantic Ocean
48	Denmark (1945)	Coastland	68	7,314	Atlantic Ocean
49	Djibouti (1977)	Coastland	516	314	Indian Ocean
50	Dominica (1978)	Island	--	148	Atlantic Ocean
51	Dominican Republic (1945)	Coastland	360	1,288	Atlantic Ocean

	Entity	*Nature*	*Land Border (km)*	*Coastline (km)*	*Ocean link*
52	Ecuador (1945)	Coastland	2,010	2,237	Pacific Ocean
53	Egypt (1945)	Coastland	2,665	2,450	Atlantic Ocean Indian Ocean
54	El Salvador (1945)	Coastland	545	307	Pacific ocean
55	Equatorial Guinea (1968)	Coastland	539	296	Atlantic Ocean
56	Eritrea (1993)	Coastland	1,626	2,234	Indian Ocean
57	Estonia (1991)	Coastland	633	3,794	Atlantic Ocean
58	Ethiopia (1945)	Landlocked	5,328	--	--
59	Fiji (1970)	Island	--	1,129	Pacific Ocean
60	Finland (1995)	Coastland	2,681	1,250	Atlantic Ocean
61	France (1945)	Coastland	2,889	4,668	Atlantic Ocean
62	Gabon (1960)	Coastland	2,551	885	Atlantic Ocean
63	Gambia (1965)	Coastland	740	80	Atlantic Ocean
64	Georgia (1992)	Coastland	1,461	310	Atlantic Ocean
65	Germany (1973)	Coastland	3,621	2,389	Atlantic Ocean
66	Ghana (1957)	Coastland	2,094	539	Atlantic Ocean
67	Greece (1945)	Coastland	1,228	13,676	Atlantic Ocean
68	Grenada (1974)	Island	--	121	Atlantic Ocean
69	Guatemala (1945)	Coastland	1,687	400	Atlantic Ocean Pacific ocean

	Entity	*Nature*	*Land Border (km)*	*Coastline (km)*	*Ocean link*
70	Guinea (1958)	Coastland	3,3399	320	Atlantic ocean
71	Guinea-Bissau (1974)	Coastland	724	350	Atlantic Ocean
72	Guyana ((1966)	Coastland	743	459	Atlantic Ocean
73	Haiti (1945)	Coastland	360	1,771	Atlantic Ocean
74	Honduras (1945)	Coastland	1,520	820	Atlantic Ocean Pacific Ocean
75	Hungary (1955)	Landlocked	2,171	--	--
76	Iceland (1946)	Island	--	4,970	Arctic Ocean Atlantic Ocean
77	India (1945)	Coastland	14,103	7,517	Indian Ocean
78	Indonesia (1950)	Coastland	2,830	54,716	Indian Ocean Pacific Ocean
79	Iran (Islamic Republic of) (1945)	Coastland	5,440	2,440	Indian Ocean
80	Iraq (1945)	Coastland	3,650	58	Indian Ocean
81	Ireland (1955)	Coastland	360	1,448	Atlantic Ocean
82	Israel (1949)	Coastland	1,017	273	Atlantic Ocean
83	Italy (1955)	Coastland	1,932	7,600	Atlantic Ocean
84	Jamaica (1962)	Island	--	1,022	Atlantic Ocean
85	Japan (1956)	Island	--	35,000	Pacific Ocean
86	Jordan (1955)	Coastland	1,635	26	Indian Ocean
87	Kazakhstan (1992)	Landlocked	12,012	--	--

	Entity	***Nature***	***Land Border (km)***	***Coastline (km)***	***Ocean link***
88	Kenya (1963)	Coastland	3,477	536	Indian Ocean
89	Kiribati (1999)	Island	11	1,143	Pacific Ocean
90	Kuwait (1963)	Coastland	462	499	Indian Ocean
91	Kyrgyzstan (1992)	Landlocked	3,878	--	--
92	Lao Peoples Democratic Republic (1955)	Landlocked	5,083	--	--
93	Latvia (1991)	Coastland	1,348	498	Atlantic Ocean
94	Lebanon (1945)	Coastland	454	225	Atlantic Ocean
95	Lesotho (1966)	Landlocked	909	--	--
96	Liberia (1945)	Coastland	1,585	579	Atlantic Ocean
97	Libya (1955)	Coastland	4,348	1,770	Atlantic Ocean
98	Liechtenstein (1990)	Landlocked	76	--	--
99	Lithuania (1991)	Coastland	1,644	90	Atlantic Ocean
100	Luxembourg (1945)	Landlocked	359	--	--
101	Madagascar (1960)	Island	--	4,828	Indian Ocean
102	Malawi (1964)	Landlocked	2,881	--	--
103	Malaysia (1957)	Coastland	2,669	4,675	Atlantic Ocean Indian Ocean
104	Maldives (1965)	Island	--	644	Indian Ocean
105	Mali (1960)	Landlocked	7,243	--	--
106	Malta (1964)	Island	--	197	Atlantic Ocean
107	Marshall Islands (1991)	Island	--	370	Pacific Ocean
108	Mauritania (1961)	Coastland	5,074	754	Atlantic Ocean
109	Mauritius (1968)	Island	--	177	Indian ocean

	Entity	*Nature*	*Land Border (km)*	*Coastline (km)*	*Ocean link*
110	Mexico (1945)	Coastland	4,353	9,330	Atlantic Ocean Pacific Ocean
111	Micronesia (Federated States of) (1991)	Island	--	6,112	Pacific Ocean
112	Monaco (1993)	Coastland	4	4	Atlantic Ocean
113	Mongolia (1961)	Landlocked	8,220	--	--
114	Montenegro (2006)	Coastland	625	294	Atlantic Ocean
115	Morocco (1956)	Coastland	2,018	1,835	Atlantic Ocean
116	Mozambique (1975)	Coastland	4,571	2,470	Indian Ocean
117	Myanmar (1948)	Coastland	5,876	1,930	Indian Ocean
118	Namibia (1990)	Coastland	3,936	1,572	Atlantic Ocean
119	Nauru (1999)	Island	--	30	Pacific Ocean
120	Nepal (1955)	Landlocked	2,926	--	--
121	Netherlands (1945)	Coastland	1,027	451	Atlantic Ocean
122	New Zealand (1945)	Island	--	15,134	Pacific Ocean
123	Nicaragua (1945)	Coastland	1,231	910	Atlantic Ocean Pacific Ocean
124	Niger (1960)	Landlocked	5,697	--	--
125	Nigeria (1960)	Coastland	4,047	853	Atlantic Ocean
126	Norway (1945)	Coastland	2,542	25,148	Arctic Ocean Atlantic Ocean
127	Oman (1971)	Coastland	1,374	2,092	Indian Ocean

	Entity	*Nature*	*Land Border (km)*	*Coastline (km)*	*Ocean link*
128	Pakistan (1947)	Coastland	6,774	1,046	Indian Ocean
129	Palau (1994)	Island	--	1,519	Pacific Ocean
130	Panama (1945)	Coastland	555	2,490	Atlantic Ocean Pacific Ocean
131	Papua New Guinea (1975)	Coastland	820	5,152	Pacific Ocean
132	Paraguay (1945)	Landlocked	3,995	--	--
133	Peru (1945)	Coastland	7,461	2,414	Pacific Ocean
134	Philippines (1945)	Island	--	36,289	Pacific Ocean
135	Poland (1945)	Coastland	3,071	440	Atlantic Ocean
136	Portugal (1955)	Coastland	1,214	1,793	Atlantic Ocean
137	Qatar (1971)	Coastland	60	563	Indian Ocean
138	Republic of Korea (1991)	Coastland	238	2,413	Pacific Ocean
139	Republic of Moldova (1992)	Landlocked	1,389	--	--
140	Romania (1955)	Coastland	2,508	225	Atlantic Ocean
141	Russian Federation (1945)	Coastland	20,097	37,653	Arctic Ocean Pacific Ocean
142	Rwanda (1962)	Landlocked	893	--	--
143	Saint Kitts and Nevis (1983)	Island	--	135	Atlantic Ocean
144	Saint Lucia (1979)	Island	--	158	Atlantic Ocean
145	Saint Vincent and the Grenadines (1980)	Island	--	84	Atlantic Ocean
146	Samoa (1976)	Island	--	403	Atlantic Ocean

	Entity	*Nature*	*Land Border (km)*	*Coastline (km)*	*Ocean link*
147	San Marino (1992)	Landlocked	39	--	--
148	Sao Tome and Principe (1975)	Coastland	--	209	Atlantic Ocean
149	Saudi Arabia (1945)	Coastland	4,431	2,640	Indian Ocean
150	Senegal (1960)	Coastland	2,640	531	Atlantic Ocean
151	Serbia (2000)	Landlocked	2,026	--	--
152	Seychelles (1976)	Island	--	491	Indian Ocean
153	Sierra Leone (1961)	Coastland	958	402	Atlantic Ocean
154	Singapore (1965)	Island	--	193	Indian Ocean Pacific Ocean
155	Slovakia (1993)	Landlocked	1,524	--	--
156	Slovenia (1992)	Coastland	1,370	47	Atlantic Ocean
157	Solomon Islands (1978)	Island	--	5,313	Pacific Ocean
158	Somalia (1960)	Coastland	2,340	3,025	Indian Ocean
159	South Africa (1945)	Coastland	4,862	2,798	Atlantic Ocean Indian Ocean
160	South Sudan (2011)	Landlocked	5,413	--	--
161	Spain (1955)	Coastland	1,918	4,964	Atlantic Ocean
162	Sri Lanka (1955)	Island	--	1,340	Indian Ocean
163	Sudan (1956)	Coastland	6,751	853	Indian Ocean
164	Suriname (1975)	Coastland	1,703	386	Atlantic Ocean
165	Swaziland (1968)	Landlocked	535	--	--
166	Sweden (1946)	Coastland	2,233	3,218	Atlantic Ocean
167	Switzerland (2002)	Landlocked	1,852	--	--

	Entity	*Nature*	*Land Border (km)*	*Coastline (km)*	*Ocean link*
168	Syrian Arab Republic (1945)	Coastland	2,253	193	Atlantic Ocean
169	Tajikistan (1992)	Landlocked	3,651	--	--
170	Thailand	Coastland	4,863	3,219	Indian Ocean Pacific Ocean
171	The Former Yugoslav Republic of Macedonia (1993)	Landlocked	766	--	--
172	Timor-Leste (2002)	Coastland	228	706	Pacific Ocean
173	Togo (1960)	Coastland	1,647	56	Atlantic Ocean
174	Tonga (1999)	Island	--	419	Pacific Ocean
175	Trinidad and Tobago (1962)	Island	--	362	Atlantic Ocean
176	Tunisia (1956)	Coastland	1,424	1,148	Atlantic Ocean
177	Turkey (1945)	Coastland	2.648	7,200	Atlantic Ocean
178	Turkmenistan (1992)	Landlocked	3,736	--	--
179	Tuvalu (2000)	Island	--	24	Pacific Ocean
180	Uganda (1962)	Landlocked	2,698	--	--
181	Ukraine (1945)	Coastland	4,663	2,782	Atlantic Ocean
182	United Arab Emirates (1975)	Coastland	867	1,318	Indian Ocean
183	United Kingdom of Great Britain and Northern Ireland (1945)	Coastland	360	12,429	Atlantic Ocean
184	United Republic of Tanzania (1961)	Coastland	3,861	1,424	Indian Ocean
185	United States of America (1945)	Coastland	12,034	19,924	Arctic ocean Atlantic Ocean Pacific Ocean

	Entity	***Nature***	***Land Border (km)***	***Coastline (km)***	***Ocean link***
186	Uruguay (1945)	Coastland	1,648	660	Atlantic Ocean
187	Uzbekistan (1992)	Landlocked	6,221	--	--
188	Vanuatu (1981)	Island	--	2,528	Pacific Ocean
189	Venezuela (Bolivarian Republic of) (1945)	Coastland	743	2,800	Atlantic Ocean
190	Viet Nam (1977)	Coastland	4,639	3,444	Pacific Ocean
191	Yemen (1947)	Coastland	1,746	1,906	Indian Ocean
192	Zambia (1964)	Landlocked	5,664	--	--
193	Zimbabwe (1980)	Landlocked	3,066	--	--
Territories					
194	Adélie Land (France)	Coastland	5,210	350	Southern Ocean
195	Akrotiri (UK)	Coastland	47	56	Atlantic Ocean
196	American Samoa (U.S.A.)	Island	--	116	Pacific Ocean
197	Anguilla (UK)	Island	--	61	Atlantic Ocean
198	Aruba (Netherlands)	Island	--	69	Atlantic Ocean
199	Ashmore and Cartier Islands (Australia)	Island	--	74	Indian Ocean
200	Baker Islands (U.S.A.)	Island	--	5	Pacific Ocean
201	Basses da India (Iles Eparses) (France)	Island	--	35	Indian Ocean
202	Bermuda (UK)	Island	--	103	Atlantic Ocean
203	Bouvet Island (Norway)	Island	--	30	Atlantic Ocean
204	British Indian Ocean Territory (UK)	Island	--	698	Indian Ocean
205	British Virgin Islands (UK)	Island	--	80	Atlantic Ocean
206	Cayman Islands (UK)	Island	--	160	Atlantic Ocean

	Entity	*Nature*	*Land Border (km)*	*Coastline (km)*	*Ocean link*
207	Christmas Island (Australia)	Island	--	139	Indian Ocean
208	Clipperton Island (France)	Island	--	11	Pacific Ocean
209	Cocos (Keeling) Islands (Australia)	Island	--	26	Indian Ocean
210	Cook Islands (New Zealand)	Island	--	120	Pacific Ocean
211	Coral Sea Islands (Australia)	Island	--	3,095	Pacific Ocean
212	Dhekelia (UK)	Coastland	103	28	Atlantic Ocean
213	Europa Island (France)	Island	--	22	Indian Ocean
214	Falkland Island (UK)	Island	--	1,288	Atlantic Ocean
215	Faroe Islands (Denmark)	Island	--	1,117	Atlantic Ocean
216	French Guiana (France)	Coastland	1,183	378	Atlantic Ocean
217	French Polynesia (France)	Island	--	2,525	Pacific Ocean
218	Glorioso Islands (France)	Island	--	35	Indian Ocean
219	Gibraltar (UK)	Coastland	1	12	Atlantic Ocean
220	Greenland (Denmark)	Island	--	44,087	Arctic Ocean Atlantic Ocean
221	Guadeloupe (France)	Island	--	306	Atlantic Ocean
222	Guam (U.S.A.)	Island	--	126	Pacific Ocean
223	Guantánamo Bay (U.S.A)	Coastland	29	18	Atlantic Ocean
224	Guernsey (UK)	Island	--	50	Atlantic Ocean
225	Heard Island and McDonald Islands (Australia)	Island	--	102	Indian Ocean

	Entity	*Nature*	*Land Border (km)*	*Coastline (km)*	*Ocean link*
226	Hong Kong (China)	Coastland	30	733	Pacific Ocean
227	Howland Island (U.S.A.)	Island	--	6	Pacific Ocean
228	Ile Amsterdam et Ile Saint Paul (France)	Island	--	28	Indian Ocean
229	Ile Crozet (France)	Island	--	36	Indian Ocean
230	Iles Kerguelan (France)	Island	--	2,800	Indian Ocean
231	Isle of Man (UK)	Island	--	160	Atlantic Ocean
232	Jan Mayen (Norway)	Island	--	124	Arctic Ocean
233	Jarvis Island (U.S.A.)	Island	--	8	Pacific Ocean
234	Jersey (UK)	Island	--	70	Atlantic Ocean
235	Johnston Atoll (U.S.A.)	Island		34	Pacific Ocean
236	Juan de Nova Island (France)	Island	--	24	Indian Ocean
237	Kingman Reef (U.S.A.)	Island	--	3	Pacific Ocean
238	Macau (China)	Coastland	0.34	41	Pacific Ocean
239	Martinique (France)	Island	--	350	Atlantic Ocean
240	Mayotte (France)	Island	--	185	Indian Ocean
241	Midway Islands (U.S.A.)	Island		15	Pacific Ocean
242	Montserrat (UK)	Island	--	40	Atlantic Ocean
243	Navassa Island (U.S.A.)	Island	--	8	Atlantic Ocean
244	Netherlands Antilles (Netherlands)	Coastland	15	364	Atlantic Ocean
245	New Caledonia (France)	Island	--	2,254	Pacific Ocean

	Entity	*Nature*	*Land Border (km)*	*Coastline (km)*	*Ocean link*
246	Niue (New Zealand)	Island	--	64	Pacific Ocean
247	Norfolk Island (Australia)	Island	--	32	Pacific Ocean
248	Northern Mariana Islands (U.S.A.)	Island	--	1,482	Pacific Ocean
249	Palmyra Atoll (U.S.A.)	Island	--	15	Pacific Ocean
250	Paracel Islands (China)	Island	--	518	Pacific Ocean
251	Pitcairn Islands (UK)	Island	--	51	Pacific Ocean
252	Puerto Rico (U.S.A.)	Island	--	501	Atlantic Ocean
253	Reunion (France)	Island	--	207	Indian Ocean
254	Saint Barthelemy (France)	Island	--	30	Atlantic Ocean
255	Saint Helena (UK)	Island	--	100	Atlantic Ocean
256	Saint Martin (Sint Maarten) (France)	Coastland	15	59	Atlantic Ocean
257	Saint Pierre and Miquelon (France)	Island	--	120	Pacific Ocean
258	South Georgia and South Sandwich Islands (UK)	Island	--	398	Atlantic Ocean
259	Spratly Islands (China, Taiwan, Vietnam)	Island	--	926	Pacific Ocean
260	Svalbard (Norway)	Island	--	3,587	Arctic Ocean
261	Tokelau (New Zealand)	Island	--	101	Pacific Ocean
262	Tromelin Island (France)	Island	--	4	Indian Ocean
263	Turks and Caicos Islands (UK)	Island	--	389	Atlantic Ocean
264	Virgin Islands (U.S.A.)	Island	--	188	Atlantic Ocean

	Entity	*Nature*	*Land Border (km)*	*Coastline (km)*	*Ocean link*
265	Wake Island (U.S.A.)	Island	--	19.3	Pacific Ocean
266	Wallis and Futuna	Island	--	129	Pacific Ocean
Other Entities					
267	Abkhazia	Coastland	Dispute	Dispute	Atlantic Ocean
268	Antarctica		--	17,968	Southern Ocean
269	European Union	Coastland	12,441	65,993	Atlantic Ocean Arctic ocean
270	Gaza Strip and West Bank	Coastland	466	40	Atlantic Ocean
271	Kosovo	Landlocked	352	--	--
272	Nagorno-Karabakh	Landlocked	Dispute	Dispute	--
273	Palestine	Coastland	466	40	Atlantic Ocean
274	South Ossetia	Landlocked	Dispute	--	--
275	Taiwan	Island	--	1,566	Pacific ocean
276	Transnistria	Landlocked	Dispute	Dispute	--
277	Western Sahara	Coastland	2.046	1,110	Atlantic Ocean
278	Vatican City	Landlocked	3	-	-

Appendix B

(Refers to Chapter 2)

Member States of International Maritime Organisation [1](2013)

1	Albania	1993
2	Algeria	1963
3	Angola	1977
4	Antigua and Barbuda	1986
5	Argentina	1953
6	Australia	1952
7	Austria	1975
8	Azerbaijan	1995
9	Bahamas	1976
10	Bahrain	1976
11	Bangladesh	1976
12	Barbados	1970
13	Belgium	1951
14	Belize	1990
15	Benin	1980
16	Bolivia (Plurinational State of)	1987
17	Bosnia and Herzegovina	1993
18	Brazil	1963
19	Brunei Darussalam	1984
20	Bulgaria	1960
21	Cambodia	1961
22	Cameroon	1961
23	Canada	1948
24	Cape Verde	1976

1 www.imo.org, accessed 23 August 2013

25	Chile	1972
26	China	1973
27	Colombia	1974
28	Comoros	2001
29	Congo	1975
30	Cook Islands	2008
31	Costa Rica	1981
32	Côte d'Ivoire	1960
33	Croatia	1992
34	Cuba	1966
35	Cyprus	1973
36	Czech Republic	1993
37	Democratic People's Republic of Korea	1986
38	Democratic Republic of the Congo (Formerly Zaire)	1973
39	Denmark	1959
40	Djibouti	1979
41	Dominica	1979
42	Dominican Republic	1953
43	Ecuador	1956
44	Egypt	1958
45	El Salvador	1981
46	Equatorial Guinea	1972
47	Eritrea	1993
48	Estonia	1992
49	Ethiopia	1975
50	Fiji	1983
51	Finland	1959
52	France	1952
53	Gabon	1976
54	Gambia	1979
55	Georgia	1993

56	Germany	1959
57	Ghana	1959
58	Greece	1958
59	Grenada	1998
60	Guatemala	1983
61	Guinea	1975
62	Guinea-Bissau	1977
63	Guyana	1980
64	Haiti	1953
65	Honduras	1954
66	Hungary	1970
67	Iceland	1960
68	India	1959
69	Indonesia	1961
70	Iran (Islamic Republic of)	1958
71	Iraq	1973
72	Ireland	1951
73	Israel	1952
74	Italy	1957
75	Jamaica	1976
76	Japan	1958
77	Jordan	1973
78	Kazakhstan	1994
79	Kenya	1973
80	Kiribati	2003
81	Kuwait	1960
82	Latvia	1993
83	Lebanon	1966
84	Liberia	1959
85	Libya	1970
86	Lithuania	1995
87	Luxembourg	1991

88	Madagascar	1961
89	Malawi	1989
90	Malaysia	1971
91	Maldives	1967
92	Malta	1966
93	Marshall Islands	1998
94	Mauritania	1961
95	Mauritius	1978
96	Mexico	1954
97	Monaco	1989
98	Mongolia	1996
99	Montenegro	2006
100	Morocco	1962
101	Mozambique	1979
102	Myanmar	1951
103	Namibia	1994
104	Nepal	1979
105	Netherlands	1949
106	New Zealand	1960
107	Nicaragua	1982
108	Nigeria	1962
109	Norway	1958
110	Oman	1974
111	Pakistan	1958
112	Palau	2011
113	Panama	1958
114	Papua New Guinea	1976
115	Paraguay	1993
116	Peru	1968
117	Philippines	1964
118	Poland	1960
119	Portugal	1976

120	Qatar	1977
121	Republic of Korea	1962
122	Republic of Moldova	2001
123	Romania	1965
124	Russian Federation	1958
125	Saint Kitts and Nevis	2001
126	Saint Lucia	1980
127	Saint Vincent and the Grenadines	1981
128	Samoa	1996
129	San Marino	2002
130	Sao Tome and Principe	1990
131	Saudi Arabia	1969
132	Senegal	1960
133	Serbia	2000
134	Seychelles	1978
135	Sierra Leone	1973
136	Singapore	1966
137	Slovakia	1993
138	Slovenia	1993
139	Solomon Islands	1988
140	Somalia	1978
141	South Africa	1995
142	Spain	1962
143	Sri Lanka	1972
144	Sudan	1974
145	Suriname	1976
146	Sweden	1959
147	Switzerland	1955
148	Syrian Arab Republic	1963
149	Thailand	1973
150	The former Yugoslav Republic of Macedonia	1993
151	Timor-Leste	2005

152	Togo	1983
153	Tonga	2000
154	Trinidad and Tobago	1965
155	Tunisia	1963
156	Turkey	1958
157	Turkmenistan	1993
158	Tuvalu	2004
159	Uganda	2009
160	Ukraine	1994
161	United Arab Emirates	1980
162	United Kingdom of Great Britain and Northern Ireland	1949
163	United Republic of Tanzania	1974
164	United States of America	1950
165	Uruguay	1968
166	Vanuatu	1986
167	Venezuela (Bolivarian Republic of)	1975
168	Viet Nam	1984
169	Yemen	1979
170	Zimbabwe	2005
	Associate Members:	
1	Faroes	2002
2	Hong Kong, China	1967
3	Macao, China	1990

Appendix C

(Refers to Chapter 3)

Evolution of Elements of National Security

Origin		*Definition Dilemma*	*Constituent Elements*	*Elements Identified for Examination*
1	Prehistoric	Survival	Physical security	Muscle power
2	Hunters	Survival	Physical security	Muscle power, primitive weapons.
3	Epics	Survival	Physical security	Campaigns
4	Spirituality	Supplements needs in the perceived security gap	Mental aspects for existential balance	Religion and inner self
5	Yale undergraduates (1790)	Earliest reference to the term national security	Fostering domestic industries	Non-military security for military security
6	Adler (1870-1937)	Apparent security	Communal living	Organised protection
7	Maslow (1908-1970)	Hierarchy of needs	Physical and psychological needs	Existentialistic deeds
8	US Senate (1945)	Security is not just defence	Other than the navy and army	Non-military aspects
9	NSC (US) (1947)	Flexible for wider use	Value based protection for freedom	Military and non-military
10	Lasswell (1950)	Balancing instruments of policy	Arms, diplomacy, information, economics	Military, and non-military

Origin		*Definition Dilemma*	*Constituent Elements*	*Elements Identified for Examination*
11	Wolfers (1962)	Absence of threats and fear	Value based protection	Military and non-military.
12	IDSA (India) (1965)	Ambiguity	National defence and national security	Military and non-military
13	International Encyclopaedia of Social Sciences (1968)	Power to protect external threats	Value protection	Military and non-military
14	Blair (1972)	Dependency on economics	Balance of payments and foreign assistance	Non-military
15	Moss (1973)	Ill defined phrase	Freedom of information	Non-military security
16	Yale Law Review (1976)	National military capability	Military to protect interests	Military security
17	Brown (1977)	Non-military	Energy, environment, climate, economy, illegal immigration, food.	Non-military security
18	Taylor, Maxwell (1979)	Non-military threats and the State	Energy, population, economy, technology, international trade, inflation.	Military and non-military security.
19	Taylor, William (1981)	Larger scope than physical security	Protection of values and vitality	Military and non-military
20	Ullman (1983)	Threat based perception	Quality of life, policy choices	Military and non-military

Origin		*Definition Dilemma*	*Constituent Elements*	*Elements Identified for Examination*
21	Buzan (1983)	Power maximisation	political and military power as leverage for domestic affairs	Power: military and political
22	Mathews, Jessica (1989)	Broadening definition	Resource, demography, environment	Military and non-military
23	Maier (1990)	Power to control domestic and foreign conditions	Self-determination, autonomy, wellbeing, prosperity,	Military and non-military
24	Moran (1990/91)	Cold War fixation	Soviet Union, International relations, globalisation, energy, economics, narcotics	Military and non-military
25	Lippman (1993)	National military capability	Military to protect other interests	Military security
26	NDC seminar (India) (1996)	Multidimensional	Politics, environment, economics, defence, culture, technology, resources, military	Military and non-military
27	Chinoy, Anuradha (2000)	State security	Maintaining political and other structures with military might	Military security

Origin		Definition Dilemma	Constituent Elements	Elements Identified for Examination
28	Saighal (2000)	Overstretched. Need to redefine.	Military, economics, global power support, strong UN institutions, unidentified factors	Military and non-military security
29	Saighal (2000)	Insecurity model	Economic vulnerability, reduced military might, political unrest, social unrest	Chaotic situation edging towards disorder
30	Kargil report (2001)	Military security	Military security against intelligence	Military security
31	Report of the Group of Ministers, India (2001)	Military security	Border security, intelligence, unified command concept	Military security combined with non-military
32	Paleri (author) (2002)	Apparent wellbeing of the people of a nation measurable through National Security Index (NSI)	15 identified elements	Military security through intelligent military might, and non-military security. NSI needs to be researched.

ANNEXURE

(Refers to preface)

SAGAR MANTHAN AND THE SYMBOLISM OF OCEAN PROPERTY

Sagar manthan or *samudra manthan* means churning of the ocean.[1] According to the story depicted in the ancient Indian scriptures, *Bhagavata Purana*, *Mahabharata* and *Vishnu Purana,* whose exact dates are not known but estimated to be around 4,000 years into the past, *suras* and the *asuras,* the juxtaposed power seeking deities jointly churned the ocean for accruing untold benefits using a mountain as the churning rod and a snake as the rope.[2]

The process of churning was at the cosmic level that produced many things precious as well as toxic according to the different versions of the scriptures, ultimately generating the ambrosia (*amrit),* the nectar of immortality, the desire ultimate for which fierce fighting ensued between both the parties.

The allegorical description of the story points out towards the awakening of self through meditation with symbolism of concentrating the mind for achieving "immortality" or the ultimate bliss in a controlled life. Here the ocean is the mind or the consciousness. The *suras* and *asuras* combine the juxtaposing pleasure and pain principles within

1 *Sagar or Samudra.*

2 The mountain was *Mount Mandarachala* and the snake was the king of *serpents Vasuki.*

the self. The mountain as the churning rod stands for concentration and the snake for the force of controlled desire. There is more.

But the interest of this study is in the depiction and understanding of the ocean by a human system, nearly 40 centuries or so old, if not older, as a realm of infinite hope and prosperity that is difficult to conquer. The description of ocean as an allegory of the complex human mind, as a provider of everything, in such an ancient treatise is a find by itself. Thousands of years back humans were aware of the importance of the ocean to the extent that they used it as an allegorical symbol to describe what they considered complex. Humans were aware of the ocean and the treasures and dangers associated with it, and more so as a provider of life and its necessities.

They are hidden in the "ocean property."

But does it also have a discrete message that the ocean cannot be exploited without conflict? It cannot be, because the description here is about the complexity of human mind, not the ocean.

SELECT BIBLIOGRAPHY

1. Adams, James, *The Next World War,* London, Arrow, 1998.
2. Addington, Larry H., *The Patterns of War since the Eighteenth Century,* Bloomington, Indiana University Press, 1984.
3. Adler, Alfred, *Understanding Human Nature,* New Delhi, Research Press, 1999.
4. Allen, Benedict, (ed.), *The Faber Book of Explorations,* London, Faber and Faber, 2002.
5. Allison, Graham T., *Essentials of Decision: Explaining the Cuban Missile Crisis,* Harvard, Harper Colins Publishers, 1971.
6. Armesto, Felipe Fernandez, *Civilizations,* London, Macmillan, 2000.
7. ----, *Millennium,* New York, Touchstone, 1996.
8. Armstrong, Karen, *A History of God,* London, Mandarin, 1994.
9. Arunachalam, B, (ed.), *Essays in Maritime Studies,* Mumbai, Maritime History Society, 1998.
10. ---, *Riding the Waves,* New Delhi, National Institute of Science Communication, 1997.
11. Audi, Robert, (ed.), *The Cambridge Dictionary of Philosophy,* Cambridge, Cambridge University Press, 1999.
12. Balasubramanian, *Corporate Governance and Stewardship,* New Delhi, Tata McGraw-Hill Education Private Limited, 2010
13. Basu, Durga Das, *Short Constitution of India,* Agra, Wadhwa and Company, 1999.
14. Bergman, Charles, *Orion's Legacy-- A Cultural History of Man as a Hunter,* New York, Plume, 1996.

15. Berkowitz, Bruce D., *Strategic Intelligence for American National Security*, Princeton, Princeton University Press, 1991.
16. Bhagawat, Vishnu, *Betrayal of the Defence Forces,* New Delhi, Manas Publications, 2001.
17. Bhandarkar, K. R., *Maritime Law of India,* Mumbai, Bhandarkar Publications, 1979.
18. Blainey, Geoffrey, A *Short History of the World,* New Delhi, Penguin Books, 2000.
19. Briggs, John, and F. Davit Peat, *Turbulent Mirror,* New York, Harper and Row, 1990.
20. Brown, Paul, *Global Warming: Can Civilisations Survive?,* Hyderabad, University Press (India) Ltd., 1998.
21. Brown, R.A.M., M.S.V. Namboodiri, N. K. Negi, and Santosh Rawat, (eds.), *From Surprise to Reckoning—the Kargil Committee Report,* New Delhi, Sage Publications, 1999.
22. Burrows, William E. and Robert Windrem, *Critical Mass,* New York, Simon and Shuster, 1994.
23. Butler, Richard, *Saddam Defiant,* London, Phoenix, 2000.
24. Byres, Terrence J, (ed.), *The Indian Economy,* New Delhi, Oxford University Press, 1998.
25. Capra, F., *The Turning Point, Science, Society and the Rising Culture,* London, Flamingo, 1982.
26. Castledon, Rodney, *World History,* London, Paragon, 1994.
27. Chandra, Bipan, *History of Modern India,* Hyderabad, Orient Blackswan, 2009.
28. Chairman, Commission on the Bicentennial of the United States Constitution, *The Constitution of the United States*, Washington, D.C., 1986.
29. Chairman, Joint Chiefs of Staff, United States of America, *Joint Pub 1: Joint Warfare of the US Armed Forces,* Washington, D.C., National Defence University Press, 1991.
30. Chaliand, Gerard, and Jean-Pierre Rageau, *The Strategic Atlas: A Comparative Geopolitics of World Powers,* New York, Harper Perennial, 1992.

31. Charney, Jonathan I, and Alexander M Lewis, (eds.), *International Maritime Boundaries,* 3 Vols., London, The American Society for International Law, 1996 (Vols. 1 & 2), 1998 (Vol. 3).
32. Chaudhary, P. N., and W. Selvamurthy, (eds.), *Battle Scene in Year 2020,* New Delhi, Defence Institute of Psychological Research, (Year not mentioned).
33. Chomsky, Noam, *Deterring Democracy,* London, Vintage, 1992.
34. Churchill, Winston S, *The Second World War,* London, Penguin, 1959.
35. Clavel, James, (ed.), *The Art of War by Sun Tzu,* New York, Delta, 1988.
36. Cleary, Thomas, *The Japanese Art of War,* Boston, Shambala Publications, 1992.
37. ----, *The Lost Art of War--Sun Tzu II,* New York, Harper, 1996.
38. Coakely, Thomas, P., *Command and Control for War and Peace,* Washington, D.C., National Defence University Press, 1992.
39. Congdon, Don, (ed.), *Combat: World War I,* New York, Dell Publishing Co., Inc., 1965.
40. Cookson, John, and Judith Nottingham, *A Survey of Chemical and Biological Warfare,* New York, Modern Reader, 1969.
41. Corbett, Julian S., *Some Principle of Maritime Strategy,* Annapolis, Naval Institute Press, 1988.
42. Cotterell, Arthur, (ed.), *World Mythology,* London, Paragon, 2000.
43. Cronin, Patrick M., *From Globalism to Regionalism: New Perspectives on U.S. Foreign and Defence Policies,* Washington D.C., National Defence University, 1993.
44. Curry, Patrick, and Oscar Zarate, *Machiavelli for Beginners,* Cambridge, Icon Books Ltd., 1998.
45. Daft, Richard, L. *Leadership,* New Delhi, Cengage Learning, 2005.
46. Danino, Michel, and Sujata Nahar, *The Invasion that Never Was,* Mysore, Mira Aditi, 1996.
47. Davidson, Mike, *The Grand Strategist,* London, Macmillan, 1992.
48. Dawkins, Richard, *The Selfish Gene,* New Delhi, Oxford University Press, 2007,

49. De Bono, Edward, *Tactics: the Art and Sceince of Success,* London, Fontana/Collins, 1985.
50. Deibel, Terry L, and John Lewis Gaddis, (eds.), Containment: *Concept and Policy*, Vols. I and II, Washington, D.C., National Defence University Press, 1986.
51. Demarest, Geoff, *Geoproperty,* London, Frank Cass, 1998.
52. Detter, Ingrid, *The Laws of War,* Cambridge, Cambridge University Press, 2000.
53. Dissanyake, Wimal, and Sunil Sarath Perera, *Self, Environment, and Communication,* Sri Lanka, Ministry of Environment and Parliamentary Affairs, 1991.
54. Dixit, K.N., *Across Borders,* New Delhi, Picus Books, 1998.
55. Dozier, Rush W. Jr., *Why We Hate: Understanding, Curbing and Eliminating Hate in Ourselves and Our World,* New Delhi, Tata McGraw-Hill Publishing Company Limited, 2003.
56. The Economist, *Pocket World in Figures,* London, Profile Books, 1999.
57. Ellen, Eric, *International Maritime Fraud,* London, Sweet & Maxwell, 1981.
58. Eyesenck, H. J., *Sense and Nonsense in Psychology,* Harmondsworth, Penguin Books, 1958.
59. Finley, M. I., *The World of Odysseus,* London, Pimlico, 1999.
60. Fromkin, David, The *Way of the World: From the Dawn of Civilisation to the Twenty-First Century*, New York, Vintage Books, 2000.
61. Gaston, James C., (ed.), *Grand Strategy and the Decision Making Process,* Washington, D.C., National Defence University Press, 1992.
62. George, T. J. S., (ed.), *India 1000 to 2000,* Chennai, Express Publications (Madurai), Ltd., 1999.
63. Gilbert, Martin, *Challenge to Civilisation: A History of the 20th Century--1952-1999,* London, HarperCollins, 1999.
64. Gill, Brinda, *Passage to India,* New Delhi, Jetwings, 2000.
65. Golden, James R, *Economics and National Strategy in the Information Age—Global Networks,* New Delhi, Macmillan India Ltd., 1994.

66. Gopal, S, (ed.), *Selected Works of Jawaharlal Nehru--Second Series, Vol. 6,* New Delhi, Jawaharlal Nehru Memorial Fund, 1987.

67. Government of India, *Report of the Group of Ministers on National Security, Recommendations on Reforming National Security System,* (Unclassified), New Delhi, 2001. Government of India, *Report of the Group of Ministers on National Security, Recommendations on Reforming National Security System,* (Unclassified), New Delhi, 2001.

68. Greene, Robert, *The 48 Laws of Power,* New Delhi, Viva Books Private Limited, 2000.

69. Greider, William, *One World Ready or Not,* New York, Touchstone, 1998.

70. Griffiths, David, N., *The Human Face of Marine Piracy—Consequences and Policy Options,* Islamabad, Fazaldad Human Rights Institute, 2012.

71. Gupta, Ranjan, *The Indian Ocean: A Political Geography,* New Delhi, Marwah Publications, 1979.

72. Haig jr., Alexander M, *Caveat,* London, Weidenfeld and Nicolson, 1984.

73. Hall, Nina, (ed.), *The New Scientist Guide to Chaos,* London, Penguin Books, 1992.

74. Hart, Liddell, B. H. *Strategy,* New York, Meridian, 1991.

75. Hawksley, Humphrey, *Dragon Fire,* London, Macmillan, 2000.

76. Hiro, Dilip, *War without End—The Rise of Islamist Terrorism and Global Response,* New Delhi, Roli Books, 2003.

77. Hitler, Adolf, *Mein Kampf,* New Delhi, Jaico Publishing House, 2004.

78. Ho, Joshua, (ed.), *Realising Safe and Secure Seas for All,* Singapore, Select Publishing, 2009.

79. Horowitz, Donald, L., *The Deadly Ethnic Riot,* New Delhi, Oxford University Press, 2002.

80. Huntington, Samuel P., *The Clash of Civilizations,* New Delhi, Penguin Books, 1997.

81. Hurdman, Charlotte, (ed.), *The Last 1000 Years,* Great Bradfield, Miles Kelly Publishing Ltd., 1999.

82. The Indian Express Team, *Inside 26/11,* New Delhi, Rupa and Co., 2009.

83. Institute for National Strategic Studies, *Strategic Assessment 1999: Priorities of a Turbulent World,* Washington, D.C., National Defence University, 1999.

84. Iyer, Subramania G, *Some Economic Aspects of British Rule in India,* Madras, Swedesamitran Press, 1903.

85. Jacob, J. F. R., *Surrender at Dacca: Birth of A Nation,* New Delhi, Manohar, 1997.

86. Jane's Information Group Limited, *Jane's Exclusive Economic Zones 1999-2000,* 1st ed., Surrey, 1999.

87. Kalam, Abdul, A. P. J. with Y. S. Y. Rajan, *India 2020: A Vision for the New Millennium,* New Delhi, Viking penguin India, 1998.

88. ---, and Sivathanu Pillai, *Envisioning an Empowered Nation—Society for Technological Transformation,* New Delhi, Tata McGraw-Hill Publishing Company Limited, 2004.

89. Kartha, Tara, *Tools of Terror,* New Delhi, Knowledge World, 1999.

90. Keay, John, *China—a History,* London, Harper Press, 2009.

91. ---, *India—A History: from the Earliest Civilisations to the Boom of the 21st Century,* London, Harper Press, 2010.

92. Keegan, John, *War and Our World,* New York, Vintage, 2000.

93. Ketelbey, C.D.M., *A History of Modern Times from 1789,* Calcutta, Oxford University Press, 1998.

94. Keylor, William R, *The Twentieth Century World--An International History,* New York, Oxford University Press, 1996.

95. Keys, David, *Catastrophe--An investigation into the Origins of the Modern World,* New York, Ballentine Books, 1999.

96. Khalilzad, Zalmay and Ian O. Lesser, (eds.), *Sources of Conflict in the 21st Century—Regional Futures and U.S. Strategy,* Dehradun, Nataraj Publishers, 1998.

97. Koithara, Verghese, *Society, State and Security—the Indian Experience,* New Delhi, Sage Publications, 1999.

98. Kurup, K. K. N., and K. M. Mathew, *Native Resistance against Portuguese--the Saga of Kunjali Marakkars*, Malappuram, Calicut University Central Co-operative Stores Ltd., 2000.

99. Kux, Dennis, *Estranged Democracies: India and the United States,* Washington, D.C., National Defence University press, 1993.

100. Lahiri, Nayanjot, (ed.), *The Decline and Fall of Indus Civilization,* Delhi, Permanent Black, 2000.

101. Landes, David, *The Wealth and Poverty of the Nations,* London, Abacus, 2000.

102. Langwiesche, William, *The Outlaw Sea—A World of Freedom, Chaos and Crime,* New York, North Point Press, 2004.

103. Machiavelli, Niccolo, *The Prince,* New York, Mentor, 1935.

104. Madan, K. D., *Life and Travels of Vasco Da Gama,* New Delhi, Asian Educational Services, 1998.

105. Mahapatra, Chintamani, *Indo-US Relations into the 21st Century,* New Delhi, Knowledge World, 1998.

106. Mangekar, D. R., *The Guilty Men of 1962,* New Delhi, Penguin Books, 1988.

107. Mangold, Tom, and Jeff Goldberg, *Plague Wars—A True Story of Biological Warfare,* London, Pan Books, 1999.

108. Mansingh, Surjit, *Historical Dictionary of India,* New Delhi, Vision Books, 1999.

109. Menon, Raja, *Maritime Strategy and Continental Wars,* London, Frank Cass, 1998.

110. ---, *A Nuclear Strategy for India,* New Delhi, Sage Publications, 2000.

111. Mishra, Rishi Kumar, *Before the Beginning and After the End: Beyond the Universe of Physics,* New Delhi, Rupa and Co., 2000.

112. Morgenthau, H. J., and K. W. Thompson, *Politics among Nations: the Struggle for Power and Peace,* New York, Alfred Knopf, 1973.

113. Niazi, A. A. K., *The Betrayal of East Pakistan,* New Delhi, Manohar, 1998.

114. Nussbaum, Martha C, and Amartya Sen, (eds.), *The Quality of Life,* New Delhi, Oxford University Press, 1993.

115. Paleri, Prabhakaran, *Coast Guards of the World and the Emerging Maritime Threats,* Tokyo, Ocean Policy Research Foundation, 2009.

116. ---, *Marine Environment—Management and People's Participation,* New Delhi, KW Publishers Private Limited, 2009.

117. ---, *Maritime Security, The Unlawful Dimension*, New Delhi, Magnum Books Private Limited, 2010.

118. ---, *National Security: Imperatives and Challenges*, New Delhi, Tata McGraw-Hill Publishing Limited, 2008.

119. ---, *Role of the Coast Guard in the Maritime Security of India*, second edition, New Delhi, Knowledge World, 2009.

120. Palmer, Norman D, and Howard C Perkins, *International Relations,* New Delhi, A.I.T.B.S. Publishers and Distributors, 1997.

121. Paret, Peter, *Makers of Modern Strategy,* Princeton, Princeton University Press, 1986.

122. Parritt, B. A. H., (ed.), *Crime at Sea*, London, The Nautical Press, 1996.

123. Pascale, Richard T., Mark Milleman, and Linda Gioja, *Surfing the Edge of Chaos,* New York, Crown Business, 2000.

124. Pearson, Simon, *Total War 2006,* London, Coronet Books, 1999.

125. Penrose, Roger,*The Emperor's New Mind—Concerning Computers, Minds, and the Laws of Physics,* New York, Oxford University Press, 1990.

126. Peters, Tom, *Thriving on Chaos,* London, Pan Books, 1989.

127. Prabhakar, Lawrence W., Joshua H Ho and Sam Bateman, (eds.), *The Evolving Balance of Power in the Asia-Pacific—Maritime Doctrines and Nuclear Weapons at Sea,* Singapore, Institute of Defence and Strategic Studies, 2006.

128. Prigogine, Ilya, *Order Out of Chaos,* New York, Bantam, 1984.

129. Quaderi, Fazlul Quader, (ed.), *Bangladesh Genocide and World Press,* Dacca, Begum Dilfaroz Choudhary, 1972.

130. Rachman, Tanley, *The Meanings of Fear,* Harmondsworth, Penguin Education, 1974.

131. Raghavan, V. R., *Internal Conflicts: Military Perspectives,* New Delhi, Vij Books India Pvt. Ltd, 2012.

132. Rana, Mohammed Amir, *Gateway to Terrorism,* London, New Millennium, 2003.

133. Ranganathan, R, *Indian Naval Strategy for 2000 AD,* Madras, Ambikai Printers, 1994.

134. Rangarajan, L.N., (ed.), *Kautilya: the Arthasasthra,* New Delhi, Penguin Books, 1987.

135. Rao, T.S.S., and Ray C Griffiths, *Understanding the Indian Ocean,* Paris, UNESCO Publishing, 1998.

136. Rapoport, Anatol, (ed.), *Carl Von Clausewitz: On War,* London, Penguin Books, 1968.

137. Regan, Geoffrey, *The Guinness Book of Naval Blunders,* London, Guinness Publishing, 1993.

138. Robbins, Stefan P, *Organizational Behaviour,* New Delhi, Prentice-Hall, 2000.

139. Roberts, Adam, and Richard Guelff, (eds.), *Documents on the Laws of War,* Oxford, Clarendon Press, 1989.

140. Romm, Joseph J, *Defining National Security--The Nonmilitary Aspects,* New York, Council on Foreign Relations Press, 1993.

141. Roonwal, R.S., *Oceanic Minerals,* New Delhi, National Institute of Science Communication, 1999.

142. Roy-Chaudhury, Rahul, *India's Maritime Security,* New Delhi, Knowledge World, 2000.

143. Roy, Mihir K, *War in the Indian Ocean,* New Delhi, Lancer Publishers, 1995.

144. Russian Consulate Publication, Mumbai. *Afanasy Nikitin's Voyage beyond Three Seas—1466-1472.*

145. Sabharwal, Gopa, *The Indian Millennium: AD 1000-2000,* New Delhi, Penguin Books, 2000.

146. Sagan, Carl and Ann Druyan, *Shadows of Forgotten Ancestors,* London, Arrow Books, 1993.

147. Sahay, Baldeo, *Indian Shipping: A Historical Survey,* New Delhi, Publications Division, Ministry of Information and Broadcasting, 1996.

148. Saighal, Vinod, *Restructuring South Asian Security,* New Delhi, Manas Publications, 2000.

149. Sandhu, Gurcharan Singh, *A Military History of Ancient India,* New Delhi, Vision Books, 2000.

150. Schmidt, Karl J., *Atlas and Survey of South Asian History,* New Delhi, Vision Books, 1999.

151. Sharma, S.L., and T.K. Oomen, (eds.), *Nation and National Identity in South Asia,* New Delhi, Orient Longman, 1999.

152. Shourie, Arun, *Governance and the Sclerosis that has Set in,* New Delhi, Rupa and Co, 2004.,

153. Shuman, Howard E., and Walter R Thomas, (eds.), *The Constitution and National Security,* Washington, D.C., National Defence University Press, 1990.

154. Simon, Jeffrey, (ed.), *The Challenge of Change,* Washington, D.C., National Defence University Press, 1993.

155. Singh, Jaswant, *Defending India,* Bangalore, Macmillan India Ltd., 1999.

156. Smith, S.E, (ed.) *The United States Navy in World War II,* New York, Ballantine Books, 1967.

157. Sridharan, K., *A Maritime History of India,* New Delhi, Publications Division, Ministry of Information and Broadcasting, 1982.

158. Stevens, Edward F, and C.S. J. Butterifield, *Shipping Practice,* Mumbai, Sterling, 1999.

159. Subramanaian, Lakshmi, *Medieval Seafarers,* New Delhi, Roli Books, 1999.

160. Sunderji, K., *A Soldier Remembers,* New Delhi, Harper Collins Publishers, 2000.

161. Tandon, M. P., and Rajesh Tandon, *Public International Law,* Faridabad, Allahabad Law Agency, 1999.

162. Tofler, Alvin, *Future Shock,* New York, Bantam, 1970.

163. Toynbee, Arnold J., *A Study of History,* Vol. I and II, New York, Dell Publishing Co,., Inc., 1978.

164. United Nations, *Handbook on the Peaceful Settlement of Disputes between States,* New York, United Nations, 1992.

165. United Nations, *The Law of the Sea,* New York, UN Publication, 1983.

166. Vas, Eric. A., *ABC of Peace and Security,* Pune, Paragon Advertising, 2001.

167. Vego, Milan N., *Naval Strategy and Operations in Narrow Seas*, New Port, Naval War College, 1996.

168. Walker, Martin., *The Cold War*, London, Vintage, 1994.

169. Walmer, Max, *An Illustrated Guide to Modern Naval Warfare,* London, Salamander Books, 1989.

170. Watson, James, *DNA—The Secret of Life,* London, Arrow Books, 2004.

171. Wee, Chow-Hou, Khai-Sheang Lee, and Bambang Walujo Hidajat, *Sun Tzu: War and Management—Applications to Strategic Management and Thinking,* Singapore, Addison-Wesley Publishing Company, 1996.

172. Weigly, Russell F., *The American Way of War,* Bloomington, Indiana University Press, 1973.

173. Wells, Samuel F, Jr. *The Challenges of Power--American Diplomacy, 1900—1921,* New York, University Press of America, 1990.

174. Wells, Spencer, *The Journey of Man: A Genetic Odyssey,* Princeton, Princeton University Press, 2002.

175. Wilson, Colin, *A Criminal History of Mankind,* London, Granada Publishing Limited, 1984.

176. ---, *From Atlantis to the Sphinx*, London, Virgin Books, 1999.

177. Wing, R.L., *The Art of Strategy: A New Translation of Sun Tzu's Classic—The Art of War*, New York, Doubleday, 1988.

178. Wolfson, Richard, *Nuclear Choices,* London, The MIT Press, 1993.

179. Yousaf, Mohammad, and Mark Adkin, *The Bear Trap: Afghanistan's Untold Story,* Lahore, Jang Publications, 1992.

180. Zeldin, Theodore, *The Intimate History of Humanity,* New Delhi, Penguin Books, 1999.

Index

D

E

F

G

H

I

N

O

P

Q

R

S

T

U

V

W